Zoo Conservation Biology

In the face of ever-declining biodiversity, zoos have a major role to play in species conservation. Written by professionals involved in *in-situ* conservation and restoration projects internationally, this is a critical assessment of the contribution of zoos to species conservation through evidence amassed from a wide range of sources.

The first part outlines the biodiversity context within which zoos should operate, introducing the origins and global spread of zoos and exploring animal collection composition. The second part focuses on the basic elements of keeping viable captive animal populations. It considers the consequences of captivity on animals, the genetics of captive populations and the performance of zoos in captive breeding. The final part examines ways in which zoos can make a significant difference to conservation now and in the future.

Bridging the gap between pure science and applied conservation, this is an ideal resource for both conservation biologists and zoo professionals.

JOHN E. FA BSc, DPhil (Oxon) is Chief Conservation Officer at the Durrell Wildlife Conservation Trust and Visiting Professor at the Division of Biology, Imperial College London. He specialises in endangered species biology and protection and on the impact of hunting on wildlife in Africa and Latin America.

STEPHAN M. FUNK BSc, MSc, MSc, PhD is a co-Founder and Director of Nature Heritage, a consultancy for conservation biology and anthropology, and a Research Fellow at the University of Puerto Rico's Centre for Applied Tropical Ecology and Conservation. He specialises and works worldwide in conservation biology, genetics and ecology.

DONNAMARIE O'CONNELL BSc, MSc is Senior Programme Manager (Africa) at RSPCA International. Her work in southern Africa focuses on integrating animal welfare into wildlife conservation and development programmes. She has an academic background in zoology and conservation biology.

ECOLOGY, BIODIVERSITY AND CONSERVATION

The world's biological diversity faces unprecedented threats. The urgent challenge facing the concerned biologist is to understand ecological processes well enough to maintain their functioning in the face of the pressures resulting from human population growth. Those concerned with the conservation of biodiversity and with restoration also need to be acquainted with the political, social, historical, economic and legal frameworks within which ecological and conservation practice must be developed. The new Ecology, Biodiversity, and Conservation series will present balanced, comprehensive, up-to-date, and critical reviews of selected topics within the sciences of ecology and conservation biology, both botanical and zoological, and both 'pure' and 'applied'. It is aimed at advanced final-year undergraduates, graduate students, researchers, and university teachers, as well as ecologists and conservationists in industry, government and the voluntary sectors. The series encompasses a wide range of approaches and scales (spatial, temporal, and taxonomic), including quantitative, theoretical, population, community, ecosystem, landscape, historical, experimental, behavioural and evolutionary studies. The emphasis is on science related to the real world of plants and animals rather than on purely theoretical abstractions and mathematical models. Books in this series will, wherever possible, consider issues from a broad perspective. Some books will challenge existing paradigms and present new ecological concepts, empirical or theoretical models, and testable hypotheses. Other books will explore new approaches and present syntheses on topics of ecological importance.

Ecology and Control of Introduced Plants
Judith H. Myers and Dawn Bazely

Invertebrate Conservation and Agricultural Ecosystems
T. R. New

Risks and Decisions for Conservation and Environmental Management
Mark Burgman

Ecology of Populations
Esa Ranta, Per Lundberg, and Veijo Kaitala

Nonequilibrium Ecology
Klaus Rohde

The Ecology of Phytoplankton
C. S. Reynolds

Systematic Conservation Planning
Chris Margules and Sahotra Sarkar

Large Scale Landscape Experiments: Lessons from Tumut
David B. Lindenmayer

Assessing the Conservation Value of Freshwaters: An international perspective
Phil Boon and Cathy Pringle

Insect Species Conservation
T. R. New

Zoo Conservation Biology

JOHN E. FA
Durrell Wildlife Conservation Trust
Imperial College, London

STEPHAN M. FUNK
Nature Heritage
Center for Applied Tropical Ecology and Conservation, University of Puerto Rico

DONNAMARIE O'CONNELL
RSPCA International

CAMBRIDGE
UNIVERSITY PRESS

CAMBRIDGE
UNIVERSITY PRESS

University Printing House, Cambridge CB2 8BS, United Kingdom

Cambridge University Press is part of the University of Cambridge.

It furthers the University's mission by disseminating knowledge in the pursuit of education, learning and research at the highest international levels of excellence.

www.cambridge.org
Information on this title: www.cambridge.org/9780521534932

First published 2011

A catalogue record for this publication is available from the British Library

Library of Congress Cataloguing in Publication data
Fa, John E.
Zoo conservation biology / John E. Fa, Stephan M. Funk, Donnamarie O'Connell.
    p.   cm. – (Ecology, biodiversity, and conservation)
Includes bibliographical references and index.
ISBN 978-0-521-82763-8 (hardback) – ISBN 978-0-521-53493-2 (pbk.)
1. Zoos – Philosophy.   2. Animal diversity conservation.
3. Captive wild animals – Breeding.   I. Funk, Stephan M.
II. O'Connell, Donnamarie.   III. Title.
QL76.F32   2011
333.95'416 – dc23   2011017495

ISBN 978-0-521-82763-8 Hardback
ISBN 978-0-521-53493-2 Paperback

Contents

Foreword

There are many great books on conservation biology and many great books on zoos, as well as shelves full of academic journals and other literature that deal with these topics and their areas of overlap. It is a vast body of work, and for a new entrant to the field, one that is hard to navigate. Here is the answer to that problem. Fa, Funk and O'Connell have brought together all the various strands related to zoos and their roles in animal conservation. The book includes detailed treatments on the full range of relevant topics, ranging from the background to the current species extinction crisis through to the contributions that zoos can make to address it.

Of course, there are critics of zoos in general and critiques of the conservation roles that zoos play. The authors tackle these head on and highlight the areas of captive breeding, public education and being ambassadors for wildlife that zoos uniquely contribute. Over the past 30 years zoos have made major contributions to the science and practice of animal conservation in a number of ways, and contributed individually and collectively to the conservation success for a number of endangered species. Of particular significance is the role that zoos play in conservation that other organisations could not. Generally, this is where well managed living collections of wild animals contribute to conservation theory or practice. Their key roles come from educating and inspiring visitors through well-designed, self-sustaining animal exhibits, contributing to scientific knowledge through observations of animals in their care, developing and communicating expertise in the biology of small populations, and of course through captive breeding programmes. Over time, the zoo community has come to better understand what their conservation priorities should be, how to undertake their unique roles better, and then how to apply these skills through acting individually, collectively or collaboratively in order to maximise the benefits for animal conservation. This book is a testament to the body of knowledge and expertise that the work of zoos and people working in related areas have contributed. Here you will find authoritative and systematic information on all these key areas as well as pointers to more information.

It should come as no surprise that this book on zoo conservation biology largely emanates from Jersey Zoo – now the animal collection component of the Durrell Wildlife Conservation Trust (Durrell). Jersey Zoo was well established in the animal conservation world before most other zoos were even thinking about conservation. Through leadership that began with the vision of Gerry and Lee Durrell and has continued with a clear sense of purpose ever since, Durrell has contributed remarkable success stories showing how dedicated attention to detail, and effective links from the zoo to the wild really can save species from extinction. At the same time Durrell has been a flagship for conservation, attracting support and resources directly through beautifully designed and managed animal collections.

One key part of the Durrell programme has been to train conservation biologists, especially to support those from areas of the world with many endangered species. Running over more than 30 years this training programme has brought conservation management skills to a generation of wildlife managers, who represent a network with shared commitments to species conservation and the skills necessary to achieve it. Passing on knowledge and experience, and bringing the next generation of conservation practitioners to a point where they have the skills and resources necessary to act effectively is going to be more important as we enter a period of even greater environmental change with potentially serious consequences for the world's species. This book will be a key resource for the very important work that is to come.

Georgina Mace CBE FRS
London

Preface

Zoos are becoming increasingly important centres, not just for exhibition and recreation, but also for promoting and actively engaging in animal conservation. Emphasis is now placed on educating the visiting public, alongside entertaining them. However, zoos continue to play an important role in *ex-situ* breeding and reintroduction of endangered species.

The efficacy of zoos as institutions capable of maintaining healthy individuals and populations has undoubtedly grown in recent years, as a result of the development of scientifically based techniques. There is a wealth of information now available on zoo management, animal husbandry techniques, captive propagation of species as genetically and demographically viable populations, as well as on the importance of zoos in biodiversity conservation. Some of this knowledge is contained in specialised publications, such as the journal *Zoo Biology*, or the *International Zoo Yearbook* but the literature is dispersed and there are no dedicated texts currently available. No book, however, has directly focussed on what we describe as 'zoo conservation biology'. Zoo conservation biology, distinct from zoo biology which is much more to do with the 'how to' of breeding, behaviour and maintenance of animal species in captivity, is a discipline which studies how zoos can best contribute to biodiversity conservation. Alongside books and literature that support the technical aspects of captive animal management, zoo conservation biology pays more attention to achieving clarity on how best science can be applied within zoos to achieve species recovery and environmental awareness at a global scale. Thus, the object of this book is to provide an up-to-date review of the potential of zoos to actively support the conservation of biodiversity. It is an introduction to conservation biology from within zoos as it relates to the management of animals in captivity and how zoos can function as well-coordinated educational and commercial establishments.

In general, this book is written with the student in mind. However, it is meant to reach a wide audience, requiring no university science prerequisite. The book should guide any reader by providing him/her with the basics required to understand all topics involved, by providing the elementary learning blocks for the uninitiated and a bolster to those with some background.

Acknowledgements

This work has been inspired by our involvement with an organisation, originally the Jersey Wildlife Preservation Trust now Durrell, the worldview and charisma of its founder, Gerald Durrell, as well as the countless friends and colleagues within it (past and present). In particular, we are indebted to the many students from all over the world that have attended courses at the International Training Centre at Durrell, and whom we have taught, for always arousing our enthusiasm and giving us hope. We know they are **all** 'making a difference'. Many collaborators across numerous other organisations have also motivated us and bettered our thinking over the years, we thank them all.

In the production of this book, we are especially grateful to Michael Usher for his constant and wholehearted steer. Michael read and commented on all earlier drafts of the chapters. To David Bowles, Mark Brayshaw, Trevor Coote, Lee Durrell, Ann-Katrine Garn, Susie Ellis, Richard Frankham, Georgina Mace, Constantino Macias, Miranda Stevenson, Phillip Seddon, Benjamin Skolnik, Mark Stanley Price and Colin Tudge, we are thankful for taking the time to read all or separate chapters. Their insights, comments and positive criticism have improved the final manuscript incalculably. Thomas Dixon, Fiona Fisken, Kristen Leus, Matthew Smith, Miranda Stevenson and Pritpal Soorae allowed us to use their unpublished data, and we thank them for entrusting these to us. Amy Hall was most generous in helping us with redrawing figures and maps.

Archiv Hagenbeck and Elsevier kindly gave permission for reproduction of Fig. 3.1 and Fig. 6.5 respectively. We are grateful to Quentin Bloxam, Jenny Daltry, Joanna Durbin, Michael Dvorak, Colm Farrington, Nick Garbutt, Gerardo Garcia, Matt Morton, Goutam Narayan, Paddy Ryan and especially Gregory Guida for lending us the use of their excellent animal photographs.

We thank Durrell, Nature Heritage and RSPCA for the time afforded to the authors in preparation of this book. The views expressed are entirely our own. We also greatly appreciate the support and guidance of Dominic Lewis and Megan Waddington for enabling the process of turning manuscript into book.

1 · *Biodiversity and zoo conservation biology*

'It may well be true that Sumatran tigers and Hyacinthine macaws seem to contribute very little to our daily lives. There is, though, a strong group of arguments . . . which say that wild animals and plants can be good for us and this is a good reason to hang on to them' (Colin Tudge)

1.1   Introduction

In practical terms, species conservation initiatives must be directed at protecting the largest number of forms as cheaply as possible. Economy, not just in monetary terms but also in achieving parsimonious ways of protecting species, is important, since resources are often limited. Debates rage over whether one or another approach is more appropriate, often with much time and effort expended and little results in hand. Biodiversity conservation has to proceed along various fronts achieved by the integration of methods to halt the current extinction of species. This book attempts to undertake this task for conservation biologists working in zoos. Zoos argue that their role is increasingly concerned with the preservation of species yet the information required for zoo staff to make informed decisions on any aspect of captive animal care, population management, etc., is not readily accessible.

This book collates and evaluates numerous papers and books published on the subject to produce a theoretical and practical document that understands the reality of keeping animals in captivity and the potential that these institutions have in biodiversity conservation. The need for such a textbook is further emphasised by the fact that although there has been a certain growth in literature that deals with the application of science to techniques for the optimal maintenance and breeding of animals in captivity, there is no text that examines the fundamental concepts underlying captive animal management. Therefore, this is not a book on the techniques of managing animals in captive collections, but one that takes a more 'aerial view' of the subject of how zoos do and can contribute further to species conservation. This book covers some subject matter that has to do with the 'biology of the management of animals in captivity', as Hediger (1950) put it (Chapter 3), but its main purpose is to review (both numerically and qualitatively) what zoos are, what they are doing and what they can do as healthy educational and research establishments.

In this first chapter, we present information on the world's biological diversity in order to place zoos firmly within this framework. Understanding what is meant by biodiversity, where it is found and how it is being lost, is crucial to clarify what needs to be done to conserve species and habitats worldwide. Here, we summarise these main issues first, starting with what we mean when we talk of a species. We then examine what factors make species rare, and what we know about past and present rates of species extinctions. We then examine why it is important to value conserving biodiversity. Finally, we set the context of the book by characterising what we are calling zoo conservation biology – or how zoos can truly engage in the conservation of biodiversity.

1.2 Species definitions

In biology in general, a species is the smallest basic taxonomic unit used to define living organisms (Box 1.1). Traditionally, a species has been defined in one of two ways, as a group of individuals that is morphologically, physiologically, or biochemically distinct from other groups (the **morphological species** concept) or as a group of individuals that can potentially breed among themselves and do not breed with individuals of other groups (the **biological species** concept).

Understanding how to differentiate geographic patterns of biological variation is critical for conservation, because of its essential role in delimiting discrete taxonomic units in nature (Ryder, 1986; Barrowclough & Flesness, 1996). Decisions about allocating space for captive breeding in zoos, or breeding programmes for maximising genetic diversity, depend on being able to distinguish correctly the different taxonomic forms. How we view the species concept therefore has consequences on how we perceive patterns of diversity and endemism, how variation is apportioned between and among groups, and in some cases how population sizes of various taxonomic entities might be determined. This is not easy and debates over what is a species are long-standing (see Davis, 1996). Mallet (2007) discussed a few of the major alternative concepts and definitions in terms of the most important practical effect of species concepts in taxonomy. More detailed discussions and critiques of various species concepts can be found in Mallet (2001) and Coyne & Orr (2004).

Box 1.1 · *Naming species and the 'taxonomic impediment' question*

Scientific species names essentially consist of two words. This system, known as binomial nomenclature, was developed in the eighteenth century by the Swedish biologist, Carl von Linnaeus. In the scientific name for the tiger *Panthera tigris*, *Panthera* is the generic or genus name and *tigris* is the specific epithet often referred to as the species. The genus name can be compared to a person's family name in that many people can have the same family name, while the species name is similar to a person's given name. *Panthera tigris* refers to just one of the four species of big cats. Scientific names are written in a standard way to avoid confusion. Sometimes scientific names are followed by the authority's name, as in *Panthera tigris* Linnaeus 1758 indicating that Linnaeus was the person who first proposed the scientific name and published it in 1758. Most scientific names have Latin or Greek roots; *Panthera* is Latin, from the Greek word for leopard.

Tiger subspecies represent an interesting example of how systematics can assist conservation. No comprehensive modern analysis of geographic variation had been undertaken until Cracraft *et al.* (1998) studied the various forms. Using DNA sequencing techniques,

Cracraft *et al.* (1998) considered the Sumatran Tiger to have a sufficiently distinct mitochondrial DNA to warrant species status. Mazák & Groves (2006) also considered the Sumatran tiger a separate species on the basis of morphology, as well as the Javan Tiger. But also based on body characteristics, however, Kitchener (1999) considered that there is little evidence for discrete subspecies and morphological variation was best characterised as clinal. Luo *et al.* (2004) later confirmed the division of tigers into six extant subspecies on the basis of distinctive molecular markers.

Biodiversity science has emerged as one of the frontier areas of research with expanding concepts, testable hypotheses and ever-refining methodologies. Being a synthetic discipline, it is primarily 'fed' by the established fields of biological sciences, such as taxonomy, biogeography, ecology, evolution, genetics, and the like. Taxonomy, which essentially deals with discovery, description and classification of living organisms, underpins the basic understanding of biodiversity on Earth (McNeely, 2002). The identification of organisms within communities to species level is one of the greatest constraints in terms of time and costs in ecological studies. Though some studies have suggested that working at a taxonomic level higher than species does not result in an important loss of information (taxonomic sufficiency) it does, however, lead to an inaccuracy of biodiversity evaluation. This is especially important when comparing different areas, and can lead to an *a priori* exclusion of some entities before understanding their role in ecology.

Some authors argue that taxonomy has been considered a marginal science even during the pioneer descriptive period of ecology, and traditionally has received little financial support, that there is a taxonomic impediment (Giangrande, 2003). The result was the production of many misidentifications and erroneous records. During recent years, the developing experimental ecological approach has led to an improvement in scientific methods, but concurrently to a reduction in the number of expert taxonomists for many invertebrate groups. Such a worldwide shortage of taxonomists, who can be called upon to identify species, describe those that are new to science, determine their taxonomic relationships, and make predictions about their properties (Gaston & May, 1992), is concerning and is expected to worsen. This is because the taxonomic workforce is aging, coupled with a decline in students being trained in taxonomy. To complete the picture, there is a decline in the number of paid positions that allow a person to spend time doing basic taxonomy. What is NOT lacking is an interest in taxonomy by potential taxonomists. The argument is often made that even the existing number of trained taxonomists are under-utilised due to insufficient commitment of funds to taxonomic study. Every major museum suffers from a backlog of unstudied specimens and undescribed new species, while curators often cite the loss of students who were interested in taxonomy, but could not get sufficient fellowship support or failed to find a paying job.

The decline in taxonomists available to study biodiversity seems puzzling since in the 1990s there was a promotion of inventory, use, and protection of biodiversity as never before. The recognition then was that taxonomic information is a prerequisite to understanding biodiversity and maximising its use and protection. It is also widely accepted that, outside mammals, birds, and some plant groups, we know only a fraction of the species on earth. The groups that are the least-known are those with the most potential for discovery of products of use to humankind, and for understanding emerging diseases and agricultural pests.

However, since the advent of molecular techniques, the species debate has become even more complicated because phylogeneticists have their own opinions on how a species should be defined. Thus, little consensus on species concepts has yet been reached. Some argue that named Linnean ranks, including species, are no longer useful in taxonomy at all (Mishler, 1999; Hendry et al., 2000a). However, attempts at consensus have been made. Poulton (1904), Simpson (1951) as well as Templeton (1989) have argued that a combination of morphological, ecological, phylogenetic, and reproductive criteria should be used. Sokal & Crovello (1970) and Mallet (1995) attempted the reverse argument: that one could arbitrate between conflicting 'concept' arguments by using the results of clustering processes on phenotype or genotype, rather than by specifying the processes themselves. Some authors, like de Queiroz (1998), have argued that conflict between species concepts is illusory, because different concepts represent criteria applicable to different stages in the lineage-splitting process. However, this attempt at consensus does not help with the practical question of whether to use inclusive or diagnostic criteria in taxonomy; that is, whether to be a lumper or a splitter. It seems likely, therefore, that species concepts and criteria will continue to be debated for some time. Until a practical solution is widely agreed, nomenclatural databases for comparative biology and biodiversity are essential. On a more practical basis, conservation that can continue to provide useful information, while fashions in the taxonomic rank considered species fluctuate, is required. Because of uncertainty of the species rank (Hey, 2001) and because the term 'species' can mean different things in different taxonomic groups; species counts on different continents or of different organisms will give only a roughly comparable idea of biodiversity. Isaac et al. (2004) were watchful of the problem that 'taxonomic inflation' can cause when assessing whether rates or risks of extinction have changed over time. This is so because much conservation planning depends on numbers of species, reflecting richness, diversity, endemism, threat and many other attributes that can be compared across locations and taxa. Hence, species numbers will increase (because more are recognised), potentially masking extinction, but taxonomic inflation will also result in a higher proportion of threatened or extinct species, because the average geographical range and population size will decline (Agapow et al., 2004). Isaac et al. (2004) suggest that these effects will make global targets very hard to meet.

In conservation studies such as those discussed in this book, we are generally concerned about the underlying mechanisms that can allow managers to make prudent decisions. Thus, the importance of what we call a species cannot be underestimated because the issue becomes one of what are we to protect or manage if we do not know how to recognise it? Despite the fact that many biologists' attitude toward the debate is one often bordering on complacency, species concepts have consequences for determining units for captive breeding and management, specifying units to be protected under law, or regulating trade in endangered taxa (Cracraft et al., 1998). The main controversy within conservation seems to be between those who prefer to view the problem of units-in-nature from a position of formal taxonomy and those who wish to avoid formal taxonomy altogether and apply another set of terms considered to be relevant to conservation action. Among the latter are ESUs, 'management units' and other such expressions. ESUs are difficult to recognise and according to Cracraft (1997) they have no status within taxonomy, because the concept is not backed-up by centuries-old scholarship, tradition or widely accepted rules of procedure. In any case, ESUs are not dissimilar to several other formal species concepts, particularly the phylogenetic species concept. The ESU concept has gained support because the biological species concept could not provide a consistent terminological solution to the units-in-nature problem (Ryder, 1986). Biological species are problematic to use as a unit of conservation because too many biological species contain multiple, differentiated, and often geographically isolated taxa. Subspecies, moreover, are not easily used because although some are distinct, geographically localised units, others are arbitrary subdivisions of continuously distributed geographic variation and are not distinct units. Because of this, some taxonomists have supported the notion that some form of phylogenetic species concept is more appropriate for conservation (Cracraft, 1997). Phylogenetic species are diagnosably distinct taxa; one or more populations that share a combination of characters that distinguish them from other units (Sites & Crandall, 1997).

1.3   What is biological diversity?

Biological diversity means the wealth of life forms found on earth: millions of different plants, animals and microorganisms, the genes they contain and the intricate systems they form. However, life on earth contains much greater variety than that measured by species alone. A single species may contain different races or breeds and differences may also exist at the individual level. Species come together to form communities which, in turn, combine in ecosystems. Many species survive in only one specific ecosystem and thus discussions involving biological diversity must define the concept at least at three distinct levels: genetic, species and ecosystem diversity. Human cultural diversity could also be considered part of biodiversity since human cultures represent 'solutions' to the problems of survival in particular environments.

Genetic diversity. Genes are the biochemical information packages passed on by parents to determine the physical and biochemical characteristics of the offspring. Genetic diversity can refer to the variation found in genes within species. Although most of the genes are the same, subtle variations occur in some. The expression of these variations may be obvious, such as size and colour; they may also be invisible, for example, susceptibility to disease. Genetic variability allows species to adapt to changes in their environment and can be manipulated to produce new breeds of crop plants and domestic animals.

Species diversity. Species are usually recognisably different in appearance, allowing an observer to distinguish one from another, but sometimes the differences are extremely subtle. Species diversity, or **species richness** (McIntosh, 1967), usually measures the total number of species found within one geographical area. The problem in measuring species diversity is that it is often impossible to enumerate all species in a region.

Ecosystem diversity. An ecosystem consists of communities of plants and animals and the non-living elements of their environment (soil, water, minerals, air, etc.). The functional relationships between the communities and their environment are frequently

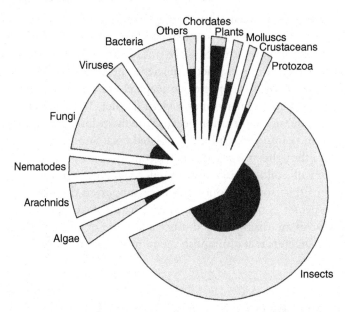

Fig. 1.1 Species richness in major groups of organisms. The main 'pie' shows the species estimated to exist in each group; the black area within each slice shows the proportion that has been formally described. From Purvis & Hector (2000), data from Hawksworth & Kalin-Arroyo, 1995).

complex, through the mechanisms of major ecological processes such as the water cycle, soil formation, nutrient cycling and energy flow. These processes provide the sustenance required by living communities and so lead to a critical interdependence. Two different phenomena are frequently referred to under the heading of ecosystem diversity: the variety of species within different ecosystems (the more diverse ecosystems contain more species) and the variety of ecosystems found within a certain biogeographical or political boundary.

1.4 How many species are there?

It is difficult to quantify the world's genetic diversity. Estimates have varied from 2 million to 100 million species, with the most common estimate of somewhere near 10 million. Diversity at the species level is somewhat better known, but current estimates of the number of species only serve to underscore our degree of ignorance. The problem defining the limits of current knowledge of species diversity is compounded by the lack of a central database or list of the world's species. A recent compilation (Wilson, 1988) has shown that since the beginnings of the science of taxonomy, scientists have identified and named about 1.4 million species of living organisms (Fig. 1.1). Of the described forms around 1.03 million are animals and 248 000 are higher plants. The best studied and most completely known groups are birds and mammals (roughly 9000 and 4000 species respectively) although together they account for less than 1% of all known species. About 80% or more of all species of birds, mammals, reptiles, amphibians and fishes have been described. Insects, however, are still little known despite the fact that they account for a high proportion of all known species. The number of insect species was estimated by C. B. Williams in 1969 to be around 3 million. By 1988, Stork (1988) estimated that insects comprised 57% of the total named species and one group of insects, the beetles, comprised 25%. Using knockdown insecticides, Erwin (1982) astonished the ecological world with his estimate of how many insects live in tropical forests. Working in Barro Colorado Island, Panama, Erwin sampled 19 individual *Luehea* trees (Family Tiliaceae) at different seasons. He collected 9000 beetles belonging to more than 1200 species. Erwin extrapolated from these data to estimate that 13.5% of these beetles (about 162 species) live only in Luehea trees. He then deduced that since roughly 50 000 species of tree live in tropical rainforests around the world and 'guácimo colorado' represents an average tropical tree, there must be about 1.8 million beetle species specialising on single tree species. Because some beetles live on more than one tree species (Erwin thought about 2.7 million of them) a total of 10.8 million species of canopy beetles was possible. If all these estimates are correct, as many as 30 million species of insects are possible. Each step in Erwin's calculation of species diversity is so speculative that many scientists do not accept this estimate and keep to the earlier figure of 10 million total species (Gaston, 1991). Two other approaches have been employed in estimating biological diversity. The first, **biological rules**, involves determining how many species are involved in biological relationships. May (1988, 1992) estimated that in Britain and Europe there are about six times more fungi than plant species. Thus, if this ratio applies throughout the world there may be as many as 1.6 million fungus species growing on the world's 270 000 plant species. A second method, of associated specialists, assumes that if each species of plant and insect has at least one species of specialised bacteria, protist, nematode and virus, estimates of the number of species should be multiplied by five – a grand total of 25 million using traditional estimates, or 150 million if Erwin's estimates are accepted.

New species are still being discovered – even new birds and mammals. On average, about three new species of birds are found each year. Although many assume nearly all mammal species are known to scientists, since 1993, 408 new mammalian species have been described, around 10% of the previously known fauna (Ceballos & Ehrlich, 2009). Other vertebrate groups are far from being completely described: an estimated 40% of freshwater fishes in South America have not yet been classified. Additionally, environments such as soil and the deep sea are revealing an unsuspected wealth of new species. Scientists believe that the deep sea floor may contain as many as a million undescribed species (Grassle, 1989). Hydrothermal vent communities discovered less than two decades ago contain more than 20 new families and subfamilies, some 50 genera and 100 new species.

1.5 Where is biological diversity found?

Biological diversity occurs within all habitats, because genetic diversity has allowed life to adapt to different environments. However, species are not spread evenly over the earth and biological diversity is greater in some areas than in others. Some habitats, particularly tropical forests among terrestrial systems, possess a greater number or density of species than others. For example, a 13.7 km^2 area of the La Selva Forest Reserve in Costa Rica contains almost 1500 plant species, more than the total found in the 243 500 km^2 of Great Britain, while Ecuador harbours more than 1300 bird species, or almost twice as many as the USA and Canada combined (Myers, 1988). Global biodiversity generally follows four clear patterns: (1) species diversity increases towards the tropics for most groups of organisms; (2) patterns of diversity in terrestrial species are paralleled by patterns in marine species; (3) species diversity is affected by local variation in topography, climate and environment; and (4) historical factors are also important.

In general, the number of species (more cautiously called inventory of species by Rosenweig, 1997) declines as you move away from the equator, north or south. Examples of these latitudinal gradients, as the effect is known, abound. Since first described by Alfred Russell Wallace in 1878, around 14 different hypotheses have been proposed to explain this phenomenon (Pagel et al., 1991). It has been found in plants and animals in both aquatic as well as terrestrial environments. There are exceptions, such as marine algae in the North/Central American Pacific (Gaines & Lubchenco, 1982), but these are indeed departures from the general pattern. Latitudinal gradients in species richness have also been found for fossil forms, in the Foraminifera for data stretching for 70 Myr and in flowering plants in a data set of around 110 Myr.

Concerns were raised about whether increasing species diversity along the tropics was an artefact of disproportionate interest by temperate area scientists describing the patterns in tropical areas. This worry was dispelled by comparing similar species in studied communities. For instance, one hectare (1 ha) of Atlantic rainforest in Bahia Province, the richest in the world, has 450 tree species (Thomas & de Carvalho, 1993). In other more typical tropical forests, one hectare can have around 200–300 tree species. A test of latitudinal gradient in species richness comes from a study by Terborgh et al. (1990) which meticulously compared the avifauna of a 97 ha tropical forest in Peru with a similar-sized area in the temperate region of North America. They believed that even though gamma diversities (the number of species in a region) have been shown to differ considerably between tropical and other areas, others like MacArthur (1965) conjectured that the alpha diversity (the diversity of species in a particular geographical point) could be the same. The results showed that whilst in the tropical forest there were 160 bird species, the richest temperate forest had four to five times fewer species. Such wealth occurs although the number of individual birds per hectare is quite similar in the two biomes.

A corollary to the observed increases in species richness towards the equator is the latitudinal gradient in geographic range size, or Rapoport's rule (Stevens, 1989). Rapoport's rule has been demonstrated for a large variety of different taxa, although some exceptions have been found. The rule essentially describes how species' ranges at the polar end of a continent are larger than those at the equatorial end. An explanation for Rapoport's rule for mammals is that an individual animal at the polar end of a continent experiences a much wider range of climatic conditions than one at the equator. Thus unlike tropical species, the more temperate species cannot specialise on a narrow set of climatic conditions. In addition, Pagel *et al.* (1991) demonstrated that more northerly species were also more generalist which correlates with the greater variability of habitats found in those environments. Theories to explain species richness in the tropics include the following.

- **Stability** – tropical climates are more stable than temperate zones.
- **Age** – tropical communities are older, therefore have had more time to evolve.
- **Environmental conditions** – the warm temperatures and high humidity in the tropics provide favourable conditions for many species that are unable to survive in the temperate areas.
- **Control** – ever-present populations of pests, parasites and diseases prevent any species or group from dominating communities.
- **Productivity** – tropical regions are highly productive, thus can provide a greater resource base that can support numerous species.

1.6 Loss of biological diversity

No species will exist forever. Species evolve and some forms disappear after some time. Extinction usually refers to the total disappearance of all individuals of a species. However, the meaning of the word 'extinct' can vary according to the context in which it is used (Estes *et al.*, 1989). A species can be said to be extinct in the wild if individuals of a species remain alive only in captivity. A species can also be locally extinct if it is no longer found in an area which it previously inhabited. Ecologically extinct is another term that focuses on species which are found in such low numbers in a community that their impact is insignificant.

The fossil record shows that since life originated four billion years ago the vast majority of species that existed are now extinct. By the early nineteenth century, geologists had unearthed so many extinct species that as much as 82% of all species known to science were extinct. By the mid twentieth century, Romer (1949) estimated that probably more than 99% of known tetrapods from the mid Mesozoic became extinct without leaving any descendants in our age. Periods of mass extinctions have taken place due to sudden changes in sea level, climate (including the impact of a colliding comet), and volcanic activity (see Sepkoski, 1989; Jablonski, 1991). During these periods of sudden change, those species which were better adapted to new circumstances than others left descendants. Species that evolved fast enough to colonise new habitats in time and space survived and flourished.

Two broad processes influence the dynamics of populations and cause extinction: deterministic (or cause and effect relationships, e.g. glaciation or direct human interventions such as deforestation) and stochastic (chance or random events, which may act independently or influence variation in deterministic processes). Rosenweig (1997) refers to these deterministic and stochastic processes as accidents and population interactions. In other words, species may disappear for no predictable reason or both predation and competition can force populations to succumb in time. The magnitude of the effects of these causes of extinction depends on the size and degree of genetic connectedness of populations. Four types of stochastic process can be distinguished: (1) **demographic uncertainty** – this is only a hazard for relatively small populations (numbering tens or hundreds of individuals); (2) **environmental uncertainty** – due to unpredictable changes in weather, food supply, disease and the populations of competitors, predators or parasites; (3) **natural catastrophes** – floods, fires or droughts; and (4) **genetic uncertainty** – random changes in genetic make-up to which several factors contribute (Shaffer, 1987).

Agents of decline of species have been classified under four main headings: (1) overkill; (2) habitat destruction and fragmentation; (3) impact of introduced species; and (4) chains of extinction. Diamond (1984, 1989) described these terms as 'the evil quartet'. Of these factors, introduced species and habitat destruction are responsible for most known extinctions and threatened species of vertebrates (Jenkins, 1992). Thirty-nine per cent of species have become extinct through introductions and 36% through habitat loss. Hunting and deliberate extermination have also contributed significantly (23% of extinctions with known causes) (see below).

Overkill. This results from hunting at a rate above the maximum sustained yield. The most susceptible species are those with low intrinsic rates of increase (i.e. large mammals such as whales, elephants and rhinos) because of their limited ability to recover quickly. Although such species usually have a high standing biomass when unharvested, they have a low maximum sustained yield which is easily exceeded. They are even more vulnerable if they are valued either as food or as an easily marketable commodity. An example of this comes from work in Equatorial Guinea in which meat extraction from the bush was proportional to the purchasing power of the urban markets. The volume of bushmeat serving Malabo, the administrative capital in Bioko, was 70% greater than that being sold through Bata, in Rio Muni, though there was little difference in population size between the two centres (52 000 and 55 000 respectively) (Fa et al., 1995). Actual harvests far exceeded potential extraction on the island and have led to the drop in numbers of many species (Albrechtsen et al., 2007).

Habitat destruction and fragmentation. Although habitats may be modified, degraded or eliminated, they are more commonly fragmented. A large tract is often converted piecemeal to another land-use. This practice is widespread throughout the world. Loss of habitat by a given proportion does not increase the vulnerability of a species, nor does it decrease the number of its members by that same proportion (except in the particular case of habitat cleared from the edge inward). Frequently, modification produces a patchwork pattern as it erodes the tract of habitat from inside and changes micro-climates (Saunders et al., 1991). Initially, the areas occupied by the new land-use form islands which later multiply and enlarge until the new land-use provides the continuous phase and the original habitat the discontinuous one. The vulnerability of species then increases disproportionately. A clear example of this comes from a study by Ranta et al. (1998) on the Atlantic rainforest fragments remaining in Pernambuco, Brazil. Their analyses of size, shape and distribution of the forest fragments showed that a large proportion of these (48%) were less than 10 hectares while only 7% were >100 hectares (Fig. 1.2). A recent review of the literature on the effects of fragmentation (Turner, 1996) provides empirical evidence from different parts of the world that in nearly all cases there is a local loss of species. Isolated fragments suffer reduction in species richness with time after excision from continuous forest, and small fragments often have fewer species recorded for the same effort of observation than large fragments or areas of continuous forest. The mechanisms of fragmentation-related extinction include the deleterious effects of human disturbance during and after deforestation, the reduction of population sizes, the reduction of immigration rates, forest edge effects, changes in community structure and the immigration of exotic species.

Impact of introduced species. Some species which have been introduced intentionally or unintentionally become invasive. These plants or animals often adversely affect the habitats and bioregions they invade economically, environmentally, and/or ecologically. In a large number of well-recorded cases, these alien invasives have proceeded to exterminate native species by competing with them, preying upon them, or destroying their habitat. A review by Atkinson (1989) demonstrated that 22 species and subspecies of reptiles and amphibians have disappeared worldwide as a direct result of alien animals. In New Zealand alone, nine species of reptiles and amphibians and 23 bird species have become extinct since AD 1000 through introductions. On the Pacific island of Guam the result of the introduction of one single alien species, the brown snake, has caused the extinction of most avifauna (Pimm, 1987).

The invasion of ecosystems by non-native species has occurred most significantly on islands, where indigenous species have often evolved in the absence of strong competition, herbivory, parasitism or predation. As a result, introduced species thrive in those optimal insular ecosystems affecting their plant food, competitors or animal prey. As islands are characterised by a high rate of endemism, the impacted populations often correspond to local subspecies or even unique species. A small number of mammal species is responsible for most of the damage to invaded insular ecosystems: rats, cats, goats, rabbits, pigs and a few others (Courchamp et al., 2003). The effect of alien invasive species may be simple or very complex, especially since a large array of invasive species, mammals and others, can be present simultaneously and interact among themselves as well as with the indigenous species. In most cases, introduced species generally have a strong impact and they often are responsible for the impoverishment of the local flora and fauna.

The impact of introduced predators on islands has been clearly shown by the work carried out by Case & Bolger (1991). They analysed lizard population sizes in tropical Pacific islands with and without mongooses. On islands invaded by mongooses, there was a significant depression of diurnal lizard populations, increasing the risk of extinction. Similarly, in the case of the black rat, the pre-eminent invasive species, introduced to Pacific islands, there was a highly significant correlation between the arrival of the rat and the decline and extinction of five endemic genera of *Pomarea* monarch flycatchers (Thibault et al., 2002). The extinction of monarch populations after colonisation by black rats tended to take longer on larger islands than on smaller ones, and on islands without black rats, monarchs persisted even where forests have been reduced by more than 75%.

(a)

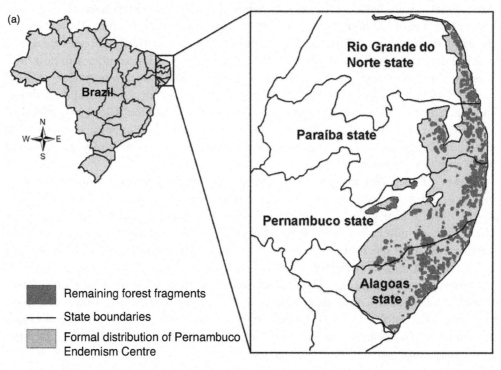

Remaining forest fragments

State boundaries

Formal distribution of Pernambuco Endemism Centre

(b)

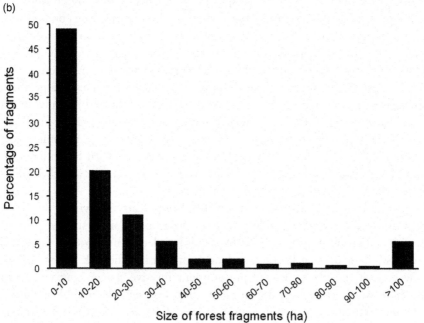

In contrast, Thibault *et al.* (2002) found no relation between presence of Polynesian rats and monarch distribution.

Chains of extinction. The extinction of one species may bring about the demise of another; this is known as secondary extinction. Diamond (1989) illustrates this chain of events with the example of the near extinction of a plant (genus *Hibiscadelphus*) resulting in the disappearance of several of the Hawaiian honey creepers, its pollinators. There are several instances of predators and scavengers dying out following the disappearance of the species which represented their source of food (see keystone species). Another example of the loss of species interactions has been demonstrated by the effect of the loss of pollinators on populations of the endangered Japanese primrose. Washitani (1996) showed, with the use of modelling techniques, that pollinator extinctions (bumblebees, butterflies and other insects) can lower the genetic variability of the flower populations through the loss of heterostyly (different positioning of stigmas and anthers).

1.7 Vulnerability of species to extinction

There is considerable evidence that the number of species in an isolated habitat will decrease over time. The crucial issue for conservationists is whether it is possible to predict those species which are most at risk of extinction from knowledge of their biology and ecology. Some taxa are more affected than are others, resulting in clades of species with differential extinctions of populations. Survival capability and extinction vulnerability can vary by geological time periods, though the probability of a species becoming extinct is independent of the age of its clade (Van Valen, 1973). As put across by Raup (1986) 'the victims and survivors are not random samples of the pre-extinction biotas'. Some interrelated features make species susceptible to extinction. Several ecological or life history traits have been proposed as factors determining an animal species' sensitivity to

←——

Fig. 1.2 Forest fragmentation in the Pernambuco Endemism Centre, Brazil. (a) Location of the Pernambuco Endemism Centre, the biogeographical area of the Atlantic rain forest located to the north of the São Francisco River, encompassing the States of Alagoas, Pernambuco, Paraíba and Rio Grande do Norte. The area has a long history of fragmentation, which started with extensive logging in 1500, subsequently intensified by sugar cane cultivation. Map adapted from Asfora *et al.* (2009). (b) The number of rain forest fragments ($n = 1839$) in different size classes within a portion of the Atlantic rain forest in the north-eastern state of Pernambuco, Brazil. Forest fragments were surrounded by sugar cane. Size and shape analyses showed that the fragments were relatively small and close to each other. Approximately 48% of the rain forest fragments were <10 ha, while only about 7% were >100 ha. Forest fragments located 50 m or less apart formed groups that included *c.* 50% of the total forest area. At 350 m inter-fragment distance, 98% of the rain forest area was included in groups of fragments. Due to the small size and irregular shape of the fragments, the total area of edge zone exceeds that of the interior habitat when the edge width is *c.* 60 m. At an edge width of 300 m, *c.* 94% of the total fragment area, is edge zone. For conservation purposes, ways of establishing networks of forest fragments connected by corridors and stepping stone fragments are essential. Adapted from Ranta *et al.* (1998).

Table 1.1 *Ecological features which make species susceptible to extinction. Compiled from Ehrenfeld (1970), Terborgh (1974), Pimm et al. (1988), Karr (1991) and Laurance (1991)*

Features	Explanation
Large body size	Associated with low birth rates (r), low population densities (N), and great disparity between r and N (Diamond, 1984). These species have thus few individuals per unit of area and are not able to expand rapidly after population slumps. Large-bodied species also require larger home ranges and are more predisposed to die off when part of their range is fragmented or damaged by human activity.
High trophic level	Animals at higher trophic levels are less abundant therefore more prone to extinction because of rarity.
Diet or habitat specialists	Ecological specialists often exploit resources which are patchily distributed in space and time and, therefore, tend to be rare. Specialists may also be vulnerable to successional changes in fragments and to the collapse of co-evolved mutualisms and food webs. Conversely, species adapted to, or able to tolerate, conditions at the interface between different types of habitats may be less affected by fragmentation than others. For example, forest edge species may benefit from habitat fragmentation.
Poor dispersal abilities	Animals capable of migrating between fragments or between 'mainland' areas and fragments are able to mitigate the effects of small population size. Good dispersers are not as likely to become extinct in fragmented habitats.
Restricted geographic range	Abundance of the species before fragmentation is a significant predictor of extinction. Newmark (1991) found that after fragmentation, rare understorey birds occupied fewer forest fragments per species than common ones. Fewer individuals of a rare species than of a common species are likely to occur in fragmented habitats.

extinction (Table 1.1). Some species are more susceptible to rapid extinction through fragmentation of tropical rain forest than others. Laurance (1991) tested the efficacy of seven ecological traits (body size, longevity, fecundity, trophic level, dietary specialisation, natural abundance in rain forest and abundance in the surrounding habitat matrix) for predicting responses of 16 non-flying mammals in tropical rain forests in Queensland. The proneness of mammals to extinction appears to be inversely related to tolerance towards conditions in the prevailing matrix vegetation of the fragmented landscape. The ability of species to use modified habitats surrounding fragments appeared to be an overriding determinant of extinction proneness. Laurance argued that 'matrix abundant' is a good predictor of extinction proneness primarily because species that occur in the matrix should be most effective at dispersing between fragments. These mammals could either recolonise fragments following extinction or have lower rates of extinction because small populations in fragments were bolstered by the demographic and genetic contributions of immigrants. Secondly, species that tolerate or exploit modified habitats may be adapted for ecological changes in fragments, particularly edge effects. For example, the arboreal folivores most abundant in modified habitats fed upon secondary trees that proliferated along corridors and fragment margins. Hence, in addition to being effective dispersers, these folivores probably responded positively to edge conditions in fragments.

Of course, the characteristics of extinction-prone species are not independent, but tend to group together into categories of characteristics. For example, species of certain body sizes are similar in terms of their population densities, gestation length, birth rates and other life history features. Furthermore, populations of species that have already undergone changes in their genetic variation will have a greater tendency to go extinct when a new disease, predator or some other change occurs in the environment. O'Brien & Evermann (1988) have indicated that the lack of genetic variability in the cheetah is a contributing factor to the lack of disease resistance. Given the above, the most susceptible species according to Ehrenfeld (1970) would be a large predator with narrow habitat tolerance, long gestation period and few young per litter, hunted for a natural product and/or sport, subject to inefficient game management, with a restricted distribution, yet travels across international boundaries, is intolerant to humans, and has non-adaptive behaviours – something like a polar bear.

1.8 The meaning of rare species

The protection of rare species is an important focus of conservation efforts. Definition of categories of rarity must be based on geographic distribution, habitat specificity, and local population size. Distribution of a species can be quantified by the number of sites in which it is present, or on a biogeographic scale by the area of the distributional range. Abundance refers to the local population density, the number of individuals found in a given site. By virtue of their scarcity or restricted range, rare species are more prone to extinction (Terborgh, 1974; Terborgh & Winter, 1980). This fact is supported by theory and by empirical data. Several demographic models show that the probability of extinction of a local population declines as its size increases, and field studies have supported these models. From a genetics viewpoint, low abundance means higher probabilities of depleting genetic variation and lower chances of long-term survival. However, rarity is not the only factor promoting extinction (see above). Karr (1982), for example, found little support for the idea that initial rarity was the cause of the majority of bird extinctions in Barro Colorado Island, Panama. Burke & Humphrey (1987) found that rarity is only one of a series of variables determining the endangerment of some vertebrates of Florida.

A classification of species according to their rarity based on geographic distribution, habitat specificity, and local population size was proposed by Rabinowitz (1981) for plants in the British Isles, one of the biologically best-known areas in the world. Rabinowitz et al. (1986) used these to distinguish eight species categories but rejected that these three ways of being rare were correlated (at least for British plants). However, the magnitude of correlation between distribution and abundance is of prime importance, as suggested by

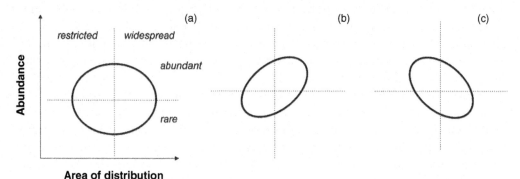

Fig. 1.3 Relative frequency of the types of rarity determined by local density (LD) and area of distribution (AD) with: (a) no correlation between AD and LD – equal number of species in each category; (b) a positive correlation between AD and LD – more widespread/abundant and restricted/rare species; (c) negative correlation between AD and LD – more restricted/abundant species and widespread/rare species. From Arita et al. (1990).

Arita et al. (1990). If rarity is seen as a combination of area of distribution (AD) and local density (LD), the number of species in each of the four possible categories is determined by the association between the variables (Fig. 1.3).

Arita et al. (1990) tested the correlation between AD and LD of species using available data on Neotropical mammals. They found a negative correlation between AD and LD for all species pooled but coefficients varied from positive to negative in subsets defined by taxonomic and trophic characteristics. When classified into the four categories in Fig. 1.3 (using the medians of area of distribution and abundance), the slight negative correlation between AD and LD produced an apparently higher frequency of restricted/abundant and widespread/rare species than the other types. From the observed correlations, larger animals tended to fall in the lower right corner of the graph (widespread/low local density species); the upper right and lower left corners having animals of intermediate sizes, the exact position being affected by other factors. Arita et al. (1990) concluded that because AD/LD correlation vanishes when body size is taken into account, rarity can be better classified by comparing only species of similar size. However, such a dichotomous classification can still be used even if the correlation between the variables is different from zero (Rabinowitz et al., 1986). Species in the restricted and locally rare category are of major concern in terms of conservation because they are likely to be at risk of extinction for demographic or genetic causes and an absence of other secondary sources.

1.9 Extinctions in recent history

Most recent extinctions have been associated with European expansion in the fifteenth and sixteenth centuries (Fig. 1.4). However, in some parts of the world some species are known to have become extinct before the arrival of the Europeans. For example, the

Polynesians who colonised the Hawaiian Islands in the fourth, fifth and sixth centuries may have been responsible for the loss of around 50 of the 100 or so species of endemic land birds in the period between their arrival and that of the Europeans.

The number of species lost during the past 500 years, as documented by the IUCN is around 785 extinctions worldwide. Many other extinctions, not included in this number, have likely occurred, but they have not yet been documented adequately enough to be formally listed as extinct. The list of extinct species is therefore likely to be an underestimate. Those listed provide the most detailed evidence on extinction available.

An analysis of the IUCN database by Sax & Gaines (2008) on species extinctions revealed several emerging patterns for terrestrial vertebrate and plant species. First, the general pattern which emerges is a preponderant loss of island forms (Fig. 1.4a). This holds true generally when all causes of extinction are pooled (Fig. 1.4a) or when only extinctions that exotic species are believed to have contributed to are considered (Fig. 1.4b). Second, terrestrial vertebrates have disproportionately gone extinct compared with plants (Fig. 1.4a), both in absolute terms and relative to the taxonomic richness of their respective groups. Third, the presumed causes of these extinctions are not evenly distributed among types of species interactions. Predation has been a far more important species interaction in causing extinctions than competition (Fig. 1.4c). Indeed, predation alone, i.e. in the absence of other factors like habitat destruction or pollution, is listed as being responsible for the extinction of >30% of vertebrate species (Fig. 1.4c). In contrast, competition is never listed as being the sole factor responsible for species extinction (Fig. 1.4c). Further, predation is listed as one of several contributing factors in >40% of terrestrial vertebrate extinctions, whereas competition is listed as a contributing factor in <10% of terrestrial vertebrate extinctions (Fig. 1.4c). This means that predation acting alone, or in concert with other factors is believed to have contributed to the extinction of close to 80% of all terrestrial vertebrate species, whereas competition has contributed to <10% of these extinctions (Fig. 1.4d). These patterns suggest that terrestrial vertebrates are much more likely to go extinct from predation than competition.

There are difficulties in documenting extinctions in the past. Often the precise mechanisms for any individual extinction are difficult to confidently determine because extinctions are often caused by multiple factors (species invasions, habitat destruction, human exploitation, pollution, and infectious disease) and most 'documented' extinctions actually involve some speculation about the factors responsible. Additionally, disagreement over species concepts, and disagreement over phylogenetic classifications of individual species, may alter numbers.

Generally, if a taxon is not located for 50 years it is considered extinct. It is impossible to eradicate an element of bias since it is not easy to state unequivocally that a species is no longer present when animals are known to persist unrecorded despite intensive efforts to locate them. The number of recorded extinctions could easily be an underestimate. Species that have never been described may have become extinct in historic times but scientific taxonomy only began in the mid eighteenth century and our knowledge of the more diverse tropics is just emerging. According to the Millenium Ecosystem Assessment

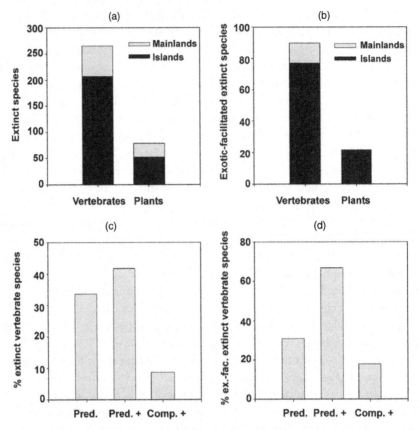

Fig. 1.4 Extinction patterns over the last 500 years, from the IUCN database. (a) The majority of documented extinctions have been on islands, as opposed to mainlands, for both terrestrial vertebrates (birds, mammals, reptiles, and amphibians) and plants; (b) extinctions facilitated by exotic species (i.e. in which exotics are listed as at least one of the factors contributing to a species extinction) show the same pattern, with more extinctions on islands, as opposed to mainlands; (c) among the 204 vertebrate species with listed causes of extinction, some form of predation (including human hunting, carnivory, and infectious disease) is cited as the sole factor responsible for species extinctions in 69 (33.8%) of extinctions, predation together with other contributing factors is cited for 85 (41.7%) of extinctions, and competition together with other factors is listed for 18 (8.8%) of extinctions. In no case is competition listed as the sole cause of species extinction; (d) extinctions facilitated by exotic species show similar patterns, with predation listed alone in 31 of 100 extinctions, predation together with other factors listed in 67 extinctions, and competition together with other factors listed in 18 extinctions. From Sax & Gaines (2008).

(2005) the rate of known extinctions of species in the past century is roughly 50–500 times greater than the extinction rate calculated from the fossil record of 0.1–1 extinctions per 1000 species per 1000 years (Fig. 1.5). The rate is up to 1000 times higher than the background extinction rates if possibly extinct species are included.

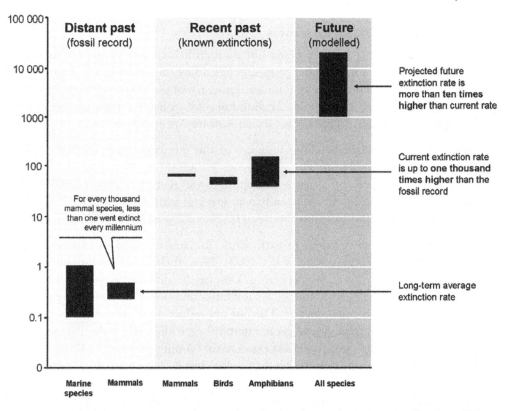

Fig. 1.5 Species extinction rates expressed as per thousand species per millennium. 'Distant past' refers to average extinction rates as estimated from the fossil record. 'Recent past' refers to extinction rates calculated from known extinctions of species (lower estimate) or known extinction plus 'possibly extinct' species (upper bound). A species is considered to be 'possibly extinct' if it is believed by experts to be extinct but extensive surveys have not yet been undertaken to confirm its disappearance. 'Future' extinctions are model-derived estimates using a variety of techniques, including species–area models, rates at which species are shifting to increasingly more threatened categories, extinction probabilities associated with the IUCN categories of threat, impacts of projected habitat loss on species loss with energy consumption. The time-frame and species groups involved differ among the 'future' estimates, but in general refer to either future loss of species based on the threat that exists today or current and future loss of species as a result of habitat changes taking place over the period of roughly 1970–2050. Estimates based on the fossil record are low certainty; lower-bound estimates for known extinctions are high certainty and upper-bound estimates are medium certainty; lower-bound estimates for modelled extinctions are low certainty and upper-bound estimates are speculative. The rate of known extinctions of species in the past century is roughly 50–500 times greater than the extinction rate calculated from the fossil record of 0.1–1 extinctions per 1000 years. The rate is up to 1000 times higher than the background extinction rates if possibly extinct species are included. From Millennium Ecosystem Assessment (2005).

1.10 Present-day extinction rates

Estimates of how many species are being lost through habitat destruction are hampered by our ignorance of the total number of species (see above) and their distribution, as well as the patterns of habitat loss. In addition, our ignorance of the effects of deforestation on species also limits our ability to predict extinctions due to habitat loss and degradation. Currently, the estimates for species loss vary enormously, primarily because:

- authors choose different baseline estimates of the number of species in the world (between 10 and 30 million);
- the proportion of species that reside in tropical forests (between 25% and 70%);
- the shape of the relationship between habitat loss and extinction;
- the rate and extent of habitat loss (between 0.5% and 2% annual global deforestation).

All these sources of uncertainty in extinction estimates can lead to extremely large errors (Simberloff, 1986; Heywood et al., 1994). Nonetheless, it is indisputable that a large extinction event is currently occurring. Despite the different ways in which these estimates were calculated, at minimum, a substantial number of the world's species are likely to go extinct in the next decade. The current reduction of diversity is believed to be destined to approach that of the great catastrophes at the end of the Paleozoic and Mesozoic eras – in other words the most extreme for 65 million years. As Wilson (1989) has said, the ultimate result is impossible to predict, but it is not something with which humanity will want to gamble.

A most significant point on the interpretation of extinction rates was made by Heywood et al. (1994). The issue revolves around the definition of what is meant by 'becoming extinct', as different authors attach distinct meanings to this. Using data for the comparatively well-studied birds and mammals (around 13 000 species), extinction rates for this century have been estimated at one species per year. Were this rate maintained, it would correspond to the average 'species lifespan' of around 10^4 years; about two to three orders of magnitude shorter than estimated from the fossil record (Raup, 1992). Contrastingly, the inferred extinction rate is almost two orders of magnitude longer than the impending extinction times (200–400 years). These extinction times have taken into account concepts such as habitat loss and species–area relations (Wilson, 1992; Reid & Miller, 1989; Simberloff, 1992), or have been derived from extrapolations of rates of species 'climbing the ladder' of IUCN-defined categories of threat from 'vulnerable' to 'endangered' to 'extinct' (Smith et al., 1993). Others have used assessments of species-by-species extinction probability distributions as functions of time to calculate the expected times when half of the species in each of ten vertebrate taxa (Mace, 1994a, 1994b) will be extinct.

Although all these theoretical estimates are beset by many uncertainties, Heywood et al. (1994) suggest that the discrepancy largely disappears if the notion of species committed to extinction is seen in the correct context, i.e. that both species–area and 'ladder-climbing' estimates are projected numbers of species. For example, Simberloff's (1992) estimate of 1350 species of birds committed to extinction by the year 2015 cannot be misinterpreted as the predicted number to become extinct between 1986 and 2015 (an average of

45 extinctions per year) since it would be implausibly high. A more empirical approach is to interpret 'committed' to extinction as referring to any species whose populations in the wild are no longer viable and will inevitably become extinct, unless major conservation actions reverse current trends (by habitat restoration, elimination of introduced predators, captive breeding and reintroduction, etc.). Using this approach, Heywood & Stuart (1992), estimated that 450 bird species will be committed to extinction by 2015, with 27 of these already probably extinct.

1.11 Why conserve biodiversity?

There are two good reasons for conserving biological diversity. The first is moral: it is right to do so. The second is practical: biological diversity supports human survival, notably through health, food and industry (McNeely et al., 1990). The fundamental social, ethical, cultural and economic values of biological resources have been recognised in most human disciplines, from religion to science. Given these multiple values it is not surprising that most cultures accept the importance of conservation. Despite this, and in order to compete for the attention of government decision-makers worldwide, policies regarding the protection of biological diversity must embrace economic values. Some conservationists take the view that biological resources are beyond quantification because they provide the biotic raw materials for every type of economic endeavour, as well as the life source for numerous indigenous and local communities (Oldfield, 1984; Oldfield & Alcorn, 1987; Bélair et al., 2010).

There is a multiplicity of ways of assessing the value of biological resources. Economists, in particular, have tried several approaches but problems arise when applying a common formula to the myriad resources used by humans. A forest's value in terms of logs would be measured differently from its value for recreation purposes or for watershed protection. Five main approaches are used to determine the value of biological resources (McNeely et al., 1990).

- **Consumptive value**: the value of natural products, e.g. firewood, fodder and game meat – these are consumed directly and do not pass through a market.
- **Productive value**: the value of products that are commercially harvested, such as game sold in a market, timber, and medicinal plants.
- **Non-consumptive value**: indirect values of ecosystem functions, such as watershed protection, photosynthesis, regulation of climate and soil production.
- **Option value**: intangible values of keeping options open for the future.
- **Existence value**: value attached to the ethical feelings of existence.

In 1992, numerous countries signed the United Nations Convention on Biological Diversity in recognition of the present and future value of biological diversity and its significant reduction around the world. Signed by 150 government leaders at the 1992 Rio Earth Summit, the Convention on Biological Diversity is dedicated to promoting sustainable development. Conceived as a practical tool for translating the principles of Agenda 21, a programme run by the UN related to sustainable development, into reality, the Convention recognises that biological diversity is about more than plants, animals and microorganisms and their ecosystems – it is about people and our need for food security, medicines, fresh air and water, shelter, and a clean and healthy environment in which to live. Signatories have legal obligations to develop national strategies and action plans for biodiversity conservation. The intention is for the Convention to be a powerful catalyst drawing together existing efforts to protect biological diversity and to provide strategic direction to the whole global effort in this area. The Convention thus provides a framework for worldwide action to conserve and use biodiversity sustainably. It addresses the full range of biological diversity at genetic, species and ecosystem levels in all environments, both within and outside protected areas. The Convention contains guiding concepts, such as the precautionary principle (Box 1.2) and gives each country the responsibility for the conservation and sustainable use of its biological resources. Most importantly, the Convention provides for the needs of developing countries to enable them to implement the Convention measures, including the provision of new and additional financial resources and appropriate access to relevant technologies.

In April 2002, at the 6th Conference of Parties to the CBD, governments committed themselves 'to achieve by 2010 a significant reduction of the current rate of biodiversity loss at the global, regional and national level as a contribution to poverty alleviation and to the benefit of all life on Earth' (Decision VI/26). This '2010 Biodiversity Target' was later endorsed at the World Summit on Sustainable Development (WSSD), and has been included in Millennium Development Goal 7 (MDG 7) under the *reducing biodiversity loss* target.

The 2010 BIP has contributed to the new 2010 Millennium Development Goals Report, to assess international efforts in reducing extreme poverty. The report, released on the 23rd June, highlights results from 60 indicators selected to measure progress towards the eight MDGs. The 2010 BIP has developed and contributed information for two of the indicators under MDG 7b; 'to reduce biodiversity loss, achieving, by 2010, a significant reduction in the rate of loss'.

The report features the BIP's 'proportion of terrestrial and marine areas protected' (Coverage of Protected Areas and overlays with biodiversity) indicator, created in partnership with UNEP-WCMC. It shows that while the proportion of protected areas has increased to 12% of the earth's land area and almost 1% of its sea area, more than two thirds of areas designated as critical for conservation remain unprotected or only partially protected.

Also included are the findings of the BIP's 'proportion of species threatened with extinction' (Red List Index) indicator, developed in partnership with Birdlife International, IUCN and ZSL. These findings are equally alarming and show that the number of species facing extinction is increasing, with mammals in developing countries particularly at risk. Both BIP indicators presented in the report show that the world has failed to meet the 2010 biodiversity target.

1.12 The science of conservation

Many creative scholars and policymakers from previously unconnected disciplines have recently converged on the problems of international conservation. Their concerns over today's perceived accelerated loss of biodiversity are based on the realisation that present threats to nature are unprecedented, that many more species are threatened with extinction than ever before (Wilson, 1988), and that the threat to biodiversity is increasing because of the demands of a rapidly growing human population, exacerbated by unequal distribution of the world's wealth and crushing poverty in many countries (Soulé, 1985). Moreover, threats to biodiversity are synergistic; several independent factors combine to make a situation worse (Myers, 1979), and especially in concert with climate change (Lovejoy & Hannah, 2005).

Thirty years ago, saving endangered species from extinction was only a small part of maintaining biological diversity. The focus of conservation was on forest, soil and water protection, fish and game management and other related disciplines. At present, with so many species at risk and the knowledge that biological diversity extends to genes and ecosystems, conservation biology has emerged as a multidisciplinary science. It is a science applied to maintaining the earth's biological diversity. Conservation biology has some unusual and unique characteristics that separate it from other sciences. It incorporates subjects which have been normally associated with the social sciences such as philosophy, psychology, economics and sociology; it also stretches into law and education, since they impinge upon ways of implementing conservation actions (Soulé, 1985). Conservation biology also relies on the pure sciences such as chemistry, mathematics and biology (i.e. genetics, habitat–animal relationships, environmental physiology). Soulé (1985) labelled conservation biology a 'crisis discipline'. In such crisis disciplines, action is better than inaction even though decisions may need to be made with incomplete information. Such immediate response requires working with available data with the best intuition and creativity one can muster, while tolerating a great deal of uncertainty. This, of course, runs counter to the way that scientists are trained, but is nonetheless necessary given the practical matters at hand. Furthermore, conservation biology is value-laden and as such rests on a number of underlying ethical assumptions that are well accepted, essentially that species diversity is good, extinction is bad, and that biological diversity has value in itself (Soulé, 1985).

Box 1.2 · *UN Convention on Biological Diversity*

The following are excerpts from the United Nations Biodiversity Treaty that was signed by every nation.

Article 8: *In-situ* conservation (on-site preservation)

Each Contracting Party shall, as far as possible and as appropriate:

- Establish a system of protected areas or areas where special measures need to be taken to conserve biological diversity;
- Develop, where necessary, guidelines for the selection, establishment and management of protected areas or areas where special measures need to be taken to conserve biological diversity;

- Regulate or manage biological resources important for the conservation of biological diversity, whether within or outside protected areas, with a view to ensuring their conservation and sustainable use;
- Promote the protection of ecosystems, natural habitats and the maintenance of viable populations of species in natural surroundings;
- Promote environmentally sound and sustainable development in areas adjacent to protected areas with a view to furthering protection of these areas;
- Rehabilitate and restore degraded ecosystems and promote the recovery of threatened species, inter alia, through the development and implementation of plans or other management strategies;
- Establish or maintain means to regulate, manage or control the risks associated with the use and release of living modified organisms resulting from biotechnology, which are likely to have adverse environmental impacts that could affect the conservation and sustainable use of biological diversity, taking into account also the risks to human health;
- Prevent the introduction of, control or eradicate those alien species which threaten ecosystems, habitats or species;
- Endeavour to provide the conditions needed for compatibility between present uses and the conservation of biological diversity and the sustainable use of its components;
- Subject to its national legislation, respect, preserve and maintain knowledge, innovations and practices of indigenous and local communities embodying traditional lifestyles relevant for the conservation and sustainable use of biological diversity, and promote their wider application with the approval and involvement of the holders of such knowledge, innovations and practices, and encourage the equitable sharing of the benefits arising from the utilisation of such knowledge, innovations and practices;
- Develop or maintain necessary legislation and/or other regulatory provisions for the protection of threatened species and populations;
- Where a significant adverse effect on biological diversity has been determined pursuant to Article 7 (Identification and Monitoring), regulate or manage the relevant processes and categories of activities; and
- Co-operate by providing financial and other support for in-situ conservation outlined above, particularly to developing countries.

Article 9. *Ex-situ* conservation (off-site preservation)

The Contracting Parties, taking into account the special needs of developing countries, shall:

- Adopt measures for the ex-situ conservation of biological diversity, preferably in the country of origin of such components;
- Establish and maintain facilities for ex-situ conservation of and research on plants, animals and microorganisms, preferably in the country of origin of genetic resources;
- Adopt measures for the recovery and rehabilitation of threatened species and for their reintroduction in their natural habitats under appropriate conditions;
- Regulate and manage collection of biological resources from natural habitats for ex-situ conservation purposes so as not to threaten ecosystems and in-situ populations of species, except where special temporary ex-situ measures are required as above.

The birth of conservation biology is commonly attributable to the First International Conference on Conservation Biology held at the University of San Diego in 1978 (Brussard, 1985), and the ensuing publication of the *Conservation Biology* volume by Soulé & Wilcox (1980). Despite its relative youth, conservation biology has advanced rapidly along two main sets of ideas or paradigms according to Caughley (1994). The first set of ideas, the small-population paradigm, deals with the risk of extinction inherent in low numbers. The second set, the declining-population paradigm, is concerned instead with the processes by which populations are driven to extinction by agents external to them. The new ideas about conservation emerging in the 1980s were almost without exception produced from within a small-population paradigm, the concern being with the population consequences of rareness and smallness (see Soulé & Wilcox, 1980). This paradigm deals with the population genetics and population dynamics problems faced by a population at risk of extinction because its numbers are small and those numbers are capped. A population on a small island, or in a zoo, transmits the appropriate image. According to Caughley (1994) this paradigm is well served by theory but its links with reality are as yet poorly developed. The declining-population paradigm revolves around detecting, diagnosing and halting a population decline. By this paradigm the problem is seen as a population in trouble because something external to it has changed, the current size of the population being of no great relevance. The research effort is aimed at determining why the population is declining and what might be done about it. Because the declining-population paradigm is rooted in empiricism it provides most of the means by which practical conservation problems might be solved. Its weakness lies in an almost complete lack of theory. It comprises mainly case studies and recovery operations, often short on scientific rigour according to Caughley (1994), that provide few opportunities for advancing our general understanding of the processes of extinction. Although Caughley's dichotomy served to point out the prevailing scientific approaches found in conservation biology, his review nonetheless advanced the idea that these two fronts overlap little. Hedrick *et al.* (1996) considered this to be false and divisive since they believe that the melding of the two paradigms is crucial. The different approaches discussed by Caughley are considered to have much in common because they both focus on the fate of a given species. Hedrick *et al.* (1996) believe that the separation is artificial because factors under the small-population paradigm are stochastic and result in the proximate cause of extinction, and those under the declining population paradigm are the deterministic (or ultimate) ones which reduce the population size so that it becomes vulnerable to random events and phenomena. They suggest an overall and comprehensive effort, which they term inclusive population viability, would be more appropriate.

1.13 Zoo conservation biology

Zoos are institutions which possess and manage collections that primarily consist of wild (non-domesticated) animals of one or more species. Zoos display at least a portion of this collection to the public for at least a significant part of the year, if not throughout the year (Chapter 3). The term zoo biology was coined by Heini Hediger (Hediger, 1969) to embrace the multitude of disciplines that come together within a zoo setting. Since as early as 1942, with the publication of Hediger's *Wildtiere in Gefangenschaft. Ein Grundriß der Tiergartenbiologie* (Hediger, 1950) significant changes have taken place in re-thinking the role of zoos. Central to the change in the role of zoos is that science is essential in understanding the basics of how to manage animals in captivity.

Zoos have been regarded as important institutions that have or are changing from mere exhibitors of wildlife to contributing directly to conservation (Chapter 4). Although the best strategy for the long-term protection of biological diversity is the preservation of natural communities and populations in the wild (*in-situ* conservation), *ex-situ* conservation can also play a crucial role. Keeping animals in captivity for solely display, a typical zoo biologist would need only to learn the ways of breeding and maintaining the species in a zoo. He or she would measure such as things as the behaviour of the animals and document their pedigree but would go no further in attempting to maintain their natural instincts and behaviours. The challenge of breeding animals in captivity for their eventual release to the wild is one which should not be shunned (Chapter 4). Our success in this aspect and the transfer of skills and knowledge developed through management of animals in zoos to manage species in the wild is a central role that zoos can play in species survival. However, the key question for zoo biologists to resolve is how we, as scientists, deal with increasing numbers of vulnerable populations. This book concentrates on this important issue, and by doing so creates a new position for biologists working in zoos or *ex-situ* breeding programmes. We have titled this new discipline *Zoo Conservation Biology*. This is a term denoting an approach that has not been described formally, though at least one university course, at the University of Plymouth, focusing on zoos, uses it. We suggest that zoo conservation biology should focus on an interdisciplinary approach, not dissimilar to what has been suggested by Hediger for zoo biology but with a different ultimate aim. Although animals in captivity need to be maintained in the best possible way, zoo conservation biology aims to do this not as its final endeavour but as a tool to conserve species from extinction. Thus, zoo conservation biologists should meld and use elements of at least four main disciplines (Fig. 1.6). These are captive animal management (Chapter 4), small population biology (Chapter 5 and 6), re-establishment of populations in the wild (Chapter 7) and relaying the importance of all this through the active education of the visiting public (Chapter 8). Each of these fields within zoo conservation biology encompasses a small part of a wider holistic and strongly cross-disciplinary domain, desirable for success in conservation.

The zoo conservation biologist must therefore, as Meffe & Carroll (1994) suggest for conservation biologists in general, think 'probabilistically' and understand the nature of scientific uncertainty. He or she must promote a non-invasive but quasi-experimental statistical investigation of the dynamics and interactions of captive individuals and populations. In this book we commit ourselves to analysing what our challenges are in conserving biodiversity, what attributes zoos have to help in this venture and more importantly how zoos can help fulfil their conservation mandates.

Although we are critical in our examination of what zoos have achieved, we offer insights into new ways of organising these institutions to become active conservation

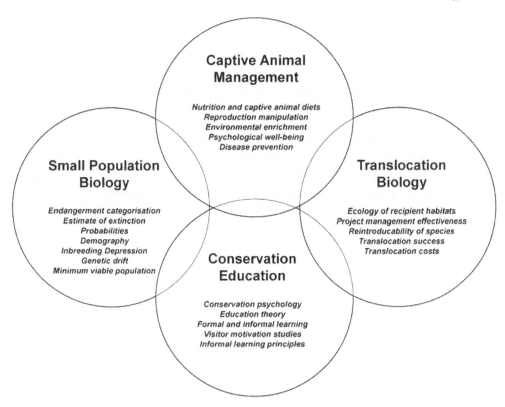

Fig. 1.6 The different fields merging in zoo conservation biology. The list of relevant sub-disciplines shown in italics is not exhaustive.

centres. This not only means encouraging zoos to continue assisting wild species through remote funding and linking with conservationists in the field, as well as educating the public, but more importantly getting zoos more involved in captive breeding **and** re-establishment of new populations of endangered taxa in the wild.

Key concepts
(1) Biodiversity is the degree of variation of life forms within a given ecosystem, biome, or an entire planet. Life on earth today consists of many millions of distinct biological species, but estimates of numbers vary significantly. Biodiversity is not consistent across the earth; it is richer in the tropics and in some specific regions but less rich in polar regions where conditions support much less biomass.
(2) The fossil record shows that since life originated the vast majority of species that existed are now extinct. The rate of known extinctions of species in the past century is roughly up to 1000 times greater than the extinction rate calculated from the fossil record.

(3) Since the emergence of humans, species have disappeared particularly through the destruction of plant and animal habitat. In addition, human practices have directly caused species extinctions through overexploitation, or indirectly through the introduction of alien predators. Survival capability and extinction vulnerability of different taxa can vary according to their ecological or life history traits.

(4) Biological resources are valuable to humans in terms of their commercial value, their importance in protecting ecosystem functions, or more intangibly in keeping options open for the future, or because of their ethical meaning.

(5) Zoos and *ex-situ* conservation can contribute directly to species conservation. Zoo conservation biology embraces this through promoting the active propagation of captive animals, the re-establishment of endangered species populations in the wild, and educating the public.

2 · *Protecting species and habitats*

'The beauty and genius of a work of art may be reconceived . . . but when the last individual of a race of living things breathes no more, another heaven and another earth must pass before such a one can be again' (William Beebe)

2.1 Introduction

The roots of the modern environmental movement can be traced to nineteenth-century Europe and North America in which a mix of passion, power, calculation and even remorse motivated elites to safeguard wildlife. It was through the emergence of the 'penitent butcher' (Beinart & Coates, 1995), epitomised by the 'repentance' of prominent hunters, themselves the cause of much megafauna to plummet (tigers, lions, elephants and rhinos in Africa and Asia, bison, moose and bear in North America), that the need for species conservation, albeit only of large-bodied species, emerged (Adams, 2004; MacKenzie, 1988). The result was the creation of influential NGOs such as the Sierra Club in the USA in 1892 (Carter, 2007), or the UK's Society for the Preservation of the Fauna of the Empire (now Fauna and Flora International) in 1903 (Fitter & Scott, 1978).

Equally, the start of WWF in 1961, amid fears that habitat destruction and hunting would soon bring about the extinction of much of Africa's wildlife, was a landmark for species conservation. But, by the end of the 1970s, WWF's work had broadened to encompass not only the conservation of wildlife and habitats, but also the wider implications of human activities on the environment. Although of course such expansion of efforts is warranted, there has been concern that attention given to species conservation has diminished. Some, as demonstrated through initiatives like the Mohamed Bin Zayed Species Conservation Fund (2010), maintain that conservation of endangered taxa has become a peripheral preoccupation (and therefore is less funded!).

The claim of those in favour of addressing the bigger environmental issues, or crises, is that by conserving ecosystems, species-status will also benefit in the long-term. Indeed, conservation is not just about avoiding extinctions but about restoring or recovering habitats and landscapes. After all, habitats must meet the needs of species that depend on them in order to ensure populations reach secure levels, whilst preventing other species from reaching such a perilous situation in the first place. Thus often, single-species conservation programmes can be used as a means towards protecting larger numbers of species and natural habitat using targeted taxa as representatives or symbols for habitat and sympatric fauna and flora. The latter concept revolves around the description of a single species that can be used to represent others, either from an ecological perspective (Caro & O'Doherty, 1999), i.e. keystone, or umbrella species, or which can have a public relations role, i.e. flagship species.

The value of focusing on measurable objectives in conservation is receiving increased attention, due in part to a demand for accountability (Salafsky & Margoluis, 2003; Parrish et al., 2003). Identifying and securing biodiversity priority areas should form the framework upon which to build other conservation actions. This process, known as systematic conservation planning, employs the analyses of numerical data on the distribution of biodiversity (Margules & Sarkar, 2007). Such quantitative methods can be applied to measures of biodiversity value, including phylogenetic diversity, species, higher taxa, vegetation or land classes, or most other biodiversity surrogates (Gaston & Blackburn, 1995). Identification and prioritisation of these areas have been achieved at national and global scales by a variety of quantitative methods. These area-selection methods are sets of rules designed to achieve particular goals efficiently and with accountability. They also have the ability to promote flexibility in the planning process, aid communication and facilitate exploration of alternative values, goals and data (Williams et al., 1996).

There is no single objective way to measure the importance of the various components of biodiversity, and equally difficult to choose priorities for managing them (Caldecott et al., 1994). Since the pioneering work of Myers (1988), there has been much emphasis on developing strategies to best allocate resources for species and habitat conservation at a global scale. Recent papers on optimal preservation policy have tried to integrate three main considerations: the relative uniqueness of different species or habitats, the degree of risk to their continued survival, and the cost of the resources needed to enhance their prospects for survival.

In this chapter, we first review the range of methods used in systematic conservation planning, and argue that these schemes have been crucial for conservationists to identify high priority areas for conserving biodiversity, from the global level down to individual sites. We then introduce and examine the IUCN Red List as the accepted standard for species global extinction risk. For more than four decades the list has not only served to highlight species at greatest risk of extinction, but also to guide conservation responses. We present data and analyses on the distribution of threatened species worldwide, and discuss regions of greatest concentration of these taxa. Finally, we discuss the two broad strategies used in conserving species: protected areas and surrogate approaches. By doing this, we aim to direct attention to high priority areas for both *in-situ* and *ex-situ* conservation activities.

2.2 Systematic conservation planning

2.2.1 The science of selection

The key question for conservationists is how best to focus conservation efforts for maximum effectiveness and answering 'which is the minimum set of areas within a region required to represent all species of a taxonomic group to be protected'? It may often be more appropriate to pursue goals for maximising biodiversity representation as a maximal-covering set of areas (Humphries *et al.*, 1995). This idea asks 'what is the greatest number of species that can be represented in a certain percentage of the total area in question?' (Vane-Wright *et al.*, 1991). The practical outcome of area-selection methods is to point out 'high priority areas' for *in-situ* conservation. This is important in deciding which combinations of available areas could represent the most biodiversity value for the future. Though this is a useful tool for finding the 'where first' and 'how much', it does not of course solve the 'how' — this is another issue.

The selection of priority areas for biodiversity protection employs two widely accepted principles for prioritising conservation action: 'vulnerability' or 'threat' (i.e. the likelihood that the biodiversity in that site will be lost) and 'irreplaceability' (i.e. the degree to which options for conservation are lost without the site) (Margules & Pressey, 2000). In most approaches species endemism rather than species richness is targeted. This may be so because although species richness is easier to quantify than endemism, it is driven by widespread and non-endangered species and is thus normally not, or only indirectly, used for priority setting (Brooks *et al.*, 2006; Ceballos *et al.*, 2005). Endemic species (see issues around definitions of endemism, Box 2.1) not only have restricted distributions and a limited number of sites suitable for conservation management, but they often have smaller population sizes than widespread species. Thus, they are more vulnerable to anthropogenic impacts and to extinction. Global conservation priorities based on richness alone have been regarded as 'of little practical use for conservation' as they 'overlook many endemic species' and therefore fail the 'irreplaceability' criteria (Lamoreux *et al.*, 2006). Indeed, the extensive literature on the development of methods for the selection of priority areas has focused on finding the minimum set of areas that represent all species in occurrence locations (Williams, 1998; Cabeza & Moilanen, 2001), or, recently, on finding appropriate areas that maximise probabilities of species persistence (Bonn *et al.*, 2002). This view has become so predominant, that the performance of existing protected area systems is commonly measured in terms of the proportion of the regional, threatened or endemic species pool that it encompasses. However, complete representation of overall species diversity will not be achieved by area selection based on indicator groups alone (see, for example, Moore *et al.*, 2003).

Box 2.1 · *Definition of an endemic species*

The concept of endemism is useful in quantifying the biological uniqueness of an area, and has been used by many authors as a meaningful alternative to simple species richness. The traditional definition of endemism included those species with ranges restricted to a particular region, and therefore it is useful only in reference to that region. To compare different regions, a standardized approach is required. Several authors have used an areal definition of endemism, such that a species in less than a certain area (e.g. $50\,000$ km^2) is considered endemic. Townsend & Watson (1998) have noted that there are several problems with this approach, largely to do with scaling issues; as the area threshold changes, the picture of endemism that appears also varies. Most importantly, the areal definition of endemism assumes equal levels of heterogeneity in different landscapes which over-emphasises fine-grained regions.

Table 2.1 *Global biodiversity conservation prioritisations. For each proposal, definitions, the primary conservation organisation utilising the template, and the most relevant references are included. From Brooks et al. (2006)*

Proposal/Organisation	Description	References
Crisis ecoregions *WWF-US*	305 ecoregions with ≥20% habitat conversion and within which the percentage conversion is ≥2 times the percentage protected area coverage.	Hoekstra *et al.* (2005).
Biodiversity hotspots *CI*	34 biogeographically similar aggregations of ecoregions holding ≥0.5% of the world's plants as endemics, and with ≥70% of primary habitat already lost.	Mittermeier *et al.* (1998, 1999, 2004); Myers, (1988, 1990, 1991); Myers *et al.* (2000).
Endemic bird areas *Birdlife International*	218 regions ≥2 bird species with global ranges of <50 000 km², and with more of these endemic than are shared with adjacent regions.	ICBP (1992); Crosby (1994); Long *et al.* (1996); Stattersfield *et al.* (1998).
Centres of plant diversity *IUCN*	234 mainland sites holding >1000 plant species, of which ≥10% are endemic either to the site or the region; or islands containing ≥50 endemic species or ≥10% of flora endemic.	WWF; IUCN (1994–7).
Megadiversity countries *CI*	Countries holding ≥1% of the world's plants as endemics.	Mittermeier (1988); Mittermeier *et al.* (1997).
Global 200 ecoregions *WWF-US*	142 terrestrial ecoregions with biomes characterised by high species richness, endemism, taxonomic uniqueness, unusual phenomena, or global rarity of major habitat type.	Olson & Dinerstein (1998, 2002).
High-biodiversity wilderness areas *CI*	5 biogeographically similar aggregations of ecoregions with ≥0.5% of the world's plants as endemics, and with ≥70% of primary habitat remaining and ≥5 people per km².	Mittermeier *et al.* (2002, 2003).
Frontier forests *WRI*	Forested regions large enough to support viable populations of all native species, dominated by native tree species, and with structure and composition driven by natural events.	Bryant *et al.* (1997).
Last of the wild *WCS*	10% wildest 1-km² grid cells in each biome, with wildness measured with an aggregate index of human density, land transformation, access, and infrastructure.	Sanderson *et al.* (2002).

High vulnerability

Low vulnerability

High irreplaceability

UNEP WCMC maintains an updated database and detailed overview of published areas of biodiversity importance (see UNEP WCMC, 2011).

2.2.2 Institutional approaches to global biodiversity conservation

The number of different approaches to global conservation championed by conservation organisations has increased in number, scope, and complexity in recent years (Redford *et al.*, 2003). According to Brooks *et al.* (2006), since 1988, at least nine major institutional templates of global biodiversity conservation prioritisation, developed exclusively by nongovernmental organisations, have emerged (Table 2.1). Most of these (six out of the nine) prioritise highly irreplaceable regions, and can be classified into areas of high (reactive) or low vulnerability (proactive). Irreplaceability measures generally refer to species endemism, but other aspects of irreplaceability may include taxonomic uniqueness, unusual phenomena or global rarity of major habitat types (Olson & Dinerstein, 1998). The logic behind protecting these areas is that the greater the number of endemic species in a region, the more biodiversity is lost if that region vanishes.

Because of the differences in emphasis on irreplaceability or vulnerability, resulting priority maps may cover less than one-tenth of the globe or more than a third of the earth's land surface. Some authors have shown concern about this, suggesting that this has bedevilled conservation and its supporters, and have called for greater collaboration between conservationists and less duplication of efforts (Mace *et al.*, 2000; Olson *et al.*, 2001). However, Conservation International's hotspots, WWF's Global 200 Ecoregions, BirdLife International's EBAs and the IUCN and WWF's centres of plant diversity are highly congruent despite their differing scales of analysis (da Fonseca *et al.*, 2000).

Despite the general congruence that may exist between the nine main global approaches, organisations may wish to promote their particular slant to endorse their 'unique selling point'. Approaches may also diverge because of the organisations' histories and values. On the other hand, for some institutions, as shown by Redford *et al.* (2003), conservation aims are less precisely specified or are left vague. Also, sometimes targets are confined to those that are non-human, or 'natural', or sometimes extended to include humans as well as in conserving particular human communities. In some cases the category of species is parsed, with some approaches targeting all species (Global 200) and others giving priority to endemic species (hotspots), landscape species (landscape-species approach), or certain taxa such as birds (endemic bird areas). The same is true with communities or ecosystems, with the hotspots approach focusing on threatened areas, Global Forest Watch focusing on forested ecosystems, and Wetlands of International Importance focusing on wetlands. Other approaches, typically with the word 'landscape' in their names, have targets that extend from species to communities and ecosystems and include ecological processes (e.g. landscape species, site-conservation planning, and designing sustainable landscapes). Biodiversity, usually undefined, is also commonly a specified target. When it is specified, it is often in conjunction with non-biological targets. For example, the ecosystem approach focuses on conserving biological diversity while assuring sustainable use and full sharing of benefits arising from functioning ecosystems. Species are identified as the target of 15 of the approaches surveyed in Redford *et al.* (2003), masking nonetheless important differences, connected with species targets and principles. Finally, many approaches have multiple targets following the often unstated logic that single-species approaches are by themselves necessary but insufficient to achieve conservation.

Box 2.2 · *Biodiversity hotspots – a conservation icon*

The 'biodiversity hotspot' approach has been the dominant conservation paradigm for over two decades. This approach has been highly successful in mobilising donors; Brooks *et al.* (2006) give the figure of $750 million of funding for these regions. Kareiva & Marvier (2003) allude to the following limitation in the hotspot approach; one that Myers *et al.* (2000) explicitly acknowledge and attempt to address.

The hotspots Myers originally identified were based entirely on the distribution of vascular plants. Those identified more recently are based on a more extensive database, including vascular plants, mammals, birds, reptiles, and amphibians – no fish, no insects, no arachnids, no fungi, no lichens, no mosses, and no microorganisms. Unless the distribution of species in different major groups of taxa corresponds to a high degree, it is possible that the hotspots Myers *et al.* (2000) identified are hotspots for vascular plants and tetrapods, while the hotspots for insects or microorganisms would be found in very different places. Their data suggest a fairly high degree of congruence between vascular plants and tetrapods, but their analysis cannot tell us how well their approach would work for the vast array of species not included in their analysis.

Over and above the data limitations of the hotspots approach, its global application has been disputed because decision-makers may see it as a cure all (a risk with all well-promoted strategies), and the world outside the hotspots would remain or become a 'cold spot'. This is particularly so in complex areas of international policy, such as biodiversity conservation, where strategies need to be applied in different ecological, political and cultural situations, against a background of urgency, irreversibility and scientific uncertainty. The notion of a 'biodiversity crisis' combined with such complexity increases the appeal of conceptually simple strategies such as the hotspots scheme. It was appropriate for CI, a US based non-government organisation with a global vision, to choose a single strategy as their focus. However, governments or public bodies are charged with delivering values to which society aspires (e.g. peace, economic growth, nature conservation, good governance, equity), and should therefore evaluate carefully such strategies before incorporating them into their national policy.

2.2.3 Selecting priority areas for species conservation

'Priority areas' are those areas considered most important for the conservation of biodiversity (Margules *et al.*, 2002). The main roles are to represent patterns and/or processes of biodiversity and to protect them from threats to their persistence (Gaston *et al.*, 2002; Margules *et al.*, 2002). The selection of priority areas is driven by the interpretation of underpinning biological data on species, habitats and biodiversity and may include socio-economic projections such as cost analysis, economics, likelihood of managing negative human interference and projections of anthropogenic induced threat (McBride *et al.*, 2007; Lee & Jetz, 2008). It takes place in a context of subjective belief systems (human attitudes, public appeal, focus on phylogenetic unique species as opposed to species-rich taxa), which may be specifically accounted for or not (Miller *et al.*, 2006). Global priority setting has focussed on individual species and groups of species or habitats and ecosystems. The two dominant approaches used today in setting priorities for biodiversity conservation across large geographic regions are by and large complementary. One focuses on conserving individual species and groups of species, the other on conserving habitat and landscapes.

The most often used metrics to identify and prioritise the importance of areas for conservation of biodiversity are species richness and endemism. In both cases, the relative biological importance of the areas being evaluated is commonly gauged by species richness per unit area though other inputs may include the number of endemic species, the number of places having ecological or evolutionary phenomena, or the condition of habitats (Jennings *et al.*, 2004). But often the predominant underpinning paradigm is species protection of rare and endangered taxa rather than the representation of overall species diversity (Bonn & Gaston, 2005). Guidelines for the selection of priority areas for conservation, however, have focussed principally on species protection, and especially that of rare or endangered species.

The strength of correlation in species richness between taxa is context and scale dependent (Grenyer *et al.*, 2006; Hess *et al.*, 2006). The mismatch between grid-based mapping and species occupancy can wrongly quantify spatial patterns of species richness and endemism, and thus significantly contribute to the misidentification of hotspots and thus non-congruence of different types of hotspots (Hurlbert & Jetz, 2007). Hurlbert & Jetz (2007) show a mismatch between the presumed (range maps) and actual occupancy of species at resolutions less than two degrees (approx. 200 km): range maps overestimate the area of occupancy of individual species and mischaracterise spatial patterns of species richness, resulting in up to two-thirds of biodiversity hotspots being misidentified.

Instead of analysing spatial patterns of biodiversity based on spatial grids, Lamoreux *et al.* (2006) used ecoregions as biological sample units. They showed that patterns of species richness among major terrestrial vertebrate taxa are correlated and that aggregate regions selected for high levels of endemism capture significantly more species than expected by chance. More recently, a global gap analysis of priority areas for conservation has highlighted a serious absence of small tropical islands (Rodrigues *et al.*, 2004a). Such islands have typically high levels of endemism, have often experienced high levels of extinctions in the near past and the remaining faunas are highly threatened (Pimm *et al.*, 1995). However, small islands are naturally species-poor 'and as such tend to have low absolute numbers of threatened species, even if these are a high proportion of their entire fauna' (Rodrigues *et al.*, 2004a). Empirical logit transformation of endemicity, or delta endemism (Fa & Funk, 2007; Funk & Fa, 2010) which jointly accounts for endemicity and species richness, identifies exactly these circumstances. Here, ecoregions with relatively high values of delta endemism tend to be isolated areas, such as islands and highlands, which have generated endemic species even if absolute species richness is low.

Several analyses of worldwide species distributions have demonstrated non-congruence of different indicator (surrogate) taxa, and non-congruence of hotspots of species richness, endemism, and extinction threat. However, other studies indicate good cross-taxon surrogacy and good performance of existing global conservation strategies. Prendergast et al. (1993a) concluded that patterns of species richness among major taxa are not well correlated. For example, they found places of high bird species richness differed from places of high butterfly species richness at a 10 km^2 resolution in Britain. Similarly, Qian & Ricklefs (2008) showed that numbers of species of vascular plants and of four terrestrial vertebrate taxa (mammals, birds, reptiles and amphibians) vary in parallel across 296 geographic areas covering most of the globe, even after accounting for sample area, climate, topographic heterogeneity and differences between continents. Similarly, Fjeldså (2000) discovered that richness 'hotspots' covered only a small fraction of the endangered species of 798 Andean bird species, recorded in 15 × 15′ grid cells. 'Hotspots of endemism' provided better guidance, and complementarity was decidedly best, but with generic data neither of these approaches was effective. Thus, 'hotspots' in terms of representing all features of interest is problematic, but endemism and complementarity are better performing principles (see Pressey & Nicholls, 1989).

Areas with the greatest numbers of endemic or restricted range species are considered of high conservation value, because protecting rare species is analogous to conserving extraordinary works of art. In this context, assessment is often based on single-country endemics, or some identifiable region within a country. Although not biologically meaningful, the use of country boundaries when assessing endemicity makes great practical sense since conservation action is usually administered at the national level. From a wider conservation perspective, the question of interest is whether levels of endemism in one taxon are correlated with those of others. If endemism patterns are similar for a variety of groups then conservation measures focusing on high endemism areas will protect a larger proportion of biodiversity. Bibby et al. (1992) examined available data for other groups to compare with bird data, and showed that endemism in the larger vertebrates is often, though not always, related.

2.3 Targeting endangered species

2.3.1 Defining endangerment

The purpose of categorising species endangerment is to highlight taxa with a high extinction risk. The IUCN has published lists of species at risk of disappearance since the 1950s, compiling these as Red Data Books in the 1960s and as Red Lists since the 1980s Collar (1993–4, 1996). Started as general compendia about endangered mammals and birds, the books first appeared in 1966 (Munton, 1987). Initially, species were assigned to qualitatively defined categories. Because of the inherent subjectivity in the Red Data Book categories and the resulting differences in the quality and quantity of information needed to support the assessment, the categories had to be reassessed (Fitter & Fitter, 1987). In 1990, IUCN began a process to redefine the categories of threat used in the Red Data Books. Mace & Lande (1991) put forward a set of categories, fewer in number than those existing at the time, and which described the probability of extinction of a species within

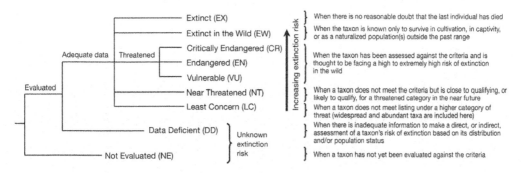

Fig. 2.1 The IUCN Red List categories. From Hoffmann *et al.* (2008), adapted from IUCN (2001).

a specified time-frame. With increasing threat levels the probabilities increase and the time-frame shortens. This makes sense both in biological and in practical terms.

In contrast to the original Red Data books, the Mace–Lande assessments of species endangerment were based on general principles of population biology with broad applicability, as well as being appropriate across a wide range of life forms. Having said this, the process of assigning species to categories is always an evolving one (though one which must be closely controlled and upon which a formal probabilistic analysis can be based). Even when considerable information does exist there may be substantial uncertainties in the extinction risks obtained from population models containing parameters that are difficult to estimate accurately. Parameters such as environmental stochasticity (temporal fluctuations in demographic variables such as age or development stage-specific mortality and fertility rates), rare catastrophic events, as well as inbreeding depression and genetic variability and, in particular, characteristics required for adaptation are all difficult to estimate accurately. Because of these reasons, it may not be possible to do an accurate probabilistic viability analysis even for some very well studied species. The categorisation of many species can nonetheless be based on more qualitative criteria derived from the same body of theory as the definitions above. This was incorporated in the Mace–Lande risk-ranking system, integrating quantitative categories and criteria. This system presented several advances, notably: (1) enabling consistent application by different people; (2) being based around probabilistic assessment of extinction risk; (3) incorporation of a time-scale; (4) flexibility of data required and population units to which it applied; and (5) ability to handle uncertainty.

The Mace–Lande system was formally adopted in 1994 by IUCN (IUCN, 1994). Whereas the first IUCN Red List assessments depended on knowledge complemented by a large dose of subjective common sense, these new categories and criteria improved repeatability and consistency in the listing process. The most recent revision to the criteria (Fig. 2.1, Table 2.2) was approved by IUCN in 2001 (IUCN, 2001). Since then, there has been considerable emphasis on improving the taxonomic coverage, rigour, justification, and transparency of IUCN Red List assessments. For example, partly in response to criticisms (see Mrosovsky, 1997), assessments are now underpinned by mandatory

Table 2.2 *Simplified overview of thresholds for the IUCN Red List criteria. Adapted from Butchart et al. (2004). AOO = area of occupancy; EOO = extent of occupancy; na = not applicable*

Criterion	Critically endangered	Endangered	Vulnerable	Qualifiers and notes
A1: reduction in population size	≥90%	≥70%	≥50%	Over 10 years/3 generations in the past, where causes are reversible, AND understood AND have ceased.
A2–4: reduction in population size	≥80%	≥50%	≥30%	Over 10 years/3 generations in the past, future or combination.
B1: small range (EOO)	<100 km^2	<5000 km^2	<20 000 km^2	Plus 2 of (1) severe fragmentation/few locations (1, ≥5, ≥10), (2) continuing decline, (3) extreme fluctuation.
B2: small range (AOO)	<10 km^2	<500 km^2	<2000 km^2	Plus 2 of (1) severe fragmentation/few locations (1, ≥5, ≥10), (2) continuing decline, (3) extreme fluctuation.
C: small and declining population	<250	<2500	<10 000	Mature individuals. Continuing decline either (1) over specified rates and time periods or (2) with (a) specified population structure or (b) extreme fluctuation.
D1: very small population	<50	<250	<1000	Mature individuals.
D2: very restricted population	na	na	<20 km^2 AOO or ≥5 populations	Capable of becoming Critically Endangered or even Extinct within a very short time-frame.
E: quantitative analysis	≥50% in 10 yr/3 generations	≥20% in 10 yr/5 generations	≥10% in 100 yr	Estimated extinction risk using quantitative models (e.g. population viability analyses).

supporting documentation, including information on geographic range and abundance, habitats, threats, and conservation actions (IUCN, 2010); these assessments are consultative, now increasingly facilitated through workshops and web-based open-access systems (e.g. BirdLife International's Globally Threatened Bird forums), and peer-reviewed.

The regular publication of Red Lists continues to serve as a means of generating public interest and to focus attention on the listed species. They have a very important role in publicity for, and planning of, species-based conservation programmes. Red Lists are used by different groups (lay public, national and international legislators and conservation professionals). In fact, Scott *et al.* (1987) argued that in many cases the mere inclusion of a species in the Red List has had as much effect on raising awareness as any of the supporting data (see also Fitter, 1974).

2.3.2 Threatened species according to the IUCN Red List

The IUCN Red List in 2000 included assessments for 16 507 species, 1406 of which were listed as threatened (Hilton-Taylor *et al.*, 2000). By 2004, the list incorporated 38 047 species, 15 589 of which were threatened (Baillie *et al.*, 2004); and by 2008 the list included 44 838 species, 16 928 of which are threatened (Vié *et al.*, 2009). However, the conservation status for most of the world's species remains poorly known, and there is a strong bias in those that have been assessed so far towards terrestrial vertebrates and plants and in particular those species found in biologically well-studied parts of the world. Efforts are underway to rectify these biases and comprehensive assessments (in which every species has been evaluated) are now available for an increased number of taxonomic groups, namely amphibians, birds, mammals, cycads and conifers, warm water reef-forming corals, freshwater crabs, and groupers. In addition, taxonomic coverage is being broadened through a randomised sampled approach which provides representative samples (Collen *et al.*, 2009). Closer examination of some of these taxonomic groups reveals that the proportions of threatened species differ markedly between groups (Fig. 2.2), with the percentage threatened ranging from 12% for birds to 52% for cycads. Generally, it seems that the more mobile groups (birds and dragonflies) are less threatened, although once the status of the Data Deficient dragonflies is resolved that group may have a much higher proportion of threatened species. Currently the two groups with the highest proportions of threatened species are the amphibians and cycads. Species in these groups generally have smaller ranges and are hence more easily impacted by threats, e.g. a pathogenic disease (chytridiomycosis) caused by the chytrid fungus in the case of amphibians, and illegal collection in the case of the cycads.

2.4 Conserving species

2.4.1 Definitions

Conservation of biodiversity can be achieved in a number of complementary ways. These methods can be broadly classified into: (1) *in-situ* conservation, which includes

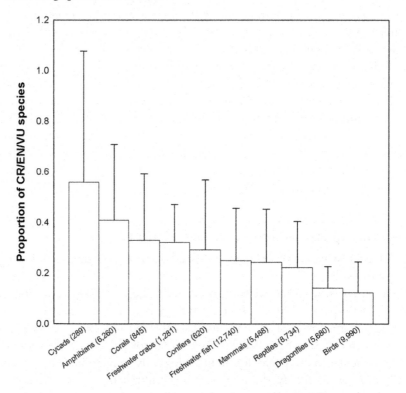

Fig. 2.2 Proportion of species threatened with extinction in different taxonomic groups. Asterisks indicate those groups in which estimates are derived from a randomised sampling approach. The estimates assume that Data Deficient species are equally threatened as non-Data Deficient species; error bars show minimum and maximum estimates if all Data Deficient species are Least Concern or Threatened, respectively. Numbers on the horizontal axis indicate the total number of described species in each group. Corals include only warm water reefbuilding species. From Hilton–Taylor *et al.* (2009).

conservation of plants and animals in their native ecosystems or even in man–made ecosystems, where they naturally occur and (2) *ex-situ* conservation, which includes conservation of samples of genetic diversity (particularly representing endangered species) away from their natural habitats.

Since the 1992 Earth Summit in Rio, *in-situ* conservation has been designated, expressly, as the legal and institutional priority with the maintenance of ecosystems, habitats and component species as the main emphasis. Thus, the prevailing regulation, the CBD, addresses a range of practices relating to *in-situ* measures for conservation, with *ex-situ* in a secondary role (Chapter 1). Other conventions also establish the prevalence of *in-situ* conservation methods with some appreciation of the benefits of *ex-situ* strategies. For example, Article VII of CITES acknowledges that *ex-situ* approaches in captive breeding endangered species can facilitate some trade in a species whilst its wild populations remain subject to an outright trade ban.

The *in-situ* conservation focus derives primarily from scientific considerations regarding the conservation and ecosystem benefits which accrue from protection of integrated habitats and ecosystems. Although there is no doubt that the maximum amount of biological diversity can be best conserved through long-term conservation of landscapes that collectively encompass diverse ecosystems and the variety of species therein, some species are so greatly diminished that the remnant populations are at an unacceptably high risk. For these species, *ex-situ* care and biotechnology are crisis responses to the threat of extinction.

Ex-situ conservation in zoos, aquaria, botanic gardens and germplasm banks should compliment *in-situ* techniques in pursuit of maintaining viable populations of species in natural habitats. This involves conservation of genetic resources, as well as wild and cultivated species, and draws on a diverse body of techniques and facilities which include: (1) gene banks, e.g. seed banks, sperm and ova banks; (2) *in-vitro* plant tissue and microbial culture collections, as well as (3) captive breeding of animals and artificial propagation of plants, with possible reintroduction into the wild.

Out-of-the-wild contributions to species conservation are indeed constrained by technical issues, infrastructure, limited or conflicting organisational missions, and perceived prohibitive costs (Chapter 6). However, the increasing body of evidence for current and predicted higher extinction rates from climate change (Gregory *et al.*, 2009) fundamentally challenges the wisdom of a heavy dependence on *in-situ* strategies, and dictates that *ex-situ* tools are brought much more to the forefront.

Key elements of the international conservation community acknowledge an evolution in the application of *ex-situ* conservation (Chapter 6). The major shift has been in the acknowledgment of *ex-situ* conservation as a set of techniques to support integrated management of wild and captive populations. For its part, the IUCN, through its published guidelines on *ex-situ* conservation, has stressed that such practices must be adopted because *in-situ* conservation will not always be sufficient to ensure the long-term existence of many species. The *ex-situ* conservation instruments are those organisations that hold wild plant and animal species, primarily zoos and botanical gardens.

2.4.2 Area-based conservation

Traditionally, one of the most widely used, and arguably, the most effective tool for achieving conservation goals at the landscape level, protected areas, today play a key role in supporting local, national and international biodiversity policies (Coad *et al.*, 2009; Jenkins & Joppa, 2009). They also serve as places for scientific research, wilderness protection, and maintenance of ecosystem services, education, tourism and recreation. In India, protected areas have existed since the fourth century BC with the establishment of Abhayaranxyas or forest reserves. The first modern examples of protected areas were established towards the end of the nineteenth century. By the beginning of this century many countries had either already established protected areas or were contemplating doing so.

The concept, however, was slow to develop since no country had in place a comprehensive network of actively managed protected areas until the 1940s. After World War

II, the number of areas established continued to be low, and the rate at which land was being incorporated into the system did not increase above World War II levels until the early 1960s. In 1962, the establishment of protected areas began to increase dramatically. An important stimulus for this may have been the first World Parks Congress held in Seattle, USA in 1962. The world's system of protected areas has grown exponentially since the 1970s, particularly in developing countries where biodiversity is greatest. The creation of the 97 million ha Greenland National Park in 1974 and of the Great Barrier Reef Marine Park in the 1980s (34 million ha) had a marked effect on the global area designated for conservation. Concurrently, the mission of protected areas has expanded from biodiversity conservation to improving human welfare. The result is a shift in favour of protected areas allowing local resource use (Naughton-Treves et al., 2005).

There are considerable regional contrasts in how protected areas are developed. This variation can be accounted for by differences in:

- cultural and historical factors;
- development of interest in wildlife and conservation;
- patterns of settlement and land-use.

However, for most regions, networks of protected areas are a recent phenomenon, with only Africa and North America having areas established before 1962.

Protected areas provide an effective means to conserve biodiversity (see Brandon et al., 1998; Bruner et al., 2001; Sánchez-Azofeifa et al., 1999). For this reason, conservationists at the 1982 World Parks Congress in Bali recommended that all nations strive to place 10% of their lands under protection for conservation (McNeely & Miller, 1985). By 2008, the amount of the earth's terrestrial surface covered by parks reached 11.6%; protected areas now cover from a low of 3% in Oceania to a maximum of around 21% in Latin American and Caribbean countries (WDPA, 2010). In contrast, marine protected areas occupy less than 6% of the earth's territorial seas and only 0.5% of the extraterritorial seas.

The critical step for ensuring persistence in protecting biological communities is to establish legally designated protected areas. This, of course, is not enough without active management, but it is a valuable starting point. Most countries have areas of natural ecosystems or habitats which are subject to some degree of control and protection. Many different legal and administrative mechanisms are used by governments to manage habitats for the conservation of biodiversity but protected area systems are central to this management. Protected areas can be established in a variety of ways, but the two most common are through government action (often at a national, regional or local level), and purchases of land by non-governmental organisations or even private individuals (e.g. APNR, is an association of privately owned nature reserves bordering on the Kruger National Park, South Africa).

Although there is much variation in the mechanisms used to create and maintain systems of protected areas, some standards for making international comparisons have been used. The IUCN, through the CNPPA, has developed a classification for different types of areas, based upon management objectives. The system has ten different classes of protected areas, two of these, World Heritage Sites and Biosphere Reserves, being international designations (WDPA, 2010). Five of these categories are truly protected areas, with the habitat managed for biological diversity. Areas in three categories are not managed primarily for biological diversity but they still may contain many or even most of their original species. These managed areas may be particularly significant since they are often much larger than protected areas.

Among nations there is a great deal of variation in protection: only 45% of the 236 countries and territories assessed had more than 10% of their terrestrial area protected, and only 14% had more than 10% of their marine area protected. Managed nature reserves/wildlife sanctuaries are the most prevalent category in terms of protected sites. National parks cover more area than any other category. The prevalence of different categories also varies according to region. In Europe, for example, most protected areas are managed as protected landscapes in contrast to Australia, where the predominant protected area category is national park (tracts of land set aside for human recreation and enjoyment, animal and environmental protection and restricted from most development). This discrepancy is a reflection of the amount of land surface left untouched.

Although overall protected area coverage is increasing gradually, the size distribution of protected areas is heavily biased towards relatively small sites. The most common size for a protected area on a worldwide basis is only 10–30 km^2. However, the majority of the world's 7.7 million km^2 of protected area is contained in relatively few large sites. These figures suggest that fragmentation may be a problem in providing protection to many of the world's natural habitats. The country's economy and the number and size of protected areas contained in it are related. Based on per capita income, for example, protected areas are evenly spread regardless of the country's wealth. Average size of protected areas is smaller for the large low-income group. OECD countries also have small protected areas probably reflecting the high population densities of these countries.

Besides protecting biodiversity and habitats (Rodrigues et al., 2004b), protected areas are also increasingly recognised for their role in protecting ecosystem services such as carbon, water, climate and soil stabilisation, and various timber and non-timber products (Raudsepp-Hearne et al., 2010). However, there is considerable debate on the extent to which protected areas deliver conservation outcomes in terms of species and habitat protection (Meir et al., 2004; Rodrigues et al., 2004a), largely because many protected areas are present only 'on paper', having no effective management on the ground (Chape et al., 2005).

Researchers recently completed the first systematic gap analysis of the entire global network of terrestrial protected areas (Rodrigues et al., 2004a,b). In simple terms, their study compared distribution maps for 11 633 vertebrate species – comprising mammals, amphibians, freshwater turtles and tortoises, and globally threatened birds – with maps of the world's protected areas. In the first step of the global gap analysis, all species lacking any coverage in protected areas were identified, revealing 1424 that the analysis classified as full gap species (Rodrigues et al., 2004b). The global gap analysis identified 1396 cells in the global grid as priority locations for the expansion of the network of protected areas. Geographically, the vast majority of these gap cells (85%) occur in the tropics, primarily

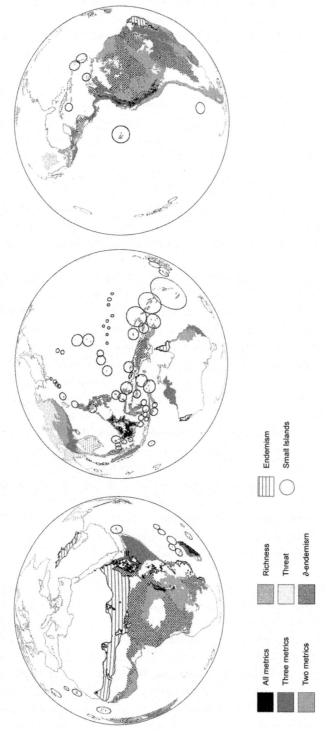

Fig. 2.3 Global maps of areas of importance for species richness, endemism and threat of terrestrial vertebrates. The maps were derived from distribution data of amphibians, reptiles, birds and mammals found in terrestrial ecoregions. Total, endemic and threatened species richness and an estimator for richness-adjusted endemism were used as metrics in continuous prioritisation. Using the top 100 ecoregions as defined by these metrics, the maps below show separate areas endemism, richness, and threat, and those areas where two, three or all metrics overlap. Small islands, which are too small to be seen on the map, are highlighted by light circles (∂-endemism) or dark circles (two overlapping metrics). Given such contrasts in the areas selected by the different metrics, major efforts to protect global biodiversity must involve complementary conservation approaches in areas of unique species as well as those with highest diversity and threat. From Funk & Fa (2010).

in tropical and subtropical moist forests. Islands also are heavily represented in the priority gap cells (31%), as are mountainous areas. The species group best covered by the current global system of protected areas is mammals, followed by freshwater turtles and threatened birds, with amphibians the least covered (Rodrigues et al., 2004a,b).

In the second step of the analysis (Rodrigues et al., 2004a), those species with very limited protected area coverage were identified and designated as partial-gap species. The world's unprotected terrestrial area was then split into half-degree (longitude–latitude) cells. Initially, these cells were roughly square and 56 km to a side at the equator, decreasing in size towards the poles, with the shapes of many becoming irregular after sections covered by protected areas were removed. These gap cells were then evaluated in terms of two variables: (1) their irreplaceability, or the degree to which they are necessary to complete the protected area network in representing all species according to their pre-defined targets; and (2) their threat, or the likelihood that the species in the cell will be lost. High priority cells were those of very high irreplaceability and very high threat – cells requiring immediate conservation attention in order to prevent the loss of unique biodiversity.

A more recent analysis aimed at comparing and integrating prioritisation approaches was undertaken by Funk & Fa (2010). Using global vertebrate distributions in terrestrial ecoregions, Funk & Fa (2010) examined how continuous and categorical ranking schemes target and accumulate endangered taxa within the IUCN Red List, AZE, and EDGE programmes. By employing total, endemic and threatened species richness and an estimator for richness-adjusted endemism as metrics in continuous prioritisation, and WWF's Global200 and CI Hotspots in categorical prioritisation, results demonstrated that all metrics target endangerment more efficiently than by chance. However, each scheme selects unique sets of top-ranking ecoregions, which overlap only partially, and include different sets of threatened species. Using the top 100 ecoregions as defined by continuous prioritisation metrics, Funk & Fa (2010) developed a map for global vertebrate conservation that incorporated important areas for endemism, richness, and threat (Fig. 2.3).

2.4.3   Surrogate species approaches

Resource managers are tasked with developing management plans that provide ecosystem services and commodity resources while retaining native species. Designing management to meet the individual needs of so many species is simply not feasible. Thus, the challenge is to reduce the many dimensions of multi-species requirements to a workable number that will adequately represent the ecological needs of a larger set of species of management concern.

In response to this challenge, various surrogate approaches – umbrella species, flagship species, indicator species, focal species, or species groups chosen on the basis of taxonomy, habitat, life-history features, or other ecological functions – have been proposed to reduce the burden of addressing the requirements of individual taxa (Marcot & Flather, 2007). Such terms for surrogate approaches are often used interchangeably, which can lead to confusion (Armstrong, 2002; Caro, 2003). So-called coarse-filter approaches, with vegetation types, ecological communities, or ecosystems as their conservation or management targets, are an extension of this consolidation in which entire ecological systems rather than species or species groups serve as surrogates for the species assemblages in an area (Groves, 2003). We do not address the use of such coarse-filter approaches or of surrogate measures of habitat condition–resource availability, water quality, '*ecosystem health*', and the like because these have been discussed extensively elsewhere (see Landres *et al.*, 1988; Groves, 2003).

Despite (or perhaps because of) the proliferation of approaches to define groups or surrogate species, the conceptual foundation and use of these approaches have generated substantial criticism (Landres *et al.*, 1988; Simberloff, 1998; Andelman & Fagan, 2000; Lindenmayer *et al.*, 2002; Roberge & Angelstam, 2004). Not surprisingly, much of the criticism focuses on the failure of surrogate approaches to consider the unique characteristics of individual species and the multiplicity of factors affecting their distribution and abundance (Carroll *et al.*, 2001). Critics argue that the assumption that management of surrogate species will adequately address the factors that enhance or threaten the persistence of individual species is unfounded, or that the effectiveness of the approaches has not been rigorously tested.

Some biologists (Paine, 1966; Terborgh, 1986; Howe, 1984) have used the term 'keystone species' to identify those species which may influence the ability of large numbers of others to persist in the community. The basic assumption is that within biological communities, certain species are important in determining the ability of large numbers of other species to persist in the community. Examples of keystone species include the starfish, the Ochre sea star in rocky tidal communities (Paine, 1974), lobsters in subtidal communities (Mann & Breen, 1972), sea otters in marine kelp forests (Estes *et al.*, 1989) or Old World fruit bats in tropical forests (Cox *et al.*, 1991). Protecting keystone species is seen by some as a priority because if such a species is lost, numerous others may disappear – causing an 'extinction cascade'. The term has also been applied to resources, to denote elements of a habitat that are critical to many species in the community (e.g. dead standing trees, salt licks and mineral pools).

While top predators are obvious keystone species (since they often control herbivore populations) others may be quite inconspicuous. Raven (1976) argues that the extinction of each tropical plant species leads potentially to the loss of another 10–30 insect species. This is because many tropical insects appear to be highly specialised in their feeding behaviour, often only existing on one single plant species. Some ecologists have tried to quantify the impact a species must have on its community in order to be considered a keystone, but it is not currently possible to assign a specific numerical criterion to the term. Owing to the difficulties in determining a precise and quantifiable definition, many ecologists do not feel that the keystone concept is currently useful to applied conservation efforts. However, others have high hopes that the keystone species concept may bridge the gap between single-species conservation and the whole ecosystem approach by converging on a species whose preservation could help conserve many other species.

Umbrella species, or their protection, has also been advocated as a means of creating a multiplier effect in conservation. Umbrella species are used to delineate areas of habitat for protection, thus they are usually species that have relatively large ranges so that protection will automatically be conferred on other sympatric species. Wilcox (1984) suggested that an umbrella species should 'provide a protective umbrella... such that its minimum area requirement is at least as comprehensive as the rest of the community'. Caro & O'Doherty (1999) argue that the attributes of an umbrella species are that it should represent other species' needs, its biology should be well known and it should be easily sampled or observed. In addition, an umbrella species will be characterised by large body size, long persistence time, wide geographical range (relative to sympatric species) and it should be a habitat specialist. Large population size and migratory habit (thus increasing the area of protection) have also been suggested as important in defining umbrella species. Fleishmann et al. (2000), however, emphasised three main attributes of umbrella species: (1) co-occurrence with other species, (2) degree of ubiquity and (3) sensitivity to human disturbance. These authors also provided a formula for calculating an 'umbrella index' to assess the suitability of a species as an effective umbrella. Lambeck (1997) recommended selecting species that are vulnerable and that need habitat restoration to persist by being area-limited, resource-limited, dispersal limited or process limited, in order to encourage active management of an area. Umbrella species examples include the use of the migratory range of wildebeest to delineate the borders of the Serengeti and Ngorongoro parks, and the preservation of viable populations of African wild dogs and cheetahs to conserve large African faunal communities.

Box 2.3 · *Trigger approaches in conservation planning*

Two recent, and well publicised, approaches that focus on distinct and threatened species worldwide highlight the use of distinct elements of biodiversity in need of imminent protection to highlight sites that contain them. One approach, the AZE, which employed the term 'trigger species' is a joint initiative of biodiversity conservation organisations from around the world, and aims to prevent extinctions by identifying and safeguarding key sites, each one of which is the last remaining refuge of one or more EN or CR species. The purpose of the alliance of conservationists was to identify sites in most urgent need of conservation, and to act together to prevent species extinctions. AZE first focused on species that face extinction either because their last remaining habitat is being degraded at a local level, or because their tiny global range makes them especially vulnerable to external threats (Ricketts et al., 2005). To identify priority sites, a site must contain at least one EN or CR species, as listed on the IUCN Red List; should only be designated if it is the sole area where an EN or CR species occurs, contains the overwhelmingly significant known resident population of the EN or CR species, or encloses the overwhelmingly significant known population for one life history segment (e.g. breeding or wintering) of the EN or CR species; and must have a definable boundary within which the character of habitats, biological communities, and/or management issues have more in common with each other than they do with those in adjacent areas.

AZE scientists working in collaboration with an international network of experts have so far identified 595 such sites that must be effectively protected to prevent the extinction of 794 of the world's most threatened species (many sites have more than one AZE 'trigger species' confined to them). To date, AZE has identified sites for those taxonomic groups that have been globally assessed for threat level: mammals, birds, some reptiles (crocodilians, iguanas, turtles, and tortoises), amphibians, and conifers. Other taxa will be added as data become available.

Another similar approach, which selects unique taxa, is the EDGE of Existence programme, initiated by the ZSL, which is the only global conservation initiative to focus specifically on threatened species that represent a significant amount of unique evolutionary history (Isaac *et al.*, 2007). Using a scientific framework to identify the world's most evolutionarily distinct and globally endangered species, the EDGE of Existence programme highlights and aims to protect these taxa. EDGE species have few close relatives on the tree of life and are often extremely unusual in the way they look, live and behave, as well as in their genetic make-up. They represent a unique and irreplaceable part of the world's natural heritage, yet most of them are not adequately protected; 70% of the world's top 100 EDGE mammals are currently receiving little or no conservation attention (Isaac *et al.*, 2007).

The EDGE of Existence programme is centred around an interactive website that features information on the top 100 EDGE mammals, amphibians and birds, detailing their specific conservation requirements. Ten focal species from each class are highlighted each year. Each of the top 100 species is given an EDGE-ometer rating according to the degree of conservation attention they are currently receiving, as well as its perceived rarity in its natural environment. The main goal of the EDGE of Existence programme is to ensure that appropriate research and/or conservation actions are implemented for each of these species by 2012. The programme puts these species on the map and triggers conservation action to secure their future.

As a means of marketing or symbolising conservation to draw attention and funding support to conservation programmes, some taxa can be used as a symbol or icon to lead the protection of a habitat (Box 2.3). The term 'flagship species', according to Leader-Williams & Dublin (2000), was used as early as 1986 in relation to charismatic species. The significance of a flagship species is essentially that it can draw financial support more easily (Meffe & Carroll, 1997) or raise public awareness (Leader-Williams & Dublin, 2000; Bowen-Jones & Entwistle, 2002). Flagship species have no inferred ecological role in conserving their wider ecosystem. According to Caro & O'Doherty (1999) flagship species should be single species that represent other species, tending to be large-size but rules for selecting flagships species are not strict, the only issue being that they are popular (or made popular through appropriate marketing) and evoke public sympathy. Several authors suggest that flagship species can also be selected that do have other surrogate roles (Simberloff, 1998; Entwistle, 2000), with Bowen-Jones & Entwistle (2002) arguing that local communities should be engaged fully and the ecological or economic values of a species explained. However, species selected as flagships may appeal to a Western audience but may be inappropriate to raise positive awareness in a local/national context. For example, large carnivores make excellent fundraisers but may be feared or disliked in their country of origin, other species may be considered pests or food. A further criticism of the Flagship species approach is that it may lead to too much emphasis on, and conservation effort towards, the selected species, which detracts from protection of other species and the ecosystem (Entwistle, 2000).

2.5 Costs and benefits of conservation efforts

Theory and practice can, of course, be very different things. It may be possible to advise conservation organisations on which species and locations to direct their efforts, but it can be quite another for them to implement such a policy. One of the problems often observed in implementing conservation policy in many countries beyond the absence of legal institutions for adequately establishing and defending landscapes, is the impact of political corruption (Smith & Walpole, 2005). Political corruption, defined as the unlawful use of public office for private gain, can be an important obstacle to both economic and social development. Corruption reduces levels of international and national investment, lowers government spending on public services and favours the establishment of projects that allow the misappropriation of funds. Smith *et al.* (2003) showed that countries with high levels of corruption are losing biodiversity faster than better-governed ones. They showed that governance scores were correlated with changes in total forest cover, but not with changes in natural forest cover. They also found strong associations between governance scores and changes in the numbers of African elephants and black rhinoceroses, and these socio-economic factors explained observed patterns better than any others. More crucially, countries rich in species and identified as containing priority areas for conservation had lower governance scores than other nations. The main explanation for this seems to be that poorly paid officials in developing countries can be bribed to ignore conservation laws. Another reason is that government conservation departments often lack the political clout to enforce regulations. These results stress the need for conservationists to develop and implement programmes which consider and where necessary ameliorate the effects of political corruption.

Despite the encumbrance of corruption and lack of resources for protection, there is evidence that direct approaches are working. Bruner *et al.* (2001), for example, demonstrated that many areas (93 protected areas in 22 tropical countries) which some deride as 'paper parks' are, in fact, effective in stopping land clearing, and to a lesser degree effective at mitigating logging, hunting, fire, and grazing. Park effectiveness correlates with basic management activities such as enforcement, boundary demarcation, and direct compensation to local communities, suggesting that even modest increases in funding would directly increase the ability of parks to protect tropical biodiversity.

Unsurprisingly, the costs of effective field-based terrestrial conservation vary enormously between countries, and more than do the likely benefits. Balmford *et al.* (2003) calculated direct costs for projects (though opportunity and transactions costs and wider landscape costs were unavailable) and showed that it cost from less than $0.1 km^{-2} y^{-1} in the Russian Arctic to over $1 000 000 km^{-2} y^{-1} for some western European programmes in which restoration is needed to recover conservation value. Conservation costs were correlated with high wilderness scores and increase closely with economic activity, as measured by mean per capita GNP (Fig. 2.4a) or the ratio of GNP to country area and local human population density. Thus, for the 'last of the wild' areas (per Sanderson *et al.*, 2002), such as the Gobi Desert, the Himalayas, and the Amazon, costs of effective reserves

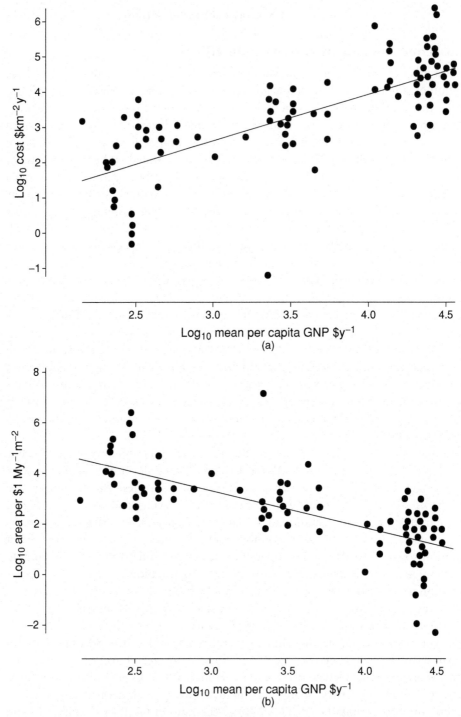

Fig. 2.4 Variation in the annual management cost of conservation projects and in the estimated benefits of field-based conservation projects: (a) annual cost km^{-2} vs. mean per capita GNP; (b) area that could be effectively conserved for $1 000 000 versus mean per capita GNP. From Balmford *et al.* (2003).

are low, \$1–60 km^{-2} y^{-1}, but typically around \$20 km^{-2} y^{-1}. However, costs of effective protected areas in more densely settled regions of Latin and Central America, Africa, and Asia ranged from \$130 to \$5000 km^{-2} y^{-1}, with typical costs of \$1000 km^{-2} y^{-1}. In the developed world, costs differed from \$5000 to \$40 000 km^{-2} y^{-1} for sampled US nature reserves, and \$15 000–50 000 km^{-2} y^{-1} for UK reserves and agrienvironment programmes.

Although being able to predict the costs of effective conservation is useful, prioritisation also depends on the distribution of conservation benefits in relation to development. Balmford et al. (2003) used a benefit measure as the total area that could be effectively conserved for a fixed annual spend per capita GNP (Fig. 2.4b) and GNP per unit area (of course the reciprocal of annual cost per unit area and as such increases with wilderness value, PPP, and a project's areal extent and decreases with local population density). Dollar costs decreased with increases in the local buying power of a US dollar (measured as PPP). Costs per unit area also decreased with the areal extent of projects, with the slope of the regression of log (annual cost, in dollars km^{-2} y^{-1}) against log (area, in km^2) found similar to a recent figure for the Cape Floristic Region (Frazee et al., 2003). For comparison, Balmford et al. (2003) showed that ex-situ conservation in three well-respected UK and US zoos cost between \$6 000 000 and \$160 000 000 km^{-2} y^{-1}, reinforcing the point that, where possible, zoos could increase the cost-effectiveness of their contribution to conservation by supporting field-based initiatives (Chapter 6).

These findings suggest that much greater conservation investment is needed by the global conservation community in places where the costs of effective conservation are relatively low and the benefits generally high. Priority areas for increased investment include developing country sites where, despite high threat, costs are still generally lower than in Europe and North America. Results provide support for calls for high priority to be afforded to some more isolated areas as well, where conservation benefits can be substantial and conservation costs are often extremely low (Olson & Dinerstein, 1998; Funk & Fa, 2010).

Key concepts

(1) The selection of priority areas for biodiversity is based on the vulnerability and irreplaceability of the biodiversity in a particular site. In most approaches species endemism rather than species richness is targeted. Areas with the greatest numbers of endemic or restricted range species are considered of high conservation value. At least nine major institutional templates of biodiversity conservation have been developed, most prioritise irreplaceable regions.

(2) The IUCN publishes the Red List which compiles species at risk of extinction. It uses the Mace–Lande system, which describes the probability of extinction of a species within a specified time-frame. Assessments for each species in the Red List are based on its geographic range and abundance, habitats, threats and conservation actions in place. By 2008 the list included 44 838 species, 16 928 of which are threatened.

(3) Conservation of biodiversity can be achieved by *in-situ* conservation and *ex-situ* conservation. *In-situ* conservation derives primarily from the conservation and ecosystem benefits which accrue from protection of integrated habitats and ecosystems. *Ex-situ* conservation in zoos, aquaria, botanic gardens and germplasm banks should compliment *in-situ* conservation and is increasingly recognised as a set of techniques to support integrated management of wild and captive populations.

(4) Protected areas provide an effective means to conserve biodiversity and are increasingly recognised for their role in protecting ecosystem services such as carbon, water, climate and soil stabilisation and various timber and non-timber products. However, a lack of management and enforcement often limits their value.

(5) Surrogate approaches include umbrella species, flagship species, indicator species, focal species or species groups selected on the basis of taxonomy, habitat, life-history traits or other ecological functions. Critics argue that surrogate approaches may not adequately address the factors affecting individual species.

3 · Zoos in focus – public exhibition or conservation

'Times are hard for zoos. If they would dedicate themselves wholeheartedly to entertaining the public, life might be easier at least financially, but almost all say they exist for the purpose of conservation' (Jeremy Cherfas)

3.1 Introduction

Contact or involvement with animals has been a dominant feature of many civilisations for centuries (Bostock, 1993; Cherfas, 1984). Collections of wild animals in private and public institutions, zoos, have been in existence since antiquity. However, zoos have long been a source of controversy. Many people feel that the keeping of animals for public display is inhumane and unethical, while others argue that zoos serve as wildlife education, by providing the opportunity for individuals to view and learn about animals they would not otherwise have the chance to see (Mazur, 2001).

Over recent years, there is no doubt that zoos have been subjected to much criticism regarding the ethics of displaying wild animals for public pleasure. Even among environmentalists, the attitude towards zoos is divided: while some activists feel that zoos play an increasingly active role in conservation and education efforts and are therefore beneficial to the environmental movement, others feel that zoos' recent emphasis on wildlife conservation is just a façade to cover up their profiteering nature. However, in general there is consensus that natural history institutions (botanic gardens, arboretums, public aquariums, marine parks, zoos, and a variety of specialist natural history museums) have a fundamental responsibility to tackle environmental problems, largely to educate visitors to create a citizenry with a better knowledge base, greater sense of compassion, a stronger commitment to care, and a deeper connection to the world of nature (Miller *et al.*, 2004). They can, and some do already, participate more directly in the protection of biodiversity.

The history of modern zoos started some 200 years ago with the creation of the first public institutions. Since that time large numbers of zoos have appeared in many different parts of the world, and a great diversity has arisen among these organisations, which now vary from zoos with general collections to specialised institutions such as aquaria, bird parks, primate zoos, and safari parks. Significant changes have taken place in the world since the establishment of the first public zoos, including an increase in the amount of free time, an elevation of the overall educational level and increased travel opportunities. These and other changes have had far-reaching consequences pushing zoos to evolve from mere menageries into more complex, professionally managed zoological parks.

The latter decades of the twentieth century saw a dramatic metamorphosis in the appearance of zoos and their involvement in species and habitat conservation. Advances in public knowledge of wildlife conservation, environmental and animal welfare issues, together with increased legislation regarding animal welfare and participation in conservation activities have pushed zoos to dramatically alter their operations and refocus their missions. However, collectively, the zoos' capacity to display animals adequately, and engage in conservation or education activities varies dramatically between countries, with some countries often lacking in resources, legislation or trained personnel (see Waugh & Wemmer, 1994). Most zoos are still found within Europe or the United States. Only ten countries account for 50% of the world's botanic gardens, including the USA and Europe (Stanley Price et al., 2004), the rest fall within the tropics where we also find the majority of species that, as conservation organisations, zoos and botanic gardens are intent on saving.

Despite the challenges facing zoos worldwide and notwithstanding their critics, these institutions remain very popular, as revealed by attendance figures, and how the press in some cities of the world express much pride about their zoos. Attendance at many zoos is steady, and in some cases rising. And with the natural world in increasing peril – overexploitation of wildlife, climate change threatening habitats worldwide, and children increasingly sealed off into safe suburban bubbles – many zoo officials feel that zoos are there to remind people why wildlife matters, before it is too late.

This chapter first broadly examines the development of zoos through time and their current positioning. We follow this by presenting statistics and trends of world zoos to understand composition of animal collections. We discuss the evolution of zoos towards conservation, and present some opposing views on how zoos can achieve conservation. We end the chapter by highlighting two main issues that affect zoos' credibility in conservation, their use of wild animals, and whether visitor enjoyment and conservation can be adequately reconciled in zoos.

3.2 Exhibiting animals – changes through time

The first examples of exotic animal collections were the royal menageries of wealthy rulers such as Egyptian pharaohs and Chinese emperors. However, the history of the present day zoo under the definition of the WAZA began in the late eighteenth and early nineteenth centuries with Vienna Zoo opening in 1752, Paris in 1793 and London Zoo in 1826 (Chapter 1). It is interesting to note that these establishments, and the others which soon followed, were founded primarily due to the interest of zoological society members [IUDZG/CBSG (IUCN/SSC), 1993]; it was only later that fee-paying visitors became a common and necessary part of zoos.

Before home entertainment such as television, and computers, and increased travel opportunities, zoos functioned as primary leisure destinations. With the absence of natural history films, the Internet, wildlife magazines and books, zoos were also the only place where people could learn about exotic wildlife. However, the underlying concept was entertainment and leisure, not education.

3.2.1 Zoos as menageries

European and American zoos in the nineteenth century have been likened to stamp collections in that there was often a single example of each species. This was the 'menagerie' period with a focus on taxonomy; exhibits displayed the diversity of life and the main preoccupations were species husbandry and propagation (Rabb, 1994). Exhibits were primarily arranged taxonomically and separated within the zoo into the 'bird house', 'reptile house', 'monkey house', hoof stock, etc. Housing was basic and functional, and usually consisted of little more than a wire cage or bars with bare floors. There was little knowledge of appropriate diets, breeding behaviours or natural social groupings. Zookeepers were essentially unskilled labourers, not trained in animal management techniques. Indeed, this regrettably continues to be the case in many zoos in different parts of the world.

Animal welfare was not carefully considered; the detrimental effects of poor housing including physical and psychological problems were yet to be fully recognised – either by legislators, keepers or the wider public. It was not until the twentieth century that zoos realised that improved husbandry conditions would reduce the animal mortality rate, which was therefore of economic advantage (Stevens & McAlister, 2003).

3.2.2 Hagenbeck's panoramic designs

In the late nineteenth century, when zoos were being built at a rate of almost one per year, a Hamburg-based entrepreneur Carl Hagenbeck (1844–1913) was hailed as the world's leading supplier of wild animals. His name, less well-known today, was once as evocative and celebrated as those of P. T. Barnum and Buffalo Bill (Ames, 2009). The infrastructure that enabled Hagenbeck to capture and trade wild animals also became a platform for his venture into public entertainments, beginning with his so-called 'anthropological-zoological exhibition'; a high-sounding name for the practice of grouping together 'exotic' humans and animals in the same space of display, that soon became a regular attraction of world fairs.

Between 1874 and 1913, Carl Hagenbeck sponsored and exhibited as many as one hundred different troupes of 'foreign people', becoming the most important ethnographic showman of the period (Fig. 3.1). Hagenbeck brought Laplanders or Sami, Sudanese, Greenlanders, Sri Lankans, Indians, East/West and North Africans and others and took them to major European cities as well as around Germany (Rothfels, 2002). Thousands of people would pay to view the 'ethnographic exhibitions' where the native peoples would demonstrate the techniques of their everyday tasks such as milking reindeer and hunting. Rothfels (2002) explains that Hagenbeck contended that these exhibitions were not shows, in that they were not theatrical representations of the culture of these different nationalities, but rather that they were authentic, the people were shown carrying on their normal activities. The exhibition of people, abhorrent as it was, was not restricted

Fig. 3.1 A monumental set from Hagenbeck's 1912 Egyptian Exhibition, 'On the Nile'. The photo depicts the Cliff Temple of Abu Simbel, the Great Sphinx, and the Pyramids of Giza – all in one place. Spectators are visible at the foot of the temple's façade.

to Hagenbeck's institution. In fact, the most appalling case of exhibition of ethnic peoples in zoos was that of 'Ota Benga', a pygmy from the Congo, who was displayed in New York's Bronx Zoo monkey house (alongside an orang-utan) in 1906 (Verner Bradford & Blume, 1992). The *New York Times* declared that 'Ota Benga' had been brought 'from his native land of darkness, to the country of the free, in the interest of science and of broad humanity'.

In 1907, Hagenbeck unveiled his revolutionary Tierpark (or 'animal park') on the outskirts of Hamburg, fundamentally changing the way that live animals were displayed and observed by staging them in natural settings and so-called open enclosures (cage-less displays). Both of these practices would later be imitated by zoos around the world (Hancocks, 2001). The designs were innovative and the ambitiously landscaped areas contained groups of mixed species, i.e. several species were housed together. The emphasis was on creating panoramic vistas by using controlled sight lines, carefully obscured moats and extensive rockwork (artificially constructed landscaping to appear like rock) along with water areas to give visitors the impression of whole habitats (Hancocks, 2001).

Hagenbeck's design principles were copied across the world, but often resulted in ill-conceived enclosures with poor use of materials, which contradicted his aim of creating realistic replicas of wild habitats. This was a move forward in terms of representing animals in at least semi-natural environments and thereby helping visitors to make the link between the animals and their natural environment. However, the complexity and volume of space available to the animals was still second to the experience of the visitors. Rothfels (2002) emphasises the 'element of dramatic entertainment', which was fundamental to Hagenbeck's park.

Hagenbeck's designs are frequently quoted in the literature as a major turning point and positive advance in zoo exhibition, which is perhaps difficult to reconcile with the fact that he was also a major animal trader, circus owner and, more shockingly, exhibitor of indigenous peoples. Despite Hagenbeck's revolutionary animal exhibits, zoo design in the early twentieth century did not build on the concept of the naturalistic enclosure, but rather took a step backwards in terms of animal welfare. Architects developed 'modern', sterile buildings with a seeming emphasis on style rather than a suitable habitat in which to keep animals. Such exhibits typically housed animals in easy-to-clean inside areas with tiled or concrete floors and plate glass windows to ensure easy viewing for the public, e.g. the 1934 Zoological Society of London's Lubetkin art deco penguin pool. These areas were devoid of cage furniture, since there were concerns about disease transmission and empty cages made them easier to keep clean (Hancocks, 2001). Animals continued to be arranged taxonomically and with little regard for social groupings. Many European elephant houses built in the twentieth century typified this emphasis on appearance and aesthetics of the house to the public and the architect, rather than the buildings' suitability for housing highly social and intelligent animals.

3.2.3 Heini Hediger's zoo biology

Heini Hediger, in his two books (Hediger, 1950, 1969) described a ground-breaking view of animal management and care. Rather than looking at the architectural merits of a zoo building, or the ease of maintenance for the staff, Hediger approached zoo design from a biological perspective (Hediger, 1950). He explained the fundamental behavioural characteristics of animals such as 'flight distance' and the consequent need to consider the 'psychological space' in an enclosure, not merely the volume or area. It seems impossible that until this time terrestrial and arboreal mammals were housed in a similar fashion, but Hediger was the first to detail the importance of tailoring an enclosure to suit the natural habits of the resident animals.

Hediger went further; he extolled the value of providing a natural diet, with varied feeding times; using natural materials rather than the traditional steel and concrete. He proposed that animals should be kept in appropriate social groupings and be provided with areas to escape from each other and the public when they chose to. These views were firmly based on his studies of animal behaviour and a conviction that the best way to care for and exhibit animals was in the way that was most natural for the species concerned. Hediger described the goals and function of zoos as: 'In contradistinction to earlier times it is not just live curiosities – as it were museum preparations in motion – that are sought in a zoo; the public now feels a growing need of, and has a right to, relaxation and recreation in a zoo – in a zoological garden. There lies and remains the primary function. Added to this are three others, viz. popular information, research and nature conservation also in terms of offering sanctuary to jeopardized species, and the preservation of their living space' (Hediger, 1969).

Table 3.1 *Main characteristics (expressed as per ha) of zoos reporting to the Zoos and Aquariums*

Region/Country	Africa			Asia			Australia and Oceania			Central America and the Caribbean		
	Median	Min	Max	Median	Min	Max	Median	Min	Max	Median	Min	Max
Employees	4.0	0.1	165.5	3.9	0.1	157.9	2.5	0.1	96.7	13.0	1.1	22.9
Attendance	14 047.7	8.3	763 636.4	41 583.3	92.8	6 157 225.6	25 000.0	38.9	1 297 200.8	32 000.0	1 709.4	72 916.7
Mammals Species	3.2	0.1	34.0	2.0	0.1	51.5	2.2	0.1	19.2	2.6	0.3	14.6
Mammals Specimens	23.4	0.7	146.0	12.7	0.1	177.6	12.0	0.3	83.2	13.5	1.6	849.2
Birds Species	10.2	0.2	97.1	2.3	0.1	93.9	3.2	0.3	47.3	7.5	0.5	25.4
Birds Specimens	36.2	0.1	595.8	16.5	0.2	454.5	13.2	0.1	283.8	54.4	2.9	187.5
Reptiles Species	3.3	0.3	80.0	1.1	0.1	115.0	1.8	0.1	40.0	3.9	0.1	15.0
Reptiles Specimens	14.5	1.6	97.6	4.4	0.1	1091.7	8.4	0.2	285.0	29.2	2.1	175.0
Amphibians Species	0.2	0.1	9.3	0.9	0.1	50.4	0.3	0.1	15.8	1.1	0.4	3.6
Amphibians Specimens	1.2	0.3	65.0	2.9	0.1	499.0	3.1	0.1	145.7	20.4	4.0	29.2
Fishes Species	0.9	0.1	270.9	4.5	0.1	1564.1	0.4	0.1	414.8	15.4	0.2	64.5
Fishes Specimens	92.8	1.3	4058.2	84.2	0.1	79 217.9	3.2	0.1	6911.1	224.6	3.3	1477.5
Invertebrates Species	61.3	37.2	85.5	46.2	0.1	473.7	0.7	0.1	226.7	6.0	0.4	38.0
Invertebrates Specimens	4.6	0.5	1818.2	653.0	0.3	33 550.2	2.2	0.2	7208.0	105.4	0.8	363.5
Total Species	135.0	0.0	705.0	987.0	0.0	9087.0	88.0	0.0	700.0	94.5	41	272
Total Specimens	139.5	0	1168	1027	0	163 273	505.0	0.0	12 926.0	1056.5	187.0	3955.0

Although he did not coin the phrase, much of what Hediger proposed would now be termed 'environmental enrichment', now recognised by skilled animal keepers as a vital component of good captive animal management. Although the basic concepts of environmental enrichment (Chapter 4) have now been around for several decades, some zoos continue to regard enrichment merely as an 'add on' rather than an integral element of animal management, or worse still are unaware of the techniques altogether.

3.2.4 Immersion exhibits

The most recent phase in zoo enclosure design has produced 'immersion exhibits'. Immersion exhibits aim to closely replicate the natural habitat of the animals in the enclosure, but to go a step further and also involve the visitors in the exhibit. This is achieved by considering the public areas as part of the exhibit; landscaping the public area in a similar way to the animal enclosure to give a feeling of continuity. Immersion exhibits are designed to encourage visitors to note the connections between humans, animals and the environment, and also to provide a more interesting and memorable experience. Immersion exhibits often use techniques such as screening part of the enclosure and providing only small viewing spaces, which provides the animals with some respite from the visitors' constant gaze and encourages visitors to be more active in searching for the animals.

3.3 Modern zoos

3.3.1 General characteristics

There is no complete census of world zoos, but there is evidence to indicate that generally zoos are found primarily in higher-income countries and outside high-biodiversity *of the World list published in the* International Zoo Yearbook *(data from Fisken et al., 2010)*

Europe			Middle East and North Africa			North America			South America		
Median	Min	Max	Median	Min	Max	Median	Min	Max	Median	Min	Max
3.3	0.1	4000.0	3.6	0.1	18.2	3.3	0.1	326.9	5.8	0.2	750.0
17 289.6	11.0	7 432 432.4	12 300.0	0.6	263 636.4	21 734.2	22.3	3 416 300.6	45 727.3	15.3	2 192 150.0
2.9	0.1	200.0	2.2	0.1	25.9	2.1	0.1	16.5	3.6	0.1	28.3
16.5	0.1	2297.3	13.7	0.7	131.6	7.8	0.1	520.0	18.5	0.2	98.9
4.2	0.1	194.9	2.7	0.1	38.8	2.5	0.1	338.0	7.4	0.3	50.0
24.0	0.1	526.1	27.0	1.2	384.7	9.1	0.1	1452.0	40.7	2.1	87.2
1.6	0.1	503.7	0.8	0.1	17.4	2.3	0.1	263.5	2.6	0.1	2650.0
6.1	0.1	2264.6	3.7	0.5	137.6	5.4	0.1	873.6	16.8	0.3	9550.0
0.5	0.1	561.1	0.4	0.2	3.7	0.6	0.1	161.1	0.3	0.1	850.0
2.4	0.1	3300.3	0.5	0.1	6.3	2.7	0.1	1217.0	1.4	0.1	3000.0
3.2	0.1	4909.1	1.1	0.2	9.3	1.3	0.1	1844.8	2.5	0.1	3250.0
33.8	0.1	41 666.7	22.6	0.3	116.2	10.3	0.1	77 447.3	18.9	0.1	21 950.0
1.4	0.0	7515.2	0.3	0.2	10.2	0.9	0.1	981.0	0.8	0.1	1800.0
20.7	0.1	39 100.0	0.8	0.1	47.9	10.9	0.1	26 461.6	6.3	0.1	7000.0
140	0	1463.0	148	0	266	169.5	0	1433	207	68	371
140.0	0.0	51 010.0	1395.5	0.0	4589.0	915.5	0.0	135 701.0	1097	251	17 706

regions (Leader-Williams *et al.*, 2007). Although there are many institutions which hold wild animals that could come under the term 'zoos', there are more than one thousand officially recognised zoos belonging to zoo associations. Such associations, about 20 or so, exist at the national level in many countries throughout the world, and at a regional level on several continents and subcontinents [IUDZG/CBSG (IUCN/SSC) 1993]. Most countries have at least one national zoo, and according to the WAZA Network, perhaps the foremost membership organisation which includes leading zoos and aquariums, regional and national associations of zoos and aquariums, as well as some affiliate organisations, there are 1300 institutions spread all over the world. But, there are dramatic differences in the number of zoos per country, with countries like Germany with over 700, about one zoo per 500 km^2 (Quantum Verzeichnis, 2009), and India despite its larger size with around 350 recognised institutions or one zoo per 9000 km^2 (Central Zoo Authority, 2010).

General characteristics of around 800 zoos found in different parts of the world can be found in the listing of *Zoos and Aquariums of the World* available annually in the ZSL's *International Zoo Yearbook*, first published in 1960. Zoos and aquariums, together with important animal collections, such as primate research centres, universities and bird parks, are listed alphabetically under the towns in which they are situated. Main attributes of world zoos by region are shown on a per hectare basis in Table 3.1. Median number of visitors per ha. was highest in South American and Asian zoos with maxima of over one million people per annum. Lowest numbers of visitors are typical of African and Central American institutions. Staffing levels are highest in Middle East/North African zoos, but lowest in North American and European zoos. Median number of species and specimens in zoos by world region are surprisingly similar, with around 2000 specimens from 200 species. Explanation for staffing may be partly related to the type of animals held in zoos, since costs of keeping birds, for example, are relatively less than for mammals (Chapter 6). Naturally, labour costs and the importance of staff–animal ratios also affect numbers of keeper staff employed.

3.3.2 Composition of animal collections

Information derived from the ZAW (Fisken et al., 2010) for the seven main global regions shows that most zoos keep higher numbers of mammals and birds than reptiles, amphibians, fishes and invertebrates (Table 3.1). For the most abundant groups, mammals, birds and reptiles, most zoos kept on average around 35% mammal specimens, 50% birds, but not more than 5% reptiles (Fig. 3.2). Animal collections according to geographical regions are also consistently similar with most zoos harbouring mostly bird specimens (mean 49%) and mammals (mean 32%), but fewer reptiles and amphibians (mean 18%).

As expected, larger zoos hold proportionately larger numbers of specimens, but there is much variation in numbers. Equally, there is a positive correlation between the overall number of specimens kept per taxon and the number of species in zoos. However, the number of specimens of mammals increases at a significantly higher rate, about three animals per hectare change in zoo size, compared to birds (two animals per ha), or reptiles (Fig. 3.3). This can be explained by the greater emphasis on keeping mammals over other taxa; large zoos will increase the number of mammals kept over other taxa. Thus, zoos generally have a larger number of spaces dedicated to mammals, because of the perception that this is more attractive to the public (especially larger-bodied species) and because mammals cannot be housed in the larger numbers typical of birds (and other taxa). This means that larger zoos are not tending towards self-sustaining populations, but merely increase the number of species. But, the implications on staffing level in zoos differ dramatically according to whether more mammals or birds are kept. Staff numbers increase with zoo size ($r^2 = 0.19$, $P = <0.001$, $n = 823$; personnel figures refer to administrative staff as well as animal-keeping employees).

3.3.3 Rare species in captivity

If zoos are actively involved in species conservation, one might expect that endangered species would comprise a significant proportion of a collection. Rahbek (1993) had already indicated that for the 1990s, zoos worldwide held less than 3% of the described species, with 878 zoos holding more than 20 000 specimens of 140 threatened mammal species. Rahbek (1993) showed that only 20 mammals were held in sufficient numbers to have viable captive populations. The situation for birds, reptiles and amphibians was even worse. In a more recent study, Zimmerman & Wilkinson (2007) found that in 72% of institutions ($n = 190$ zoos and aquariums in 40 countries), fewer than 30% of their species were listed in an IUCN category of threat. Similarly, only 49 individuals of 10 species of critically endangered vertebrates out of over 49 000 specimens of more than 1200 species were held in 188 zoos from six South American countries (Stanley Price & Fa, 2007).

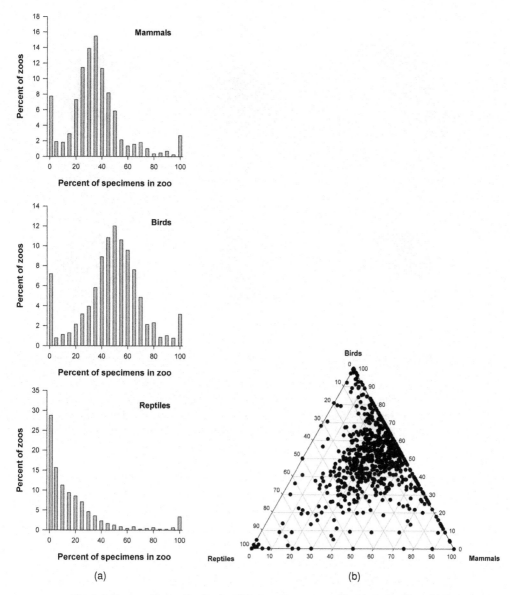

Fig. 3.2 Composition of animal collections in zoos worldwide indicating: (a) Percentage number of zoos by percentage number of mammal, bird and reptile specimens per collection; (b) ternary plot of number of mammal, bird and reptile specimens held in zoos by global regions. Data from Fisken *et al.* (2010).

Most specimens (85%) in these zoos belonged to non-threatened species, within which 73% of non-native and 88% of native specimens were of non-threatened taxa.

Unpublished census data on rare species in captivity (CRSC) for 417 world zoos for 2005 (Table 3.2) indicated that zoos housed on average around 16 rare species (median 11);

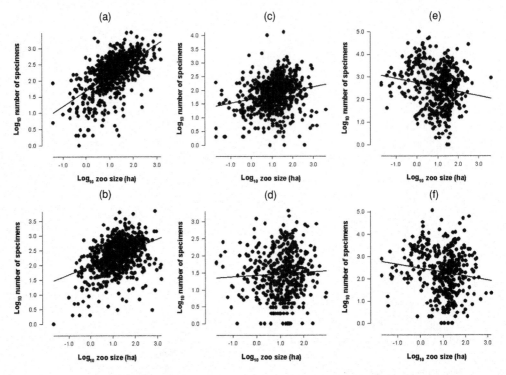

Fig. 3.3 Relationship between the number of specimens held relative to the size (in ha) of zoos worldwide, shown as $\log_{10}$ zoo size and $\log_{10}$ of specimen numbers for (a) mammals, (b) birds, (c) reptiles, (d) amphibians, (e) fishes and (f) invertebrates. Data from the *International Zoo Yearbook* (Fisken *et al.*, 2010). All correlations were highly significant.

each species with a mean of about 100 specimens (median 46). Among mammals ($n =$ 23 774), the three most abundant orders represented over 80% of specimens in collections; primates (37%), followed by ungulates (23%) and carnivores (22%). This same pattern of distribution of specimens was observed for mammals in captivity in the 1990s (Magin *et al.*, 1994). Rare birds ($n =$ 5600 specimens) in the CRSC were largely represented by storks (20%), cranes (20%), parrots (17%) and eagles and hawks (11%), whereas reptiles ($n =$ 4722) were mostly tortoises and turtles (44%), snakes (23%), lizards (16%) and crocodilians (15%). Amphibians ($n =$ 482), were mostly anurans (72%). The bias seen towards certain groups amongst the mammals, birds and reptiles could indicate perceived public popularity rather than endangerment of those particular groups (Chapter 4).

Of the 90 species that had a combined total of more than 100 specimens (an arbitrary number of population viability) registered in the CRSC database, most were mammals ($n =$ 64), 15 were birds and 11 reptiles. By global regions (Fig. 3.4), 31 mammal species with 100 or more specimens were held in European zoos, 16 in North American zoos, and only one in Australasian institutions. For birds, six rare species with over 100 specimens were found in European zoos, three in North America, and none in the other regions.

Table 3.2 Number of specimens, n, of threatened taxa held in captivity according to data from the International Zoo Yearbook Census of Rare Animals in Captivity (Fisken, personal communication)

	Region															
	Europe		Africa		N. America		C. America		S. America		Asia		Australasia		Total	
Class	Zoos	n	Zoos	n	Zoos	n	Zoos	n	Zoos	n	Zoos	n	Zoos	n	Zoos	n
Fish	–	–	1	21	25	6919	–	–	–	–	–	–	1	2	27	694
Amphibians	14	238	1	1	17	112	–	–	–	–	17	87	2	23	51	46
Reptiles	233	1202	10	277	385	2140	3	71	16	128	53	575	17	291	717	468
Birds	475	2619	34	207	360	1599	–	–	28	106	196	880	36	188	1129	559
Mammals	2245	12 498	73	510	1425	6795	4	11	82	349	470	2770	168	840	4467	2377
Unidentified	12	418	–	–	5	2	1	–	–	–	2	3	–	–	20	42
Total	**2979**	**16 975**	**119**	**1016**	**2217**	**17 567**	**8**	**82**	**126**	**583**	**738**	**4315**	**224**	**1344**	**6411**	**4188**

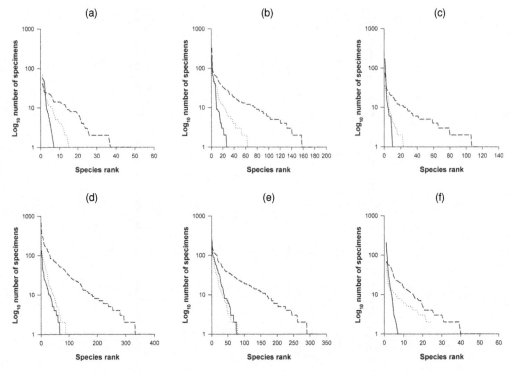

Fig. 3.4 Plots of ranked number of specimens of rare species of mammals (dash lines), birds (dotted lines) and reptiles (solid lines) held in zoos in the different global regions: (a) Africa; (b) Asia; (c) Australasia; (d) Europe; (e) North America; (f) Central/ South America. Data from Fisken (personal communication).

In contrast, only three reptile species with 100 or more specimens were held in North American zoos, followed by two in European zoos, and one each in Australasia, Asia and Africa.

Reproductive success of rare species in zoos is more complicated to assess. However, a simple measure using the percentage of specimens in collections that are captive-born may indicate degree of achievement (or difficulty) in breeding the various groups. Data from Fisken *et al.* (2010) clearly show that fish numbers are mostly captive-born (97%), followed by mammals (92%), birds (79%), amphibians (76%) and reptiles (66%).

3.3.4 Specimens-per-species trends

Data on numbers of specimens (even without breakdown by sex) per species found in zoos can be derived directly from zoo inventories. However, general trends of how average numbers of specimens per species, as a surrogate measure of the potential zoos may have to maintain viable animal populations, is possible from zoos reporting to the IZY total numbers of specimens and species. For example, information for 149 European, North

American and Japanese zoos over the period 1970–2000, showed that average numbers of animals per species were around 4–5 specimens in North American and Japanese zoos, and just slightly higher (5–6 specimens per species) in European institutions and this was consistent across decades (Stanley Price & Fa, 2007). Although variation around the mean was large for some decades (but numbers only ranging from 2–7 specimens per species), specimen numbers by species did not increase significantly. This may be an indication of zoos collaborating more, because they hold enough specimens between them, or simply an emphasis on exhibiting variety rather than attaining sufficient breeding numbers. By taxonomic group, average specimens per species for mammals was highest with 7.6 (median 4.7), followed by birds (7.5, median 5.0), but lower for amphibians (6.2, median 3.3) and reptiles (5.4, median 3.7). These data indicate that animal population sizes in zoos globally are low and probably not viable within collections. The argument that zoos may be keeping self-sustaining populations under collaborative management arrangements, by maintaining large metapopulations, may be true, but this is unlikely for all species involved. An evaluation of whether the average number of specimens per species was reflecting large metapopulations or just low numbers per zoo was tested for 118 South American zoos from the six largest countries (Stanley Price & Fa, 2007). These analyses, representing around 95% of all zoos in the continent and close to 50 000 specimens of more than 1200 species showed that most taxa were found in only one collection, with very few species present in more than 10% of all zoos. Moreover, only 8% of total population sizes for all represented species of mammals, birds and reptiles had combined populations of more than 100 specimens. Additional data from IZY also indicate that the numbers of specimens per species increase significantly for mammals and birds as number of species in collections increases, but specimens per species drop significantly in reptiles, amphibians, fishes and invertebrates as shown in Fig. 3.2.

3.3.5   Visitor attendance

Zoos worldwide are amongst the top recreational destinations, visited by a high percentage of the population. Davey (2007) compared attendance figures for zoos around the world with several socio-economic variables, to reveal a significant positive relationship between a country's population size, country income and zoo-attendance figures. Highest average attendance per ha was in South America, followed by Asian, and North American zoos (Table 3.1). European and Australasian zoos had high attendance numbers with the lowest in Africa and Central America/Caribbean. This confirms the finding of Leader-Williams et al. (2007) that demonstrates that visitor attendance was highest in wealthier nations (Fig. 3.5). Additionally, there was a negative correlation between number of zoo visits per million and combined bird and mammal species richness in different countries (Leader-Williams et al., 2007). Most zoos and zoo visitors are not in biodiversity-rich countries.

WAZA states that over 600 million people visit zoos around the world each year (WAZA, 2005). Zoos within the AZA network in the USA receive over 175 million visitors, more than the combined attendance at all major sporting events (AZA, 2010a,b).

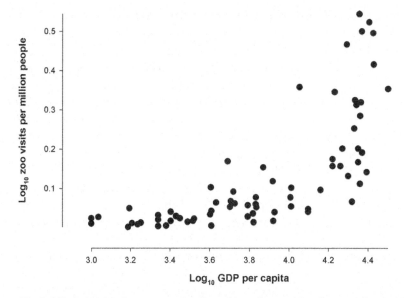

Fig. 3.5 Relationship between national wealth and zoo visits, shown as $\log_{10}$ GDP per capita and $\log_{10}$ zoo visits per million people, based on data from the *International Zoo Yearbook*. The correlation was highly significant ($r_s = 0.72$, $P < 0.001$, $n = 71$). From Leader-Williams *et al.* (2007).

This represents over half of the approximately 309 million estimated US population (US Census Bureau, 2010). In the UK, 23.7 million people visited BIAZA collections in 2008 (BIAZA, 2010), approximately one third of the UK resident population of 61 million (Office for National Statistics, 2009). In Australia, nearly 36% of the population aged over 15 years visited a zoo at least once in the year 2005–6, more than any other cultural activity except for cinema visits (Australian Bureau of Statistics, 2008, as cited by Aegis Consulting Australia & Applied Economics, 2009). Interestingly, this attendance rate was virtually the same as ten years earlier. When international visitors and children below the age of 15 years are included, there are approximately 15.4 million visits to Australian zoos per annum (Aegis Consulting Australia and Applied Economics, 2009).

Membership to a zoo may suggest a greater commitment to it or at least an intention to visit regularly. In 2008, over 679 000 people held memberships or season tickets to BIAZA zoos and aquaria (BIAZA, 2010); approximately one percent of the UK population. There are 9.4 million paying members of AZA institutions (AZA, 2010a,b), equating to around 3% of the population. For comparison, figures supplied to the Office for National Statistics (UK) for 2003 show that the combined membership of BIAZA organisations exceeds that of non-collection based environmental organisations such as WWF (320 000), and Greenpeace (221 000). However, it is lower than the Royal Society for the Protection of Birds (1 022 000) to which membership gives access to several nature reserves and significantly lower than the 3 million membership of the National Trust, membership of which provides access to around 300 historical properties (Office of National Statistics,

2003). The Association for Leading Visitor Attractions, which publishes visitor numbers for visitor attractions in the UK each year, showed that for 2009, Kew Gardens (an internationally renowned botanical gardens), Chester Zoo, London Zoo and the Eden Project (biomes of plants and animals emphasising conservation) were four of the seven fully fee-paying attractions in the top 20 attractions by visitor numbers (ALVA, 2010).

Zoos naturally depend on visitors not only because entrance fees and other revenues generated during visits are an important source of income, but also because attendance figures gauge public perceptions and popularity of zoos (Davey, 2007). Some zoos are self-financing and depend almost solely on visitors for funding. But, zoos currently operate in a highly competitive visitor attraction market in which all organisations compete fiercely for their share of customers (Swarbrooke, 2001). Attendance figures are important because they gauge indirectly the popularity and public perceptions of zoos (presumably, the less the people who visit, the less popular the zoos). This has become an issue in recent years because of the growing concern and criticism on animal-welfare issues and the ethics associated with maintaining animals in captivity (Singer, 1995).

Some authors claim that zoos are popular; for example, Kellert (2002) reaffirmed the fashionable phrase that 'the popularity of zoos is reflected in the suggestion that more Americans visit zoos annually than attend all professional football, baseball and basketball games combined' and he labelled this as an 'extraordinary popularity'. There have also been attendance increases in zoos in the United States (Morey & Associates, 2000, 2001, 2004). In contrast to the view that zoos are popular, it is also claimed that zoo attendance is declining (Mason, 2000). For instance, the British Tourist Board's annual analysis, via a national survey of visits to UK visitor attractions indicates that zoo attendance declined during the 1990s, whereas attendance to other visitor attractions increased (BTA/ETB, 1997). There have also been several zoo closures in the UK since the 1990s.

Given these conflicting views, it is difficult to judge how popular zoos really are and how they are positioned in the visitor-attraction market compared with their competitors. Davey (2007) investigated zoo-attendance patterns from zoos reporting to the IZY and factors that could account for them for data since the 1960s from a large number of zoos across the world. Results showed that attendance had generally declined in most world regions during the 40-year period, particularly marked during the 1960s and 1970s. However, there were increases at North American and British zoos since the 1980s.

3.4 Zoos and conservation

3.4.1 Evolution of zoos

Tudge (1995) asserts that if zoos did not already exist, any good conservation strategy would invent them. But, zoos in their original form were actually deleterious to conservation. The on-going collection of wild caught animals to replace those dying prematurely due to poor animal husbandry was unsustainable. In addition the poor knowledge of the species' natural behaviours resulted in enclosures, which could only provide a warped perception of animal behaviour and did nothing to connect the caged animal to their wild habitats. Of course, a major trigger for self-sustaining populations in zoos was the adoption of CITES, also known as the Washington Convention, by many countries as a result of a resolution adopted in 1973 at a meeting of members of IUCN. Its aim is to ensure that international trade in specimens of wild animals and plants does not threaten their survival, affording varying degrees of protection to more than 33 000 species of animals and plants. CITES made movement of rarer species more difficult, and alongside increased legislation on animal health restrictions, this made import of wild caught animals more difficult, and forced zoos to develop more self-sustaining populations.

We recognise presently that zoos have moved from animals caged for our delight, to a more enlightened conservation message, and finally to the notion that zoos can actually change human behaviour by teaching the visiting public about the natural world and pressures on it. Seal (1991) recognised a number of phases in the recent participation of zoos in species conservation, which chart the progress of zoos from being consumers of wildlife to leaders of captive animal propagation (Box 3.1).

Box 3.1 · *Phases in the evolution of zoos*

According to Seal (1991) there has been a number of clear phases in the evolution of zoos.

Phase 1. Breeding animals in captivity as a source of stock e.g. the New York Zoological Society supply of American bison to the wild in the early 1900s.

Phase 2. Systematic keeping of records and preparation of studbooks. Earliest studbooks were for the Przewalski's horse, Siberian tiger and the wisent.

Phase 3. Development of central databases for the management of species as global populations to achieve sufficient numbers and genetic founder stock. The International Species Inventory System expanded to include a sizeable number of the world's collections and provides the raw material to initiate new studbooks.

Phase 4. Development of species survival plans by zoo federations based upon population biology to provide efficient management guidance to achieve genetic and demographic goals for species conservation.

Phase 5. Participation with wildlife agencies to rescue critically endangered species from oblivion by bringing all specimens available into captivity (e.g. black-footed ferret). Benefits from rapid development of co-ordinated breeding programmes and population viability analyses have been stimulated by the increasing recognition that we are losing the battle in developed countries.

Phase 6. Collaboration with conservation biology and wildlife management communities to develop new captive populations with adequate founder stock of species.

Phase 7. Return of species to the wild. This requires the development of new knowledge about most of the species in the face of scepticism by ecologists and wildlife biologists.

Phase 8. Participation in support and protection of reserves and parks to sustain species in natural ecosystems.

However, despite their evolution, zoos remain a form of entertainment, with the animals unwittingly playing the main roles. So if zoos are trying more than ever to do right for the animals in their care, providing them in many cases with hyper-naturalistic, state-of-the-art exhibits and greater attention to what the animals might actually need, or attempt to contribute to biodiversity conservation, then there are some tough questions. Which animals should be exhibited and why? How much do we invest in actual direct conservation? Selection of species for captive breeding and zoos will be dealt with in more detail in Chapter 4.

3.4.2 Mission impossible?

Objections to the operations of zoos and captive breeding programmes come from wildlife biologists, ecologists, animal rights groups, animal welfare groups and conservation groups. The concerns expressed revolve around the success of captive breeding programmes and the allocation of funds for these (Chapter 6). Indeed, to date, efforts to breed endangered species for conservation or maintaining genetic diversity among non-threatened species have been limited in their success. Another major criticism against zoos is that captive breeding programmes are essentially a misallocation of conservation funds. There is undoubtedly a disparity in the money spent on captive breeding efforts in comparison with that spent on similar *in-situ* programmes, as suggested by various authors (e.g. Rahbek, 1993; Snyder *et al.*, 1996). Some, like Leader-Williams (1990) have gone further to advocate that it would cost 50 times as much to keep African elephants and black rhinos in zoos than to manage the same number of individuals in the wild. Furthermore, the argument is often made that keeping captive individuals of one species does not benefit other species, as an *in-situ* programme focusing on habitat conservation would.

These views are strongly held and even nowadays any open discussion of options is rejected in favour of the status quo. According to Bertram (2004) the main objections to zoos are of three types. The first set consists of arguments that zoos in general ought not to exist, as being fundamentally wrong:

- zoos are a drain on wild populations and help to endanger them;
- zoos distract attention from efforts to conserve animals in the wild;
- the money spent on zoos should be spent on conservation in the wild instead;
- rather than shutting them up, species should be allowed to die out in dignity;
- it is wrong to restrict animals' freedom;
- confining wild animals makes them suffer;
- it is degrading to animals to be gawped at;
- keeping animals for entertainment is wrong.

The zoo world often counters these with justifications, particularly in relation to the conservation and education work that zoos carry out. The second set of anti-zoo arguments attack these justifications:

- we should be conserving habitats, not single species as zoos do;
- it is more cost effective to conserve animals in the wild than in zoos;
- zoos can only save a tiny proportion of all the species that are under threat;
- reintroduction back into the wild doesn't work;

- zoos are not really educational because they give the wrong messages;
- fine modern films and television programmes make zoos unnecessary;
- people can always go and look at animals in the wild;
- no useful research is possible in the unnatural conditions of zoos.

The third set is essentially arguments about what happens in practice in zoos:

- some zoos are clearly bad;
- zoo staff don't care about their animals' welfare;
- zoos do bad things like culling animals;
- some species should never be kept in zoos.

Such arguments have been counteracted, as undertaken by Bertram (2004), but there are many articles and some books that make a case for their closure. Pros and cons against zoos still abound, as exemplified in Table 3.3. But, persistently, the most fundamental objection to zoos, understood and expressed by only a small segment of today's animal rights movement, is that zoos are an immoral enterprise because they exploit and abuse living creatures for the entertainment of the crowd, and in so doing cause and perpetuate immeasurable suffering. The issue about absolutes is probably irresolvable since it depends on whether the basic premise of the argument is from an animal rights perspective, such as first put forward by the Australian philosopher Peter Singer in the 1970s (Singer, 1995).

Modern zoos, through the *World Zoo and Aquarium Conservation Strategy* [IUDZG/CBSG (IUCN/SSC) 1993, 2005], an initiative of the WAZA and the CBSG, have declared that the zoo and aquarium community is prepared to support the conservation of species, natural habitats and ecosystems. The document recognises the evolution of zoos from menageries, and exhorts zoos to become modern conservation centres by becoming more engaged in captive or 'conservation breeding', education and research for wildlife conservation. Most people recognise that zoological collections have a key and active role to play in maintaining biological diversity, as pronounced in individual organisations' mission statements and joint declarations by global entities such as the IUCN. In a global survey of zoos, Zimmerman & Wilkinson (2007) found that 77% of 190 zoos which responded had biodiversity conservation in their mission; the majority (82%) said they participated in conservation activities. Patrick *et al.* (2007) also examined the mission statements of 136 AZA accredited zoos and found that in most the predominant themes were education and conservation. To explore the relation between these two themes, the authors present a literature review of the roles and purposes of zoos and discuss how the literature compares with the roles and purposes of zoos as found in the zoo mission statements. They conclude that with more than 134 million visitors a year, zoos are in a unique position to provide environmental education and conservation education to large numbers of people.

The scope of activity that zoos perform in order for them to become a force of benefit to conservation has been summarised by various authors (e.g. Seal, 1991; Rabb, 1994; West & Dickie, 2007) as encompassing the following:

Table 3.3 *Arguments for and against zoos. From Dixon (2005)*

Against zoos	For zoos
1. Animals belong in their natural habitat in the wild. It is a breach of their natural rights to take them by force into captivity for our own purposes.	Animals do not have rights. In any case, zoos, as we will see below, exist to protect endangered species and to help us understand and protect our animal cousins more successfully. One of the reasons animals are taken into captivity in zoos is because they are under threat if they stay in their natural habitat (see point 4).
2. Whatever the good intentions of zookeepers, animals in zoos suffer. They are inevitably confined in unnaturally small spaces, and are kept from the public by cages and bars. They suffer psychological distress, often displayed by abnormal or self-destructive behaviour. Aquatic animals do not have enough water, birds are prevented from flying away by having their wings clipped and being kept in aviaries.	There have in the past been many bad zoos and cruel zookeepers. It is imperative that these are reformed and weeded out. Good zoos in which animals are well fed and well looked after in spacious surroundings are becoming the norm and should be encouraged. Zoos can exist without cruelty to animals, however, and so the fact that there are animal welfare problems with some zoos does not mean that all zoos should be shut down.
3. Adults and children visiting zoos will be given the subliminal message that it is OK to use animals for our own ends, however it impinges on their freedom or quality of life; thus zoos will encourage poor treatment of animals more generally. People do not go to zoos for educational reasons; they simply go to be entertained and diverted by weird and wonderful creatures seen as objects of beauty or entertainment. As a form of education the zoo is deficient: the only way to understand an animal properly is to see it in its natural environment – the zoo gives a totally artificial and misleading view of the animal by isolating it from its ecosystem.	Zoos nowadays are not marketed as places of entertainment – they are places of education. Most modern zoos have their main emphasis on conservation and education – the reason that so many schools take children to zoos is to teach them about nature, the environment, endangered species, and conservation. Far from encouraging bad treatment of animals, zoos provide a direct experience of other species that will increase ecological awareness.
4. There are two problems with the claim that zoos are beneficial because they help to conserve endangered species. First, they do not have a very high success rate – many species are going extinct each week despite the good intentions of some zoos. This is partly because a very small captive community of a species is more prone to inter-breeding and birth defects. Secondly, captive breeding to try to stave off extinction	One of the main functions of zoos is to breed endangered animals in captivity. If natural or human factors have made a species' own habitat a threatening environment then human intervention can preserve that species where it would certainly go extinct if there were no intervention. There are certainly problems with trying to conserve endangered species in this way but it is right that we should at least try to conserve them. And as long as animals are

(*cont.*)

Table 3.3 (cont.)

Against zoos	For zoos
need not take place in the context of a zoo, where the public come to look at captive animals and (often) see them perform tricks. Captive breeding programmes should be undertaken in large nature reserves, not within the confines of a zoo.	treated well in zoos there is no reason why conservation, education, and cruelty-free entertainment should not all be combined in a zoo. There is also, of course, a valid role for breeding in different environments such as large nature reserves.
5. As above, research into animals (when it respects their rights and is not cruel or harmful) may be valuable, but it does not need to happen in the context of confinement and human entertainment. Also, the only way really to understand other species is to study them in their natural habitat and see how they interact socially and with other species of flora and fauna.	As above we should take a 'both–and' approach rather than an 'either–or' approach. Animals can and should be studied in the wild but they can be studied more closely, more rigorously, and over a more sustained period of time in captivity. Both sorts of study are valuable and, as in point 4, there is no reason why this should not be done in the context of a cruelty-free zoo as well as in other contexts.

Direct conservation

- Preservation of populations of endangered species, and through these the conservation of natural habitats and ecosystems. *In-situ* conservation projects to protect endangered species, i.e. those run by a zoo or those which a zoo funds.
- Individuals from *ex-situ* populations can be periodically released into the wild to maintain numbers and genetic variability in natural populations.
- By ensuring that *ex-situ* populations are self-maintaining the need to collect animals from the wild for display and research purposes can be dramatically reduced.

Research

- Zoos have been presented by some authors as unique venues for scientific research (Kleiman, 1992; Hutchins *et al.*, 1996; Wharton, 2006, 2007). Research in zoos has allowed the acquisition of scientific facts relevant to *in-situ* conservation, as well as enabling the accumulation of knowledge useful for improving animal care.

Education and training

- Public and political awareness with respect to the need of conservation and natural resource sustainability.
- Individuals on display can help to educate the public about the need to preserve the species, and so protect other members of the species in the wild.
- As conservation centres, zoos must also address sustainable relationships of humankind and nature, explain the values of ecosystems and the necessity of conserving biological diversity.

- Training of *in-situ* and *ex-situ* conservationists enabling the transfer of skills from experienced zoo personnel to field staff in a variety of disciplines e.g. veterinary medicine, research staff, educators, animal keepers.

3.4.3 Direct contribution to conservation

Policies and structures that encourage zoos to contribute directly to conservation can be found in the *World Zoo and Aquarium Conservation Strategy*, but are also embedded in legislation such as the European EU Council Directive (1999/22/EC) which requires zoos to contribute to conservation. Contribution to conservation has a wide interpretation, from educating the public, undertaking research and direct involvement in *in-situ* activities. In fact, the European legislation does not explicitly state that it requires direct *in-situ* conservation by zoos (Rees, 2005; Wehnelt & Wilkinson, 2005).

Estimates of the amounts spent on field projects (in the zoo's country as well as overseas) by *ex-situ* institutions are hard to find, although some attempts have been made by regional zoo organisations, e.g. EAZA, BIAZA, or AZA. In an email survey sent to 725 zoos and aquariums from 68 countries (to which 26% of the institutions from 40 countries answered), approximately $49 million per year was being spent in conservation-related field activities (Zimmerman & Wilkinson, 2007). Conservation expenditure was positively correlated with zoo income, with over half of zoos generating more than three quarters of their conservation funds from their own income (i.e. gates and earnings), rather than from externally sourced funds (e.g. statutory funding, trusts and foundations). Zimmerman & Wilkinson (2007) found that over a third of zoos relied entirely on their income to fund field projects. Their results also showed that conservation expenditure was comparable between high and low-GDP countries. However, the inclusion of Latin American zoos in Zimmerman & Wilkinson's study, which are known to contribute considerable sums to field projects despite being in low-GDP countries, may have biased results. In any case, the contribution made to field conservation projects may have little to do with a country's general wealth and more to do with the zoo's philosophy and commitment to conservation.

There is no denying that large sums of money are invested by zoos worldwide in the pursuit of their conservation objectives (Zimmerman & Wilkinson, 2007). For instance, more than $38 million are spent in direct conservation projects by the EAZA per annum (Anne-Katrine Garn, personal communication). Among the UK federated zoos, which actually contribute 42% of the EAZA's spend on *in-situ* conservation projects, approximately $4.5 million were spent in 1995, rising to over $16 million by 2008 (BIAZA, 2010). In addition, specific EAZA campaigns since 1996 have raised a further $1 million from public donations for other conservation projects for a range of species from tigers to medicinal leeches. Individually, relatively small zoos such as Durrell can have relatively high conservation spends; Durrell's conservation budget for 2009 was approximately $5 million; representing close to half of the gross income of the zoo and the Trust (Durrell, 2010). This covers overseas projects and the International Training Programme where zoo/conservation professionals from around the world are trained in endangered

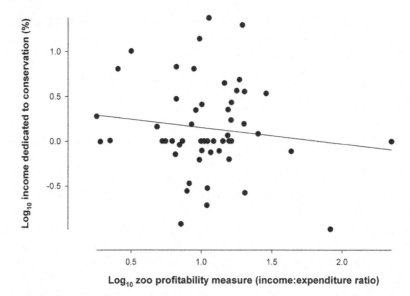

Fig. 3.6 Plot of the relationship between the percentage of a sample of UK zoos' income dedicated to conservation activities, and their declared income to expenditure ($y = -0.18x + 0.32$; $r^2 = 0.02$, $P = 0.35$, $n = 56$). Data from BIAZA (M. Stevenson, personal communication).

species conservation techniques (Waugh & Wenner, 1994; Fa *et al.*, 1996; Fa & Clark, 1998). Other notable examples, such as the much larger London Zoo/ZSL in the UK or the Bronx Zoo/WCS in the US, invest over $6 million in projects in 50 countries and $8 million in 500 field conservation projects in 60 countries respectively; in both cases more than 20% of their operating income. Perth Zoo in Australia, in 1999/2000, out of a total revenue of $5 909 138 spent $1 066 951 associated with producing seven threatened species for reintroduction programmes; 18% of gross income (Tribe & Booth, 2003).

However, many zoos are still apparently contributing little in financial terms to conservation projects. A report on percentage of operating budgets by Bettinger & Quinn (2000), revealed that in American zoos in 1999 the average expenditure on conservation (including zoo-based research and staff time) was only 0.1% of budget. Some zoos, for example Auckland Zoo in New Zealand, dedicate a fixed proportion of their earnings (1%) from gate and all commercial revenue to a conservation fund. Income and expenditure for 2009 as well as amounts spent on conservation for a sample of UK zoos ($n = 66$) (Stevenson, personal communication) showed that on average 3.6% (median 0.8%; range 0%–65%) of their income was spent on conservation projects, with only two institutions investing more than 20% of their gross income. Over 82% of all sample zoos spent less than 5% of their income on conservation and 27% none at all. Moreover, the proportion of gross income spent on conservation was not greater, but in fact tended to be less, in the more profitable zoos (Fig. 3.6). Although no data were given, Miller *et al.* (2004) asserted that conservation expenditure among most 'collection-based institutions' was less than 5%. This corroborates our figures for UK zoos.

If they are to make a real contribution to biodiversity conservation, some authors have proposed that a minimum amount of an institution's income should be dedicated to conservation. For example, Kelly (1997) suggested that a minimum of 10% of operating income should be committed to research and conservation activities. Miller *et al.* (2004) proposed that a quarter of an institution's gross income should be dedicated to conservation. This figure was derived from the amount that WCS invests which the authors considered the benchmark for 'collection-based institutions'.

Whether a significant proportion of a zoo's operational budget can be contributed to conservation requires further scrutiny. Of course, some are already achieving this, as we have seen above, but not necessarily because they are more profitable. But, most zoos argue that they have great difficulty finding additional resources to direct to conservation programmes (Mitchell, 1994). One reason given is that many zoos have experienced declining attendances (Chapter 3) which has affected their financial ability to improve the visitor experience and their capacity to contribute to conservation (see Mallinson, 2003).

Other means of raising additional revenue for conservation in zoos includes receiving donations from individuals or institutions (even competitive funding). Several zoos in the USA have conservation contribution machines for visitors to donate cash towards the conservation of their chosen species. In Australia, some zoos offer behind-the-scenes tours for 'gold coin donations' to channel funds directly to regional *in-situ* conservation projects. Many institutions receive funding from governmental agencies (e.g. the UK's Darwin Initiative Fund, the US Fish and Wildlife Service) or from multilateral institutions (e.g. European Union, MacArthur Foundation).

The crucial dilemma (or even worry) for some zoo directors is whether zoo participation in conservation affects visitor levels. Information is limited on the expectation, interest, or satisfaction of visitors regarding the role of zoos in conservation. Without a proven link, some zoos seem reluctant to fully embrace their conservation potential, apparently believing that money spent on conservation will not be compensated for by increased visitor revenue. In so doing, such zoos may in fact be missing out on important marketing and fund-raising opportunities (Tribe & Booth, 2003). As Jo Gipps, then Director of London Zoo, made plain in an interview to the UK newspaper *The Independent* (White, 1993) the problem with zoo management is that it does not realise that 'conservation can sell tickets'. If zoos are to attract visitors and private and public financial support, then in the future they will have to work harder at promoting their conservation activities. Likewise, Conway & Hutchins (2001) cite that sound support for conservation will greatly benefit an institution since conservation and education programmes provide incentives for donors.

3.5 Colliding paradigms in the zoo world

A scheme for species and habitat preservation was proposed by William Conway (Conway, 1995). The main tenet of Conway's strategy was that multiple populations of threatened species could be managed effectively by including populations in nature and in captivity. Although the principle of interactive metapopulation management for key species is relatively simple (Foose, 1991), its use as a means of preserving habitat is more complex (May, 1991; Stanley Price, 1991). This is because all metapopulations of a wild-zoo programme are aimed at ensuring the survival of both the species and its habitat in nature. Interactive management, according to Conway, would support key species' subpopulations in an integrated fashion, using their study in nature as a way to understand wildlife habitats, ecological processes and conservation threats. In the face of rising human populations and habitat destruction, the survival of many species and habitats will depend upon the utility of fragments of habitat and the survival of relatively small populations whose habitats are reduced or altered and whose numbers are capped. Under such conditions, interactive wild-captive metapopulation strategies may increase the security of key species. Thus, a crucial objective in zoo evolution is to focus upon the species and its habitat as the unit of conservation, not the species alone.

Conway's (1995) emphasis on interactive management resonates with many conservationists, primarily because it has stimulated thinking around a pathway that can promote better communication between zoos and the wild. In reality, interactive management as a strong discipline has faltered; there is not much evidence of a serious take-up of these ideas by the zoo world (see Conway, 2007). This is evident from the lack of attention paid to interactive management as a discipline since the 5th World Conference on Breeding Endangered Species in Captivity in 1988 (Dresser et al., 1988), which purported to consolidate the relations between the captive and wild. Perhaps a major barrier to such an approach has been the formulation of a different posit for zoos, essentially emerging from Hutchins et al. (1995) plea for zoos to move away from the Noah's ark paradigm, which is the idea that zoo collections should emphasise threatened or endangered taxa over common taxa (Conway, 1987; Balmford et al., 1996). Hutchins et al. (1995) presented the case against this paradigm, suggesting it as too restrictive and that taxa in zoos should contribute to a broader conservation goal, one that goes beyond the emphasis on captive breeding and public education to a greater involvement in field conservation. Hutchins & Conway (1995) presented examples in which members of the AZA are contributing to a more holistic approach to conservation in the field. These include fund-raising to support habitat protection and/or restoration, public education, ecotourism, scientific research, development of relevant technologies, professional training and technological transfer and political action (Hutchins & Wemmer, 1991). Indeed, support of nature protection in-country can be achieved through innovative linkages between western zoos and conservation in the wild, such as the Minnesota Zoo's *Adopt a Park* programme in Indonesia (Tilson, 1995). In 1990, Minnesota Zoo charted a new course for wildlife conservationists in zoos worldwide by 'adopting' an Indonesian National Park, Ujung Kulon. Through this *in-situ* project, which ran for more than 15 years, the zoo provided direct assistance to Indonesian forestry rangers to better manage and protect their national parks. This park, the last refuge of the one-horned Javan rhinoceros, of which fewer than 60 animals are believed to exist in the wild, also protects one of the last remaining fragments of lowland forest on Java, many species of rare plants, hundreds of bird species (several of which were displayed in Minnesota Zoo's Asian Tropics), numerous rare amphibians, fish and reptiles. By using the rhino as a 'flagship' and 'umbrella species', Minnesota Zoo attracted attention and funds to help conserve a significant combination of Javan wildlife, as well as an entire ecosystem of global importance. Examples of direct conservation activities initiated and sustained by zoos abound and have been increasing in the past decade (see Leader-Williams et al., 2007 and below).

Thus, Hutchins et al. (1995) argued, although not explicitly, that an emphasis on a Noah's ark paradigm would preclude zoos from using a variety of taxa, including non-endangered ones, to contribute to conservation. A clear target for Hutchins et al. (1995), however, were processes such as CAMPs (Seal et al., 1994), which were perceived as advocating that hundreds of species could be saved through captive breeding. Ellis (1995), in her response to Hutchins et al. (1995), asserts that their assessment of CAMPs was equivocal, given that these processes, according to their instigators (CBSG), were meant to assemble practitioners and guide appropriate captive breeding actions (Chapter 4). Hutchins et al. (1995) do not, of course, deny the contribution that captive breeding can make to species recovery in 'carefully selected' cases.

3.6   Two remaining fundamental questions

3.6.1   Are zoos still consumers of wild animals?

Generally, modern zoos consider it unacceptable not to have self-sustaining populations. Data on whether populations of species kept in animal collections are self-sustaining are complicated to assess (although see below for viability assessments of European bird and mammal studbooks). It may be true that in most modern zoos, situations typical of the past, such as in the Paris menagerie from 1830 to 1959 when nearly 4000 monkeys perished (Baratay & Hardouin-Fugier, 2004), do not occur. However, data from South American zoo inventories in Stanley Price & Fa (2007) suggest that very few captive populations are self-sustaining since most species are found in small numbers and in only one collection; very few species are found in more than 10% of all zoos. In fact, when total population sizes for mammals, birds and reptiles in South American zoos were examined, only 8% of all species had combined populations larger than 100 specimens. This suggests that self-sustaining populations for most captive populations in this part of the world do not exist, and therefore imports from the wild would be needed to sustain them. But, most specimens (88%) in the South American zoo sample were common taxa, often the result of confiscations (see Cuarón, 2005); hence breeding programmes for endangered species would be the ones requiring supplementation with wild animals.

The declared acquisition of wild animals to supplement zoo collections is likely to be an underestimate. For example, according to the Brazilian illegal animal traffic monitoring institution, *Rede Nacional de Combate ao Tráfico de Animais Silvestres* (RENCTAS, 2001) traffickers will '*launder*' wildlife through zoos or so called 'scientific/conservation' or commercial breeding institutions – legal or not – which provide false certificates attesting the animals were born in captivity, which enables them to be imported or exported. Data available from the CITES Trade Database which contains information about the legal international trade in endangered species, managed by the UNEP-WCMC on behalf of the CITES Secretariat, showed that during 1975–2008, 140 314 specimens of 1308 CITES species were taken from the wild to supply zoos; 79 284 were Russian tortoises (65 000 to German institutions). More worrisome, however, was the import of 570 wild African elephants of which 45% were imported to three countries (99 to Germany, 91 to the USA, 65 to Belgium). These elephant imports are propping up zoo populations of the species, and as has been shown for Asian elephants in North American zoos (Weise, 2000), the captive population may not be self-sustaining, and would therefore require a number of imports per year, including from the wild.

There are, of course, some examples of captive populations of endangered species that are not a drain to the wild. This is the case for the giant panda, whose captive population has improved substantially since the early 1990s, removing its need for demographic or genetic augmentation from wild-born stock (Traylor-Holzer et al., 2008). Improved reproductive success and higher cub survival have resulted in 10% annual population growth in recent years. The current global captive population of 241 pandas is comprised primarily of captive-born animals and is self-sustaining. Most captive pandas are maintained within China by the Chinese Association of Zoological Gardens or the State Forestry Administration, who work collaboratively to administer the cooperation breeding programme. Genetic management has maintained a high level of gene diversity with little inbreeding and is accomplished through an annual population analysis and breeding strategy. Planned natural matings as well as successful artificial insemination efforts have enabled the retention of additional founder lines from previously non-reproductive wild-caught animals. This captive population is demographically and genetically viable and is projected to reach its target size of 300 animals to function as a backup against population decline in the wild.

3.6.2 Can visitor enjoyment and conservation be reconciled?

Although few dispute the primary role of zoos should be species conservation (Tudge, 1991), zoos must still balance this aim with the need to attract visitors (Hutchins et al., 1995). Although the world's zoos have considerable resources at their disposal – their operating budgets were suggested to be four to six times that of all protected areas in the tropics (CBSG, 1992) – attraction of large numbers of people, simply to remain open, remains the elementary challenge (Balmford, 2000a). Assuring funds to guarantee financial viability of the institution may conflict with making resources available for conservation. Magin et al. (1994) argue that this consideration may be one of the main reasons for low numbers of threatened mammal species in zoos.

The question of what sorts of species are best able to attract visitors into zoos has been much investigated (Morris, 1960; Surinova, 1971), with what constitutes animal 'charisma' long debated. There has been research into which species visitors enjoy viewing in zoos, and which species offer the greatest visitor enjoyment per zoo dollar spent (Ward *et al.*, 1998; Balmford, 2000b). These studies have primarily focussed on body size, some authors reporting a positive relationship between a species' size and its popularity (Ward *et al.*, 1998; Balmford, 2000b). However, recent findings suggest that small mammal displays yield a higher cost to benefit ratio, in terms of exhibit popularity per unit cost, than large mammal displays (Balmford, 2000a). However, other studies have indicated that additional factors influence visitor enjoyment of exhibits, e.g. activity (Bitgood *et al.*, 1986), exhibit design (Birney, 1991) and perceived danger of animal (Bitgood *et al.*, 1986). Interest in visiting a zoo may be as much motivated by curiosity in preferred species, as fascination for disliked animals (such as snakes and spiders). Surinova (1971) concluded that visitors prefer mammals over all other animal groups. Although consensus has not been reached, the finding that large mammals are not always favoured over small has led to hopes that zoo attendance may not be adversely affected if zoos decreased their numbers of larger mammals (Balmford *et al.*, 1996). Large charismatic taxa, such as primates, cats and ungulates, may be generally important in drawing the public, but they may not be the most profitable species for zoos, because more popular, large-bodied animals will cost more to keep. Yajima (1991) showed unequivocally, by comparing attendance before and after the opening of the 'insect ecological land' in Tama Zoo in Japan, that imaginative displays of small-bodied species can substantially increase zoo attendance.

This study also suggests that species most suitable for captive breeding need not be unpopular with visitors, especially since such species not only tend to be small, but also have shorter generation times and may be kept in larger (and in some cases, more social) groups. Greater visitor interest in animals in larger groups has been found by previous studies (Marcellini & Jenssen, 1988). By including opportunities for animal activity (e.g. ropes/trees/pools/etc.), and increasing their interaction, zoos could maintain popular displays of smaller animals in need of captive breeding.

What interests the public once inside zoos has been examined by Balmford *et al.* (1996) and Balmford (2000a) by looking at the distribution of visitors across a number of main exhibits in a sample of zoos. The logic is that the mean percentage of visitors at each exhibit is a direct reflection of how the average visitor distributes his/her time within the zoo. Balmford *et al.* (1996) showed no relationship between percentage visitors per exhibit and body size, with reptiles and small mammals more popular than ungulates, elephants or rhinos. These data to some extent dispel the widely held notion that displays of large-bodied species are necessarily more interesting to the general public.

How specific factors and their relative importance to each other affect visitor preference in zoos, however, is still largely unresolved. It may not be the species *per se* the public like, but those from which they gain the most pleasure viewing in a particular zoo environment. No study to date has addressed whether zoo visitor preferences, attitudes and behaviour vary across the range of zoo types now in existence, and what can be learnt from the non-zoo-going public. In the only relatively recent study in which this sector was involved, it was found they were unlikely to be aware of ongoing improvements in zoos, such as collection changes (Reade & Waran, 1996).

Even though the general public may perceive a change in the role of the zoo as it moves away from the traditional type and concentrates more on conservation, the public's reasons for visiting them may not change. The factors of overwhelming importance are still apparently for visitors to have a day out and to see animals. Many studies conclude that the major reasons for attending zoos are entertainment-based (Kawata & Hendy, 1978; Kellert & Dunlap, 1989; Reade & Waran, 1996) and that zoos must provide species and exhibits to give an enjoyable experience (Hancocks, 2001). Thus, these are compelling arguments made by zoos for introducing species into their collections primarily for entertainment value.

The major crowd-puller without any doubt has been the giant panda, described as one of, if not, the most, sought after of animals for zoos. Loans of giant pandas to American and Japanese zoos formed an important part of the diplomacy of the People's Republic of China in the 1970s, as it marked some of the first cultural exchanges between China and the West. This practice has been termed 'Panda Diplomacy'. By 1984, however, pandas were no longer used as agents of diplomacy. Instead, China began to offer pandas to other nations only on 10-year loans. The standard loan terms included a fee of up to US$1 000 000 per year and a provision that any cubs born during the loan are the property of the People's Republic of China. Zoos that have exhibited pandas have reported exorbitant increases in attendance figures and profits of millions, some from the sale of souvenirs. An example of this is the two baby pandas from China imported to Zoo Atlanta in 1999. Visitor numbers doubled, and overall revenue (including concessions and gift-shop sales) increased from $4 million to $7.7 million in a year (Shropshire, 2000). Although some of these profits, not just from Zoo Atlanta, may have gone towards panda conservation, many believe that the loan fee has not been used appropriately. At the height of the 'rent-a-panda' controversy (when numerous zoos were having pandas on short-term display), conservationists, including George Schaller, a foremost ecologist who has studied pandas in the wild, criticised the use of money raised through zoo loans to fund panda breeding stations in China. Since 1998, due to a WWF lawsuit, the US Fish and Wildlife Service only allows a US zoo to import a panda if the zoo can ensure that China will channel more than half of its loan fee into conservation efforts for the giant panda and its habitat. There are no published data on how such funds are deployed.

Such crowd-pleasing 'powers' are also attributable to species more economical to display, although they may be of less conservation concern. The flurry of interest in meerkats, for example, is a tribute not just to the species' undoubted charisma, but also to the exposure they have received through the media (Box 3.2). Meerkats are currently a potent example of a species selected almost entirely as a crowd pleaser in zoos since they are not threatened and so fulfil no direct conservation role.

Box 3.2 · *How meerkats have ruled the world*

Meerkats are mongooses that live in colonies of up to 30 members. They are distributed throughout most of the Kalahari Desert in Botswana and in South Africa. The species is not threatened.

Simon Usborne writing for the UK newspaper *The Independent* (15 October 2009) summed it up well by saying 'meerkats are beyond compare'. Britain, like Europe and the USA, has gone mad for meerkats. They have colonised billboards, cinemas and television screens. Their adorable faces, quizzical disposition and trademark posture make them seriously cute (and seriously attractive to marketing professionals) but some even claim that, in gloomy times, meerkats have a unique power to make people happy. In Germany, they call them *erdmännchen*, or 'little earth people'.

When did this madness begin? Although the popularity of meerkats reached its height in 2005, the animals first became popular in 1987 with the release of the BBC documentary, 'Meerkats United'. The film captivated a generation and has been voted the most popular nature documentary of all time. In 2008, the big-budget Hollywood film 'Meerkats – The Movie' was released, backed by the Weinstein brothers, and narrated by the late Paul Newman. This film builds on the popularity generated by the British television programme produced by Oxford Scientific Films for Animal Planet International that premiered in September 2005 and ran for four series until its cancellation in August 2008. Blending more traditional animal documentary style footage with dramatic narration, the series told the story of the Whiskers, one of more than a dozen families of meerkats in the Kalahari Desert being studied as part of the Kalahari Meerkat Project, a long-term field study into the ecological causes and evolutionary consequences of the cooperative nature of meerkats.

But there is one personality that has done more to propel the meerkat into celebrity than any other – Aleksander Orlov, a computer-generated Russian aristocrat (meerkat) with a thick accent and a smoking jacket from a series of TV ads for a price comparison website, Comparethemarket.com. The agency behind the campaign, VCCP, have made Orlov the world's most famous (and, depending who you ask, most annoying) meerkat. 'He' regularly updates his Twitter feed and Facebook page and boasts more than half a million followers. A Flickr album of black and white family portraits reveals his noble heritage and a biography tells how Orlov's *'greatest grandfather'*, Mikhail, fought in the Meerkat–Mongoose war of 1728, while his grandparents survived the Furry Terror of 1921. In the latest ads, Orlov is joined by his web technician, Sergei, a veteran of the Soviet space programme (he designed the *'Mir(kat)'* space station). The inspired, brilliantly silly campaign has been heaped with industry awards and Orlov has transformed the fortunes of a website that used to struggle to be distinctive in a competitive field.

In zoos meerkat-mania has resulted in more investment in meerkat exhibits and corresponding merchandise and an increase in adoptions. Zoos more used to receiving donations for lions and tigers are swamped with requests for meerkat adoptions. Such is the demand that some zoos like the Yorkshire Wildlife Park launched *Comparethemeerkatbabies.com* for prospective parents to choose a meerkat 'child'. Meerkats in adoption programmes in many zoos are the most popular animals.

Although crowd-pulling species do precisely that, the evidence that any (or some) species in zoos can be exhibited to raise commercial revenue to fund scientific research, conservation efforts and education is lacking. There are few reports by zoos as to whether exhibit investment costs are really recovered through a greater footfall, and whether the improved footfall does indeed create a surplus that the zoo then channels to these activities. A superficial review of new exhibits at some zoos shows construction costs to be staggering. One case in particular, the *Lied Jungle* at Henry Doorly Zoo, Omaha, which opened in 1994 at a cost of nearly $20 million, serves as an example. To offset this investment alone would require the equivalent of 1.7 million paying visitors; the reported visitor attendance to the zoo is currently around 1.4 million per annum.

Other examples of high-end exhibits include the Cleveland Zoo rainforest exhibit and the Bronx Zoo's *Jungle World* both requiring outlays of about $30 million (Hancocks, 2001). The declared expenditure on new exhibits in zoos accredited by the AZA for 2001 was over US$ 245 million for 171 exhibits (AZA, 2001), which was three times higher than the current annual contribution to conservation of AZA accredited zoos of nearly $90 million supporting 4000 projects (AZA, 2010c).

Key concepts

(1) The modern day zoo began in the late eighteenth and early nineteenth centuries. The 'menagerie period' in the nineteenth century focused on taxonomy with little appreciation for animal needs. Hagenbeck revolutionised zoo exhibits in the early twentieth century using innovative landscaping but animal welfare was still poor. Heini Hediger described the fundamental behavioural characteristics of animals and the importance of species-appropriate enclosures and care.

(2) Zoos do not keep a proportionately higher number of endangered species; in most collections less than one third of the species are listed as threatened by IUCN. Most zoos maintain higher numbers of mammals and birds than other groups. Zoos worldwide are amongst the top recreational destinations. However, most zoos and zoo visitors are not in biodiversity-rich countries. Entertainment remains a primary reason for visitors to attend the zoo and education campaigns have not changed this. Zoos argue that species selection must balance conservation needs and visitor enjoyment. Zoos argue that crowd pleasers such as giant pandas and meerkats can draw additional visitor revenue, which can be used to support conservation efforts.

(3) Arguments against zoos include 'they are fundamentally wrong' for example because they divert attention from *in-situ* efforts and using animals for entertainment is wrong; 'conservation and education claims by zoos are unjustified' for example because zoos can only save a small proportion of threatened animals and TV and other media make zoos redundant educationally; 'zoos are operationally poor' for example because some zoo staff do not care about animal welfare and some species should never be kept in zoos.

(4) Zoos are involved in direct conservation through: support of *in-situ* projects directly or through funding; reintroduction to the wild of zoo animals; actively ensuring self-sustaining *ex-situ* populations to reduce the need for wild-caught animals for display and research. Research in zoos can provide data for *in-situ* conservation as well as *ex-situ* animal care. Zoo education can use individual animals in the zoo to address the importance of conserving biological diversity and train conservationists in skills necessary for field work and zoo animal care.

(5) Investment in conservation by zoos is generally low. Available data point to less than 5% of income being spent on conservation. Most zoo associations trumpet their investment in conservation through declaration of sums of money dedicated to conservation. However, if zoos allocated more of their income to outcome-oriented conservation projects, some argue 10%–25% of world zoos could become a veritable force in saving species from extinction.

(6) The idea that zoos can directly contribute to conservation of species through captive breeding and reintroduction, the 'Noah's Ark' paradigm, has been dismissed as too restrictive. Opponents argue this is too restrictive and propose a broader conservation goal beyond captive breeding and public education to a stronger involvement in field conservation. The departure from a clear dedicated commitment to direct conservation by zoos may have slowed the pace by which zoos contribute to species conservation.

4 · *Keeping animals in captivity*

'Our animals in captivity don't fight for food. They don't have to travel long distances for food, water and shelter . . . They have a specially prepared diet weighed to the gram, and they have animal care staff checking them every day for injury' (Barbara Baker)

4.1 Introduction

If animals are to be kept in the best possible state for exhibition, propagation and eventual release into the wild, what are the consequences of keeping small numbers of individuals in less complex environments? Since Hediger stressed the importance of studying the reactions of animals to their confinement as early as 1934 (Meyer-Holzapfel, 1968), much research has focussed on the behaviour of vertebrates in captivity. Much is known about the conduct of captive primates and carnivores, but much less about other mammals, birds, reptiles and amphibians. The last 20 or so years have seen a substantial growth in the number of behavioural studies undertaken in zoos; some are basic research on ethology and behavioural ecology, but most are applied and designed to understand how captive environments influence behaviour (Hosey, 1997). However, interpreting the results of these studies, particularly those on the influence of the captive environment, can be difficult, because it is by no means clear what benchmark should be used for evaluating behaviours seen in captivity.

Generally, most investigations indicate that captive environments affect the animal (see Hosey, 2005, on captive primates) but this is simplistic. At one extreme we know that animals in impoverished settings exhibit behaviours considered to be 'abnormal'. But, the concept of abnormality has proven very difficult to define since many believe such behaviour may be an adaptation by the animal to help it cope with the environment. Abnormality is therefore usually demonstrated by comparing captive animals with their wild counterparts, which frequently reveals stark differences in their time budgets and behavioural repertoire. Although well studied in their developed form, there is a distinct lack of research behind the origins of abnormal captive behaviour, the risk factors that predispose to them, and from which particular behaviours or conditions they arise. With our increased understanding of the psychological as well as the physical needs of animals, it is imperative that these source behaviours and environmental conditions are identified and ameliorated to improve the welfare of captive animals and perhaps even aid conservation efforts in the long term.

One of the biggest concerns regarding *ex-situ* populations is that they remain representatives of their taxa (Snyder *et al.*, 1996). However, captive-bred animals often exhibit deficiencies in foraging, predator avoidance and reproductive behaviour, which can present major difficulties when attempting to restore wild populations using captive-bred animals (Chapter 7). Behavioural differences between wild and captive-bred animals can arise through both intentional and unintentional processes. Intensive rearing practices often aim to maximise production by selecting preferred traits, such as enhanced growth rate, which can indirectly affect correlated traits such as aggression (Price, 1988). Adaptation to the captive environment (domestication) can also promote behavioural traits that are advantageous in captivity but maladaptive in the wild, such as tameness and a reduced response to stress (Frankham, 2008). Furthermore, captive environments often differ substantially from wild habitats, causing behavioural differences to arise as a result of differential experience (Price, 1999).

Captive animals exist in a very different environment to that of their free-living counterparts (see reviews by Huntingford, 2004; Price, 1999). Animals living in captivity do not need to devote a large proportion of their time to searching for food because they have a regular supply of good quality food available to them. Mate choice is sometimes absent in intensively managed animals so that reproduction occurs without the need to attract mates or compete with rivals, and in some systems it goes unchecked. Animals in captive environments are also protected from their predators (except humans) and therefore do not need to trade-off predation risk with other activities such as foraging and courtship behaviour (Huntingford, 2004).

In the wild, animals must learn to survive by adapting to live in complex and challenging environments. Institutions that hold animals in captivity, such as zoos, safari parks or research facilities, control for or remove the major environmental factors that encourage and preserve species-typical behaviour in the wild (Markowitz, 1982). These factors include such behaviours as foraging, finding shelter, intraspecific relationships and anti-predator behaviour. The challenge thus lies in how institutions can promote these behaviours in captive animals. There are two reasons for achieving this. Firstly, if eventual reintroduction of the individual into its natural habitat is the aim, then an animal that exhibits species-specific behaviours is more likely to survive in the wild. Secondly, many institutions make it their aim to provide educational opportunities for people to learn about the natural behaviour of species in their care. This is not possible unless the animals are able to exhibit similar behaviours to their wild counterparts.

Issues to do with the genetics of animals in captivity are briefly introduced here, but further discussed in the next chapters. Here, we first focus on what is meant by captive conditions, i.e. what variables are under management control, and how these changes to an animal's environment affect the way it eventually looks and behaves. We review what is understood to be mind and body, how we assess well-being in captive animals, and as an extension we touch upon the issue of animal rights and zoos. We end the chapter by presenting a synopsis of the use of environmental enrichment techniques as a means of keeping animals physically and psychologically active in captive situations, not just as an add-on but as an integral part of progressive captive animal management. However, we broach the question of whether environmental enrichment is sufficient to keep a captive animal 'natural'.

Most examples used here refer to mammals and birds, and in some cases fish. This is because most of the literature available relates to these taxonomic groups. The lack of emphasis on how captivity affects the behaviour of insects, for example, has been implicitly led by the supposition that these animals are 'hard-wired', unlike more sentient study subjects (e.g. primates, bears and cats). However, studies of crickets (Bailey et al., 2010) show how the effects of juvenile social experience on adult male morphology, reproductive investment, and behaviour influence sexual selection and phenotypic evolution.

4.2 Consequences of keeping animals in captivity

4.2.1 Variables under management control

An animal's environment can be defined as including all internal (e.g. parasites), external (e.g. social interactions) and non-hereditary conditions under which an animal lives (Besch & Kollias, 1994). In the wild, animals are able to thrive by way of having control over their surroundings via regulatory behavioural adjustments (Poole, 1995, 1998). Replicating an animal's complete natural environment in captivity is virtually impossible as the variables to take account of are infinite, although many believe this is not actually important for the animal's well-being.

At the most basic level, for a wild animal to survive in captivity it must be provided with an environment that is appropriate to its basic physiological needs, must be supplied with regular food and water, and is often spatially managed to permit encounters with potential mates for breeding, for example (Table 4.1). Catching and restraining for routine husbandry checks, veterinary care or transportation will also take place. All such variables are under direct management control by staff. In the case of daily feeding times, for example, this can be predicted by some animals. The long-term constancy of these variables will modify the behaviour and well-being of animals in captivity (Basset & Buchanan-Smith, 2007), and result in a range of 'domestication' processes. Changes in the nature of any variable can have immediate consequences on the animals' behaviour and general health status, but can also include morphological and physiological changes which could have important implications for reintroductions and the management of wild and captive populations as a whole.

4.2.2 Selection and adaptation to captivity

Humans have controlled wild animals' breeding and living conditions for multiple generations. Animals of use to humans are the oldest documented instance of keeping wild species in captivity. This process has not just resulted in habituation of wild animals to survive in the company of, or by the labour of human beings, but has also led to the modification of the domesticated animals' behaviour, life cycle, and physiology. Probably the earliest known domestication of an animal is the dog; likely to be as early as 15 000 BC

Table 4.1 *Variables under management control for animals in captivity*

Variable	Description
(1) The physical environment	
Lighting	Both quality and quantity are of paramount importance both for psychological (e.g. nocturnal, diurnal) and physiological (e.g. UV for vitamin D synthesis, heliothermic) needs. Photoperiod has an important impact on the major hormone-mediated systems of the body (e.g. seasonal reproduction, reproductive condition).
Humidity	Largely of physiological relevance. Variation to mimic seasonality (e.g. cue for aestivation).
Temperature	Provision of adequate temperatures for even the largest of species during inclement or extreme seasons. Where possible a temperature gradient should be provided as this will give the animal choice (e.g. provision of shade and shelter).
(2) Spatial confinement	
Boundary type	That is, moat, window, fence. Shape curved, square, etc. Determines visual and vocal contact with conspecifics, other species and the public. The minimum flight distance of a species must be considered to ensure that an appropriate distance from the public and other animals is possible. Suitability of the barrier for an animal's safety, e.g. glass for birds and water for apes may lead to injury or even death if not properly managed.
Dimensions	Often regarded as the most important however quality of the enclosure is more so. The size of the area must be appropriate to the species and the size and structure of the animal group(s) in it.
Furnishings	Enclosures must facilitate natural behaviours, e.g. climbing, swimming, running, etc. and make provision for refuge areas so that animals can evade both each other and the public. Where mixed species exhibits are established, furnishings should provide natural type niche divisions and thus reduce competition for space and resources.
Substrate	This should be chosen with both health and maintenance in mind so that it is both good for the animal and not too difficult to keep clean, e.g. hard stands for hoof stock to prevent hoof overgrowth and the use of carefully monitored deep litter.
(3) Maintenance	
Maintenance	Cleaning routines, etc., a sterile environment is unrealistic and not necessarily ideal. Temporal aspect of great importance with many species, the development of a daily routine to which the animals can become accustomed.
Feeding	Basic nutritional requirements must be assessed and where possible diet formulated based on the wild one. Supplementary in cases where species are left to their own devices to acquire the bulk of their diet, e.g. grazers (seasonal variation in grazing for hoofstock).

(*cont.*)

Table 4.1 (cont.)

Variable	Description
	Non-nutritional considerations: presentation of foods in natural forms, bones and fur for carnivores to maintain tooth condition, items to gnaw for rodents and birds to prevent tooth/bill overgrowth.
Special dietary requirements	Dictated by condition of individuals, e.g. young, sick and old may need extra feeds and for presentation and composition to be different.
Feeding methods	Both temporal and spatial aspects are vital to ensure individuals in groups receive appropriate rations.
Water	Clean drinking water should always be available for all animals.
(4) Routine management	
Interaction with animal staff	This is an important aspect of the management of any animal, both for the confidence of the animal and assessment of its condition by the keeper. If an animal is calm and relaxed in the presence of a keeper it will be easier to manage, observe, mix, etc.
Social groups	Contact with conspecific animals maintained in natural conditions is likely to be more attractive.
Seasonality	Mating breeding cycles must be considered. Groups may have to be split or rearranged as a result of oestrus.
Pregnancy/egg laying and incubation	Provision of nest boxes, cubbing dens or appropriate nesting areas is vital for reproductive success.
Birth/hatching	Routines may have to change to reduce disturbance during this particularly sensitive time and for a period after.
Development and care of young	Changes in management will be required whilst young are being reared both in the provision of food, water and the conspecific mixing of certain species. Hand rearing techniques must be appropriate and staff competent both for adequate rearing and future well-being of the individual if this course of action is taken.
(5) Handling	
General handling	A policy should be developed to control animal handling. Even in the case of apparently tame animals, it can cause stress and should be avoided unless necessary.
Catching/restraining	This should be undertaken by experienced staff or under supervision. Appropriate techniques and equipment should be used to minimise risk of injury to both staff and animals.
Transportation	This should be as quick as possible and container should be an appropriate size and contain food and water for long trips. If it is to be flown then the crate must comply with IATA Live Animal Regulations.

among hunter-gatherers in several locations (Drake & Klingenberg, 2010). Domestication generally acts through a process of intentional artificial selection by humans, in mammals promoting changes in body and brain size, alteration of external appearance (often a reduction of the facial region) and a thicker fat layer beneath the skin (Clutton-Brock,

1999). The majority of these changes are believed to be a side effect of the selective pressure of human-directed breeding of some 5000 to 15 000+ years.

Captive environments are very different from wild environments. Thus, natural selection acts very differently in the two environments. Moreover, captive management introduces artificial selective pressures such as selection for tameness or selection against intraspecific aggression and disease. Selection for animals that are behaviourally more suited to captivity will result in concomitant morphological, physiological and/or behavioural changes, with severe consequences for the successful reintroduction of captive-bred endangered species to the wild. Two types of adaptation are relevant for captive breeding: (1) non-heritable adaptation to captive conditions; and (2) genetic adaptation to captivity (see Appendix 5 for definitions).

Non-heritable adaptation. Some species show a remarkably high degree of phenotypic plasticity, allowing them to morphologically, physiologically, or behaviourally adapt to their environment. The best documented cases come from 'headstarting' programmes, which involve the harvesting of eggs from wild animals and rearing these in captivity before release to the wild (Perrow & Davy, 2002). For example, Schultz *et al.* (2009) reared individuals from two wild populations of the Puget blue butterfly in Washington, USA. The researchers collected eggs from the wild or from adult females brought into indoor facilities for oviposition. Survival from egg to adult was similar (<10%) across all captive groups which survived past diapause. As captivity did not lead to increased survivorship, headstarting is not suitable for population augmentation in this case under current methods. Moreover, captive-reared individuals were lighter and had smaller wings and shorter body lengths than their founding populations for both sites, which will likely directly impact flight physiology and fitness. Headstarting can also impact the behavioural competence of animals after release (Section 4.2.3). These findings point to the importance of comparing characteristics of reared individuals to individuals from the founding population to quantify possible effects of captive conditions.

Whether observed differences in morphology or phenotype result from different environments or reflect genetic differences is often difficult to infer without experimentation. Such testing is not possible when dealing with endangered species, as in the case of the two forms of whiptail lizards in St. Lucia (Funk & Fa, 2006). Hence, observations of how wild animals change in captivity are instructive. In the case of the black-footed ferret, one of the world's most endangered mammals, which has been captive-bred and released to the wild (Chapter 6), morphological changes in captivity were expressed after 10 years in captivity. Ferrets maintained in captive conditions were 5%–10% smaller in body size, had smaller skulls and a different skull shape compared to pre-captive animals. The reasons for this change remained elusive (Wisely *et al.*, 2002). However, a comparison of *ex-situ* animals after reintroduction with their *in-situ* descendants demonstrated that reintroduced individuals quickly returned to their pre-captive size. This suggested that the observed morphological changes were a temporary effect of captivity and therefore not heritable (Wisely *et al.*, 2005). Moreover, cage type affected the overall size and shape of the ferrets; implying that small cage size and environmental homogeneity inhibit the mechanical stimuli necessary for bone development (Wisely *et al.*, 2005). In a study of captive Coho salmon, rearing conditions reduced sexual dimorphism and captive fish had smaller heads but larger bodies than wild salmon (Hard *et al.*, 2000). More importantly perhaps, male salmon reared in captivity were discriminated against by wild and captive female fishes, and were therefore less likely to reproduce than wild males. These differences might be due to a lack of environmental stimuli such as seawater, migration or increased density in the captive populations, but a genetic difference between the populations could not be ruled out (Hard *et al.*, 2000). Another study on Coho salmon used individuals from wild stocks, hatchery stocks and hybrids and reared them in the wild or captivity. There were no detectable phenotypic differences in fish of different origin, but there were significant differences in reproductive output, survival, physiology and behaviour according to rearing environment, indicating non-heritable adaptation (Chittenden *et al.*, 2010). But, the lack of observed genetic differences between wild- and hatchery-born salmon could be due to the long-term admixture of wild and hatchery genotypes or strong selection in the wild, demonstrating the practical difficulties of distinguishing between genetic adaptation and phenotypic plasticity.

Genetic adaptation to captivity. The effects of genetic adaptation to captivity are similar to domestication regarding the direct or indirect genetic changes from selection, whether intentional or non-intentional. While in domestication artificial selection dominates, genetic adaptation to captivity may occur without any deliberate artificial selection. It also includes situations where genetic change in captivity is different from the wild e.g. due to a relaxation of selection by improved veterinary care. Genetic adaptation has been described in many species, including mammals, fish and insects (reviewed by Frankham, 2008). Observed effects range from behavioural to morphological and physiological changes. For example, a study of wild and captive-bred marsupial feathertail gliders found that captive-bred individuals differed from two wild populations (Geiser & Ferguson, 2001). Captive-bred individuals which had been in captivity for four generations had longer tails and snouts than those of wild individuals, but most importantly, they differed in their ability to enter torpor. Feathertail gliders enter torpor for up to several days in any season during periods of low air temperature. The captive-bred animals were active for much longer periods, and entered torpor at lower temperatures (15 °C) than the wild animals (20 °C). In addition, captive-bred gliders became hypothermic and had to be warmed externally at lower temperatures, whereas the wild-caught animals were never hypothermic. Geiser & Ferguson (2001) inferred that the captive-bred gliders' inability to maintain a stable body temperature in ambient temperatures they would encounter in the wild could threaten their survival, if they were not fully acclimatised to the local environment. Release programmes to the wild that use captive animals that have maladapted physiologies will obviously fail in their conservation aims and are ethically unjustifiable. Effects of genetic adaptations can be very large. In large white butterflies, captive butterflies were not only significantly heavier than wild butterflies, but fecundity of females increased approximately 13-fold during 150 generations in captivity (Lewis & Thomas, 2001).

A recent study on experimental fruit fly populations revealed that loss of heterozygosity at microsatellite loci was not only large (12%) but also significantly faster than predicted from pedigree information (Montgomery *et al.*, 2010). Microsatellite loci are important genetic markers. They are normally not under selection, i.e. selectively neutral. This neutrality is essential for captive breeding because: (1) the management of captive populations by minimising mean kinship (Section 6.7), and (2) modelling retention of genetic diversity in captive breeding programmes (Section 5.7.2) assume neutrality. The larger-than-predicted loss was in sharp contrast to the wild population from which the experimental populations were derived. The most parsimonious explanation for the unexpected behaviour of the neutral loci is that genome-wide selective sweeps of the initially rare fitness alleles had occurred. A selective sweep is the change in genetic variation at a genetic locus, which is neighbour of a locus that is under strong selection. Thus, neutral loci might show the signature of selected loci if they are linked (i.e. in near neighbourhood) with selected loci. As there is widespread evidence for rapid genetic adaptation to captivity across a broad array of taxa, it is unlikely that selective sweeps are restricted to fruit flies. The deviation from neutrality of supposedly neutral genetic markers not only highlights the large effects genetic adaptation might have, but it also questions the assumptions of most modern approaches to captive breeding, in particular the use of pedigree-derived estimation of the retention of genetic diversity in captive breeding programmes, which is the standard approach for captive management (Section 5.7.5, Box 5.2).

There is little published literature on morphological changes in wild animals in captivity. Skeletons are often viewed as rigid, genetically defined entities, but in reality, they are entirely plastic, responding significantly to behavioural and environmental stimuli. Hence, the variety of environmental and genetic influences on captive-bred animals will have an effect on their morphology and ultimately affect the conservation and management of wild-living and captive populations, especially when managed together as metapopulations (Chapter 6). Most studies of morphological changes resulting from an animal's reaction to captivity, and there are still few, focus on cranial changes and are often linked to diets, more often than not to inappropriate ones (O'Regan & Kitchener, 2005). Fortunately, some of the morphological differences between wild and captive animals can be rectified with appropriate changes in husbandry such as dietary nutrition and abrasion. However, others imply a much greater modification in captive animals than may previously have been expected, e.g. brain size or speed of development, that may impede the adjustment of released animals to the wild if their morphology has adapted to captivity over many generations. Several studies in carnivores, comparing morphology of wild, captive and feral animals, have shown significant differences in cranial morphology. In polecat and feral ferrets, Birks & Kitchener (1999) demonstrated significant differences in cranial volume and postorbital breadths, suggesting that these differences were not just the result of phenotypic plasticity. Similarly, Lynch & Hayden (1993) reported that captive American mink have larger skulls, shorter palates and narrower postorbital constrictions than feral mink (Kruska, 1996). The skulls also displayed reduced sexual dimorphism, which suggested that there might be a relaxation of sexual selection, owing to selective breeding for larger animals and lack of competition for resources in captivity. Kruska & Sidorovich (2003) reported heritable changes explaining phenotypic change in the species.

There are few published examples of changes in internal physiology occurring in animals kept in captivity. In captive birds, shortening of intestines has been reported (Liukkonen-Anttila et al., 2000). Such alteration in gut dimensions may have negative consequences on the ability of released birds to adapt to wild foods. Whether similar modifications occur in captive mammals is still largely unknown, but the observed plasticity in gut morphology in wild European rabbits (Sibly et al., 1990), or gut length differences between domestic and wild cats (Schauenberg, 1977; Kitchener, 1998) may hold further clues. To understand whether these modifications only occur in the lifetime of individual captive animals, i.e. the modification is not inherited, is also important.

Genetic changes vary considerably not only in terms of effects but also regarding time scale, from slow to very fast. For example, whilst agonistic, sociopositive and courtship behaviours differ significantly between domestic and wild guinea pigs, wild animals, which were captive-bred over 30 generations, still did not show any such behavioural differences (Künzel et al., 2003). In other species, such as the steelhead trout, after only two generations in captivity, fish exhibited a reduction in reproductive performance of ∼40% per captive-reared generation (Araki et al., 2007a,b). Similarly, Sockeye salmon became reproductively isolated from wild counterparts in less than 13 generations (Hendry et al., 2000b). Such changes may be linked to increased fitness in captive individuals. This effect has also been shown in the common fruit fly; the relative fitness of a captive population was double that of a wild population in only eight generations (Frankham & Loebel, 1992). However, despite this rise in fitness, adaptation to captivity may impede animals from surviving in the wild upon release. Some evidence for this may be found in the fact that reintroductions with captive animals are generally half as successful as reintroductions using wild-caught individuals (Breitenmoser et al., 2001; Fischer & Lindenmayer, 2000; Chapter 7).

Fitness in captivity versus *in the wild after reintroduction*
The effects of genetic adaptation to captivity play a major role when captive-bred animals are returned to the wild. The benign environment in captivity generally masks negative effects, which are normally stronger in wild, more stressful environments (Frankham, 2005a; Woodworth et al., 2002). Traits favoured by captive conditions are overwhelmingly disadvantageous in wild environments as reported for birds, amphibians, fish and biocontrol insects (reviewed by Allendorf & Luikart, 2006; Frankham, 2008).

The negative effects of loss of genetic diversity, inbreeding depression and mutational meltdown are, on average, highest at small population size and lower at larger population size for both *in-situ* and *ex-situ* populations (Woodworth et al., 2002). Conversely, genetic adaptation to captivity shows remarkably different dynamics, which is of high relevance for captive breeding for conservation (Woodworth et al., 2002). Because natural selection is most efficient in large populations, the resulting genetic adaptation is positively correlated with population size. In captivity, the genetic adaptation leads to higher fitness benefits at high population size and lower benefits at lower size (Fig. 4.1: solid lines). This relation reverts after reintroduction or introduction to wild environments. This results

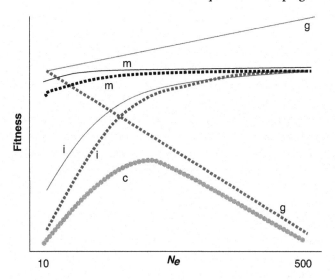

Fig. 4.1 Expected relationships between reproductive fitness and population size (N_e) due to inbreeding depression (i), mutational accumulation (m), genetic adaptation (g) and combined (c). The effects are shown for populations maintained for ~50 generations in benign captive conditions (solid lines), and after these populations were translocated to the wild environment (dotted lines). Modified from Woodworth *et al.* (2002).

in a surprising expectation for combined fitness effects of captivity after return to the wild, namely that combined fitness is low at both low and high population size but higher at medium population size (Fig. 4.1). The exact shape of this curvo-linear relationship depends on the characteristics of the species, captivity and the wild environment. Woodworth *et al.* (2002) tested the theoretical expectations under controlled conditions using the fruit fly as a model organism. The experiments confirmed the theoretical expectations outlined in Fig. 4.1. Reproductive fitness rapidly deteriorated when captive populations were translocated to more stressful or wild conditions. Genetic adaptation to captivity was more important in large populations and inbreeding depression in smaller populations.

Reintroduction programmes are both expensive, time consuming and fail more often than they succeed (Chapter 7). If captive-bred animals are to be released to the wild, O'Regan & Kitchener (2005) suggest, rightly, that our growing knowledge of observed changes in captive animals means it is essential to determine if captive-bred animals are able to survive in the wild. Surprisingly, the problems of adaptation for subsequent reintroduction are largely underestimated for both genetic adaptation (Frankham, 2008; Woodworth *et al.*, 2002) and non-heritable adaptation (Schultz *et al.*, 2009). Although the negative effects of adaptation for reintroduction can be very large (Frankham, 2008), there remain significant gaps in our empirical knowledge to understand the effects of adaptation: (1) distinguishing genetic adaptation from phenotypic plasticity; (2) identifying the relative importance of genetic adaptation *versus* other genetic and non-genetic factors; and (3) quantifying the effects of adaptation for reintroductions. For example, many zoos have become actively involved in captive rearing and headstarting of butterflies, but the effects of captive conditions are still poorly understood. It is rare that traits in the founding wild population and the captive-reared population are assessed and compared. The careful evaluation of butterfly programmes is urgently needed because captive rearing for augmentation purposes might not result in enhanced population size as in the case of the Puget blue butterfly (Schultz *et al.*, 2009). The development of optimal husbandry conditions and re-location needs to be matched by scientific evaluation in order that these programmes can play a significant role in butterfly population recovery.

4.2.3 Behavioural changes

Comparing the behaviour of captive and wild populations of conspecifics should allow *ex-situ* managers to create artificial settings that promote natural physical and psychological development. Without such adequate environments, aberrant morphologies and behaviours can result and contribute to poor fitness or even domestication. Animals may also suffer physically and psychologically if they are unable to perform a full repertoire of natural behaviours (Veasey *et al.*, 1996). But understanding how to maintain animals in captivity so that they behave like their wild counterparts is not easy, complicated by how to understand (and measure) how a typical wild animal behaves.

Often, comparisons of captive *versus* wild animal activity budgets are calculated under the implicit assumption that wild animals always show the 'correct' set of behaviours. Since activity budgets of wild animals may be biased due to observational difficulties or low sample sizes, but more importantly activity of a species may vary according to geographic location or time of the year, captive–wild comparisons are problematic. In wild primates, for example, a number of studies have shown that intra-specific contrasts in the amount of time spent in different behaviours correlate, expectedly, with environmental conditions. More specifically, time spent feeding is the major variant within activity budgets, and of course correlated with food supply (not just quantity and quality, but also predictability in space and time). Hence, in situations where food provision is predictable, high-volume and high-quality such as in artificially provisioned settings, e.g. Indian rhesus macaques (Seth & Seth, 1986) or Barbary macaques at a tourist site in Gibraltar (Fa, 1986), or in captivity, animals spend significantly less time feeding compared to wild animals and generally overfeed (Box 4.1). So, amount of time spent feeding in the wild or in captivity is the fundamental pivot determining time spent in other activities (see Fa & Southwick, 1988; Asquith, 1989). Yet, some studies that compare activity budgets of captive *versus* wild animals conclude that captive animals 'can exhibit wild-type activity budgets' (Melfi & Feistner, 2002). This, of course, may be true in some contexts, but equally, there are also wild animals that exhibit what may be considered typically 'captive' activity budgets.

Deciding what sets of behaviours and at what frequency they should be expressed by a captive animal is therefore not clear-cut. Extrapolating from observations of a species in a specific ecological situation to all members of that taxon may not be useful. However, increasing the amount of time spent foraging (and moving) as well as modulating nutritional levels (not encouraging animals to overfeed) needs to be addressed. Investigations of calorific intake and energy use of captive animals are uncommon but one study of provisioned Barbary macaques showed that animals consumed from 9% to 382% more than energy expended (Fa, 1986). Decreased activity levels have a significant effect on captive animals, from pathology to increasing amounts of subcutaneous and deposited fat. Kitchener (1999) found that captive Rodrigues fruit bats accumulated subcutaneous fat steadily throughout their lives, until it comprised 30+% of body weight by the age of 20 years, which would probably have prevented or severely affected flight capability.

A study of individual food consumption and food item preference of 12 St. Lucia parrots tested the hypothesis that subjects would select foods in relation to their presumed nutritional needs (Fa & Cavalheiro, 1998). Diets in zoos are normally prepared around what is acknowledged to be the 'optimal' diet for that species (Crissey, 2005). The parrots were offered mostly fruits, vegetables and pulses but also processed foods and commercial parrot pellets. Each day all birds were presented with the same selection of foods and no novel items were introduced during the study period. Birds varied in their average food intake per feeding session from as low as 15 g kg^{-1} to 89 g kg^{-1}. Diversity of food items eaten per session was determined by the Simpson's index of diversity. Food preferences were measured by Ivlev's electivity indices from the total amount of each food type consumed relative to the total amount of that food type offered during all sessions. Foods were classified as 'disliked' when electivity indices were negative and 'rejected' if not consumed at all. The order in which food types were consumed by each parrot was also analysed. Results showed that diet diversity and food intake were significantly higher for females than males. Wild-born parrots consumed less but ate a wider variety of foods than captive-born ones. Significant sexual differences in overall food intake as well as in the percentage of disliked and rejected foods were found among captive-born birds but not in wild-born parrots. However, because all wild-born birds in the present study were twice as old as the captive-born ones, age of bird and origin were confounding variables. Older birds disliked less food than younger ones but younger parrots ate more than older birds. Within paired birds, females were more aggressive towards males than vice versa. This may have influenced the lower feeding levels observed by subordinate males but single males ate even less than those kept in pairs. The results of this study suggest that it is not possible to make generalisations to satisfy optimal diet requirements of the species because of the considerable individual variation found. Quantifying intake and preference from direct observations of the birds during feeding can be a useful technique to help with the formulation of diets. Further studies are required to determine the roles of sex, age and origin on food consumption and preference. The behaviour of paired and single birds should also be assessed in order to identify suitable methods for feeding dominant and subordinate birds in an attempt to optimise nutritional intake of each individual.

Box 4.1 · *'Nutritional wisdom' in animals*

Animals have many nutritional needs (in addition to energy), and their requirements may not be met simultaneously when animals are kept in captive conditions. Classical foraging theory focuses on energy acquisition, and individuals of some species appear to feed so as to maximise net energy acquisition. 'Nutritional wisdom' has been suggested as a trait by which animals obtain a nutritionally balanced diet (Richter, 1943). The hypothesis proposes 'specific hungers' permitting a sensing of nutrients in the diet, and selection of a diet including the elements required. However, few studies have demonstrated the ability to forage for particular elements although exceptions include deer foraging with appetites for certain minerals (Ceacero *et al.*, 2009). The idea that captive animals select a diet based on nutrient composition, or that they possess nutritional wisdom, is frequently implied but seldom tested.

A number of studies have demonstrated that rearing environment can promote aggressive behaviour in fishes (reviewed by Ruzzante, 1994). For example, steelhead trout grown in structurally enriched hatchery tanks or stream environments have increased competitive ability and achieve higher dominance ranks than fish reared in conventional hatchery tanks (Berejikian *et al.*, 2001). Rearing environment can also affect the development of neurological processes, which are an important determinant of behaviour; hatchery-reared trout for example, have smaller brains than their wild-reared counterparts (Marchetti & Nevitt, 2003).

In butterfly splitfins, an endangered freshwater fish (Chapter 6), Kelley *et al.* (2006) investigated whether captive breeding results in the behavioural divergence of wild and captive individuals. In a first experiment, they examined whether the captive environment allows for the similar expression of behaviours observed in wild fish. The foraging, courtship and aggressive behaviours of fish in their natural habitat (in Mexico) were compared with those of their counterparts that have been bred at London Zoo, UK, for 40 years. The *in-situ* observations revealed that wild fish were preoccupied with searching for food whereas captive fish engaged more in aggressive interactions. In a subsequent laboratory experiment, the behaviour of wild-caught and captive-bred fish under standard conditions in two novel habitats: structured (enriched) and unstructured (bare) aquaria showed that captive-bred butterfly splitfins displayed higher levels of aggression than wild-caught fish. The relationship between aggression and habitat structure was influenced by density; captive-bred males were more aggressive when observed in structured habitats than unstructured ones, but only when they were stocked at a high density. There was no effect of captive breeding or habitat structure on courtship behaviour. The findings from this study suggest that the captive rearing of endangered fishes can promote the expression of particular behavioural traits, such as increased aggression. This could cause problems if captive-bred individuals are released into the wild. In the case of the butterfly split-fin, aggressive males may have problems reproducing if attacks are directed towards females (in black-footed ferrets; see Wolf *et al.*, 2000), or they may be at greater risk of predation through reduced vigilance and increased conspicuousness. Aggression is often correlated with other traits such as boldness; in sticklebacks for example, aggressive individuals take greater risks to acquire resources and consequently have higher growth rates (Ward *et al.*, 2004). Comparisons of the behaviour of wild and captive-bred species under standard conditions can be advocated as a simple method for assessing a species' suitability for reintroduction (Mathews *et al.*, 2005).

Behavioural competency for survival and reproduction after reintroduction is of uttermost concern for any captive breeding for conservation. Headstarting programmes (see Section 4.2.2) highlight potential problems with behavioural incompetency particularly well, because headstarting is done solely for re-location to the wild and normally aims at very short times in captivity. Certain behaviours, such as predator avoidance or searching for food in reptiles are regarded as innate, but headstarting clearly demonstrates that this is not always the case (Taubes, 1992). For example, five months after release Kemp's ridley sea turtles did not successfully acquire any of the escape and avoidance response to humans that wild individuals typically have (Meylan & Ehrenfeld, 2000). As always in biological systems, variation is large: in contrast to Ridley turtles, headstarted loggerhead sea turtles behaved similarly to wild animals (Nagelkerken *et al.*, 2003). Species-specific training and the provisioning of a well-designed captive environment can help to foster behavioural competency (e.g. rock iguanas: Alberts, 2007; Pérez-Buitrago *et al.*, 2008). Such facilities are typically located in range countries and are run by or with the support of zoos.

Survivorship is typically used for assessing or declaring success of headstarting. This can, however, be highly misleading. For example, increased local density following headstarting of Mona island rock iguana indicated that the programme was successful. However, most headstarted iguanas returned to the headstart facility without establishing territories typical for adult wild Mona island rock iguanas, indicating that longer-term success remains unknown and may even be in doubt (Pérez-Buitrago *et al.*, 2008). A general lack of data on behaviour of released animals is commonly highlighted. This is notable even for turtles, for which headstarting was first utilised (see Mitrus, 2005; Pérez-Buitrago *et al.*, 2008). Thus, it remains difficult to assess the impact of headstarting on natural populations, highlighting the urgent need for future research and monitoring.

4.3 Well-being of zoo animals

4.3.1 Mind and body

Until relatively recently it was believed that so long as the few basic necessities required to keep an animal alive were provided this was sufficient. It is now regarded as essential that captive conditions allow animals to exhibit a natural repertoire of behaviours and activity patterns.

When discussing animal well-being it is very difficult to separate the physical from the psychological aspects. Mind–body dualism (Thomas & Lorden, 1989) is a term coined to express the reciprocal relationship between the two. If an animal's physiological needs are unsatisfied it is extremely unlikely that the psychological ones can be and vice versa. The failure to meet the needs of an animal results in the experience of stress, a condition with both physiological and psychological components. Some degree of stress is experienced in nature as a result of natural environmental stimuli and regarded as being beneficial. This has been termed **eustress** as opposed to **distress** which has a negative effect (Selye, 1974).

When keeping an endangered species in captivity, conditions must approximate the natural state in order to achieve a natural level of fitness of the animal in question, if release into the wild is the intention. In other cases, where the animal is to be maintained in captivity for other ends, it may be necessary to encourage behaviours better adapted to captive conditions in order to reduce stress in the animal. Whatever the situation, a good general understanding of the animal's biology and natural history is vital.

By definition animals in captivity are restricted in their range and as a result their ability to select their environment. Provision for an animal's needs is the responsibility of the carer and the facility in which it is kept. Physical considerations are important but the provision of behavioural needs has been argued for by Ewbank (1985). Certain environmental conditions and management techniques may encourage the expression of specific behaviours; however, in some cases their absence may not be detrimental to the animal. In an experiment by Dawkins (1976) it was found that provision of litter trays to battery hens initiated dust bathing, but their absence, however, did not cause any increase in stress levels. Trays were regarded as being a 'developer' stimulus which encouraged a behaviour to be expressed. It was also found that prior to egg laying the birds would exhibit nesting behaviour when provided with appropriate materials. The omission of such materials resulted in an increase in aggressive and stress-related behaviours. The requirement of nesting material prior to egg laying should be regarded as a 'behavioural need'. Behavioural needs of an animal are real and as such demand equal consideration to the physical ones. There are numerous variables which must be controlled to maintain the health of a specimen and ensure that its life is 'happy' and productive.

4.3.2 Assessment of well-being

Bayne (1989) recognised that although the assessment of well-being may include measures of reproductive success, general physical condition (body weight), physiological indices (cortisol ACTH levels) and general behaviour, it is not easy. This is clearly apparent from the fact that reliable guidelines (clinical signs) for the recognition of distress in most captive animals are not available. Most research into signs of distress has been carried out on primates (Morton & Griffiths, 1985). A list of examples of responses to inadequate conditions published by the American Psychological Association's CARE may include the following.

Behavioural responses
- Apparent inability of non-aged primates to move quickly without strain or difficulty when appropriately stimulated to do so.
- Chronic self-mutilation or abnormal pattern of repetitive motor acts of the limbs or whole body which fit within the general accepted definition of stereotypic behaviour.

- Persistent pattern of avoiding or ignoring novel stimuli within the immediate living space.
- Failure to respond in species-typical fashion to social partners.
- Repeated species-specific fear or avoidance behaviour in the absence of noxious stimulation.

Physical responses
- Characteristics such as skin condition (flaky, scaly, rashes, smooth), coat (sparse, patchy, full), colour and consistency of urine and faeces, appearance of eyes (swelling, crusts, clear, opaque, etc.), gait pattern (shuffling, limping, stiff walk, normal) and rate of growth or ageing.
- Various physiological variables such as hormones typically measured in blood, urine and faeces.
- Immune function.
- Physical criteria may be applied to all species in captivity with relative ease; however, behavioural criteria are less simple. The more complex the natural behaviour patterns of a species are the more complicated and distinct the identification of indicators of distress is likely to be. Knowledge of behavioural patterns display the shortcomings of the environment in which an individual is kept. In the case of species with simpler behavioural repertoires, e.g. many reptiles, physiological cues may be more important. Thus, even in species whose basic physiological requirements have been understood and catered for, reproduction may still be poor and longevity shortened due to insufficient knowledge of their behavioural needs.

4.3.3   Stereotypic behaviours

The exhibition of 'stereotypic' behaviour is one of the most common arguments used against confinement of animals and for the improvement of captive conditions (Shepherdson, 1989). 'Stereotypies are a series of movements of the whole or part of the animal's body which are repeated regularly and which serve no apparent function' (Danzer & Mormede, 1983). Pacing, head flicking, weaving, bar gnawing, crib biting, wind sucking, spot pecking and excessive grooming may all be stereotypic if exhibited at high frequencies.

It is generally accepted that the cause of stereotypy is an adverse or under-stimulating environment. The actual role played by stereotypy is more complex, as is its development. At its appearance a stereotypic behaviour can be directly associated with a cause, pacing being related to confinement etc. As the condition develops the behaviour may become abbreviated to an extent that its cause can no longer be identified – pacing becoming head tossing, for example. It then becomes a displacement activity and a habit which may continue long after the original cause has been rectified.

Severity of stereotypy
- The level of abnormality of the behaviour and its direction. The more normal the behaviour and the greater the link between form and cause the less serious the situation.

- Level of representation in an animal's activity pattern. It has been suggested that more than 10% of waking activity is unacceptable (Broom, 1983).
- Awareness of surroundings, if it can be distracted from its behaviour then the condition is less serious than if this is not the case.
- If the behaviour is responsive or spontaneous (Shepherdson, 1989). If the onset is linked temporally to a stimulus, the condition may be less severe.
- If a decrease in behavioural repertoire accompanies the expression of stereotypy, it indicates that the condition has degenerated.
- Stereotypies and other aberrant behaviours may be corrected in many cases by manipulation of the environment (environmental enrichment).

The assessment of animal well-being is the primary responsibility of the keeper, who must therefore be familiar both with individual animals in his/her care to identify day to day changes and with the species in order to relate the behaviour in captivity with that exhibited in the wild. Much attention has been focussed on mammals, particularly primates, because of their complex behavioural patterns. It is, however, accepted that more attention must be given to other species, especially ones that have proved particularly difficult to keep in captivity.

4.4 Animal rights, animal welfare and zoos

Some people argue not only that zoos are failing to meet their conservation objectives, but that it is inherently wrong to use individual animals for any purpose unless it is in the best interest of the individual animal. From this 'animal rights' standpoint, except in very rare circumstances, zoos are morally indefensible. Such circumstances would include the temporary protection in captivity of an animal whose life is at risk from predation from humans, followed by release of the individual to the wild when this danger had passed (Reagan, 1995). Despite any benefits to humans and the environment such as public education, scientific research, conservation of endangered species, or non-conservation related justifications such as contribution to the local economy, cultural value, etc., according to proponents of the animal rights ethic, zoos are morally indefensible because captivity restricts an animal's freedom and is therefore not of benefit to the individual animal (Reagan, 1995; Jamieson, 1995). For an analysis of the animal rights, utilitarian and holistic ethics as they relate to zoos, see Reagan (1995). Animal welfare advocates argue that animals can be used by humans, but that the animals' well-being is paramount, any suffering being minimised and always balanced against any perceived benefits to humans. The welfare of an animal can be defined as 'its state with regards its attempt to cope with its environment' (Broom, 1986), or 'its capacity to avoid suffering and sustain fitness' (Webster, 1994). Poor welfare can be caused by unsuitable environmental conditions; if an animal's environment is altered from that which it has evolved to cope with in the wild, this can result in stress, fear or frustration. In addition to the perhaps more obvious causes of poor welfare such as disease and injury, Duncan (2006) includes boredom as a state of suffering. This could be of particular relevance to zoo animals. If the enclosure and husbandry do not provide sufficient challenge and variety, allowing animals to express natural behaviours then stress and frustration can result (Mason *et al.*, 2001). Despite the contribution zoos can make towards biodiversity conservation, if the effect of captivity causes poor welfare to individual animals, we must consider the net benefits to that animal, other animals, to the environment and to humans (Broom, 2006).

There have been significant advances in the science of animal welfare in recent decades (Duncan, 2006; Kirkden & Pajor, 2006). The most important amongst these is the growing certainty, arising through a variety of fields of science, that consciousness (the capacity for awareness of pleasant and/or unpleasant feelings) is likely to be present in a wide range of species. It is now generally accepted that at least all vertebrates, and also cephalopods, are sentient; they can feel (Duncan, 2006). If an animal can feel, then it can also suffer. Another important step is that it is now possible to determine how animals are feeling by indirect means (Duncan, 2006), such as assessing their preference for and motivation to obtain certain resources (Dawkins, 2006). Thus, zoos should be striving not just to prevent suffering, but to ensure that animals in their care also experience 'pleasure'. Duncan (2006) suggests that since 'pleasure' increases the quality of life of humans, why shouldn't pleasurable activities (e.g. social grooming, playing) also be important to animals? It follows that we have a strong moral obligation to take animals' feelings into account in our dealings with them. This position was reflected, for example, by the agreement of the European Heads of State at the Amsterdam Summit meeting in 1997 to make provision in the Treaty of Rome (which established the European Community in 1957) 'to ensure improved protection and respect for the welfare of animals as sentient beings'. Other legislation such as the EU Zoo Directive 1999/22/EC, national animal welfare laws, the *Balai Directive* 92/65/EEC and IATA regulations govern the welfare of animals in zoos and the transport of animals between zoos. Jamieson (1995) contends that in the future there will be 'increasing tension between what zoos do to gain public support (entertain) and what they must do to justify themselves (preserve species)'. There are inherent animal welfare concerns in both of these pursuits.

In some countries, for example in the UK, animal welfare is explicitly included in legislation on zoos. The UK Secretary of State's Standards of Modern Zoo Practice (DETR, 2000), have adapted the *Five Freedoms* (Box 4.2), guiding principles of animal welfare which were developed by the FAWC and have been taken up widely around the world.

These 'freedoms', which recognise both physical and behavioural needs, succinctly encapsulate welfare requirements of animals and also form a framework that can be used in the assessment of animal welfare. They are ideals and it is important that there is some flexibility in their use because they can, at times, be contradictory. In their application to zoo animals, these freedoms could actually further the risk of domestication. The tension between not causing suffering to animals and allowing them to behave as they would in the wild can be challenging. For example, in social animals, freedom to express normal

Box 4.2 · *The 'Five Freedoms' in animal welfare*

The concept of Five Freedoms originated with the Report of the Technical Committee to Enquire into the Welfare of Animals kept under Intensive Livestock Husbandry Systems, the Brambell Report, December 1965 (Brambell, 1965). This stated that farm animals should have freedom 'to stand up, lie down, turn around, groom themselves and stretch their limbs', a list that is still sometimes referred to as Brambell's Five Freedoms.

As a direct result of the Brambell Report, the FAWAC was set up. This was disbanded at the same time that the FAWC was established by the British Government in July 1979, with some common membership. A list of provisions that should be made for farm animals were listed in five categories, which also became known as the Five Freedoms (despite the fact that not all the categories were actually freedoms).

The concept was subsequently refined by the FAWC so that it actually took the form of five freedoms. It has since been further updated and is now the most visited page on the Council's website (FAWC, 2010). In their current form these are as follows.

1. Freedom from thirst, hunger and malnutrition – by ready access to fresh water and a diet to maintain full health and vigour.
2. Freedom from discomfort – by providing a suitable environment including shelter and a comfortable resting area.
3. Freedom from pain, injury and disease – by prevention or rapid diagnosis and treatment.
4. Freedom to express most normal behaviour – by providing sufficient space, proper facilities and company of the animal's own kind.
5. Freedom from fear and distress – by ensuring conditions which avoid mental suffering.

behaviour may at times result in fight injuries to cage mates. Likewise, it may be impossible in practice to avoid any fear or pain because, for example, diagnosis of disease in captive wild animals (involving blood sampling, etc.) may induce both. Therefore, judgement has to be exercised in balancing the freedoms.

4.5 Which features of zoos can cause poor welfare?

The specific characteristics that define the zoo environment – regular presence of large numbers of unfamiliar visitors, the management of the animals by humans, and the restrictions of enclosure size (Hosey, 2005) can result in particular compromises to welfare over and above those associated with the captive environment *per se* (Melfi & Hosey, 2005). Daily husbandry routines, animal management for breeding programmes, preventative and curative veterinary care and adherence to legislative requirements such as marking individual animals for identification purposes can all affect the welfare of zoo animals to a greater or lesser extent. The constant presence of large active groups of visitors has been shown to cause stress in primates (Hosey, 2000). The effect of zoo conditions and routines should be considered for all animals, 'you do not need to be clever to feel pain or experience hunger' (Dawkins, 2006). However, the challenge of meeting the psychological needs of animals with greater cognitive capacity may be greater (Boyd Group, 2002).

Despite advancements in the scientific assessment of animal welfare, without detailed behavioural and veterinary studies it is often difficult to determine whether a particular environment provides good welfare (Kirkwood, 2003). The diversity of species in zoos, coupled with the often poor knowledge of their ecology means the challenge of achieving high welfare for all zoo animals is immense. In addition, the paucity of data on the effect of potential stressors within a zoo environment is a serious limitation to the development of optimum husbandry. Morgan & Tromborg (2007) provide a comprehensive review of the potential environmental stressors in the zoo environment. These include the quantity, quality and periodicity of light, presence or absence of odours, pitch, frequency and sound pressure of sounds, temperature gradients and type of substrate. Measurement of these stressors can be technologically challenging and is exacerbated by the fact that different species have varying sensitivities to different stressors. It is essential that environmental variables, e.g. temperature, are measured from locations appropriate to the animal since temperatures experienced by researchers outside an enclosure can vary widely from those in micro-climates within an enclosure (Morgan & Tromburg, 2007).

Simply meeting basic needs is not sufficient to ensure good welfare. For example, zoo animals are often fed prepared foods which require little or no foraging or manipulation behaviour. Some authors suggest that animals have a need to perform certain 'appetitive behaviours', e.g. foraging even in the absence of appropriate trigger stimuli (Morgan & Tromburg, 2007), and that restrictions of such behaviours can result in locomotor stereotypies (Mason, 1993). In a study of eight species of captive primates, Marriner & Drickamer (1994) suggested that the higher rates of stereotyping observed in omnivores compared to frugivores and folivores is due to greater food search and handling time of omnivores in the wild, which is limited in captivity. Many enrichment strategies aim to encourage foraging and extend food manipulation times through techniques such as food scattering and provision of whole foods. It has also been suggested that the predictability of the captive environment is itself stressful (Buchanan-Smith, 2006) and that situations in which animals have more control over their environment, e.g. free-ranging primates in a zoo, may be less stressful (Hosey, 2005).

The provision of larger, more complex enclosures is one of the major improvements in the management of zoo animals in recent decades. However, the effect of restricted space on welfare is still unknown for most species. Clubb & Mason (2003) investigated variables such as home range size, general activity and natural foraging patterns to determine if any are predictors of stereotypic pacing in carnivores in zoos. Their results showed that the home range size of the species in the wild predicted the degree of stereotypic pacing and level of infant mortality observed in the species in captivity. This study has serious consequences for the husbandry of wide ranging carnivores in zoos, such as polar bears. Such studies can provide invaluable guidance to responsible zoo managers in their future selection of species in collection plans. The issue of which species should be kept in zoos is further discussed in Chapter 6.

Good welfare is essential for effective *ex-situ* conservation since provision of conditions which promote good welfare aids animals' abilities to adapt to the captive environment. However, for animals involved in reintroduction programmes, their individual welfare may be compromised both in preparation for release and post-release (Box 4.3).

Box 4.3 · *Is reintroduction humane?*

It is evident that the well-being of a captive-bred animal may be compromised by releasing it into the wild, because it will be exposed to risks which are absent in captivity. Reintroduction, however, must be viewed in the broader context of the overall value of the operation. Thus, even though individuals will be put at risk, if there are good reasons to believe that a viable population of the species can be established, which could ensure the survival of the species in the wild, then the risk to an individual may be '*compensated for by the gain for conservation*'. The latter statement appeared in the UFAW guidelines for the reintroduction of captive-bred animals (UFAW, 1992). These guidelines of course strongly advocate all possible reduction of individual risk, and detail a number of steps for doing so. The statement reinforces the growing understanding of conflict between reintroduction success and the welfare of individual animals (Beck *et al.*, 1991). The conflict is not just about ensuring as much as possible the survival of the individual after reintroduction, but also striving to breed and maintain animals under conditions that will enhance reintroduction success.

The replication of natural environments, which undergo variation (sometimes extreme) in temperature and precipitation, attacks by predators and parasites, untreated illness and injury, as well as intra- and inter-specific resource competition are almost impossible. Of course, species have evolved mechanisms to cope with environmental stressors but how much this is hard-wired is very often unknown. Examples of captive-bred individuals at risk after release have been documented by some authors. In the case of the golden lion tamarin reintroduction in Brazil, for example, individuals have been found unable to cope with weather conditions, e.g. cold (10 °C), rain, become wedged in tree holes and die, or are killed by coral snakes or Africanised bees. Beck (1995) points out that reintroduction is therefore not entirely humane. So, how can zoos prepare animals to cope with the predation, starvation, parasitism, climatic extremes, locomotor and orientation challenges, and social competition they will encounter after reintroduction if we don't expose them beforehand? But, the greater challenge is how do we expose animals to all these factors without decreasing the welfare of individual animals in zoos?

Many argue that there is a need to create environments for animals specifically bred for reintroduction that will allow them to learn essential information and skills, develop adequate strength and stamina, and adapt. A large number of these attributes are genetically programmed, and will vary according to taxonomic groups. For example, the need to dedicate more time and effort in preparing animals for release is always greater for primates and especially great apes (Beck *et al.*, 2007) than for birds, reptiles or amphibians. The general consensus is that if we want captive animals to behave more naturally, we must keep them in naturalistic environments not dioramas (Robinson, 1988). To do so will mean a dramatic decrease in the welfare of zoo animals, perhaps opening up a philosophical and practical wedge between what is best for the individual, the population or the species.

4.6 Keeping the captive, wild!

4.6.1 Environmental enrichment

That captivity can have adverse effects on the behaviour of some animals has been known for some time (see Morris, 1964; Hediger, 1969). Confining an animal to a cage or enclosure reduces the complexity, and increases the predictability, of its environment. As a result of this 'environmental impoverishment', 'undesirable' behaviours increase and 'desirable' ones decrease. This degradation causes a downward spiral from unstimulating environment to suboptimal behaviour to reduced use of environment resulting in worsening behaviour (Chamove & Anderson, 1989).

Many researchers are increasingly interested in interrupting this trend. Most published works relate to animals living in small groups in zoos, some to individually housed animals (Markowitz, 1982) and yet others are laboratory studies (Erwin & Deni, 1979). Environmental enrichment describes the efforts made to alleviate the incidence of boredom, promote desirable behaviours and reduce undesirable behaviours in captive animals. Environmental enrichment, through for example improved landscaping of enclosures and increasing the foraging behaviour of animals, also serves to increase the attractiveness, entertainment and educational value of exhibits.

The need to keep animals occupied in captivity was recognised as early as 1925, when Robert Yerkes noted that apparatus for play and work improved conditions for captive primates. However, concerns to maintain easy management and good hygiene in the traditional zoo enclosure (hard concrete floors and ceramic-tiled walls) often overrode the psychological needs of the animals. The focus and motivation for enrichment have changed as our understanding of the physiological and behavioural needs of captive animals improves as well as of the cause and effect of captive behaviour.

4.6.2 What are undesirable behaviours?

Just because a captive animal behaves differently in captivity, does not necessarily mean that it is suffering, but in the absence of any criteria for judging welfare it can be said that if an animal behaves the same in captivity as in the wild, it is probably not suffering. Activities such as coprophagy, regurgitation, hair-pulling, self-injury or stereotyped movements are generally judged as undesirable whilst active exploration, play, affiliation and foraging are judged as desirable. The desirability of a behaviour displayed by a captive animal must be considered at various levels.

Normality: where possible, behavioural repertoires and activity patterns should approximate those in the wild. Because there is variation in nature and because sometimes field data are scarce, it may not always be possible to confirm what 'wild' behaviour is but the principle still holds. The preservation of a species depends on maintenance of more than just genetic material.

Public acceptability: the zoo visitor wants to see neither an inactive animal nor one exhibiting stereotyped or aberrant behaviour. Apart from any obvious benefit to the animals, environmental enrichment makes the exhibition of captive animals more interesting and more acceptable to the public. This is particularly important in the current climate where more and more doubts are being expressed about zoos and their social and ecological value.

Theoretical considerations: some enrichment work has a theoretical rationale, e.g. setting goals for calorie expenditure or pre-release training.

Practical considerations: enrichment can often be a way of improving husbandry methods. Successful techniques should see a reduction of aggression, self-injury, stereotyping and other aberrant behaviours.

4.6.3 Types of environmental enrichment

Much of the pioneering work on behavioural enrichment was initiated in the USA during the last three decades. Two schools of thought evolved, each emphasising a different way of enriching captive environments. The first is typified by Hal Markowitz working mainly in Portland Zoo, Oregon, and is referred to as behavioural engineering (Markowitz, 1982). Faced with the task of encouraging more activity and more foraging-related behaviour in animals in traditional sterile enclosures, Markowitz developed a number of mechanical devices that would deliver food to animals on completion of a task. For example:

- a system whereby Lar gibbons were able to activate a food dispenser by operating two widely spaced levers;
- a system whereby Diana monkeys could exchange plastic tokens for food at a food dispenser;
- a display in which pumas were able to trigger the release of artificial 'prey' animals. Capture of the prey activated the food dispenser.

The alternative school of thought, known as the naturalistic approach, was pioneered by Woodland Park Zoo in Washington (Hancocks, 1980). It aims to recreate the natural environment as far as possible using natural materials. The criticism levelled at the behavioural engineering approach by Hutchins *et al.* (1978/1979) is that the behaviours the devices stimulate are no more natural than the behaviours they replace. For example, a puma exhibit had to be abandoned when the target animal was hunting at a frequency of 200 hunts per day. However, Forthman-Quick (1984) suggested that the two approaches can be reconciled. Although the naturalistic approach is attractive, it is not always possible to provide a naturalistic environment within the constraints of existing enclosures, either because of lack of space or because natural materials would be destroyed too quickly by the inhabitants (a particular problem with large primates). Mechanical devices can be used to decrease the predictability of captive environments, something that a purely naturalistic approach does not always achieve (Shepherdson, 1988).

4.6.4 Aims of enrichment

Kitchener (2004) has suggested that environmental enrichment will be deemed successful when we can no longer discern any morphological differences between wild and captive-bred animals. Enrichment must aim at enhancing the social and physical environment of the captive animal. A major factor hindering the definition of simple, effective guidelines for optimising well-being in a wide variety of animals is the fact that environmental needs differ across species: husbandry techniques that promote well-being of one species will not necessarily transfer to another species (e.g. in primates; NIH, 1991). The most powerful perspective from which to devise environmental enrichment devices for a specific taxon in captivity and subsequently to evaluate their implementation is a detailed knowledge of that species' natural history (Fragazy & Adams-Curtis, 1991; Redshaw & Mallinson, 1991).

Environmental enrichment should not be regarded by modern zoo staff as an add-on, but built into the enclosure design and daily routine from the outset. However, there are particular animals or species in collections that will benefit most from a programme of enrichment (Poulsen, 1994). These are animals housed in inappropriate social groups, with special health care requirements, those hand-raised which need to acquire natural skills, animals exhibiting stereotypies or living in unnatural and environmentally impoverished environments. Of course, these situations should be prevented wherever possible as can be easily done by keeping animals in appropriate social groups. When enrichment apparatus is to be used, this should be designed and engineered according to the strength and destructive skills of the animal it is intended for. Because species and individuals respond differently to changes in their environment, enrichment needs to be introduced in such a way that does not stress the animals and cause negative behaviours e.g. displaced aggression within a group.

Box 4.4 · *Environmental enrichment*

Environmental enrichment is aimed at the following.

(1) Improvements to the social environment

Keeping animals with socially compatible individuals. Even species which in the wild are relatively solitary, e.g. orang-utans, otters and mink, may benefit from this (Poole, 1987). Compatible social groupings may be very different from those found in the wild because of changed environmental constraints. The natural socio-biology of the species should be known before changes are made to the grouping policies. The size and the structure of a social group are of great importance to its cohesion and overall health. Dominance hierarchies and age and sex distribution of a group will determine the levels of stress and competition experienced by its members.

Greater keeper input. The individual, or team, responsible for the care of an animal or group of animals may be responsible for much of the stress which they experience. Movement of animals and feeding must be established as routines in order to reduce this stress to a minimum. Routines do not have to be inflexible so long as the animals understand what they are expected to do in response to certain requests or actions. An important part of this process is the establishment of the caretaker in a dominant position whether as part of the group or as an outsider. As conditions in which animals are kept have improved, standards of acceptability have changed. As a rule, establishments are being encouraged to house specimens in natural breeding groups. The appropriate socio-environmental conditions of captive animals are now regarded more a necessity than a luxury. Having said this, the improvement of such conditions could be seen as a form of environmental enrichment.

(2) Amelioration of the physical environment

The inclusion of more stimulating substrates. Grass, shavings, peat and woodwool can be used to replace the bare concrete floors of more traditional enclosures: a move from 'hard' to 'soft' cages.

The introduction of appropriate cage furniture. The provision of appropriate furnishings within the cage facilitates locomotion and allows an animal to make full use of three-dimensional spaces within an enclosure.

The use of screens and panels. Used correctly, they subdivide space and create a series of more complex and partially compartmentalised environments.

The provision of manipulable objects. Manipulable objects such as puzzle boxes provide variability and active stimuli for the captive animals.

(3) Improvements of the psychological environment

Reduction of stress levels. Management techniques and exhibition methods may be adapted to reduce unnecessary stress. Provision for species-specific traits, e.g. flight distance and response to the public, is important.

Predictability. The spatial and temporal predictability of a captive environment may be reduced relatively easily by modifying routines. Though the necessity for a basic routine in the captive situation is indisputable, there should always be room for some flexibility. This type of enrichment very often involves an aspect of training and development of new routines. The following types of behaviours are targeted by this type of approach:

Foraging. The aim is to increase time spent searching for food in captivity to simulate nature. To this end, zoos have used a number of devices, e.g. artificial termite mounds for great apes (McEwan, 1986), food dispersal in a substrate for macaques (Anderson & Chamove, 1984), live insect prey such as mealworms for fennec foxes, meerkats and otters (Foster-Turley & Markowitz, 1982).

Manipulative behaviour. Animals are given materials to manipulate – straw, woodwool and leaves to bears and great apes to use for nest building, splash pools, ponds and streams for macaques and climbing apparatus for more arboreal species.

Learning. New behaviours may be learnt which make use of natural ability and consume time. Some may be used educationally in demonstrations, not to be confused with shows, and others may be related to food acquisition. This approach still holds greatest potential for development as it can be applied to existing enclosures and does not have to be expensive.

4.6.5 Enrichment and food

Most enrichment programmes involve changes in food presentation both spatially and temporally. Animals in captivity are now fed a number of times a day and the diversity of items fed has also increased. In the wild, foraging and feeding are activities which dominate the daily pattern e.g. mountain gorillas may spend up to 45% (Harcourt & Stewart, 1984) and bushbabies will spend from 30% to 50% of their day feeding (Bearder & Martin, 1980). Any efforts to slow feeding rates and spread them out over a longer time period are beneficial as they prevent other activities reaching unnaturally high levels. The amount of food offered does not have to be increased since presentation can be adapted instead. In many cases, the increased effort required to obtain food will in fact increase calorific expenditure by the animal.

4.6.6   Evaluating environmental enrichment

It is important to assess the benefits an animal is deriving from enrichment. Of course, it is impossible to know whether or not an animal is 'happy' or content with its environment. Ultimately, an intuitive decision has to be made based on our own experience. However, it is possible to use scientific evidence to increase the chance that our decision is correct (Dawkins, 1980). This problem can be approached by measuring various physiological parameters such as steroid levels in the blood or directly observing an animal's behaviour. Steroids (glucocorticoids such as cortisone and cortisol) are known to be associated with stress and are secreted in situations such as physical injury. The problem with these measurements is that it is difficult to decide how much stress indicates suffering. Furthermore, some of the physiological responses to excitement, which is a positive emotion, are similar to those of stress. More practically, the behaviour of an animal can indicate its emotional disposition by watching how the animal reacts to aversive situations (such as being hurt or attacked). If the same behaviour is observed in another context it can be assumed that the situation is also aversive to the animal. An alternative is to compare the captive animal with its wild counterpart under the assumption that wild animals are on the whole 'happy and contented' because they have evolved to live successfully in their environment. Thus, the more similar the captive animal's behaviour is to the wild animal's, the better. Another important observation is the extent to which the captive animal performs different or abnormal behaviours (see above).

A positive evaluation based on the above criteria will justify the continuation of the enrichment programme and further work on other exhibits and species. Such an assessment requires the study of the animals' behaviour before (known as the baseline study) as well as after or during enrichment, if it is ongoing. The following behavioural changes confirm the benefits of enrichment.

- An increase in the behavioural repertoire (other than fearful or aversive behaviours) of the subject.
- A decrease in abnormal or stereotyped behaviours.
- Positive changes in the animal's activity patterns; lethargic animals becoming more active, hyperactive ones calmer.
- Greater use of enclosure space.
- Improved locomotory activity, e.g. climbing/swimming/flying.
- Reduced aggressive or asocial behaviour.

Environmental enrichment techniques have several important roles to play in the breeding of endangered species in captivity (Shepherdson, 1994). Enrichment can help preserve the behavioural diversity of captive populations and ensure the growth of behaviourally viable populations. Enrichment can increase the success of reintroduction programmes by providing animals with the opportunity to learn skills necessary for life in the wild, and by optimising the capacity of animals to learn from, and adapt to, new environments. Free-ranging captive-born groups of animals established in protected natural surroundings, e.g. cotton-top tamarins (Price *et al.*, 1989; Chamove & Rohruber, 1989), golden lion tamarins (Bronikowski *et al.*, 1989) or Siberian polecats (Miller *et al.*, 1994) demonstrate the importance of enrichment in preparing animals for release to the wild. The skills required for survival in the wild revolve around orientation and locomotion skills, feeding and foraging, obtaining suitable resting and sleeping places, and exhibiting appropriate inter-species (including predator avoidance) and intra-specific interactions (Box, 1991). Clearly animals born and reared in the wild have superior survival skills to those reared in captivity. Wild-born animals reintroduced to the same sites as captive-born individuals adapt quicker and survive longer (Chapter 7). This contrast underlines the importance of pre-release environment and enrichment to the acquisition of behaviours necessary for survival in the wild (Shepherdson *et al.*, 1990).

Key concepts
(1) High standards of animal welfare are increasingly regarded as fundamental for captive breeding. It is now explicitly included in many national legislative frameworks on zoos. Five fundamental 'freedoms', which recognise both physical and behavioural needs, succinctly encapsulate welfare requirements of animals and also form a framework that can be used in the assessment of animal well-being. To assure animal rights, captive breeding for conservation must find a delicate balance between advantages/ disadvantages of captivity and the threat to survival of *in-situ* populations.
(2) Strong expressions of 'stereotypic' behaviour are a tell-tale sign of problems with animal welfare. However, reliable guidelines (clinical signs) for the recognition of distress in most captive animals are not available. Captive rearing can promote the expression of particular behavioural traits, such as increased aggression, changed food searching behaviour, and changed spatial and temporal behaviour.
(3) Even without any deliberate artificial selection, genetic change in captivity can be very rapid, i.e. within a small number of generations, and very intensive. Observed effects range from behavioural to morphological and physiological changes. Over the last years, a large body of evidence emerged indicating that a broad array of taxa are affected by rapid genetic adaptation to captivity. These new data all indicate that the current management of minimising loss of genetic diversity is not sufficient if captive populations are to act as sources for future reintroductions and population augmentation. Management to minimise genetic adaptation must be implemented.
(4) The benign environment in captivity generally masks negative effects of genetic adaptation and inbreeding depression, which are normally stronger in wild, more stressful environments.

(5) Environmental enrichment should be built into the enclosure design and daily husbandry routine from the outset. Several approaches to enrichment exist and need careful and case-specific evaluation and adaptation. Environmental enrichment should target the requirements for animal welfare in captivity, and for the wild-born of those captive populations destined for reintroduction. Behavioural competency for survival and reproduction after reintroduction is of uttermost concern for any captive breeding for conservation.

5 · *Viable captive populations – the numbers game*

'Setting conservation thresholds at a few hundred individuals only is a subjective and non-scientific decision, not an evidence-based biological one . . . . Many existing conservation programs might therefore be managing inadvertently or implicitly for extinction' (Lochran Traill)

5.1 Introduction

Measuring the potential for zoos to house and breed threatened species has been a cause of concern for some time, but is as yet unresolved. However, progress has been made since the 1980s around the 'small population paradigm', as Caughley (1994) termed it, the study of the dynamics of small populations that have declined owing to some (deterministic) perturbation and which are more susceptible to extinction via chance (stochastic) events (Chapter 1). Past theoretical and empirical work predicts that population viability should increase with increasing initial population size both among and within species (Reed *et al.*, 2003a). Individuals in small or fragmented populations may have fewer opportunities to locate mates because of a skewed local sex ratio and/or physical isolation from conspecifics, henceforth the Allee effect (Courchamp *et al.*, 1999, 2008). But also low demographic rates, i.e. low annual adult survival and fecundity (Beissinger, 2000) or high annual variability in these demographic rates in response to environmental variation (Stacey & Taper, 1992), can lead to extinction of small populations.

A primary issue in small population biology is how large populations need to be to ensure persistence over time. For captive breeding programmes, solving this question is fundamental since managers require knowledge of some threshold of the number of individuals that will ensure, at some acceptable level of risk, a population to persist in a viable state for a given interval of time. The concept of minimum viable populations (MVP) emerged (Shaffer, 1981) to resolve this issue, but identifying the MVP for a species is like gambling. It involves playing the odds and, if you win, the population will be self-sustaining and genetically viable, if you lose, it will not survive. Unlike gambling, however, the opportunity exists to change the odds in your favour.

In this chapter, we first review our current understanding of what constitutes a viable population. To do this, we outline the thinking first used in Soulé *et al.*'s (1986) seminal paper on the subject, and show how there has been a shift in the basic premises. We argue that there is a danger in adopting the rule of thumb blindly, and present the general genetic principles that remain fundamental for resolving the issue of minimum viable populations for the apposite implementation of captive breeding programmes. However, we argue that too often emphasis on expediency has overridden biological concerns, endangering the future success of many programmes. We identify data that have been published since Soulé *et al.*'s (1986), and discuss how these new insights may shed light on their initial thinking, and whether a re-evaluation is required. We inevitably introduce mathematical formulae and statistics, but we introduce them sparingly and encourage the reader to consult more specialist texts on population and conservation genetics.

5.2 From rule of thumb to golden standard

5.2.1 The 'millennium ark'

Animal populations, if very large, can persist indefinitely and withstand environmental and demographic stochasticity whilst maintaining evolutionary potential. The definition of 'very large' is often species-specific, strongly depending on life history traits (particularly effective population size, social organisation, breeding strategy, reproductive output and generation length). In practice, maintaining sufficient numbers of the many species that may require captive reproduction is probably unattainable due to space and financial limitations. Because of this truth, Soulé *et al.* (1986) in their parable of the 'millennium ark', which derives from the Noah's Ark image (Box 5.1), developed a series of guiding principles for captive breeding. Soulé *et al.* (1986) suggested that the main goal of captive breeding should be the 'maintenance of 90% of the genetic variation in the source (wild) population over a period of 200 years', and that in most cases, founder groups will have to be 'above 20 (effective) individuals'. The authors acknowledged that these threshold values (which could be modified if deemed necessary) were intuitive, i.e. subjective. They are based on a trade-off between the need to retain genetic diversity – a proxy for self-sustainability – and the economic constraints of long-term captive breeding. Importantly, these numbers are inter-dependent. Self-sustaining populations that can persist indefinitely and can withstand environmental and demographic stochasticity in captivity and maintain their evolutionary potential are necessarily 'very large'. The 'millennium ark' was thus premised on a number of assumptions, focussing on length of time in captivity and numbers required to preserve viable populations.

Box 5.1 · *The rise and fall of a paradigm*

Whether fable or truth, as creationists believe, the biblical story of Noah's Ark embodies many topics that are so urgent today. It highlights the interdependence between humans and nature. We are all in the same boat! Noah's Ark was the lifesaver for animal biodiversity after human behaviour doomed the whole world.

The 'Noah's Ark Paradigm' is the assumption that a large number of species can be 'saved' through captive breeding and successfully reintroduced in the future, whereby the future date is mostly unspecified. Although the story of Noah, the ark and the animals two-by-two, may have provided an attention-grabbing image of zoos as saviours of the world's species, the actual application of the tale falters for two reasons. Firstly, there was no reproduction on the ark; the biblical text even implies breeding was prevented. Secondly, Noah's Ark was clearly a short-term solution for the flood; when it receded, the extinction factor vanished. In contrast, procreation is, of course, the very essence of captive breeding and with the notable exception of some programmes lasting less than a handful of generations; most are long-term and take many decades before the species can be restored to the wild. Thus, the story of Noah's Ark and the 'Noah's Ark Paradigm' used by zoos and captive breeding are strikingly different from each other.

Whilst many zoos may have shifted their focus away from the 'Noah's Ark Paradigm' (Chapter 3), the image of the ark still persists. The symbol is employed in promotional material e.g. 'Durrell's Ark', institutional names such as 'Noah's Ark Farm Zoo' (which actually advocates creationism), in adverts (e.g. 'Art on the Ark'), for rescue programmes (e.g. 'Amphibian Ark') and is even used in zoo emblems and insignia (e.g. Chester Zoo, UK; Parco Natura Viva, Italy).

In fact, zoos often talk about 'captive assurance populations' of some species, as if these were on board an 'Ark' of sorts, secure until factors threatening their extinction are removed. Thus, the allegory of the ark, although somewhat inaccurate, may still unify zoos in reinforcing their role in captive breeding and reintroduction.

Time frame. Demographic forecasts at the time of Soulé *et al.* (1986) predicted a 'demographic winter' lasting 500–1000 years because of the mushrooming human population. The authors argued that this would eliminate most wildlife habitats in the tropics, and about 2000 species of large, terrestrial animals would disappear if they were not captive-bred. Improvements in biotechnology in a 200-year horizon could facilitate the task of protecting these species, but it would probably take decades at least before cryotechnology *per se* was a viable alternative to captive breeding. Only after 500–1500 years, the trend of habitat loss would stabilise, and habitat for wildlife could begin to increase, providing a more realistic chance of re-establishing habitats and reintroducing species. Based on this, Soulé *et al.* (1986) chose 200 years as a reasonable time-frame, which could be modified if necessary, and compensatory changes in effective population sizes made if the time-frame was adjusted.

Founding population numbers and representation. Soulé *et al.*'s (1986) case for number of founders focusses on the well-documented impact of inbreeding and loss of heterozygosity on the founder population. Empirical evidence from (domestic) animal breeders suggests that the rate of inbreeding per generation, F, needs to be 2% or less for inbreeding depression to be balanced by natural selection for target traits such as fertility. Interestingly, Franklin (1980) and Soulé (1980) are more conservative and take 1% for MVPs based on the same data. Using F, we can calculate the number of animals required:

$$F = 1/2N_e. \tag{5.1}$$

Here, N_e refers not to the total number of individuals in a population, N, but to the effective number (Appendix 5). N_e is typically smaller than its actual size. For example, non-reproducing animals do not contribute to N_e (for the different meaning of effective population size, see Appendix 4). Accepting inbreeding per generation of 2% requires 25 unrelated animals, whereas $F = 1\%$ requires 50 for founding a captive population. Soulé *et al.* (1986) suggest at least 20 founders to account for the practical difficulties of finding and securing suitable founders especially for endangered or critically endangered species. The slightly lower threshold target is possible because the suggested overall goal is to retain 90% of genetic variation. Lower founder numbers can be compensated by larger final population sizes in captivity, all achieving the same 90% target.

The founder event causes a population bottleneck, resulting in loss of heterozygosity. In an idealised population, this can be generalised as the loss of heterozygosity, Δh, from the heterozygosity immediately before the bottleneck to the heterozygosity immediately after the bottleneck within a single generation is as follows:

$$\Delta h = 1/2N_e. \tag{5.2}$$

An effective population size of 50 results in a loss of 1% heterozygosity in one generation, 25 in 2%, 6 in 8.3% and 5 in 10%, respectively. A one-generation bottleneck of five or less animals means that the long-term goal of retaining at least 90% heterozygosity cannot be met.

In terms of representation, Soulé *et al.* (1986) refer to the source (wild) population, from where founders are extracted, and which is the baseline for the monitoring of genetic variation over time. However, they do not give any further details with regard to representativeness of founders or the definition of a source population.

Maintenance of genetic diversity. There is overwhelming evidence that genetic diversity is, on average, ultimately vital for the long-term survival, evolutionary potential and future adaptability of populations (see below). Without variation there is no evolutionary change possible. Genetic variation is a much better predictor of the future of populations than population size *per se*. There is, however, no clear evidence as to how much variation can be lost before significant negative impacts arise in populations. This depends on evolutionary past and life history traits. Soulé *et al.* (1986) argued that 'it was the consensus that the 90% threshold represents, intuitively, the zone between a potentially damaging and a tolerable loss of heterozygosity'. Importantly, the correlation between variability and the future of populations is an average relationship. There are examples of species with low genetic variability which are currently doing very well after reintroduction. Therefore, there are no 'lost cases', where hope is abandoned and conservation management ceased, if the 90% goal is unachievable or founder sizes are very small, compared to the recommendation.

The actual number of effective animals which need to be maintained in captivity after founding is species-specific and case-specific, critically influenced by the size of the founder group, breeding strategy and founder contribution to the gene pool, the rate of growth of the population in captivity, and the generation time. Larger founder sizes allow lower final population sizes, are expensive at the beginning and cheaper later in the breeding programme. Lower founder numbers require larger final population sizes, are cheaper at the beginning and more expensive later.

5.2.2 The modified rule of thumb

Although Soulé *et al.*'s (1986) set of prescriptions are attractive to managers because they see these as practical suggestions based on what appears to be reliable inferences and data, conservation management is a much more complex task. Collection of relevant data and detailed analysis requires time and valuable resources, often necessitating teams of experts. Predictions on how biological systems 'behave' in the future are not only inherently complex but typically have large error margins and uncertainties. Therefore, generalisations can be dangerous and destabilising to management (Ehrenfeld, 1991; Meffe & Carroll, 1997). For example, the '50/500 rule' (Franklin, 1980) used to estimate MVPs has been controversial because of the numerous cases where it did not apply (Franklin & Frankham, 1998). However, although some authors discourage the use of the rule (Meffe & Carroll, 1997), others strongly support it because it performs well on average, and because rules of thumb are often seen as the only realistic approach to face the current biodiversity crisis (Traill *et al.*, 2010). They are also ideal to effectively communicate to policy-makers, who – realistically – are not interested in details, or may not have the time to read the fine print, or may not be conversant with detailed genetic science.

Soulé *et al.*'s (1986) rule of thumb has changed in two ways since publication. Firstly, the time frame has been reduced from 200 to 100 years, but without adjustment of the 90% heterozygosity target suggested by Soulé *et al.* (1986). Secondly, the baseline for calculating heterozygosity over time has changed from the 'source (wild) population' to a sample of the source population, i.e. the founding population. The earliest example of the use of the modified rule of thumb is found in Frankham *et al.* (2002), who suggested that there are 'economic trade-offs among... number of founders... cost of starting captive populations and the subsequent size required to maintain 90% of genetic diversity for 100 years (the current objective of captive management)'. Subsequently, Hiddinga & Leus (2006) explicitly argued that 'the retention of 90% of gene diversity (GD) for a hundred years' was a sensible compromise 'between retaining a reasonable amount of gene diversity and not needing a ridiculously high number of individuals to do this'. Likewise, Earnhardt *et al.* (2009) in proposing captive management guidelines for the Bali mynah, put forward that 'under current management conditions, population decline and extinction are unlikely and that although GD will decline over 100 years the projected loss does not exceed levels acceptable to population managers (less than 90% GD retained)'.

The 90% in 100 years is now used as THE rule of thumb in most programmes, implicitly or explicitly, but rarely justified. More surprisingly, the rationale of these modifications has not been extensively debated and is rarely critically evaluated. Nevertheless, captive programmes often make large efforts to estimate minimum population sizes that are just big enough to maintain 90% of the founding genetic diversity (Earnhardt *et al.*, 2009). Hence, the question still remains whether the current targets for captive management are adequate and sustainable. We review the evidence that has emerged since Soulé *et al.* (1986) regarding genetic adaptation to captivity (Sections 4.2.2), viable captive populations (this chapter) and effective captive breeding (Sections 6.7 and 6.8). All information indicates that these criteria might be well suited to assure viable captive populations for future exhibitions of living museum collections, but are less suitable for planned reintroductions in a time frame of 100+ years. We conclude that much shorter time-frames and less loss of genetic diversity ought to be targeted for reintroductions (Chapter 9).

5.3   Why are small populations vulnerable?

Population size matters! Mutations, selection, migration and stochastic events shape the genetic backbone of any population, small and large. Stochastic events are random events like throwing a dice. Once a population becomes small, it is particularly vulnerable to several factors which have no or little impact on large populations or meta-populations, composed of many semi-isolated small populations, as a whole. These factors are characterised by stochasticity. Therefore, not every small population will inevitably become extinct, but the likelihood of extinction will increase and will be higher than in larger populations.

Environmental and demographic stochasticity. Random fluctuations in the availability and quality of habitat and resources, predation and disease, competitive interactions and invasive species, and catastrophes can cause large variances/fluctuations in population sizes. Whilst even local extinctions can be compensated by recolonisation in a metapopulation setting, species composed of only one small population will then vanish from the earth.

Demographic stochasticity describes random fluctuations in birth rate, death rate, and sex ratio, and can push a population over the cliff without any external trigger. It is usually the major stochastic factor for populations of around 100 animals or smaller (Lande, 1993). Demographic and environmental stochasticity can act together on populations to greatly elevate extinction risk. There is a long history of models that incorporate stochasticity to examine its effect on population growth and extinction, but the combined effects remain poorly understood. Melbourne & Hastings (2008) showed in a laboratory population of the red flour beetle, that extinction risk for natural populations might have been greatly underestimated by previous models because of undetected demographic variance. These results led Melbourne & Hastings to suggest that the re-evaluation of extinction risk for many populations of conservation concern is urgent. However, to the best of our knowledge, implications for captive breeding during the founder phase have so far not been evaluated.

Allee effects. An Allee effect arises when individual fitness decreases with population density from some maximum value at high density. There can be a critical threshold density above which the population grows and below which the population dynamics are unstable, leading often to sudden and unexpected population crashes and extinctions. Factors causing Allee effects include failure to find reproductive partners, interruptions of mating behaviour (e.g. lekking behaviour), feeding efficiency, predator avoidance (e.g. schooling behaviour in fish), thermoregulation (e.g. bees or overwintering garter snakes), and other social behaviours. Allee effects can explain many sudden collapses of exploited populations (Courchamp et al., 2008).

Genetic factors. Small population size leads inevitably to inbreeding and reduced genetic diversity. Both are caused by stochastic changes of the population's genetic composition over time. The likelihood of inbreeding depression increases and this has short-term negative impacts on reproductive fitness, survival and other life history traits. The loss of genetic diversity reduces the long-term adaptability to changing environments and hampers evolutionary change (Frankham, 2005b; Frankham *et al.*, 2010).

Interactive effects. Once populations are small the population dynamics become increasingly unstable. Genetic, environmental and demographic stochasticity and Allee effects can reinforce each other and impacts become increasingly severe. Inbreeding and loss of genetic variability also increase and make the population more vulnerable. This causes a downward feedback loop, an 'extinction vortex' (Gilpin & Soulé, 1986), which drags small populations into the abyss and eventually leads to extinction. The theoretically proposed dynamics of the extinction vortex is supported by empiric data on wild vertebrate populations during decline to extinction (Fagan & Holmes, 2006). The stochastic nature of the factors increasing extinction risk has two major implications:

Firstly, these factors act upon any small population irrespective of the species or life history traits. For example, the effects of selection are small and overruled by stochasticity. There is a large body of theoretical information on dynamics at small population size. The effects can be studied by using model organisms in the laboratory or captivity and results can be extrapolated to other organisms. Moreover, extinction risk can be modelled on computers, allowing the predictions of the fate of populations as used in numerous computer programmes. On the other hand, the stochastic nature only allows the estimation of likelihoods rather than the prediction of the fate in specific scenarios. There are of course many caveats mainly caused by simplifications such as the use of idealised populations for the parameterisation of models. We have already discussed how the use of too simplistic models can falsely predict the relative importance of environmental *versus* demographic stochasticity and lead to underestimated extinction probabilities.

Secondly, the interaction between genetic, environmental and demographic stochasticity, catastrophes and Allee effects is complex and intricate, making it very difficult to disentangle the importance of these factors for extinctions. This has led to a highly controversial discussion on the importance of genetics for extinctions. Lande (1988), Caro & Laurenson (1994) and many others have argued that non-genetic factors cause extinction prior to genetic factors, and contribute significantly to the extinction vortex.

There is now overwhelming theoretical and empirical evidence demonstrating the importance of genetics for extinctions in small and isolated populations. Spielman *et al.* (2004) compared heterozygosity in 170 threatened taxa with those in taxonomically related non-threatened taxa and found a highly significant departure from the predictions of the non-genetic impact hypothesis. Heterozygosity was lower in threatened taxa in 77% of comparisons, and was on average 35% lower. If this assumption, that populations go extinct because of non-genetic factors before genetic factors can act, were true, no or minor differences in genetic diversity between threatened and taxonomically related non-threatened species can be expected. Thus, Spielman *et al.*'s meta-analysis indicates a link between extinction risk and reduced genetic variation. Computer modelling, laboratory experiments and an increasing number of case studies (next chapter) all demonstrate strong genetic effects in small population (Evans & Sheldon, 2008; Flight, 2010; O'Grady *et al.*, 2006). For example, Blomqvist *et al.* (2010) recently demonstrated serious genetic effects in a declining natural population of southern dunlins, an endangered shorebird, likely reducing the prospects for its survival.

5.4 Genetic composition of small populations

The smaller a population is, the greater is the effect on its genetic composition. Ideal, large, essentially infinite, populations have genetic compositions that remain unchanged over time. In other words, the frequencies of genotypes (here the emphasis is on individuals) and the frequencies of alleles in a population (here the emphasis is on alleles) remain constant from generation to generation. In the **real** world, however, all populations are finite. As a consequence, the frequency of genotypes and alleles will change from generation to generation because the offspring will represent an imperfect sample of their parent population as a consequence of stochastic, random processes. This is **random genetic drift**, which is not a consequence of selection or mutations. Mutation rates are in general very low. Mutations are important in the long-term but are relatively unimportant for conservation, where other short-term factors might cause much more dramatic impacts on genotype/allele frequencies.

Genetic drift and the inbreeding effect of small populations. All real populations are subject to random genetic drift. Because genetic drift is random, the direction of drift in allele frequency distributions from one generation to the next cannot be predicted. However, the magnitude of the change can be predicted. The expected magnitude is inversely related to population size: it is very small in large populations, but can be dramatically large in small populations.

One of the assumptions of the Hardy–Weinberg principle is that a population is randomly breeding. One particular form of non-random mating is **inbreeding**, the mating of related individuals within a population. In large populations it is less likely that related individuals will mate with one another. Nevertheless, inbreeding may occur due to non-random matings, for example mate selection. In small populations, particularly those which are closed to immigration, it is inevitable that related individuals will breed even when randomly mating because individuals tend to be related to each other. Inbreeding between related animals causes the decrease of heterozygosity and increase of homozygosity in their offspring.

In small populations, random genetic drift is relatively large and leads to: (1) change of allele frequencies; (2) loss of heterozygosity; and (3) loss of alleles, in particular rare ones, thus decreasing polymorphic loci, and causing large differences in all these parameters between replicate populations because of the random nature of genetic drift.

Imagine a locus with only two alleles, one of which is at low frequency in the population (say, 0.05, i.e. 5%) and the other at high frequency (i.e. 0.95). Because of chance, the low-frequency allele has an increased likelihood to get lost from the population and, therefore, allelic diversity is lost. If it is lost, the polymorphic locus (in this case, two

Table 5.1 *Methodological advantages and disadvantages of the use of random genetic drift on genetic variation to infer population history*

Measures	Advantages	Disadvantages
Heterozygosity	• proportional to the amount of genetic variance at a locus • expected proportional reduction of heterozygosity by genetic drift is independent of the number of alleles at each locus • estimates of heterozygosity from empirical data are relatively robust for sample size	• relatively insensitive to population bottlenecks
Allelic diversity	• relatively sensitive to the strength of population bottlenecks	• estimates of allelic diversity from empirical data are sensitive to sample size (if sample sizes are equalised, or the equivalent is done statistically)

alleles) changes into a monomorphic locus (one allele). Such fixation leads to a reduced proportion of polymorphic loci. Heterozygosity is also lost. Vice versa, the amount of loss of genetic variability can be used to infer population history and effective population size. These two effects of random genetic drift on genetic variation have advantages and disadvantages when used to infer population history (Table 5.1). Random genetic drift reduces both heterozygosity and allelic diversity. Both are functions of population size where: (1) the expected loss of heterozygosity per generation is $1/2N = F$ with F being the inbreeding coefficient; and (2) the probability of an allele being lost is $(1 - p)^{2N}$ with p being the frequency of the allele in the population.

If a population goes through a population bottleneck, genetic diversity is being lost by random genetic drift as follows.

- Heterozygosity, h, is lost at a rate of $1/2N$ per generation (see equation (5.2)) regardless of the heterozygosity before the bottleneck. In the extreme case of only two surviving animals ($N = 2$), only 25% of heterozygosity is expected to be lost.
- Allelic diversity is lost according to the number of alleles before the bottleneck and their allele frequencies. Rare alleles are lost on average much more often than common alleles. In the extreme case of only two surviving animals a maximum of four alleles can survive regardless of the number of alleles present in the population before the bottleneck, but it is also possible that only one allele survives purely by chance.
- Because genotypic diversity grows exponentially with allelic diversity (two alleles results in three possible genotypes, three alleles in six, four alleles in ten, etc.), loss of allelic diversity can dramatically reduce genotypic diversity.

Genetic drift, severity and length of population bottlenecks. Random genetic drift applies for every generation. Heterozygosity, h, is lost during every single generation with small population size. After n generations, the effect is multiplicative over all generations 1 to n and the heterozygosity remaining is:

$$h_{n+1} = (1 - 1/[2N_1]) * (1 - 1/[2N_2]) * \cdots * (1 - 1/[2N_n]). \qquad (5.3)$$

The length and severity of the bottleneck has a strong impact on the loss of h. Assume three populations with four generations and an initial heterozygosity of 1 (i.e. 100%). All populations have the same effective population size of 55 individuals over time.

- Population 1: $N_1 = 55$, $N_2 = 55$, $N_3 = 55$, $N_4 = 55$, $h_{remaining} = 0.96$.
- Population 2: $N_1 = 100$, $N_2 = 10$, $N_3 = 10$, $N_4 = 100$, $h_{remaining} = 0.89$.
- Population 3: $N_1 = 100$, $N_2 = 2$, $N_3 = 18$, $N_4 = 100$, $h_{remaining} = 0.72$.

In other words, the remaining h over time is determined not by the average population size, average h or cumulative h, but by the generations with smallest population size and the number of generations the bottleneck lasts. This means that it is essential that management of wild and captive populations aim to recover N_e as fast as possible. This also applies to the loss of alleles, albeit it is more complicated to predict as it depends not only on N_e but also on the number and frequency of alleles (see Appendix 4).

The effects of bottlenecks on genetic diversity have been observed in numerous natural populations, laboratory experiments with model species and with computer simulations parameterised with data from wild populations. For example, England et al. (2003) showed in systematic experiments with the common fruit fly that bottlenecks indeed reduced heterozygosity, allelic diversity, heterozygosity and proportion of polymorphic loci, and changed allele frequency distributions as expected whereby large differences among replicate populations occurred. Moreover, the experiments demonstrated the different impacts of short intensive *versus* more diffuse bottlenecks. Allelic diversity, scaled by heterozygosity, was lower in the intense than the diffuse treatments.

5.5 Heterozygosity loss or loss of allelic diversity: what is more important?

Heterozygosity is proportional to the genetic variance at loci for quantitative variation. Therefore, heterozygosity is generally assumed to determine the short-term evolutionary potential immediately after population bottlenecks (Franklin, 1980). For populations with the same heterozygosity but different allelic richness, the short-term adaptive potential to population bottlenecks and management of inbreeding depression will be the same. However, allelic diversity is assumed to determine **long-term evolutionary potential** (James, 1970; Hill & Rabash, 1986). Allelic diversity is important at quantitative loci, especially at loci associated with disease or insecticide resistance, or other loci involved in adaptation to changing environments and selective pressures (Allendorf, 1986). For example, allelic diversity of the MHC complex is crucially important for disease resistance, e.g. in Soay sheep (Paterson et al., 1998). The evidence that the loss of MHC variation negatively affects population survival is so far equivocal and difficult to separate from effects of general inbreeding (Radwan *et al.*, 2010). However, the high-profile case of Tasmanian devil facial tumour disease, a clearly identifiable genetic malfunction which has been linked with the loss of MHC diversity, is a compelling example (Siddle *et al.*, 2007). In domestic livestock, retaining allelic richness is becoming increasingly the focus of conservation strategies for rare and endangered breeds (see Simianer, 2005). The long-term selective advantage and the future potential for adaptive change will likely be higher in populations with higher allelic richness and thus a broader allelic resource on which selection can act.

Whilst the long-term evolutionary potential is difficult to test empirically, England *et al.*'s (2003) study on *Drosophila* elegantly demonstrated that **short-term evolutionary potential** after population bottlenecks relates to loss of heterozygosity and not allelic diversity. As predicted, short intensive bottlenecks resulted in more severe loss of allelic diversity than more diffuse bottlenecks. The experiments examined short-term evolutionary potential by imposing environmental stress on the bottlenecked populations by increasing concentrations of sodium chloride, and measuring which concentrations resulted in extinctions. No differences were found between the intense and diffuse bottlenecked populations. The experiments were designed to result in identical losses of heterozygosity irrespective of bottleneck dynamics whilst bottleneck dynamics resulted in different losses of allelic diversity. Thus, they demonstrate that short-term evolutionary potential relates to loss of heterozygosity and not allelic diversity.

What are short-term and long-term? The definition seems arbitrary and mainly depends on the variation of allelic effects and the intensity of selection (Caballero *et al.*, 2010). Considering the rapidly changing environment due to human-induced changes and climate change, the selective advantage and the future potential for adaptive change due to a broader allelic resource might become of crucial relevance much faster than 'long-term' might suggest. More research is clearly required.

Selection. Because individuals in a population are different in genotype and phenotype, their responses to their surrounding environment also vary. Some individuals will be better adapted than others and will therefore have a better chance of surviving and producing offspring. The phenotypic traits and the genes responsible for them will be favoured in the population and their frequencies will increase until an equilibrium level is reached. Environments, however, are prone to change and when this happens, individuals with traits which did not allow for optimal performance under previous environmental conditions may now find that they are best suited for the new environment. This will result in a shift in gene frequencies towards the newly favoured genotype until equilibrium is again reached. Removal of allelic diversity will dramatically decrease genotypic and thus phenotypic diversity, which is the unit natural selection primarily acts upon. This loss of long-term evolutionary potential will be important for changing environments especially in climate change scenarios.

Small population size interferes also in the short-term with selection processes. Natural selection becomes less effective because of random genetic drift. Except when the selection pressure is very large, the random changes of allele frequencies will override the effects of selection. When under directional selection, both advantageous alleles and deleterious alleles will act as if selectively neutral and might become either more or less abundant purely by chance. Thus, deleterious alleles can go to fixation before selection can remove them. Mutational meltdown occurs when deleterious alleles accumulate in small populations, leading to decreased size which in turn leads to a further accumulation of more deleterious alleles (Lynch et al., 1993). However, empirical evidence indicates that mutational meltdown is of minor importance in time-frames of relevance to conservation, especially in sexual species (Gilligan et al., 1997; Zeyl et al., 2001). For overdominance, random genetic drift accelerates the loss of variation if the equilibrium allele frequency is near zero or one (i.e. one allele is rare). The second major effect of random genetic drift on selection in small populations is that the effects of selections become much less predictable.

Inbreeding depression. Inbreeding depression is the reduction of fitness of offspring from related animals relative to offspring from unrelated animals. Inbreeding depression may result from two mechanisms:

- increased homozygosity and thus expression of deleterious recessive alleles;
- reduced heterozygosity at loci where heterozygosity is selectively advantageous over homozygosity (i.e. overdominance).

Studies carried out on a variety of mammal populations in captivity have shown a significant correlation between inbreeding and reduced reproductive fitness (Ralls & Ballou, 1983). As many as 41 of 44 mammalian populations showed higher juvenile mortality and lower rates of fertility among inbred than among outbred individuals. In the wild, studies on whether and how genetic factors cause population decline and extinction have, surprisingly, been lacking, but there is now an emerging number of convincing studies. The effects have been demonstrated in a wild metapopulation of the Glanville fritillary butterfly. The extinction risk increased significantly with increasing inbreeding, even after accounting for the effects of the relevant ecological factors (Saccheri et al., 1998). 'Genetic rescue' of an isolated and inbred Scandinavian adder population elegantly tested the link between inbreeding and extinction (Madsen et al., 1999). The population was at the brink of extinction, with continuously declining population size and negligible recruitment, but dramatically recovered after the introduction of new genes from a different population and the restoration of genetic variability. Similarly, the introduction of migrants into an isolated and inbred population of greater prairie chicken has restored fertility and hatching rates (Westemeier et al., 1998).

The severity of inbreeding depression can be estimated by the mean number of lethal equivalents. The effect of sublethal alleles is being added for the estimation of LEs. Ralls et al. (1988) analysed inbreeding depression in zoos on the basis of juvenile survival. LEs ranged from −1.4 to 30.3, with a mean of 4.6 and a median of 3.14. The average cost of a parent–offspring or full sibling mating, estimated as reduction of juvenile survival compared to unrelated parents, was about 33%. The median value of 3.14 diploid LEs is used as a standard in many applications. For example, it is implemented as the default value in VORTEX. Brook *et al.* (2002) used this estimate in their study across a broad taxonomic range (birds, mammals, plants and reptiles) and found a clear reduction in population viability. However, inbreeding depression affects not only juvenile survival but all components of the life cycle. A major meta-analysis of published values of empiric inbreeding depression in wild, mammalian and avian species revealed a mean diploid LEs of 3.9 for fecundity, 2.4 for first year survival and 6.0 for survival from one year old to sexual maturity, resulting in a total of 12.3 diploid LEs (O'Grady *et al.*, 2006). Thus, Brook *et al.*'s (2002) seminal analysis likely underestimates extinction risk substantially. O'Grady *et al.* (2006) warn that 'disregarding the influence of inbreeding depression on extinction risk will lead to serious overestimates of the survival prospects of threatened mammalian and avian taxa. Further, inappropriate recovery plans may be instituted if the causes of extinction risk and their relative contributions are not recognized'.

Crnokrak & Roff (1999) analysed 137 published fitness traits from 25 taxa, 20 animal and 15 plant species in the wild. Inbreeding depression was confirmed approximately 54% of the time when species are known to be inbred. The percentage might be an underestimate as many data sets were small and had thus low statistical power. When significant, inbreeding depression was similarly deleterious across major plant and animal taxa. The most important result from the study comes from the comparison with Ralls *et al.*'s (1988) data from captivity: inbreeding depression was seven times higher in the wild than in captivity. Most, but not all, studies comparing captive with wild conditions have found that inbreeding depression is greater in more stressful wild environments than in more benign captive environments (Armbruster & Reed, 2005). A meta-analysis of 34 studies revealed that inbreeding depression significantly increased under stress in almost half of the cases and that estimated LEs were ≈70% larger under stressful conditions. There is also a huge body of evidence from laboratory and domestic animals and plants showing that inbreeding has deleterious effects, especially on fitness traits (Frankham *et al.*, 2010).

The cost of inbreeding depression has not only been shown in wild and captive populations but also at an individual level in the wild. On the island of Hirta, St. Kilda, Scotland, relatively inbred Soay sheep are more susceptible to parasitism by gastrointestinal nematodes and are more likely to die during environmental stress during winter due to their increased susceptibility to parasitism (Coltman *et al.*, 1999).

Parasites and infectious diseases are important for population dynamics, adaptation and constitute a major variable in the extinction vortex of small populations. An increasing number of field studies and experimental challenges of wild populations has demonstrated that host inbreeding increases susceptibility to ectoparasitism (e.g. the Sonoran desert fruit fly *versus* a macrochelid mite (Luong *et al.*, 2007); the lesser kestrel *versus* the feather lice (Ortego *et al.*, 2007)), bacterial infection (e.g. house finch *versus* bacterial pathogens (Hawley *et al.*, 2005)), infectious clonal cancer (the Tasmanian devil *versus* Tasmanian devil facial tumour disease (Siddle *et al.*, 2007)) or immune responses (e.g. cell-mediated immune response in the song sparrow (Reid *et al.*, 2003)). Effects reflect either genome-wide effects, with no single locus contributing disproportionately to the observed effect (Ortego *et al.*, 2007), or are linked to specific loci such as MHC (Siddle *et al.*, 2007).

Purging. Inbreeding can 'unmask' deleterious recessive alleles as the frequency of homozygous genotypes increases. Natural and artificial selection can remove the carriers of these homozygous genotypes. This opens the opportunity that deleterious alleles can be removed, 'purged', from a population by natural selection in the wild or by carefully controlled inbreeding together with natural or artificial selection in captivity. Theoretically, this can result in populations with higher mean fitness than the populations from which the captive populations were founded.

For conservation breeding, hope was raised that 'inbreeding depression does not constitute an insurmountable barrier to the long-term maintenance of a species in which inbreeding cannot be avoided' (Templeton & Read, 1984). The captive breeding programme of Speke's gazelle has been widely cited as an example of how to effectively purge genetic load in captivity. The captive population was descended from one male and three females only and severe inbreeding depression was observed. The programme employed deliberate inbreeding coupled with careful selection of healthy inbred individuals for matching pairs for mating. This seems to have led to a very rapid elimination of inbreeding depression (Templeton & Read, 1984). However, the role of purging for Speke's gazelle remains highly controversial and there is mounting evidence ruling out purging to be of relevance in this programme (Ballou, 1997; Kalinowski *et al.*, 2000; Willis & Wiese, 1997; but see Templeton, 2002). A reanalysis of the data did not provide evidence that inbreeding and selection caused a reduction of inbreeding depression and that purging effects were non-significant. It seems that temporal changes in fitness due to environmental fluctuations indicated purging, but because these changes were caused by these environmental influences and not selection, purging can be ruled out.

Since then, all data indicate that purging is of minor importance for conservation. Many studies have failed to demonstrate purging, both in the wild and captivity (Leberg & Firmin, 2008). Although purging was confirmed experimentally in some laboratory experiments (Fox *et al.*, 2008), inferred from pedigree and trait analysis for stringently selected dairy cattle (Mc Parland *et al.*, 2009), and inferred for some captive populations (Boakes *et al.*, 2007), the effects are generally small and highly variable within and between species. For example, in zoo populations, the reduction in inbreeding depression averaged less than 1% across all 119 zoo populations of mammals, birds, reptiles and amphibians investigated (Boakes *et al.*, 2007). The minor importance for conservation is highlighted by the following.

- Crucially, highly inbred populations may go extinct before their genetic load can be purged, even under laboratory conditions, where inbred lines can be reared under benign and optimal conditions (Leberg & Firmin, 2008; Fox *et al.*, 2008). Thus, purging in captive endangered populations is not a practical approach because of the increased likelihood that targeted populations go extinct and because the reduction of inbreeding depression is generally low even when purging works.

- Even for those experimental studies where purging could be demonstrated, purging in captivity might not create the hoped-for positive effects on fitness in new environments after reintroductions. Purging in *Drosophila* affected only the environment in which purging occurred but had no fitness advantages in changed environments because other deleterious alleles were exposed or expressed there (Bijlsma *et al.*, 1999).

The effectiveness of purging depends on the extent of allele effects. Alleles with small effects approach selective neutrality and they are more likely to become fixed rather than removed in small inbred populations due to random genetic drift (see above). Thus, breeding aimed at purging might actually reduce fitness – the opposite of the intended effect. The low reduction of inbreeding depression by purging in zoos (Boakes *et al.*, 2007) indicates that most inbreeding depression is caused by recessive alleles with relatively mild deleterious effects.

Fitness-related traits tend to be governed by many loci and alleles with less severe effects, whereas hereditary disorders tend to be caused by alleles at single or a few loci, with strong effects. Alleles with large detrimental effects can be quickly purged without a high probability of population extinction, except when the total genetic load or inbreeding depression is very high (Hedrick, 1994; Lande, 1994). This raises the hope to purge hereditary disorders, which may be fairly common in captive populations. Published disorders range from hereditary blindness in wolves, albinism in brown bears, and chondrodystrophy, a kind of dwarfism, in captive California condor (Laikre, 1999; Ralls *et al.*, 2000). Here, single deleterious alleles cause clearly identifiable abnormal conditions in individuals that are homozygote at the particular gene. Most alleles causing hereditary disorders are recessive and are only expressed when in the homozygote state. Such homozygotes can be easily identified and removed. Although carriers are not phenotypically identifiable, pedigree analysis allows assigning to individuals likelihoods of being a carrier. A highly inbred grey wolf population in North European zoos exhibits hereditary blindness (Laikre, 1999). In this case, analysis of the pedigree and modelling showed that the frequency of the recessive allele causing blindness could be dramatically reduced without affecting the genetic variability of the population excessively. However, this is not always the situation and great care needs to be taken. In the case of chondrodystrophy in the California condor, for example, eliminating the disease-causing allele by selection of breeding animals would prevent more than half of the 146 living condors from breeding (Ralls *et al.*, 2000; Ralls & Ballou, 2004). This would come with a fairly low cost in reduction of heterozygosity (from 94.6% to 92.3%) but with a very high cost in the loss of alleles (from 12.9 to 8.9). Thus, the authors advised against removing the alleles and recommended minimising phenotypic expression. The development of new molecular tools to identify the locus and to test for carriers will change the costs of eliminating the defective allele and might, for the first time, allow the elimination of chondrodystrophy from the breeding population. Such efforts are currently underway (R. Frankham, personal communication). In addition to the potentially high associated cost of an allele's removal from the programme for future inbreeding and genetic diversity, captive breeding must also consider other practical issues. Zoo managers tend to assume that deformities observed in captive populations are heritable and select against them (Ralls *et al.*, 2000). However, heritability and the mode of inheritance is often more difficult to confirm than envisaged.

At first glance, captive breeding seems to resemble small island populations that have remained small in size over long periods of time. The zoo community often raises the hope that this demonstrates that long periods of time with small population size creates more opportunity for purging. This argument does not consider, however, that those small endemic populations observed today do not reveal the number of events where other small island populations went extinct or speciation 'attempts' failed because of extinction. On the other hand, population sizes of many island endemics have suffered because of the negative impacts of introduced non-native predators, e.g. the introduced brown tree snake drove the Guam rail to extinction. In this case, these demographic bottlenecks might be less detrimental because they have successfully sustained smaller effective population sizes than their continental sister taxa (Jamieson, 2007). However, even the population that survived inbreeding had lower fitness (Reed *et al.*, 2003b).

Outbreeding depression. Hybridisation between formerly isolated populations can result in an increase in fitness. This has been extensively utilised by animal and plant breeders applying systematic inbreeding of lineages and subsequent crossing of inbred lineages to create enhanced performance in the first hybrid generation (heterosis or hybrid vigour). There are many possible underlying mechanisms, with overdominance and the masking of deleterious recessives particularly important. Conversely, hybridisation can also cause reduced fitness, termed outbreeding depression. Negative effects are more severe in between-species hybridisation than between populations of the same species. In isolated populations different advantageous mutations may accumulate over time and alleles at several genes may co-adapt selection by epistatic interactions (i.e. interactions between alleles at different loci). Outbreeding depression may occur when hybridisation breaks up these co-adapted gene complexes (Templeton, 1986), or through loss of local adaptation, but mechanisms can vary and often remain unknown. For example, experimental crosses between individuals from isolated populations of the common frog demonstrated population-specific outbreeding depression (Sagvik *et al.*, 2005).

Whilst many cases of inbreeding depression have been described in the wild and captivity, the number of known cases of outbreeding depression remains low. In an extensive review, Edmands (2007) summarised outbreeding depression for fertility, population viability and reproductive success in 17 invertebrate species, mostly model species such as *Drosophila* spp., and eight vertebrate taxa. Worryingly, heterosis may be present in the first hybrid generation but outbreeding depression later. Further studies are urgently needed especially on the duration of fitness problems and the joint effects of inbreeding and outbreeding. Outbreeding depression has been described relatively rarely but it could be more common in taxa that exhibit strong genetic differentiation between populations. This could apply especially to amphibians, which have recently become the focus of conservation breeding and management. For example, translocation of frogs from large populations to isolated, declining populations is being suggested to increase genetic variation, but this could trigger unintended effects in the form of outbreeding depression (Sagvik et al., 2005; Seigel & Dodd, 2000).

Conservation managers are advised to minimise the risks of both inbreeding and outbreeding by using intentional hybridisation only for populations clearly suffering from inbreeding depression (Edmands, 2007). This advice, however, might turn out to be problematic. The fear of outbreeding depression may be highly exaggerated. Whilst we agree that potential outbreeding depression ought to be considered when planning management, there is general agreement between most theoretical and applied geneticists that inbreeding depression is the main problem. Small population size and random genetic drift increases population differentiation, sometimes dramatically. Consequently, population managers might shy away from mixing gene pools because of what is perceived to be a large genetic distance between populations, even when artificially created by drift. Moreover, it might dramatically inflate the number of management units within species, reinforcing the dilemma of what to conserve and whether there is enough space and resources available in captivity.

5.6   The importance of genetics for small populations

In the 1990s, the relative importance of inbreeding depression for population persistence and for conservation in general was challenged by the argument that non-genetic factors will drive a species to extinction before genetic factors can affect them (Caughley, 1994; Caro & Laurenson, 1994). Indeed, there are populations that have lost much of their genetic diversity and yet they thrive in the wild and show no detectable sign of inbreeding depression. Examples include the northern hairy-nosed wombat, beaver and others (Taylor et al., 1994). Comparing 170 threatened with related non-threatened taxa showed that heterozygosity was on average 35% lower in threatened taxa in 77% of comparisons, suggesting that most extinctions occur only after genetic factors affect populations adversely (Spielman et al., 2004). Although the study was biased against endemic island species that naturally occur at lower density and might have adapted to small population size (Jamieson, 2007), the study together with the large body of empirical and experimental evidence has finally put the controversy about the importance of genetic factors for population extinction to rest (see also Evans & Sheldon, 2008; Flight, 2010).

The stochastic nature of random genetic drift and inbreeding depression mean that some inbred lineages will show no or only little inbreeding depression. But because, as outlined above, the effects of inbreeding depression also depend on the severity of environmental stress, the fact that some populations thrive despite low genetic diversity does not exclude future negative fitness consequences when the environment changes. For example, the Mauritius kestrel dropped to only four known individuals in the early 1970s, resulting in a loss of 55% of the ancestral allelic diversity and 57% of heterozygosity. Captive breeding and intensive management of the reintroduced birds resulted in a dramatic increase of the wild population, to between 500 and 800 individuals within 20 years. This is a remarkable success and seems to constitute one of the examples where populations thrive despite loss of genetic diversity. However, the Mauritius kestrel has continued to lose genetic diversity since, and the inbreeding rate is one of the highest reported in the wild. This now has raised concerns that genetic deterioration may affect this population's long-term viability (Ewing *et al.*, 2008); re-emphasising that current 'success' might not last.

Until the appearance of Tasmanian devil facial tumour disease in 1996, Tasmanian devils were common and widespread across most of Tasmania and were doing well despite low genetic diversity (Jones *et al.*, 2007). Heterozygosity and allelic diversity were lower than other Australian marsupials or most other carnivores and indicate a population and genetic bottleneck at some point in the recent past, possibly around the time of the last ice age. The emerged devil facial-tumour disease is fast-spreading and now poses a serious threat to the species. Available data show that it is loss of MHC diversity that is allowing the disease to spread, which now threatens the overall extinction of the species (Siddle *et al.*, 2007).

5.7 Minimum viable populations, MVPs

5.7.1 Context

The theoretical and empirical data summarised above clearly show that extinction probability increases with declining population size. The relationship is non-linear, however. A stochastic decline of, say, 10% in a population of 50 000 reproducing animals is of no relevance for the population's extinction probability, whilst a 10% reduction in a population of 50 results in a proportionally higher increase of extinction risk than 10% in a population of 500. Is there a critical threshold density, which results in a 'switch' from low impact to a dramatically changed extinction probability, similar to Allee effects? A population size denoting the transition from a declining to a small population? Or is there a magic number, above which populations are relatively safe and below which populations are doomed without conservation action?

The concept of MVP (Shaffer, 1981), has been extensively used in conservation management of wild animal populations, and is of critical importance for captive ones also. The definition of an MVP for 'any given species, in any given habitat, is the smallest isolated population having a 99% chance of remaining extant for 1000 years despite the foreseeable effects of demographic, environmental, and genetic stochasticity, and natural catastrophes'.

The MVP concept addresses long-term population persistence. The goal is to maintain populations to persist in their natural environment in the face of detrimental effects of environmental change, especially human-induced. The MVP is the smallest number of individuals achieving this goal (Shaffer, 1981). The concept was first enthusiastically embraced, especially in the 1980s and 1990s, but has lately fallen out of favour for *in-situ* conservation and management (Traill *et al.*, 2010). For captive populations, it remains a central pillar. The perceived competition of 'zoo places' available for captive breeding for conservation *versus* other utilities such as visitor attraction or teaching, has created strong pressures to estimate the minimum viable population size in zoos and to breed species as marginally above that value as possible (e.g. Bali mynah, Earnhardt *et al.*, 2009).

MVP represents the upper boundary of Caughley's (1994) small population paradigm. The fate of populations smaller than the MVP is largely driven by stochasticity acting on the population's specific life history parameters and the local environmental setting. MVP size has been estimated either by modelling the impact of demographic, environmental and genetic stochasticity or by directly using population genetics data.

5.7.2 Empirical MVPs in the 'wild'

A frequently used species-specific method of risk assessment and estimating MVP size is the population viability analysis, PVA, or its extension the population and habitat viability analysis, PHVA. These are processes that determine the probability that a population will go extinct within a given number of years. PVA is a marriage of ecology and statistics that brings together species characteristics and environmental variability to forecast population health and extinction risk. The larger goal in mind when conducting a PVA is to ensure that the population of a species is self-sustaining over the long term. PVAs and PHVAs employ life-history data to parameterise a population model, and employ stochastic models to represent the main factors acting on small populations (environmental, demographic and genetic stochasticity).

A number of user-friendly generalised computer programs are available to aid the PVA practice, e.g. VORTEX (Lacy, 1993), ALEX (Possingham & Davies, 1995), RAMAS (Akçakaya & Root, 2002). Once parameters are specified by the user, the implemented models estimate the probability of population persistence (measured on the equivalent scales 0 to 1, or 0% to 100%) over a set period of time, typically 100 years, at a given MVP (Shaffer, 1981). Alternatively, MVP is estimated at a given probability of population persistence, mostly 90%. Choice of length of time, time-scale and probability of population persistence are purely arbitrary. Although extinction risk scales better to generations than years (O'Grady *et al.*, 2008), most users choose years rather than generations.

In a review and meta-analysis of published PVAs, Traill *et al.* (2007) reported that 60% of these included genetic effects, the remainder modelling environmental and demographic stochasticity only. Outcomes are strongly impacted by model assumptions and the availability of background biological information and data on the target species. For example, Brook *et al.* (2006) report that median estimates of MVP across 1198 species are almost two magnitudes of order higher for density-independent models compared with density-dependent models (Fig. 5.1). Traill *et al.* (2007) identified six variables contributing to methodological variation when computing MVPs:

- model type (individual-based or matrix/cohort-based simulation; empirical census or genetic analysis);
- probability of population persistence;
- time period for which population persistence was modelled;

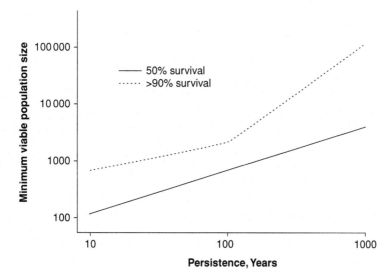

Fig. 5.1 Line plot of median minimum viable population estimates (scaled to $\log_{10}$) for 1198 species derived from time series analyses (see Brook *et al.*, 2006) along a logged timescale (10–1000 years). The full line represents median MVP size at 50% probability of persistence. The dotted line is the median MVP at greater than 90% probability of persistence. From Traill *et al.* (2010).

- density dependence;
- inbreeding depression;
- catastrophes (whether random catastrophes are modelled in addition and outside the distribution of random environmental stochasticity).

These authors used statistical modelling to account for these variables and to allow for comparison of MVPs based on different parameter settings. The median for the corrected MVPs was 4169 individuals (95% confidence interval 3577–5129). The analysis used key ecological, life history and anthropological extinction correlates as predictors for the species IUCN Red List threat category and MVP. Results indicated that body mass, generation length, fecundity, social grouping, dispersal/philopatry, distribution range, human impact, and population trend did not successfully predict MVPs. This is in line with the 'small population paradigm', which postulates that stochasticity is the main driving factor influencing extinction probability. Conversely, ecological, life history and anthropological parameters explained over 50% of the variation in IUCN Red List categories, a result aligned with the 'declining population paradigm'. This paradigm describes the factors causing smallness: systematic/deterministic parameters, which are species- and situation-specific, intricately linked with ecological and life history traits that drive population declines.

Technical aspects of PVAs and PHVAs have been intensively scrutinised by various authors (see, for example, Naujokaitis-Lewis *et al.*, 2009; Patterson & Murray, 2008).

132 · Viable captive populations

There are several categories of problems that impact on the modelling results. First, uncertainty in ecological modelling includes:

- parameter uncertainty – not knowing the current system state (e.g. limited data available or used to estimate population parameters, especially for rare species);
- model structure uncertainty – not knowing the rules for system change (e.g. assumed future stationarity of population parameters; the biological information on density-dependence of population dynamics in many endangered species is missing or severely data deficient);
- natural stochasticity uncertainty – not being able to predict environmental, genetic, and demographic stochasticity;
- future management decisions uncertainty – having a limited ability to forecast future decisions and their implications.

Sensitivity analysis is useful to explore the impact of parameterisation on model predictions. However, sensitivity analyses are surprisingly often ignored or are not suitable.

PVAs predict without bias for well-studied species (Brook et al., 2000), but many species are understudied. The latter case comes with a new set of problems relating to pre-modelling decisions:

- omission of critical parameters;
- use of computer programs as black boxes;
- systematic bias in parameterisation of critical parameters;
- use of untested assumptions;
- lack of independent model validation;
- divergent results related to particular software packages.

The omission of critical factors in the modelling process is most pronounced for genetic parameters. In spite of the well documented negative effects of inbreeding depression on population viability, and the strong evidence that it should not be omitted from PVAs and PHVAs, inbreeding depression is often absent (Frankham, 2010). Most studies that implement genetic factors limit these to the impact of inbreeding on reproduction and survival, which is not adequate to fully assess future adaptability (Visser, 2008). Inbreeding depression is typically modelled using 3.14 diploid lethal equivalents found by Ralls et al. (1988) for juvenile survival in zoo populations (Traill et al., 2007). This is particularly dominant when computer programs are used as 'black boxes', relying on pre-set default values such as 3.14 diploid lethal equivalents implemented in VORTEX. However, a meta-analysis of published values of empirical inbreeding depression revealed much higher values for all components of the life cycle (see Section 5.5). Moreover, inbreeding depression is typically greater in more stressful environments than in more benign captive ones. This has led to a systematic underestimation of the importance of inbreeding depression, leading in turn to serious underestimates of extinction probability (O'Grady et al., 2006). Similarly, most analyses do not account for all major factors contributing toward stochasticity (Melbourne & Hastings, 2008). Moreover, the failure to include all the stochastic processes can lead to a misinterpretation of the relative importance of environmental and demographic variability. Using a full stochastic model, Melbourne & Hastings (2008) observe that demographic sources of stochasticity are the prominent cause of variability in their experimental study system with the red flour beetle. Conversely, a standard, simpler model leads to the erroneous conclusion that environmental variability dominates. Demographic factors entail a much higher extinction risk for the same variability level, thus demonstrating that current estimates of extinction risk could be greatly underestimated. Population dynamics is typically complex and parameters are often difficult to estimate. The use of untested assumptions may result in biased results, especially when combined with inadequate sensitivity testing as apparently happened in the PVA of the Eastern wolf in the Algonquin Provincial Park, Canada (Theberge *et al.*, 2006), which may have led to counterproductive and inadequate management decisions (Patterson & Murray, 2008).

PVA and PHVA leave the door open to errors and misinterpretation, in the worst case intentionally to support a preconceived management strategy. Patterson & Murray (2008) point out that limited attention has been directed at ensuring that PVAs remain objective and impartial in their assessment. They list as potential problems selective use of analyses to support a particular point of view (e.g. data dredging), or slanting interpretation of results to emphasize a perceived conservation need.

5.7.3 Model-derived MVPs

Because of the large number of potential problems in PVAs and PHVAs and the lack of time to determine essential base-line information to parameterise these analyses, 'rules of thumb' based on genetic and evolutionary considerations have been widely applied as surrogates for MVP to make management decisions.

Franklin (1980) introduced a popular and widely applied 'rule of thumb', the '50/500' rule. The rule focuses on the two main considerations crucially important for endangered species to retain their evolutionary potential: (1) short-term or immediate danger to small populations due to inbreeding; and (2) long-term loss of quantitative genetic variation limiting future evolutionary change and adaptation.

Based on genetic theory and an empirical study, Franklin quantified minimum effective population size to be at least 50 in the short term and 500 in the long term, which is the '50/500' rule. The '50' in the rule comes from the experience of animal breeders that inbreeding depression is balanced by selection if inbreeding depression is less than 1%. Applying the simple formula (equation (5.1)), this requires an N_e of at least 50. Importantly, as the '50' was derived from information on the effects of inbreeding depression, it refers to the inbreeding effective size, N_{ei}. It must be stressed that the '50' does not refer to the total number of individuals or to adults or reproducing animals (see Box 5.2, definitions in Appendix 4). At least 50 'genetically effective' individuals are necessary to avoid inbreeding depression. N_{ei} can be estimated from pedigree data (rarely available) or from heterozygosity data, which can be derived from molecular genetic screening. Importantly, N_{ei} depends on population history and can be larger than census size in declining populations.

For example, Storz *et al.* (2002) tested the hypothesis that $N_{ev} < N < N_{ei}$ due to a recent demographic bottleneck in a long-term study of savannah baboons. Indeed, N_{ev} was smaller and N_{ei} larger than census size N, as predicted. Estimated N_{ei} was 2.2 to 7.2 larger than N. In northern white rhinoceros (Braude & Templeton, 2009), N_{ei} was with 61 higher than $N = 23$, $N_{ev} = 41$, and the lower Frankham boundary. In contrast, the southern subspecies' N_{ei} is less than double the size as the northern subspecies despite a census size of almost 8500 ($N_{ei} = 106$). The remaining subspecies of the black rhinoceros demonstrate impressively the impact of population history on census and inbreeding effective population size (Harley *et al.*, 2005).

- *Diceros bicornis bicornis*: vulnerable, N: $600_{(1980)}$, 1310_{now}; $N_{e(SMM)} = 1876$.
- *D. b. michaeli*: critically endangered, N: $2000_{(1980)}$, 520_{now}; $N_{e(SMM)} = 5173$.
- *D. b. minor*: critically endangered, N: $110_{(1930s)}$, $8000_{(1980)}$, 1775_{now}, $N_{e(SMM)} = 1472$.

In *D. b. minor*, the estimate of the inbreeding effective size under a mutational model appropriate for the method used (microsatellites: $N_{e(SMM)}$), indicates a N_{ei} which is an order of magnitude higher than N at the population minimum. Moreover, the effective population size for *D. b. michaeli* is more than twice that for the other two subspecies despite current census being the smallest. The N value thus primarily reflects just population numbers rather than the genetic diversity represented by N, which is determined by the genetic diversity of their ancestors and population history.

Whilst the '50' refers to the inbreeding effective size, the '500' refers to the variance effective size, N_{ev}. To retain long-term quantitative genetic variation, the rate of loss of variation due to random genetic drift must be equal to or smaller than the rate of gain by mutation. Effective population size at equilibrium between drift and mutations can be estimated on the basis of the estimation of several genetic parameters, namely:

- additive genetic variance, V_A;
- increment of additive genetic variance per generation due to mutation, V_m;
- environmental variance, VE;
- heritability, h^2.

The equations and their rationale can be found in the original literature (Franklin, 1980; Soulé, 1980) or text books. Here, these details are not essential, but it must be stressed that the derivation of the '50/500' rule and alternative rules are based on these theoretical assumptions and how the genetic parameters are estimated. Franklin excluded the role which selection plays and used a study on the abdominal bristle number in *Drosophila* to estimate h^2 and V_m. Based on these empiric data, the equations resolve as long-term $N_e = 500$. There is general agreement that the conservation of quantitative genetic variation is essential for conservation management, but the appropriate value of N_e and the underpinning parameters remain controversially discussed. Lande (1995) stresses that new mutations are mostly deleterious and comes to the conclusion that a long-term $N_e = 5000$ is required, whereas Franklin & Frankham (1998) suggest 500–1000 and Lynch & Lande (1998) 1000 as the long-term N_e. Crucially, a captive-bred or *in-situ* managed population must be bred up as fast as possible to reach a variance effective size, because the population will loose genetic variability due to drift as long as it remains lower than the variance effective size, N_{ev}, whether it is Franklin's 500 or Lynch's 5000.

Using the rule of thumb can be highly problematic and sometimes even counter-productive for animal management. It ignores demographic and ecological stochasticity and behavioural limitations (Allee effects) such as colonial breeding. An important danger is using an inappropriate effective size estimator or even census size. Despite that the lower size boundary refers to an effective size, which might be larger than the census size, it has been argued that populations are unlikely to survive once the census is below the 50 boundary of Franklin's rule. Braude & Templeton (2009) discuss in detail possible misinterpretations and dangers. They highlight the example of the northern white rhinoceros population, where the very low census population size was lower than the '50' in the '50/500' rule. Ignoring the fact that N_{ei} actually might be larger than N, concerns were raised about the long-term genetic viability (Walpole et al., 2001). Policy-makers might have interpreted this as a 'write off' with little prospect of surviving – an interpretation unfortunately not unique for the northern white rhinoceros (Allendorf & Luikart, 2006) – and this might have tragically contributed to its population's demise (Braude & Templeton, 2009).

5.7.4   The continuing value of MVP in the 'wild'

PVA and PHVA are laden with technical and philosophical problems. Evolutionary derived rules of thumb are highly sensitive to assumptions and the '50/500' rule changes to a '500/5000' rule when some assumptions are varied. On the other hand, average MVP of empirical estimates across a broad spectrum of taxa is approx 4200 (95% CI: 3577–5129) as outlined above, and converges to the upper value of total individuals contained in the '50/500' rule, which refers to genetically effective individuals. The average ratio of effective size N_e to the census size N is roughly 0.1 (Frankham, 1995) or 0.2 (Waples, 2002). Therefore, the effective population size of 500 translates to a census population of 2500 to 5000 adults. The estimation of mean N_e/N ratios over species depends on model assumptions and highlights that even the '50/500' rule cannot be elegantly translated into numbers that managers and non-biologists can easily understand and apply: N rather than N_{ei} or N_{ev}. Not to mention the large variance in N_e/N ratios or whether we should aim at a minimum long-term size N_{ev} of 500, 500–1000, 1000 or 5000. Moreover, all empirical and theoretical data indicate that identifiable threshold values or threshold bands do not exist as biological properties of populations.

Nevertheless, even the detractors of the concept stress that empirically estimated or model-based MVPs are reasonable order-of-magnitude estimates and reasonable rules of thumb if appropriate safety margins are adhered to. Excluding literal or narrow interpretations of the '50/500' rule (e.g. northern white rhinoceros), most conservation biologists now agree that the operational goal is to determine an MVP as a warning sign indicating that urgent action should be immediately considered. Importantly, the goal is not to maintain MVP, but to maintain populations well above the MVP estimate.

The main advantage of using this rule of thumb is that it represents a concrete target that can easily be communicated to policymakers. Lack of communication between science and conservation policy remains a serious problem in engaging the general public and policymakers in nature conservation. Generalities help to bridge the communication gap (Gibbons *et al.*, 2008). This applies especially to the communication of zoological gardens, both intra-organisational communication (many CEOs are now recruited from the economic sector), but also to the communication to visitors and stake-holders. Nevertheless, the caveats must be emphasised to ensure over-simplification with rules of thumb is not counter-productive. However, use of the '50/500' or similar quantitative rule of thumb must: (1) never override case-specific concrete conservation planning by detailed data analysis and modelling, and (2) assure proper in-depth training of conservation managers. Many organisations now offer training courses for wildlife conservation, both to achieve academic accreditation and to provide an out-of-university academic foundation to conservation practitioners including zoo staff. Especially, the latter courses are in danger of over-simplification and this needs to be urgently addressed.

5.7.5 MVPs for captive populations

Those captive programmes that assess genetic and demographic status and extinction risk normally use a deterministic approach, which treats genetic and demographic risks separately and which does not include stochasticity (implemented in PM2000: Pollak *et al.*, 2002). PVA analysis typically also includes environmental, demographic and genetic stochasticity. Such an approach has recently been developed specifically for captive situations (ZooRisk software; Faust *et al.*, 2008). In analogy to IUCN's Red List, the software categorises a population's risk of extinction as *Critical*, *Endangered*, *Vulnerable*, or *Low Risk* in captivity using five standardised risk tests. The threshold values are as follows.

Criteria	Critical	Endangered	Vulnerable	Low risk
Probability of extinction ($P(E)$) in 100 years	50%–100%	20%–49%	10%–19%	0%–9%
Distribution of breeding-aged, mixed-sex groups in # zoos	1	2	3	>3
Current number of breeding-aged animals (male. female)	0.0 to 3.3	4.4 to 6.6	3.3 to 10.10	>10.10
Reproduction in the last generation as # pairs reproducing	0–2	3–5	6–9	>9
Gene diversity (GD) of starting population or modelled population in 100 years	<0.75 or <0.5	<0.8 or <0.75	<0.9 or <0.9	>0.9 or 0.9

Box 5.2 · *The Bali mynah Species Survival Plan*

The Bali mynah is critically endangered, hovering immediately above extinction in the wild for several years. The last stronghold of the species is at Bali Barat National Park set up just for the Bali mynah's survival. The wild population was at an all-time low of just 6 birds in 2001, after the late 1990s wild population of 3–4 dozen was reduced by poachers for the illegal pet trade. Continuing releases raised the number of wild birds to 24 by March, 2005.

Its decline was caused by the urbanisation of the island and by illegal trapping for the caged-bird trade; indeed, the number of captive birds bought on the black market is estimated to be twice the number of legally acquired individuals in the captive breeding programme. The Bali mynah is listed in Appendix I of CITES. Trade even in captive-bred specimens is strictly regulated and the species is not generally available legally to private individuals. However, experienced aviculturalists may become affiliated with the captive-breeding programme, allowing them to legally keep this species.

The Bali mynah SSP aims to maintain a captive population size that can meet the pro-gramme's educational and conservation goals far into the future (Earnhardt *et al.*, 2009). The conservation goals of SSPs specifically include *in-situ* reintroduction, if possible (Chapter 6). Management aims to minimise the risk of extinction by minimising the loss of GD and by avoiding large fluctuations in population size and structure. The AZA Passerine TAG recommended a target population size of 250 birds but the SSP regulated population size at 200 birds, because of limited space available at zoos. Earnhardt *et al.* (2009) seek the smallest possible population size that retains 90% or more of gene diversity over the next 100 years, the threshold 'acceptable to population managers'. The authors use the ZooRisk software (Faust et al., 2008) to decide whether 200 or 250 animals are adequate. This is the first peer-reviewed analysis using the software and its underpinning assumptions.

ZooRisk's risk categorisation method rates the SSP population as *Low Risk* with an extinction risk of 0% and a GD of 93.87+-1.44% over the next 100 years under current genetic management. If genetic management would be abandoned, the gene diversity would decrease to 86.2 ± 5.6%, which ZooRisk categorises as Vulnerable. The authors contend that the SSP can be managed at 200, and that there are few or no intrinsic or extrinsic threats to future viability. Further, they argue that these results 'reinforce perceptions of population managers about long-term viability and should allay concerns of Bali mynah SSP participants about the risk of unplanned future population size decline or extinction'.

The first peer-reviewed presentation of the classification is the analysis of the Bali mynah SSP breeding programme (Box 5.2). ZooRisk is a welcome development to assess population viability in captivity and long-term exhibition needs, but needs further testing with real and simulated data. Is 9.9% likelihood of population extinction in capacity within 100 years really a low risk in captivity?

SSPs specifically aim at reintroduction and ZooRisk defines a 'reliable' population as one that meets exhibition and reintroduction needs with no genetic considerations other than extinction risk in captivity and GD. Yet, the approach ignores the problem of genetic adaptation to captivity and loss of fitness after reintroduction (Section 4.2.2), violation of neutrality of genetic loci, which is an assumptions for genetic management (Section 4.2.2), representation of the source population by founders (Section 5.2.1), loss of allelic diversity (Section 5.5), and demographic history of the source population prior to extracting founders (Section 6.8). Thus, we disagree that the sole reliance on the criteria used is meaningful to assess captive breeding for reintroduction. Not only is the reliance on the 90% gene diversity threshold value problematic, but also the time-frame as all data now indicate that captive breeding should be as short as possible to have a realistic chance of successful reintroduction (Sections 4.2.2, 6.7.4 and 6.8).

5.8   Reproductive technologies

Reproductive technologies, developed in humans and domestic livestock, can be adapted for and applied to minimise genetic drift, inbreeding and genetic adaptation in captivity (Chapter 6). Modern approaches include AI, ET, IVF, GRB, and cloning or SCNT. Cloning is very controversial, especially because of ethical issues, policy implications (giving the impression that even extinct species could be resurrected – thus we could stop worrying about extinctions, couldn't we?), the very high cost involved and the applicability to a very small number of well-researched species. The advantage of the other methods, in theory, is that the conservation of viable germplasm and embryos allows managers to hedge against random genetic drift, inbreeding, genetic adaptation and catastrophic population crashes. Despite these significant potential benefits, reproductive technologies have, to the best of our knowledge, been successfully incorporated only into the breeding plans and recovery of black-footed ferret, cheetah, giant panda, whooping crane, and Wyoming toad (Frankham *et al.*, 2010; Holt & Lloyd, 2009; Howard *et al.*, 2003; Jones & Nicolich, 2001; Wildt *et al.*, 1997; Wildt *et al.*, 2003). Not only is the application to endangered species rather complex, because of the species' biology and limiting logistical barriers, but also these technologies are species-specific or inefficient because of insufficient knowledge of the basic reproductive biology of most endangered species. Technical problems and lack of basic biological information about most non-domestic species constitute major challenges. Research is highly biased towards species similar to domestic animals such as felids, where methods have been developed, and towards a small number of enigmatic flagship species such as the giant panda. Research is urgently required, but there are major logistical, financial, legal and cultural barriers for further research (see below).

Soulé *et al.* (1986) based their modern ark framework explicitly on the hope that reproductive technologies will advance so much in 200 years that they will play a significant role in conserving biodiversity. However, judging from the current pace of the development and application of suitable reproductive technologies for conservation, there is no indication that the progress will speed up in the foreseeable future (Andrabi & Maxwell, 2007). Thus, the foundation and rationale to placing the modern ark into the 200 year time-frame or even the 100 year time-frame is in doubt.

5.9 Research constraints

Reproductive technologies have a great potential for minimising some of the most negative effects of captive breeding: inbreeding depression, further loss of genetic variability once in captivity and genetic adaptation. Yet, major gaps in knowledge remain. For example, cryopreservation of germplasm (spermatozoa, oocytes, embryo, blastomere) can significantly contribute to increased generation time in captivity, which in turn is one of the most powerful mechanisms to prevent genetic deterioration and adaptation, but too little is known (Williams & Hoffman, 2009). Especially in this field, urgently needed research is hampered by legislation and human attitudes, which aim to conserve biodiversity and are well meaning. A strong antagonism has developed in the conservation community, often expressed by a strong suspicion of technological solutions such as reproductive biotechnologies. This is partly based on lack of information on these technologies, the unease on the reliance on technological solutions, which target symptoms but not the causes of biodiversity loss, and the discrepancy between the exuberant hope some place on technological solutions, *versus* the practical limitations and the continuing urgency for further research. At London Zoo (ZSL), Holt & Lloyd (2009) expressed this dilemma most succinctly stating that: 'we frequently face the paradoxical situation whereby we are requested on the one hand to develop technologies that will contribute to the survival of a threatened species, but are prevented by the animal managers from undertaking suitable research because too few animals are available. On occasion, we have sought to overcome this problem by proposing similar research on a related, but more common surrogate species, only to be told that this was unacceptable because there was no justification to study this "nonthreatened" species. . . . This paradox is compounded by the legal system, which allows qualified veterinarians to perform procedures such as electroejaculation, AI, oocyte recovery and embryo transfer, provided the purpose is explicitly to breed the animals. If the electroejaculation or AI procedure is actually being undertaken for the development of optimal freezing protocols, the entire scenario changes into a research project. This imposes a new and nontrivial layer of bureaucracy that requires project and personal licences, designated premises, and a research outline with justifications such as the minimum number of animals needed to obtain statistically valid data'.

Such problems are widespread and not limited to UK law, which governs ZSL. For example, the conservation value of the central repository of frozen germplasm and somatic cells in Europe will be very limited because of the legal hurdles to import and export such samples. For years, we have attempted the molecular analysis of the founder stock of the pygmy hog in order to achieve clarity on relatedness as most of the founders are from a very small geographic area and might represent a single family group. Yet, all attempts have failed because the cost-efficient solution of the analysis at the laboratory at headquarters in Europe failed because the export of DNA materials from India is prohibited whilst the local analysis in a laboratory in India failed because of cost implications.

Key concepts
(1) The 'Noah's Ark' paradigm and the concept of the 'Millennium Ark' are responses to the biodiversity crisis and the loss of species in the wild. Zoos often talk about 'captive assurance populations' of some species, as if these were on board an 'Ark'. It assumes that species can be 'saved' through captive breeding and successfully reintroduced in the future, whereby the future date is mostly unspecified.
(2) Population size matters. Small populations are critically endangered because they are small. Smallness increases extinction risk through many interacting factors including demographic and genetic stochasticity and catastrophes. It has been argued that genetic factors are overemphasised and that they are irrelevant compared to demographic factors and catastrophes. However, meta-analysis of extinctions in the wild, laboratory experiments and population genetic theory all indicate a strong link between extinction risk and reduced genetic variation.
(3) Genetic diversity − both heterozygosity (i.e. gene diversity, GD) and allelic diversity − is, on average, ultimately vital for the long-term survival, evolutionary potential and future adaptability of populations. Loss of genetic diversity causes many negative effects including Allee effects, random genetic drift, inbreeding and inbreeding depression. Small populations continue to lose genetic diversity over time and the loss is in general irreversible in captivity. The theoretically only positive effect of small population size is the purging of deleterious alleles, but all data indicate that purging is of minor importance for conservation.
(4) The concept of minimum viable populations, MVPs, has been applied widely for *in-situ* conservation. However, the concept and the methods to determine MVP

values by population (and habitat) viability analysis, PVA and PHVA, are laden with technical and philosophical problems. MVP estimates are never to be understood as exact cut-off values but as reasonable order-of-magnitude estimates for the determination of warning signs that indicate that urgent action should be taken. Otherwise, populations are likely to be managed inadvertently or implicitly for extinction.

(5) Analogous to MVPs *in-situ*, the genetic target to manage captive populations for future reintroduction is defined as the 'maintenance of 90% of the genetic variation in the source (wild) population over a period of 200 years' by Soulé *et al.* (1986). Subsequently, the target has been watered down to the retention of 90% of gene diversity (GD) for 100 years. This is widely assumed as the accepted approach by zoo managers. However, this ignores the empiric and theoretical data which have accumulated over the last 20 years, which emphasise the problem of genetic adaptation to captivity, loss of fitness after reintroduction, representation of the source population by founders, loss of allelic diversity, and demographic history of the source population prior to extracting founders. Thus, the reliance on the 90% gene diversity threshold value and the time-frame of 100 or 200 years is problematic and requires urgent re-evaluation. Many breeding programmes might inadvertently or implicitly manage for failed reintroductions.

6 · Captive breeding and zoos

'What I had in mind was an almost completely new concept of the motivation of a zoological garden . . . The idea was that the captive colonies should be set up . . . as a safeguard against extinction, while at the same time the most stringent efforts should be made to preserve the wild habitat and wild populations of the species concerned and to release back to the wild captive-bred animals when their habitat had been made safe. This, it seemed to me, was a zoo's major raison d'être.' (Gerald Durrell)

6.1 Introduction

There is general agreement that captive breeding, the process of reproducing animals in human controlled environments in zoos or other *ex-situ* facilities, can save threatened species from extinction. The IUCN technical guidelines on the *Management of Ex-Situ Populations for Conservation* officially recognise the role that zoos, botanic gardens, aquariums, gene banks and research facilities could play in species conservation (IUCN, 1987a, 1992, 2002). This declaration of intent is believed to indicate an evolution in the strategic application of *ex-situ* conservation, as well as reflecting the recent developments in the science and practice associated with it (Maunder & Byers, 2005).

The first formal invocation of captive breeding was in the 1973 CITES agreement. Here, the Convention (Article VII) refers to the benefits of *ex-situ* strategies for some species by facilitating some trade whilst its wild populations remain subject to an outright trade ban. However, the strongest political context in which *ex-situ* conservation could flourish was ostensibly rooted in the IUCN World Conservation Strategy, *Caring for the Earth*, which in turn related to the United Nations Conference on Environment and Development's acceptance of the CBD at Rio de Janeiro in 1992. It was in the wake of the Rio Summit that the first strategy document, WZCS, was launched in 1993 by the global zoo and aquarium community [IUDZG/CBSG (IUCN/SSC), 1993]. The WZCS declared a commitment by zoos and aquariums to biodiversity conservation, by way of education, research and via 'establishing *ex-situ* zoo populations by providing the nucleus for re-establishment or reinforcement of wild populations in nature'. Ten years later, an updated strategy document, WZACS, defined the strategic vision of the members of WAZA in support of its overarching conservation mission. This document set out policies and standards to be reached under headings relating to the key functions and activities of all zoos and aquariums, focussing on the long-term demonstrable achievement of conservation (WAZA, 2005).

Even though the overarching documents produced by the zoo community may indeed be 'shaping strategic thinking and guide hands-on practical work' (WAZA, 2005), the crucial question is whether enough resources are dedicated to breeding threatened species in zoos, and more significantly whether species are actually being saved and whether zoos are the best option to save some species. Whether captive breeding for conservation should be the main focus of zoos is still fervently debated; some authors arguing that there is no evidence that zoos so far have devoted more space to threatened species in their collections (Magin *et al.*, 1994; Frynta *et al.*, 2010).

Animals kept in zoos are bred for four main reasons, as an aid to species conservation, to sustain animal populations for exhibition (and therefore reduce the number of animals that need to be collected from the wild), for research or for education to serve as ambassadors for their wild counterparts. But, if captive breeding is to become an effective tool for species conservation within zoos, this requires resolution at two fundamental levels. First, which species require captive breeding and, second, what space is truly available in zoos for taxa in need of captive breeding. Such questions have been tackled sporadically in the literature, some as early as Soulé *et al.* (1986). However, issues such as the selection of species for captive breeding in zoos are still unresolved, with examination of cost-effectiveness of captive breeding choices not pursued beyond analyses in Balmford *et al.* (1996). In practice, organising the zoo community to dedicate sufficient resources to endangered species breeding is perhaps less complicated than it seems, because it is possible to plan space for animals in zoos. Much debate has taken place on what zoo collection planning should be (Chapter 3), ranging from individualistic (not necessarily *laissez faire*), led by the notion that zoos are 'decentralised sovereign institutions', to slightly more prescriptive decision keys for species selection as suggested in Wemmer & Derrickson (1995).

It is correct that a more holistic institutional planning process is required, since zoos must balance the need to entertain and contribute to conservation, but there is also a need to develop realistic and systematic plans for the captive breeding of threatened animals. The latter is affected by the difficulty of obtaining sufficient numbers of very rare species for efficient demographic and genetic management; because of the difficulties (technical, infrastructure, and perceived prohibitive costs) associated with keeping threatened animals in captivity; but also because of differences in institutional understanding on how zoos should best contribute to conservation.

Clear and rational criteria for identifying which threatened taxa zoos should focus on are necessary. Ideas for strategic collection planning vary. Some plans concentrate on optimising resource use and minimising programme duration with reintroduction in mind whereas others focus on using species for conservation education or conservation research. This chapter starts by examining captive breeding successes; species that have been saved from extinction by breeding in zoos and release of captive-bred individuals to the wild. We then examine which species may require captive breeding, and how a rational system for selection can be applied. We contrast this with how zoos actually choose species to breed in their collections, and how much it costs to keep animals in captivity, using data available on vertebrates (the mainstay of zoos). Finally, we describe the types, numbers and effectiveness of managed *ex-situ* animal breeding programmes.

6.2 Captive breeding successes

In its most basic form, managed *ex-situ* populations can assist biodiversity conservation by serving as a genetic and demographic reservoir of critically endangered species; a 'last resort' strategy. Indeed, there are species that have become extinct in the wild, which have been saved (at least in the short term) through direct manipulative intervention. For several high-profile species, such as the Arabian oryx (Stanley Price, 1989), the California condor (Snyder & Snyder, 2000) and Przewalski's horse (Van Dierendonck & Wallis de Vries, 1996), zoo populations have provided source animals for their re-establishment in the wild. Despite such high-profile successes, the number of species that has actually been saved from extinction by captive breeding programmes is small. In 1990, seven species (five mammals and two birds) had been successfully captive-bred in zoos and then reintroduced to areas of their former range (Jenkins, 1992; Magin *et al.*, 1994); this number in 2010 (IUCN, 2010) rose by one mammal species only (Table 6.1).

Extinction in the wild has been recorded in 153 out of 247 territories in the IUCN Red List of Threatened Species (IUCN, 2010). A total of 36 taxa: 19 vertebrates (one mammal, two birds, one reptile, two amphibians and 12 ray-finned fishes) and 17 invertebrates (14 molluscs) are currently only found in zoos. More than half of these species were from Sub-Saharan Africa. Status in captivity of species extinct in the wild varies between taxa (Table 6.2). According to data from ISIS (ISIS, 2010), all fish species are found in relatively large numbers, ranging from around 100 groups of the Mexican black-blotch pupfish, (or *cachorrito enano de Potosí*) to nearly 400 of the *Tiro*; all except the pupfish, which is found in a single institution, are in three or four aquaria (Contreras-Balderas & Lazano, 1994; Contreras-Balderas *et al.*, 2003). The two 'extinct in the wild' amphibians are also found in large populations in captivity, but are in a relatively small number of institutions. Numbers of the Socorro dove, no longer found in Socorro Island in the Mexican Revillagigedo Archipelago, are low in captivity (only three institutions involved), but the sole mammal, the Scimitar-horned oryx, numbers more than 8000–9000 individuals in more than 100 zoos, safari parks, ranches and private collections. A proposal is currently being developed to reintroduce the Socorro dove after successful control of feral cats. The Scimitar-horned oryx, in contrast, for which there are a number of studbooks for the species including an international studbook, and three coordinated captive breeding programmes in European, North American and Australasian zoos, have already been reintroduced into areas in Tunisia (Bou Hedma National Park 1985, Sidi Toui National Park 1999, Oued Dekouk National Park 1999), Morocco (Souss-Massa National Park 1995), and Senegal (Ferlo Faunal Reserve 1998, Guembuel Wildlife Reserve 1999). Reintroduction is also planned at a site in Niger.

There are examples of species that have been rescued from the brink of extinction through a number of different techniques. Because birds are amongst the best known of

Table 6.1 'Extinct in the wild' species that have been assisted through captive breeding and release into the wild. Data from compilations for each species in IUCN (2010)

Species Red List status, trend	Pre-intervention wild status	Captive breeding	Reintroduction
Black-footed ferret Endangered, Increasing	Historically, black-footed ferrets were found throughout the Great Plains, mountain basins, and semiarid grasslands of west central North America – from southern Canada to northern Mexico wherever its obligate prey, prairie dogs, were located. Populations had declined to near extinction by the 1970s due to loss of prey and disease. A small remnant population (around 100 animals or less) was discovered in 1981 near Meeteetse, in NW Wyoming, but decimated by Disease in 1985.	The black-footed ferret captive breeding programme was initiated in October 1985. Eighteen black-footed ferrets were captured between 1985 and 1987 from the last-known population in Wyoming to start the captive breeding population. There are currently nearly 300 ferrets kept in captivity. Since 1987, over 6000 ferret kits have been produced through captive breeding. There are currently six institutions (one federal facility and five zoos) participating in the propagation programme.	To date there have been 18 reintroduction efforts, only 3 of which are self sustaining (South Dakota and Wyoming; Arizona, Colorado, South Dakota, and Utah; Arizona, Kansas, Montana, New Mexico, South Dakota, and Mexico), and three declining or extirpated populations in Montana. Over 2000 ferrets have been released. Approximately 500 breeding adults in the wild, less than 250 of which were actually born in the wild.
Red wolf Critically Endangered, Increasing	The Red wolf's historic range may have extended northward into central Pennsylvania and even further north into NE US and extreme eastern Canada. Recent genetic evidence supports a similar but even greater extension of historic range into southern Ontario, Canada.	A captive breeding programme established in 1976, using 17 animals (14 founders) captured in Texas and Louisiana. By 1985 the captive population had grown to 65 individuals in six zoological facilities; by September 2002 there were 175 wolves in 33 facilities. There are also two propagation projects on small islands off the South Atlantic and Gulf Coasts of the USA.	Captive red wolves were reintroduced to NE North Carolina in 1987, 1991 and from 1992 to 1998. By September 2002, 102 animals had been released with a minimum of 281 descendants produced in the wild since 1987. A total wild population believed to be at least 100 individuals is present in NE North Carolina.

(cont.)

Table 6.1 (*cont.*)

Species Red List status, trend	Pre-intervention wild status	Captive breeding	Reintroduction
Wild/Przewalski's horse Endangered, Increasing	Until the eighteenth century, the species ranged from Germany and Russian Steppes east to Kazakhstan, Mongolia and N China. After this time, the species went into catastrophic decline. The last wild population of Przewalski's horses survived until recently in SW Mongolia and adjacent parts of China. Wild horses were last seen in 1969, in Dzungarian Gobi Desert in Mongolia.	Several American and European zoos collaborated in breeding wild horses for reintroduction. All horses alive today are descended from only 13 or 14 individuals. While dozens of zoos worldwide still have Przewalski's in small numbers, there are also specialised reserves dedicated primarily to the species in Ukraine and China. In China, there is a large captive population of approximately 123 Przewalski's horses	Between 1992 and 2004, 90 captive-born horses were released in Mongolia. A further three males were translocated in 2007. Over 100 free-ranging horses now make up one population, and close to 200 in a second. A third reintroduction site was started in 2004 where 22 horses were reintroduced. In China, one harem group roams free on the Chinese side of the Dzungarian Gobi since 2007.
Père David's deer Endangered, Increasing	This deer was restricted to swamps and wetlands in southern China. Its range shrank and its population declined due to hunting and land reclamation as human population expanded. The last wild animal was shot in 1939. However, during the Qing Dynasty (1616–1911), deer were kept in the Nanyuang Royal Hunting Garden. In 1895, most deer escaped from the garden and were hunted; only 20–30 animals survived. In 1900, the garden was occupied by troops and the remaining deer shot.	Before the demise of the royal herd of Père David's deer in 1900, deer had been introduced into private collections in the UK, France and Germany. During the first decade of the twentieth century, the 11th Duke of Bedford in the UK gathered the last 18 Père David's deer in the world to form a breeding herd. Despite inbreeding, the captive population increased, and since WWII animals were spread through captive facilities worldwide; captive animals were sent back to Beijing Zoo in 1956.	There have been two reintroductions of Père David's deer to China. The first 38 animals from Woburn Abbey in 1985 and 1987 to the relic site of the Nanyuang Royal Hunting Garden, and a second reintroduction of 39 deer in 1986 to a site on the Yellow Sea coast in E China. This group was selected from five zoos in the UK. In 2003 and 2006 another two groups of deer were released. There were 950 Père David's deer in the reserve in 2006.

| Wisent/European bison
Vulnerable, Increasing | Historically distributed throughout western, central, and south-eastern Europe and Caucasus. By the end of the nineteenth century, there were only two populations of European bison left in the wild. Both were driven extinct in the wild in 1919 and 1927. Subsequently, the species survived only in a few European zoological gardens. | Captive populations of about 1400 individuals are well distributed in 30 different countries worldwide. Some captive animals are not recorded in the European Bison Pedigree Book, so this is likely to be an underestimate. Population structure is such that approximately 60% of individuals are sexually mature. The effective population size is smaller than the total population size, because European bison is a polygynous species, so not all males have the opportunity to breed. | As a result of reintroductions and introductions, it now occurs in free-ranging and semi-free herds in Poland, Lithuania, Belarus, Russian Federation, Ukraine, and Slovakia. The total population of free-ranging bison now stands at *c.* 1800. The free ranging population increased more or less steadily from the mid 1960s to a peak of *c.* 2000 in the early 1990s. Following a period of decline in the mid–late 1990s, the population has expanded, although ongoing growth is limited by a number of factors. |
| Californian condor
Critically Endangered, Increasing | The species declined rapidly throughout its historic range from British Colombia to Baja California during the twentieth century and reportedly disappeared from outside California, USA, in 1937. Decline has been principally attributed to persecution and accidental ingestion of lead shot from carcasses, resulting in lead poisoning. The population had dropped to an all-time low of just 22 birds by 1981. | In 1987, the species became extinct in the wild when the last of the six wild individuals was captured to join a captive-breeding recovery programme involving 27 birds. The success of the scheme has seen an increase from one chick hatched in 1988 to an annual hatch of 25–30 birds in recent years. The Peregrine Fund (at the World Center for Birds of Prey), Los Angeles Zoo, San Diego Wild Animal Park and Oregon Zoo are involved. | A total of 154 condors were released into the wild between 1992 and 2003. Overall survival of released birds has been high, although it is estimated that rates of mortality in the wild still exceed sustainable levels. By December 2006 there were 130 wild birds at five release sites, although only 44 were mature individuals (over six years old, the age at which breeding commences at the very earliest). |

(cont.)

Table 6.1 (cont.)

Species Red List status, trend	Pre-intervention wild status	Captive breeding	Reintroduction
Guam rail Extinct in the Wild	Decline and extinction in the wild result from predation by the introduced brown tree snake. Species was widely distributed until 1968 when, along with most other indigenous species, it started to decline. In 1981, the population was estimated at c. 2000, in 1983 it was reckoned to number fewer than 100 and, by 1987, it was extirpated from the wild.	Captive breeding started in 1984. Since 1987, efforts have been under way to establish a self-sustaining, experimental population on the nearby snake-free island of Rota. In 1999, birds bred there for the first time. In late 1998, some captive-reared birds were released in northern Guam, into a small area (24 ha) protected from snakes by a barrier and trapping, and these birds are also breeding. It survives in captive-breeding facilities in Guam and in 14 zoos in the USA (c. 180 birds in total).	An 'experimental population' of 22 Guam rails were released on Rota in December 1989 and January 1990. The site proved to be unsatisfactory probably due to the presence of dense grassland habitat. In February 1991, another 33 rails were released. This release appeared to be more successful than previous ones. Releases were discontinued until the spring of 1995 due to the low production of rails at captive breeding facilities. High production allowed release of 117 birds in January, August and September 2000.

Table 6.2 *Examples of threatened species surviving only in captivity. Data from IUCN (2010) and, ISIS (2010)*

Species	Cause of disappearance and current situation in captivity	Conservation recovery potential
Fishes		
Yarkon bleak Israel	Very abundant historically but declined sharply between 1950 and 1970. Population stable until 1999, when a drought resulted in the riverine habitat disappearing; species dropping to near extinction. The last remaining individuals were taken from the remnants of the river and bred in captivity.	Two groups now have been released (for conservation purposes) back into the wild from the captive stock. One group has not reproduced. It is not known if the other group has reproduced yet (surveys are required).
Butterfly splitfin Mexico	Formerly found throughout the Ameca River drainage in Mexico; the type locality is Teuchitlán River, Jalisco. The species was only ever found in an area about 15 km in diameter (Miller & Fitzsimmons, 1971). It was declared extinct in the wild in 1996. In 1997, a population was rediscovered living in springs near the town of Ameca, at the headwaters of the Teuchitlán River, the river from which all historical records of butterfly splitfins originate.	Ritchie *et al.* (2007) found that the wild population of this this fish is much more genetically diverse than stocks, which have been maintained in captivity for up to 10 years. Its effective population size is more than an order of magnitude greater. Introducing fish from captive stocks cannot substantially increase genetic diversity, and may promote the spread of deleterious alleles adapted to captivity.
Potosi pupfish Mexico	This pupfish was restricted to the '*Manantial* (Spring) *El Potosí*', in Ejido Catering Rodríguez, in the Galeana municipality. The spring was found at the foot of the Cerro El Potosí, 1900 m above sea level. The species disappeared from the spring in 1996 due to habitat destruction.	Captive breeding in 300 groups within three institutions. No releases to the wild contemplated.
La Palma pupfish Mexico	This small Mexican pupfish was only recently described in 1993; it became extinct in the wild in 1998. It was found only in '*El Charco Palmal*' spring, from the Bolsón de Sandia, Nuevo Leon. This fish originally inhabited a small pool of water that was spring fed, due to groundwater use and over-exploitation the pond dried and all fish were exterminated.	Captive breeding continued in 300 groups within 4 institutions. No releases to the wild contemplated at present.
Black-blotch pupfish Mexico	Extinct since April 1996. The species was restricted to the '*Manantial El Potosf*'.	Captive breeding in around 99 groups within one institution. No releases to the wild contemplated.

(cont.)

Table 6.2 (*cont.*)

Species	Cause of disappearance and current situation in captivity	Conservation recovery potential
Golden skiffia Mexico	The genus contains four species, endemic to the Mesa Central area of Mexico. They typically have a limited tolerance to environmental degradation, and so are susceptible to anthropogenic disturbance, especially eutrophication. The golden skiffia has been declared extinct in the wild by the IUCN.	Captive populations of the species are maintained in a variety of locations by aquarium hobbyists, research institutes and zoos. The history of this species is unclear, but believed to have descended from one stock collected in 1976. There are no current plans for re-establishing the species in the wild.
African cichlids Kenya/Tanzania	Over 200 distinct species of cichlids have evolved in Lake Victoria. Reasons for their plight are the introduction of alien predatory fish, and pollution.	Reintroduction of captive stock seems improbable.
Inconnu Russia	Fish of the nominate subspecies used to inhabit the Volga, Ural and Terek rivers, and migrate up to 3000 km upstream from the Caspian Sea to their spawning grounds in the spring. Following the construction of dams and hydropower reservoirs, the migration and natural reproduction has been impeded, and the taxon is now considered as extinct in the wild.	The stock survives in hatcheries and some populations are maintained by stocking, e.g. in the Caspian Sea.
Amphibians Wyoming toad USA	Restricted to the Laramie Basin, Wyoming; a historical range of 2330 km^2. As of 2002, extant only at Mortenson Lake National Wildlife Refuge through recent annual releases of captive-reared toadlets. Toads in this site are infected with the amphibian chytridiomycosis but predation, pesticide use, irrigation practices, and lack of genetic diversity might also limit their abundance. The cause of the original decline remains unknown but might be associated with the invasion of chytrid.	A recovery programme, using captive-bred animals and reintroductions, has been implemented in Mortenson Lake National Wildlife Refuge. There are 146 groups in 5 institutions, all in the US. The Nature Conservancy recently acquired a 800 ha tract at Mortensen Lake and has arranged a conservation easement with an adjacent landowner. Lake George is also a toad refuge. The success of the recovery programme probably depends on finding some way to combat chytridiomycosis in the wild.

Species / Country	Description
Kihansi spray toad Tanzania	Only known from the Kihansi Falls, in the Kihansi Gorge, in the Udzungwa Mountains. Its global range covered an area of less than two hectares, and searches for it around other waterfalls have not located any additional populations (Channing *et al.*, 2006). Reintroduction efforts should be preceded by an assessment of the species' habitat status and introduction of artificial sprinklers. It was not known from any protected areas. Sufficient minimum bypass flow from the dam is required to maintain the spray habitat. Captive breeding is ongoing in Toledo and New York Bronx Zoos.

Reptiles

Black soft-shell turtle India	This species is only known to exist in an artificial pond (Baizid Bostami shrine) near Chittagong, Bangladesh. In 1912, its distribution was given as between the Brahmaputra river system and the Arakan streams, but this may have been an incorrect assumption based on the distributions of other similar turtle species. The population size is estimated to be about 300 individuals, with an adult sex ratio of 1.5 male to one female; juveniles are present. There is no known plan for reintroduction of the species.

Birds

Species / Country	Description
Alagoas curassow Brazil	This curassow has been almost certainly extirpated from Alagoas and Pernambuco, NE Brazil. It went unreported between the mid seventeenth century, when found in Pernambuco, and 1951, when rediscovered around São Miguel dos Campos, Alagoas. Since the early 1970s, there are records from four forests in this region. Numbers were probably as few as 20, even in the 1960s. The most recent reports were of hunted individuals in 1984 and perhaps 1987 or 1988. A captive population, initially established in Rio de Janeiro in 1977, numbered 44 in 2003. Searches of remaining forest fragments in 2001 failed to find any trace of the species. CITES Appendix I and protected under Brazilian law. A private captive population, supplemented from the wild, was established in 1977, and divided between two well-known aviculturists in 1999 when it numbered 44, with 10 eggs in artificial incubation. A 30 km² forest remnant in Alagoas, Usina Serra Grande and Usina Leão and another site, Fazenda Petropolis, in Usina Santo Antonio have been identified for potential reintroduction attempts.
Socorro Dove Mexico	The species was extirpated from Socorro Island where it was formerly common; observations in 1957–1958 gave no indication that it was declining. The last sighting in the wild was in 1972, and all suitable habitat on the island has been surveyed subsequently without recording the dove. Captive populations were held in the USA and Germany, thought to total several hundred birds. It now appears that many are hybrids between Mourning and Socorro doves. A proposal is currently being developed to reintroduce the species. Some control of feral cats has been undertaken, but there are now plans to eradicate cats and sheep. Reports that rats have recently colonised Socorro have proved to be unfounded. Status of the birds in captivity may need further assessment.

(cont.)

Table 6.2 (cont.)

Species	Cause of disappearance and current situation in captivity	Conservation recovery potential
Mammals		
Scimitar-horned oryx Sahara	May formerly have been widespread across North Africa, at least in arid and Saharan areas, but now extinct in the wild over all its range. An estimated 500 oryx survived at least until 1985 in Chad and Niger, but by 1988 only a few dozen individuals survived in the wild and since then there have been no confirmed reports of any wild oryx surviving in the wild (Morrow in press).	The species is listed on CMS Appendix 1. A global captive breeding programme was initiated in the 1960s. In 2005 there were at least 1550 captive animals held in managed breeding programmes around the world. In addition, a large number, probably >4000, is kept in a private collection in the United Arab Emirates. Additional animals are likely held on private game ranches in the USA. Animals have been released into fenced protected areas in Tunisia, Morocco and Senegal. Reintroduction is currently also planned at a site in Niger.
Molluscs		
Partula snails French Polynesia	Species in the family Partulidae (genera *Partula* and *Samoana*) were once widespread over the high islands of French Polynesia. Between the mid 1970s and mid 1990s an estimated 56 species (two–thirds of the total of 72) have become extinct in the wild. This disastrous series of extinctions was due to the ill-judged introduction of a carnivorous snail as a bio-control agent against the giant African snail, a major horticultural pest. As a result of predation by carnivorous snails, the distribution of the surviving partulid species was rapidly reduced to tiny, isolated populations. A total of 10 (15% of total) species survive only in *ex-situ* populations. Extensive surveys have been conducted since 2003 and the situation on the ground is now well-documented. The epicentre of the species radiation of the genus *Partula* was on the Society Islands.	Two out of three known A. Samoana species are maintained in an international breeding programme. Four of the 33 *Partula* species in Raiatea survive in captivity and in 2004 a new species of *Partula* was discovered on the highest peak of the island, along with a species of *Samoana*. On Moorea, five of the original eight species are in breeding programmes and one species of *Partula* and one *Samoana* persist in the wild in a number of small, fragmented populations. Reintroduction of *Partula* has been attempted in the wild, after trial releases were undertaken in Royal Kew Botanical Gardens.

organisms, understanding which efforts have been successful in reducing deteriorating trends are instructive in understanding the role of captive breeding. Although there are caveats in determining 'what if' scenarios, Butchart et al.'s (2006) examination of what interventions significantly mitigated against bird extinctions may allow us to place captive breeding in the right context for preventing extinction of critically endangered species. Butchart et al.'s study identified those species for which conservation may have prevented extinction during 1994–2004. There were 241 Critically Endangered species of birds in 1994, out of which 27 taxa had population sizes of below 100 individuals or less than 200, but declining at a rate greater than 80% over 10 years or three generations (as specified by IUCN Red List criteria). Results showed that 16 of the 27 species that fit these criteria would probably have gone extinct in the absence of intervention. All such species had very small population sizes, a mean population size of 34 individuals in 1994 (numbers likely to be have been chosen for captive breeding programmes, see below). However, in 12 species (75%) conservation actions focussed on habitat protection and management, control of invasives (8, 50%), and in only six cases (33%) captive breeding and release was employed. In these six taxa, population estimates (ranging from 5 to 70 individuals) were significantly below the other remaining species; with one exception: the Chatham Island taiko. The salient point emerging from these data is that the importance or use of captive breeding as a tool to safeguard the species' future is variable, perhaps supporting Snyder et al.'s (1996) claim that captive breeding should not be invoked in the absence of comprehensive efforts to maintain or restore populations in wild habitats. However, there is no doubt that captive breeding has played a crucial role in recovery of some species for which effective alternatives are unavailable in the short term (Box 4.1).

6.3 Selecting species for conservation breeding

6.3.1 Triage

Despite the extensive literature on captive breeding, species selection is barely mentioned in any unequivocal manner. The only published guidelines, which merely advocate the importance of focusing on threatened or flagship species, are contained within the WZACS documents. But because of the lack of explicit criteria for captive breeding in zoos, Balmford et al. (1996) have suggested that such a system may perpetuate selection of charismatic/exhibition species. Thus, effective choice of species in zoos must not just consider biological and conservation-related variables, but also economic issues (Balmford et al., 1995; Snyder et al., 1996). This is against a background in which mammals in particular make up the majority of animals in zoos (Chapter 3); reflecting the known popularity of this over other groups (Bright & Morris, 2000; Chapter 8).

According to Ebenhard (1995), captive breeding can be labelled conservation breeding only if the ultimate goal is to recreate self-sustaining wild populations. Although it is clear that conservation breeding should be invoked for a species if its extinction is imminent, when to deploy an ex-situ conservation programme is often not clear-cut.

Box 6.1 · *Mauritius birds – time to recovery is long*

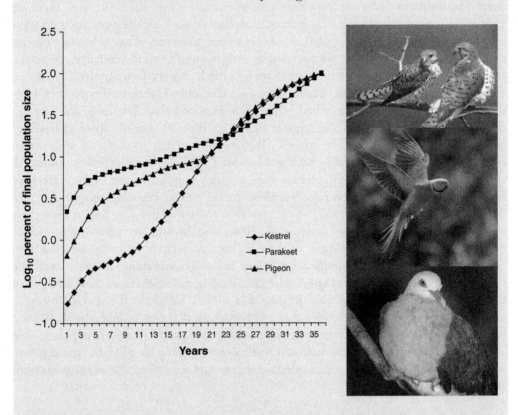

The best-known of Mauritius's endemic birds was the (now extinct) Dodo, which became very scarce on the mainland in the 1640s, persisting until c. 1662 on offshore islets. Most of the native vegetation on Mauritius has been cleared and replaced by sugar-cane, tea and conifer plantations. Only remnants of original forest remain (c. 5% of the island), mainly in the south-west around the Black River Gorge, but even here it is severely degraded by introduced animals and plants. Introduced deer, pigs and monkeys cause the most damage, but other exotics affecting forest regeneration are rats. Not surprisingly, all the endemic birds are threatened as a result of habitat loss and continuing degradation, and also because of nest-predation by introduced species. The kestrel suffered from organochlorine pesticides in the 1960s.

Without any doubt, the recovery of the three endemic birds in Mauritius is attributable to captive breeding and release efforts (Butchart *et al.*, 2006). The three species have made spectacular recoveries from very low numbers. The Mauritius kestrel was the first species to be kept in captivity, in 1973. Between late 1973 and early 1988 a total of five adults, four fledglings and three nestlings were taken from the wild for breeding (Jones *et al.*, 1995). First birds were bred in captivity in late 1978, but the first successes of the project were recorded in the 1984/1985 season when five young were reared. The involvement of the Peregrine Fund (USA) with their long experience in birds of prey recovery assisted in the programme. Three pairs were sent to Idaho, where they bred and 21 birds were returned to Mauritius (Jones *et al.*, 1995). Since then 200+ birds have been bred, using techniques such as double clutching both in the wild and in captivity, and hand-rearing of birds in captivity. Release of captive-bred kestrels started in 1984–1985. Birds hatched in the Gerald Durrell Endemic Wildlife Sanctuary (GDEWS) have been released in different areas within the Black River Gorges, Bambous Mountains and Moka range. The released birds have bred successfully and the kestrel population is now said to be stable, with a wild population estimated at between 600 and 800 birds.

The first pink pigeons were bred in captivity as early as 1977, and currently over 200 birds have been reared in the GDEWS (formerly the Black River Government Captive Breeding Centre) from 11 birds caught and a few eggs harvested from the wild. The captive population, around 200 birds, is located in Mauritius, Europe, USA, Singapore and India. Release of captive-bred pigeons into their original range has occurred since 1984. Currently, the estimated wild population is close to 500 birds in five localities (four on the mainland and one on an offshore island, *Ile aux Aigrettes*).

Echo parakeet numbers had been dwindling for decades as a result of habitat destruction and fragmentation. By 1986, the wild population was estimated at only 8–12 individuals, with three known females, limited to less than 50 km^2. In early 1993 the population was 16–22 birds including five established pairs. Since 1987 the species has been managed through the provision of nest boxes, supplemental feeding, and control of nest predators, close guarding of nest sites, and attempted captive breeding. Numbers in the wild have increased and the current population is around 150 birds.

Recovery trajectories for the systems for prioritising species' conservation, including captive breeding, are needed. The absence of such a system may explain the clear discrepancy between the number of species that may require conservation breeding, and the figure actually assisted by this. For example, Ebenhard (1995) suggested that at least 3000 species, most of them birds and mammals, were in need of conservation breeding; but at the time only 45–90 taxa were deemed to be self-sufficient in zoos. The numbers of taxa in zoos with viable populations are still low (see below), but unlike the 1990s scenario now against a background of an ever-increasing number of threatened species (Chapter 2).

Prioritising and allocating effort, in the certain knowledge that there is insufficient capital available to save and protect all of nature's diversity, has led to much discussion around the application of ecological (or conservation) triage (Bottrill *et al.*, 2008). Triage, meaning 'to sort', is a process of prioritisation first used in a medical context to allocate limited resources for the greatest good for the largest number of 'patients'; treatment of patients prioritised by injury severity. As used in conservation, triage is also a means of prioritising the allocation of limited resources to maximise conservation returns. However, the concept is enveloped in an evolving, and often acrimonious, debate at the centre of conservation biology. Much of the argument has been around how we achieve 'zero extinction' globally, engendering two fundamentally different approaches toward conservation, viz. 'no species extinction, at any cost' and 'extinction is inevitable for some species, let's manage the process rationally' (Jachowski & Kesler, 2009). The debate has a long history. Walker (1992) advocated the prioritisation of species (conservation status) according to the necessary functions that species or populations provided to ecosystem function; and the abandonment of functionally redundant, or highly diminished species. While few conservationists explicitly advocate extinction of no-hopers, triage is implicit through recognition that current threats to biodiversity outweigh the resources available to mitigate these (Bottrill et al., 2008).

Decision-makers are faced with making choices about how and where to invest conservation resources. This is not easy, given the multitude of conflicting and/or complementary benefits, values and costs. If triage is a way to define explicitly what actions need to be taken according to resources available, a number of approaches can be taken to optimise conservation effort, albeit acknowledging that preventing extinction altogether is at the very least daunting. Hobbs & Kristjanson (2003) advocated adaptive management strategies ranging from no immediate management action (say, for non-threatened species) to urgent protection or restoration, without stating that populations should be abandoned. As suggested by Pimm (2000), saving the very rarest pushes the technical frontiers of conservation biology.

6.3.2 CAMPs – a triage approach

An attempt to determine conservation actions needed for species within different taxonomic groups, and explicitly determining what level of captive breeding may be required for various taxonomic groups or species has been undertaken by the CBSG. As early as 1991, CBSG, through their CAMPs, coalesced expertise in an interactive workshop format to scope problems facing taxa or regions, the decisions emanating from participants. CAMPs often operated in conjunction with the IUCN taxa-based specialist groups to provide strategic guidance on intensive conservation for threatened taxa (Ellis & Seal, 1996). From 1992 to 2009, a total of 78 CAMPs were organised (CBSG, 2010). CAMPs assess the degree of threat for every taxon by assigning each to a category following the IUCN Red List. The ultimate goal is to promote the creation of viable populations i.e. ones which are sufficiently large and well distributed to survive stochastic risks as well as deterministic threats.

Conservation recommendations for taxa within CAMPs necessarily depend on some assessment of population status, even though in some cases population estimates can be first-attempt, order-of-magnitude approximations (Ellis, 1995). Even a 'guesstimate' of numbers sets the stage for contemplating different actions. Based on the species status, those CAMPs that have been applied already propose one of the following intensive actions:

(1) more intensive protection and management *in-situ*;
(2) a formal population viability analysis;
(3) more *in-situ* and *ex-situ* conservation;
(4) a conservation breeding programme.

Definitions of these interventions are based on a consideration of the theory of extinction times for single populations as well as on time-scales believed meaningful for conservation action. The proposal has been that if biological diversity is to be maintained for the foreseeable future at anywhere near recent levels in natural ecosystems, fairly stringent criteria must be adopted for the lowest level of extinction risk (Vulnerable). A 10% probability of extinction within 100 years was suggested as the highest level of risk that is biologically acceptable (Shaffer, 1981; Chapter 5) and was seen as appropriate for this category. Furthermore, events 100 years in the future are hard to foresee and this may be the longest duration that legislative systems are capable of dealing with effectively.

Captive breeding for conservation is unavoidably the end of the line for many species. The underpinning logic is that because it is not possible to ensure the survival of a threatened taxor *in-situ* it is necessary to use a range of complementary conservation approaches and skills including captive breeding techniques. The decision to implement an *ex-situ* conservation programme for the recovery of a species will depend on the taxon's circumstances, where reproductive propagation will enable genetic and demographic population management. CAMPs propose captive breeding programmes or other recommendations based on conservation need alone (e.g. will the intervention contribute to the species' recovery or survival in the wild?). Captive breeding programmes, broadly speaking, aim to prevent imminent extinction of declining species or populations. Their ultimate goal is to maintain the genetic diversity and fitness within populations until the threats to them are removed and they can be reintroduced as self-sustaining populations. Although recommendations for captive breeding have evolved within the CAMP process and have become more streamlined, CAMP documents essentially advocated three levels of captive programmes (Seal *et al.*, 1994; Ellis, 1995).

Level 1 – A captive population is recommended as a component of a conservation programme. This programme has a tentative goal of developing and managing a population sufficient to preserve 90% of the genetic diversity of a population for 100 years (90%/100). The programme should be further defined with a species management plan encompassing the wild and captive populations, and implemented immediately with available stock in captivity. If the current stock is insufficient to meet programme goals, a species management plan should be developed to specify the need for additional founder stock. If no stock is present in captivity, then the programme should be developed collaboratively with appropriate wildlife agencies, SSC Specialist Groups, and cooperating institutions.

Level 2 – This is similar to the above, except a species/subspecies management plan would include periodic reinforcement of the captive population with new genetic material from the wild. The levels and amount of genetic exchange needed should be defined in terms of the programme goals, a population model, and a species management plan. It is anticipated that periodic supplementation with new genetic material will allow management of a smaller captive population. The time period for implementation of a Level 2 programme will depend on recommendations made at the CAMP workshop.

Level 3 – A captive programme is not currently recommended as a demographic or genetic contribution to the conservation of the species/subspecies, but is recommended for education, research, or husbandry purposes.

Other captive recommendations included the following:

N – A captive programme is not currently recommended as a demographic or genetic contribution to the conservation of the species/subspecies. Taxa already held in captivity may be included in this category. In this case species/subspecies should be evaluated for management toward a decrease in numbers or for complete elimination from captive programmes as part of a strategy to accommodate as many species/subspecies as possible of higher conservation priority as identified in the CAMP or in SSC Action Plans.

Pending – A decision on a captive programme will depend upon further data either from a Population and Habitat Viability Assessment, a survey, or existing identified sources to be queried.

The primary difference between Level 1 and Level 2 lies in the periodic reinforcement of a Level 2 captive population with new genetic material from the wild. Recommendations are made by the biologists at the meetings. The number of species that have been recommended for captive breeding through the CAMP process has been considerable; 863 out of a total of 2863 species (30%) in seven CAMPs (Fig. 6.1) required some level of captive breeding according to the participants (Seal *et al.*, 1994).

Although CAMPs received wide recognition by the conservation community as a strategic guide to intensive management and research of threatened taxa, practically unknown until their appearance (Seal *et al.*, 1994; Ellis, 1995), they have also been severely criticised. CAMPs have been construed by Hutchins *et al.* (1995) as too ambitious, inferring that they assume that 'hundreds, if not thousands, of species can be saved' through captive breeding and returned to the wild. Moreover, Hutchins *et al.* (1995) have disputed the reasoning allegedly behind the 'Noah's Ark Paradigm', as reputedly embraced by CAMPs, for zoos to shift their collections to more endangered taxa. The approach of Hutchins *et al.* does not refute the need for captive breeding and reintroduction, but their words suggest that there are 'more immediate ways' that zoos and their living collections can contribute to conservation beyond captive breeding for reintroduction. More poignantly, Hutchins *et al.*'s interpretations of CBSG's intentions at the time and these authors' suggestions for organisational improvements to collection planning may have led to a clear split in directions in the zoo world (Chapter 3). Although there were substantial rejoinders by various members of the conservation community against the viewpoints expressed in Hutchins *et al.* (1995), some even suggesting misinterpretations, factual errors and the like (Ellis, 1995; Walker, 1995), the CAMP initiative may have suffered. Whereas at the start of the process, there were up to 12 CAMP workshops undertaken in a year (1994), numbers have gone down to around one to four per year (CBSG, 2010). Arguably, a focus on conservation through means other than direct conservation may have been responsible for creating a certain amount of release of pressure from zoos. However, other contributing factors, such as funding limitations or changes in strategic direction within CBSG, may have contributed to this (S. Ellis, personal communication.) Also, most of

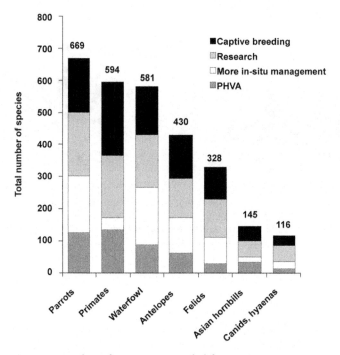

Fig. 6.1 Number of taxa recommended for intensive conservation actions from CAMP workshops. Data from Seal *et al.* (1994).

the major taxonomic groups had already been covered by CAMP processes by the mid 2000s.

6.3.3 Which species do better in captivity?

Not all animals kept in zoos reproduce unfailingly. This is not just associated with the conditions in which animals are maintained, but also relates to the species' basic biology. Ultimately, a species' breeding performance, linked to its intrinsic rate of natural increase (r_{max}), is inversely related to its average adult body size (Peters, 1983; Hennemann, 1983).

Body mass, however, does not account for all of the variation in r_{max}. For example, Hennemann (1983) observed that certain orders of mammals, such as the Lagomorpha and Carnivora, have high r_{max} values but low basal rates, which suggests that phylogeny can affect r_{max}. Robinson & Redford (1986) also showed that, at least among Neotropical mammals, phylogeny but not diet explained the observed variation in r_{max}. This association is attributable to the influence of phylogeny on reproductive characteristics of species. Given such allometric relationships, it is not surprising that population growth rates of species in zoos decline dramatically with increasing body mass. This has been shown for *in-situ* and *ex-situ* populations of mammals (Balmford *et al.*, 1995), and for a wider range of taxa (Balmford *et al.*, 1996). Estimates of *r* and lambda for *ex-situ* populations were

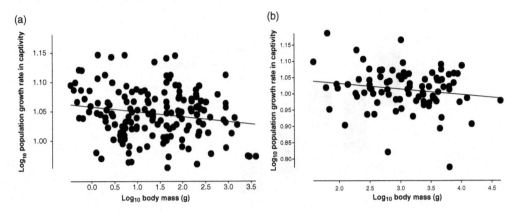

Fig. 6.2 Log–log plot of the relationship between adult body mass (g) and growth rate (lambda) for: (a) mammals in EAZA captive breeding programmes ($y = -0.003x + 0.03$; $r^2 = 0.02$; $P = 0.08$; $n = 56$); and (b) birds ($y = -0.008x + 0.03$; $r^2 = 0.05$; $P = 0.12$; $n = 87$). Data from K. Leus (personal communication).

calculated from SPARKS analyses of data supplied by studbook keepers, or from between-year census figures, excluding data for periods when zoos were actively limiting population size. Further data from EAZA studbooks for mammals shows this relationship for captive mammals (K. Leus, personal communication). Although there is much variation in captive breeding performance for mammals and birds of the same size (which can vary according to phylogeny), population growth rate falls with increasing body size (Fig. 6.2). Thus, populations of smaller-bodied species could increase more rapidly under optimal captive conditions than can populations of larger-bodied taxa.

6.3.4 Not 'curbing your enthusiasm'

One could argue that once unleashed from any 'millennium ark' option (Soulé *et al.*, 1986) or any global organisational system for selecting taxa requiring captive breeding (see Ebenhard, 1995), zoos may have eased onto species that could fulfil a conservation (albeit important) role through education and research. The counter-argument, of course, is that not all zoos can afford to put resources into breeding species for conservation, so they should contribute through other means. However, any de-emphasis on direct conservation targets could drive down commitment to captive breeding and reintroduction, because less space will be allocated to threatened species in zoos.

In agreement with Hutchins *et al.* (1995) strategic collection planning at a global, regional and institutional level is better than species selection for personal preference, or availability, that may have occurred in earlier times. But, while there is no doubt that existing organisational structures (e.g. TAGs) have improved collaboration around captive breeding (although see below), this is inconsequential if species that require captive breeding for their survival in the wild are not considered. If zoos are to maximise their contribution to conservation, even within a Hutchins *et al.* scenario in which zoos also educate and entertain the general public, they must develop rational priorities for *ex-situ* conservation (Balmford, 2000a,b). The reality is that despite a continued stress for zoos to focus on threatened and flagship species and on groups with which zoos already have experience (Seal *et al.*, 1994; Hutchins *et al.*, 1995) there is evidence that 'visceral' characteristics of the species e.g. physical size, to what extent a species is considered a 'higher form of life' (Metrick & Weitzman, 1996, 1998) or even resemblance to humans (Samples *et al.*, 1986; Gunnthorsdottir, 2001), are often more important than their threat status. A predisposition towards zoos holding species with greater appeal rather than endangerment was clearly shown by Marešováa & Frynta (2008) for boas and pythons in world zoos. For this group of species, attractiveness to humans determined the size of their populations in captivity. Variables putatively associated with species rarity (inclusion in the Red List or protection by international law, geographic range size, and commercial price) had no effect. Thus, there is a partiality for 'attractive' species in zoos; Marešováa & Frynta (2008) suggest that there could be a tendency for the selective extinction of 'unattractive' species in zoos 'as an anthropogenous macroevolutionary process'. Similarly, Frynta *et al.* (2010) confirmed a significant, positive association between perceived beauty and the size of worldwide zoo populations of parrots. Whilst they found that range size and body size were significant predictors of zoo population size, the effects of other explanatory variables, including the IUCN listing, were insignificant.

At another level, preferential focus on attractive taxa regardless of their conservation needs has also been shown to influence government decisions on whether to protect a species. The US General Accounting Office found that the US Fish and Wildlife Service generally ignored most species highest on the priority (threatened) list, concentrating instead on those with 'high public appeal' or facing 'imminent recovery' (Raloff, 1989). This has meant that many millions have been spent on species conservation, but neither uniqueness nor risk has weighed heavily in resource allocation. Instead there has been a heavy bias toward 'charismatic megafauna' – large, well-known birds and mammals ('higher forms of life' in the human value system) in contrast to species with less charisma but with potentially more scientific value, or at greater risk.

As already shown by Balmford (2000a,b) and Balmford *et al.* (1996), coordinated breeding programmes disproportionately target larger mammals and birds over smaller vertebrates. More specifically for mammals, the percentage of an order's threatened species and subspecies in *ex-situ* programmes was seen to be positively correlated with the order's average body size. A more detailed comparison of body sizes of species in European and North American zoo captive breeding programmes (see below for more details) shows that mammals, birds and reptiles are significantly larger in comparison to critically endangered and endangered taxa in the Red List (Table 6.3). For mammals, average body mass of Red List mammals was 32.5 kg (median 2.6, range 0.004–3305, $n = 537$), average body size in captive breeding programmes was significantly larger, 109.8 kg (median 12.0, range 0.013–3940, $n = 332$). Large mammals command widespread public appeal and this may indeed be the main economic reason for zoos to concentrate on these animals

Table 6.3 *Differences in distribution of body sizes (kg) of species held in North American (AZA, 2010a,b) and European (EAZA, 2010) cooperative zoo breeding programmes compared to body size distributions of threatened (critically endangered, endangered) taxa of mammals and birds. Body mass data for extant birds, which is right-hand skewed (mean 53 g, median 36 g) were taken from Blackburn & Gaston (1994). Body mass data for terrestrial mammals are significantly higher (18^3 g) than for birds, median 81 g (data from Smith et al., 2003). Threatened taxa lists taken from the IUCN Red List (IUCN, 2010)*

Group	Body mass (kg)	Red List species	AZA[a] SSP	AZA[a] PMP	EAZA[b] EEP	EAZA[b] ESB	All breeding programmes
Mammals	Mean	32.5	239.6	86.4	176.9	65.2	109.8
	Range	0.004–3305.1	0.2–3940.0	0.01–1134.0	0.24–3940.0	0.07–1417.5	0.013–3940.0
	Median	2.6	23.8	15.7	13.6	10.6	12.0
	n	537	83	117	128	80	332
Birds	Mean	0.60	3.8	2.1	2.6	2.6	2.2
	Range	0.003–8.8	0.1–12.5	0.01–44.0	0.1–12.5	0.03–44.0	0.010–44.0
	Median	0.69	1.7	0.6	1.2	0.9	0.75
	n	553	22	154	37	68	236

[a] SSP, Species Survival Plan, and PMP, Population Management Plan, both programmes of AZA; [b] EEP, European Endangered Species Programs, and ESB, European studbook.

(Chapter 8). But, the generally higher costs of keeping larger animals in captivity may limit opening up spaces for smaller endangered taxa.

6.4   Costs of keeping animals in zoos

6.4.1   General patterns

There are several components to the overall costs of long-term captive breeding programmes, but annual per capita cost of keeping an animal alive and healthy in captivity is often the simplest to measure. Although generalities of how much it costs to keep animals in captivity have been known for some time – such as to feed and house carnivores is more expensive than herbivores of the same size, or caring for heat-requiring species in cold climates is more costly – quantitative examinations of the economic constraints affecting species selection in zoos have only been recently undertaken. However, building such cost models (to calculate breeding programme outlays) has been hampered by lack of data on maintenance budgets. Conway (1986) was probably the first to publish per capita maintenance costs for a range of species at the New York Bronx Zoo and St. Catherine's Wildlife Survival Center. His results showed that even though costs clearly varied according to body size within taxonomic groups, unsurprisingly maintaining reptiles was cheaper than keeping birds or mammals. Labour was the more expensive item in all species, occupying on average around 60% of all costs whilst food costs ranged from

43% for tigers (total $4247 per individual per annum) and white-naped crane (total $847), to less than 2% for the Mauritius pink pigeon (total $924). Using available published estimates of maintenance requirements or zoo adoption fees for species ranging from snails to rhinos (22 mammals, six birds, four reptiles and three invertebrates), annual per capita costs increased strongly with body mass (Balmford et al., 1996).

More detailed maintenance cost data for a range of vertebrates at the Durrell Wildlife Park were derived from an intensive 'time-and-motion' study (J. Fa, unpublished data). A total of 90 species of amphibians, reptiles, birds and mammals were included in this study. Separate plots of annual per capita costs and body mass for the different groups (including 22 other taxa in Balmford et al., 1995, 1996) showed that the correlation was positively significant for mammals and reptiles (Fig. 6.3). For birds, annual cost per capita did not change significantly as body size increased, as shown by the fact that the largest bird on earth (around 100 kg), the ostrich, costs around $647 per individual (Scottish Agricultural College, 2010), similar to the cost of keeping a duck. This contrasts with the upkeep of an Andean bear, a mammal of similar size, which costs an order of magnitude more than an ostrich. Such contrasting cost–body mass relationships between birds, mammals and reptiles can arguably be explained by differences in the daily energy expenditure and daily food requirements of these groups. Scaling differences for various taxa, dietary, and habitat groups, have been shown by Nagy et al. (1999), where the allometric slope for reptiles was greater than that for mammals, which was greater than that for birds. The implication of this new finding is that the cost–body mass correlations derived by Balmford et al. (1996) underestimate per capita outlay for mammals and overestimate them for birds.

Generally then, smaller animals breed more rapidly than larger taxa, and generally cost less to keep. However, small-bodied taxa tend to have shorter generations and so lose genetic variability more quickly than larger species. So, to compensate for this, small species must often be maintained in larger captive populations than larger ones (Soulé et al., 1986), potentially masking the lower per capita costs associated with small size. Balmford et al. (1996) examined the combined effects of breeding rate, per capita cost, and generation length by estimating the long-term costs of hypothetical breeding programmes designed to retain 90% of founder heterozygosity over 100 years. The minimum size that each founder population had to grow to and remain at to achieve that goal was calculated using Capacity software (Ballou, 1989), using data on breeding rates (r) and generation length, the ratio of effective to census population size (N_e/N), and assuming that the proportion of heterozygosity lost per generation approximates to $1/2 N_e$. For each hypothetical programme, founder N_e was set at 25, and r and generation length calculated for each taxon. As expected, estimated programme costs will increase with body mass, those for warbiter crickets were less than 1% of those for western lowland gorillas. However, controlling for body size, breeding programmes are indeed cheaper for taxa with long generation times because they lose heterozygosity relatively slowly (Balmford et al., 1996). From the standpoint of zoo managers, therefore, both body mass and generation length should be taken into account in selecting species for cost-effective captive breeding.

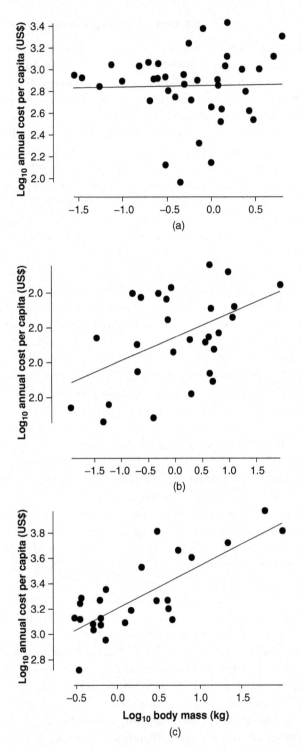

Fig. 6.3 Plot of the relationship between adult body mass (kg) and annual per capita maintenance costs of species in zoos for data from Fa (unpublished data) and Balmford *et al.* (1996): (a) birds ($y = 0.01x + 2.85$; $r^2 = 0.0003$; $P = 0.99$; $n = 47$); (b) mammals ($y = 0.34x + 3.21$; $r^2 = 0.60$; $P = 0.01$; $n = 40$); and (c) amphibians and reptiles ($y = 0.15x + 2.53$; $r^2 = 0.35$; $P < 0.0001$; $n = 43$).

6.4.2 Arks or parks?

Estimated costs for protecting large species such as mountain gorillas or rhinoceroses in the wild were argued to be less expensive per capita than maintaining these species in captivity (Harcourt, 1986; Leader–Williams, 1990). Balmford *et al.* (1995) extended this line of reasoning by using data for a number of threatened mammals, undertaking comparisons of demographic performance and costs for a species, both in captivity and in the wild. Although there were no consistent differences in the rates of population growth under effective *in-situ* protection or in established breeding programmes, there were clear-cut differences in costs for maintaining the species in one or the other setting. Even when all costs for protecting reserves were loaded onto single flagship species, on a per capita basis these taxa were still maintained far more cheaply in the wild than in zoos. Balmford *et al.*'s (1995) general conclusion was that *in-situ* protection was a more cost-effective conservation strategy than captive breeding for larger species. This being true, though, because a species' status can change dramatically in the wild, well-managed captive breeding programmes may become the lifeline for some taxa, including large species. This could have been the case for the northern white rhinoceros, now extinct in the wild (Groves *et al.*, 2010). Thus, 'cost effectiveness' of wild *versus* captive conservation is certainly a measure to take into account, but not the only consideration in terms of where to put resources to save species. Sometimes we just need a plan B!

Although in general, differentials between captive and *in-situ* costs seem to be positively correlated with size, some species fall outside the main trend line; costs were surprisingly low for species such as the gorilla, large cats, or even the black rhinoceros, but higher for smaller taxa such as the golden lion tamarin (Fig. 6.4). This actually means that Balmford *et al.*'s (1995) cost-effectiveness rule of how the cost of captive breeding programmes increases with rising body size may not necessarily be that clear-cut. Resolving this dichotomy more clearly is dependent on obtaining more data on costs. Crucial also, as Balmford *et al.* (1995) mention, is the need to assess the relative benefits of the intermediate option between initiatives based in western zoos and in the field – captive propagation *in-situ*.

6.5 Managed *ex-situ* populations

6.5.1 How to coordinate?

The reasons for keeping a species in captivity impose differing strategies for managing their populations, e.g. for those taxa to be released into the wild, time in captivity should be short. But, whatever the motives are for breeding animals in captivity, the strategies for all taxa need to be based on the development of viable populations. A viable population is defined as one that is large enough to provide some specified or acceptable level of protection against stochastic as well as deterministic threats (Foose, 1991). The minimum viable population (MVP) concept has been criticised mainly on the precision and accuracy of the estimates, and its real-world applicability (Chapter 5). However, MVPs have been applied to an increasing number of species (Traill *et al.*, 2007).

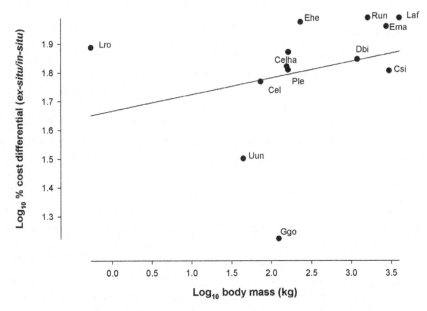

Fig. 6.4 Plot of the relationship between cost differentials of *ex-situ/in-situ* according to body size of mammals ($y = 0.06x + 1.66$; $r^2 = 0.08$; $P = 0.03$; $n = 13$). Data from Balmford *et al.* (1995). *Cel = Cervus eldi; Celha = Cervus elaphus hangli; Csi = Ceratotherium simum; Dbi = Diceros bicornis; Ehe = Equus hemionus; Ema = Elephas maximus; Ggo = Gorilla gorilla; Lro = Leontopithecus rosalia; Laf = Loxodonta africana; Ple = Panthera leo persica; Pti = Panthera tigris; Run = Rhinoceros unicornis; Uun = Uncia uncia.*

A viable population size depends on the genetic and demographic objectives of the conservation programme and the biological characteristics of the population (Nunney & Campbell, 1993). MVP targets have been used to allocate scarce resources toward the maintenance of populations, and for the derivation of minimum requirements. An example of a PVA-based study was undertaken for African wild dogs by Mills *et al.* (1998), in which it was found that populations of more than 100 individuals were likely to survive over 50 years with adequate protection from human persecution, while small populations (of 20 individuals) were unlikely to persist due to stochastic hazards (Cross & Beissinger, 2001). Such quantitative estimation of MVP allows biologists to link finite resources to a target figure or range, assuming that the persistence of a population will be assured thereafter (or for a period of time). Thus, viable population strategies should guide captive breeding programmes, but also require development of metapopulations (Box 6.2) to achieve populations that are large and widely distributed enough to have an acceptable survival probability. The metapopulation management model describes the relationships between *ex-situ* and *in-situ* populations being managed under one conservation goal. A metapopulation is a set of populations distributed over a number of patches that are connected, to varying degrees, by dispersal (Hanski & Gilpin, 1991). The dynamics of a metapopulation are a function of both within-population dynamics and among-population movement. Captive and managed wild populations also form metapopulations when people move individuals among populations to maintain genetic diversity, replenish depleted populations, and establish populations in new areas. Many metapopulation models suggest that increased movement among populations reduces the probability of metapopulation extinction.

Few metapopulation models incorporate any potential negative effects of movement among populations. Population viability analyses for a number of endangered species have incorporated a metapopulation approach suggesting that some extant populations should be subdivided into numerous subgroups with exchange of individuals among them to reduce the chance of catastrophic loss. However, routine application of a policy of extensive subdivision has been criticised, since it may have detrimental consequences for certain endangered species, such as has been suggested for the Puerto Rican parrot (Wilson *et al.*, 1994). Many endangered species have gone through a genetic bottleneck which may heighten their susceptibility to disease. Multi-species facilities are a high-risk environment favouring the transmission of pathogens, especially when the facilities are located outside the natural ranges of a particular species. Thus, population viability analyses need to acknowledge that proliferation of captive subgroups accompanied by exchanges of individuals can in themselves carry substantial risks that must be weighed against the presumed benefits of subdivision.

Components of a metapopulation management plan may include multiple regional *ex-situ* populations (or a global *ex-situ* population), in-country breeding programmes, multiple wild populations, reintroduced populations, vacant habitat suitable for re-introductions and even genome banks. Population management is accomplished through transfers between institutions in the *ex-situ* population, reintroduction of zoo-bred animals into the wild, translocation of animals among wild populations, and, for genes, artificial insemination, or embryo transfer technologies. The role of the *ex-situ* populations can vary from simply serving as a static genetic and demographic reservoir for the species, with little interaction with wild populations, to populations with extensive gene flow in both directions (reintroduction and periodic acquisition of new founders).

The ploughshare tortoise provides an excellent example for illustrating the metapopulation approach (Box 6.2). This species is one of the rarest chelonians in the world with less than 1000 individuals remaining in the wild. The wild population consists of only five small, isolated populations, all of which are restricted to a patchily distributed scrub habitat within a 30-km radius of Baly Bay in north-western Madagascar (Smith *et al.*, 1999). The species has been subject to centuries of commercial exploitation and loss of tortoises and their habitat by bush fires (Pedrono & Smith, 2003). The effects of historic exploitation on the demographic characteristics of ploughshare tortoise populations are still evident, despite the fact that few wild tortoises have been collected in recent years. In 1986, at the request of The World Conservation Union, the Durrell Wildlife Conservation Trust initiated a recovery programme for the ploughshare tortoise (Durrell *et al.*, 1994). The recovery plan included an in-country captive-breeding programme

Box 6.2 · *Wild–captive interactive management: the Madagascar ploughshare tortoise*

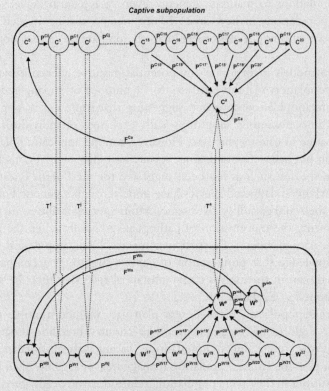

Age and class-structured life-cycle graph of the ploughshare tortoise metapopulation. Wj: number of wild individuals; Wa: number of wild adults 300–345 mm carapace length (CL); Wb: number of

wild adults 345–420 mm CL; C^j: number of captive individuals; F: size-specific fecundity; P*: age-specific transition probability; j: juveniles; a, b: adults; T^j: number of individuals translocated; P*': transition rate to a superior reproductive class. Transition rates are age-specific survival rates until maturity and size-dependent fecundity for adults. Transition to adulthood occurs between ages of 17 and 22 for wild individuals and between ages of 15 and 20 for captive individuals (from Pedrono et al., 2004).*

In order to evaluate how interactive management can be used as a conservation tool, a metapopulation viability analysis (MVA) using both wild and captive populations (defined as 'subpopulations') is necessary. In a model for wild and captive populations of the ploughshare tortoise or angonoka developed by Pedrono *et al.* (2004), the authors used projection models to address the potential effectiveness of an interactive management approach to managing captive and wild populations of the species. They examined the likelihood of the persistence of this metapopulation (both wild and captive subpopulations) under various management options. They considered a purely demographic framework of extinction probability because no genetic information was available. However, given the relatively long generation time exhibited by the ploughshare tortoise (about 30 years), general goals for the maintenance of genetic variability within a fixed time period are easier to achieve than with species with a shorter generation time.

The model predicted that catastrophic events such as bush fires would likely have a negative effect on the future of remaining wild populations. However, the model also predicted that the use of captive-born offspring to establish additional wild populations would decrease the risk of extinction of the metapopulation as a whole. A true interactive management programme seeks to address the cause(s) of the decline of a species, such as habitat loss, and in cases where remaining populations are fragmented and isolated, to use captive populations to augment wild populations. The use of captive-bred animals to supplement wild populations is controversial because of the difficulty and expense of captive breeding, the risk of spreading pathogens and the difficulty of evaluating the success of such programmes (Wilson *et al.*, 1994). However, in certain situations reinforcements can result in demographic and genetic enhancement of a wild population. Such programmes typically give priority to flagship and/or umbrella species that are threatened in the wild. While the focus on flagship or umbrella species is not a panacea, targeting management programmes at such species is often the most cost-effective mechanism to conserve biodiversity of the entire community (Conway, 1995). Furthermore, focusing conservation efforts on flagship species can generate funds to support habitat preservation.

and research on the status and ecology of wild populations. Over the course of 10 years, more than 250 offspring were produced from a founder stock of 20 tortoises at the multi-species breeding facility at Ampijoroa in Madagascar. The goal of the captive breeding programme was to produce offspring that could be used to supplement wild populations, if deemed necessary. More than 40 ploughshare tortoises have been released to part of their former range. In addition, efforts are underway to protect wild tortoise populations with the support of the local people. The ploughshare tortoise is already serving as a flagship species for the protection of the biological community around Baly Bay.

6.5.2 Coordinated breeding programmes

The necessity to manage populations of species of large enough numbers has required a new order of cooperation and collaboration among institutions, necessitating new standards of record keeping and pooling of genetic and demographic data in a form suitable for preparation of studbooks and scientific analyses (Seal, 1991). Indeed, such plans have reached an important level of biological and management sophistication, which according to Seal (1991) are unequalled in any other part of the biological world. These programmes can only work by focusing on the needs of the species (whilst paying attention to animal welfare), overriding any personal and organisational inclinations. Frequently, it is the acquisition of animals for an approved propagation programme that limits progress because it can be expensive, and long-term maintenance costs will also mount (Foose et al., 1995). Thus, successful breeding of species in coordinated zoo programmes is possible, but can be hampered by availability of space, expert personnel and other resources for breeding the species in captivity. The limitation is not necessarily technology, since this is thought to exist to breed most vertebrate species in captivity on a long-term basis (Seal, 1988).

There is agreement that in moving away from selecting animals through personal preference, availability or competition, as in the past, zoos should engage in a more systematic process for taxon selection.

Planning for this has to occur at a global, regional and institutional level. At the global scale, much of the planning was organised by the CBSG through its CAMP process (see above) with the intention of connecting all the regional breeding programmes, as well as universities and wildlife management institutions, in a global network. CBSG, as one of about 100 specialist groups within the IUCN SSC, would facilitate global assessments of the need for intensive management (including conservation breeding) in wild populations of threatened taxa (Fig. 6.5), as well as formulating global breeding strategies for species managed in regional programmes via a GCAP.

Many of the current assessments of captive breeding needs within zoos are led by individual regional zoo associations in different parts of the world. The largest and arguably the most important regional zoo associations worldwide are the EAZA (327 members) in Europe, AZA (221 members) in the USA and Canada, and the ZAA (70 members) in the Australasian region. These associations separately choose species for their captive breeding programmes based on recommendations made by association committees known as TAGs. TAGs have been established to provide advice to curators and animal management staff within each association. TAG members are professional zoo and aquarium personnel who work in member institutions and have specialist knowledge in the group of species covered by the specific TAG. The declared intention of the TAGs is to 'examine conservation needs of entire taxa' (AZA, 2010a) to ' . . . plan and manage animal collections cooperatively, in ways that promote sustainability and contribute to species conservation' (ZAA, 2010). Despite such statements, Balmford et al. (1996) and later Leader-Williams et al. (2007), who examined 'reintroducability' of species in coordinated programmes, showed that zoos did not focus on threatened species not affected by irreversible habitat loss. These

Organizational bodies and product documents (in italics), with flow of information and work input indicated by arrows

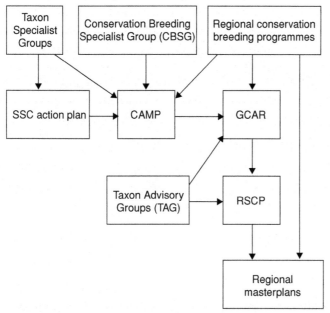

SSC action plan

The Species Survival Commission (SSC) of the World Conservation Union consists of about 100 specialist groups, networking several thousand managers, researchers and administrators worldwide. Most specialist groups attend to specific taxa. such as orders or families [Taxon Specialist Groups), make global assessments of species status, and recommend conservation efforts in global or regional action plans.

CAMP - Conservation Assessment and Management Plan

The CAMP is intended to provide strategic guidance for application of intensive management and research to threatened taxa41. In the CAMP workshop, information from published SSC action plans on threats to wild populations is used to assess whether populations need (1) more intensive protection and management in situ, (2) a formal viability analysis, (3) more in situ and ex situ research, or (4) a conservation breeding programme (see Table 1). The CAMP process is facilitated by the Conservation Breeding Specialist Group (CBSG) of SSC, but draws widely on expertise.

GCAR - Global Captive Action Recommendations

For taxa identified in the CAMP as being in need of conservation breeding, a global strategic breeding plan is worked out in a GCAR workshop41 (previously known as GCAP). The GCAR process works through the stages outlined in Box 1 to arrive at a target population size, and then distributes responsibilities among the Regional Conservation Breeding Programs, such as the North American Species Survival Plan (SSP) and the Europaisches Erhaltungszucht Programm (EEP).

RSCP - Regional Strategic Collection Plan

Within each region, a Taxon Advisory Group (TAG) evaluates the feasibility of recommendations made in the GCAR, considering the availability of space, personnel and funding in zoos of the region, producing a strategic collection plan (i.e. what species to keep and in what numbers).

Regional masterplan

The regional masterplan is the detailed individual-by-individual recommendations on breeding issued by the species coordinator, to be implemented by all participating zoos.

Fig. 6.5 Global organisation of conservation breeding. Taken from Ebenhard (1995).

species are generally more suitable for captive breeding and release, i.e. species that are affected by more reversible threats such as overhunting.

The mandate of TAGs is to advise which species should be kept in member zoos, how they should be managed to ensure viable populations; TAGs can also recommend appropriate *in-situ* conservation efforts. TAGs can propose the establishment of a studbook alone or the setting up of a breeding programme. By 2010, there were a total of 42 TAGs operating in EAZA (EAZA, 2010), 46 in AZA (AZA, 2010a) and 14 in ZAA (ZAA, 2010). Of the 102 TAGs operating within these three zoo associations, more than three-quarters centre upon distinct mammal (e.g. apes, small carnivores, equids, or felids) and bird groups (e.g. doves, turaco/cuckoos). The remaining TAGs are more general in their remit, as is the case for reptiles (e.g. crocodilians, turtles, snake), invertebrates (e.g. aquatic and terrestrial), fish (marine and freshwater), and amphibians (one TAG for all amphibians). This emphasis on mammals and birds, and in particular groups such as primates and parrots within these, mirrors the composition of taxa held in zoos, as discussed in Chapter 3.

Zoo associations like EAZA, AZA and ZAA presently operate two distinct levels of breeding programme types: (1) a most intensive type of population management for a species kept in member zoos, and (2) a less intensive programme primarily based around a studbook keeper who is responsible for gathering data on births, deaths, transfers, etc., from all zoos and aquariums that keep the species in question. Both types of programme rely on demographic and genetic analyses of the captive population to make recommendations for future management of the species. Participants of AZA's SSPs agree to implement recommendations whilst AZA's PMPs agree to consider but not necessarily to implement recommendations.

Type 1 breeding programmes, e.g. AZA's SSP programmes, aim 'to manage and conserve a select and **typically threatened or endangered**, ex-situ species population . . . ' (AZA, 2010a). AZA consider that SSP species are often 'flagship species', which the organisation defines as 'well-known animals which arouse strong feelings in the public for the preservation and protection of the *in-situ* population and their habitat, including the giant panda, California condor, and lowland gorilla'. The AZA's use of the term 'flagship species' invokes an education element alongside the establishment of these programmes but how effective these have been in supporting conservation activities for iconic species (such as the panda, condor or gorilla) would be expedient to measure (see Chapter 3). New Type 1 breeding programmes are approved by the central authority of the zoo associations if various internal advisory committees deem the species in question to require help and if sufficient dedicated staff are available. These programmes are administered by a centralised office, generating master plans for specific species and coordinating research, transfer and reintroductions. Part of this process involves designing a 'family tree' of particular managed populations in order to achieve maximum genetic diversity and demographic stability. Consideration is given to the logistics and feasibility of transfers between institutions as well as maintenance of natural social groupings. In some cases, master plans may recommend not to breed specific animals, so as to avoid having captive

Table 6.4 *Number of managed cooperative animal breeding programmes in North American (AZA, 2010a) and European (EAZA, 2010) zoos*

	AZA[a]			EAZA[b]		
	SSP	PMP	Total	EEP	ESB	Total
Mammals	83	117	200	127	80	207
Birds	22	156	178	37	68	105
Reptiles	11	37	48	7	16	24
Amphibians	3	2	5	–	2	2
Fish	1+	–	1+	–	6	6
Invertebrates	1	–	1	2	1	1

[a] SSP, Species Survival Plan, and PMP, Population Management Plan, both programmes of AZA.
[b] EEP, European Endangered Species Programs, and ESB, European studbook.

populations outgrow available holding spaces. While there are success stories, coordinated breeding programmes are still works in progress (see below).

European, North American and Australasian zoo associations administer close to 900 Type 1 and 2 breeding programmes. EAZA and AZA together run 800 of these; over half are mammals, close to 40% are birds, 9% reptiles, and the remaining, amphibians and invertebrates (Table 6.4). Invertebrates are represented only by four programmes, and there are just seven established collaborations around amphibians. Among the most common taxonomic groups in breeding programmes, only 18% of all mammal taxa ($n = 321$) and 9% ($n = 256$) of birds are critically endangered or endangered. Only five of the 71 reptile species are under threat, three of the seven amphibians, three out of the four invertebrates, and 15 (of these 13 African cichlids) of the 29 fish taxa in breeding programmes are at risk. Thus, despite the declared intention of using zoo breeding programmes in support of threatened or endangered species, most may be serving the continuity of exhibit species rather than supporting endangered taxa. As we show earlier, this is definitely corroborated by the larger body sizes of mammals and birds in the breeding programmes, in contrast to the size distributions of threatened species within these taxa. We have argued in Chapter 5 and later here, that breeding programmes can be developed for ensuring continuity of species to exhibit, but current programmes cannot be marketed by zoos as being primarily aimed at threatened animals.

6.5.3 Performance of breeding programmes

Though there seems to have been a marked increase in the numbers of threatened species held in coordinated breeding programmes between 1992 and 2003, as suggested by Leader-Williams *et al.* (2007), there is little information on how well zoos manage these populations. Individual programmes may be regularly assessed by their members to see whether recommendations have been followed for a particular species. But, as Baker (2007) noted, there has not been any systematic evaluation of effectiveness of programmes as a whole. Measures to gauge efficacy include:

- the proportion of the captive population that is captive-born or hatched;
- the demographic health of the captive population (number of animals per programme, age structure of the population and whether or not demographic goals of a stable, increasing or decreasing population are being met); and
- the genetic health of the captive population based on gene diversity or founder genome equivalents, and average inbreeding coefficients.

Together, demographic and genetic assessments can indicate whether population viability is likely. From data in ISIS, Baker (2007) calculated that over three-quarters of mammals (79% of around 126 000 specimens) and more than half of birds (63% of 162 000 specimens) were captive-bred. Less than half (41% of 57 000 specimens) of reptiles and around a quarter only of amphibians (27% of 23 000 specimens) were captive-hatched. The situation for mammals is probably adequate, because most mammals in zoos are large and therefore long-lived (see above), wild-caught animals are therefore less important in sustaining these populations. The situation for reptiles and amphibians is less encouraging, with large numbers of animals still harvested from the wild (Baker, 2007). This may indicate a lack of coordinated captive-breeding programmes for these taxa. The conclusion that Baker (2007) comes to is that many of the *ex-situ* breeding programmes examined were not viable long-term, suffering not just from an insufficient founder base but also from unstable demographics. Of 89 SSPs in 2002, 25% reported gene diversity of less than 90%, and close to three-quarters had population sizes of less than 100. For Old World monkeys, particularly, none of the 10 taxa targeted for captive breeding had founder genome equivalents of more than three wild-caught animals (Baker 2007). Earnhardt *et al.* (2001) examined 17 PMP and 46 SSP populations with similar conclusions.

A more recent assessment of the sustainability of 87 mammal species managed in captivity through SSPs, EAZAs and ARAZPA Species Management Plans (Lees & Wilcken, 2009) indicated that 48% of the programmes are breeding for replacement and 55% currently retain the levels of genetic diversity at or above the recommended threshold of 90%. Laurie Bingaman Lackey and Kristin Leus performed an assessment of EAZA avian studbooks to look at the sustainability of those captive populations and found a similar trend (K. Leus, personal communication). Out of 92 avian studbooks evaluated, 24 species were in excellent or fairly good shape in terms of population size, growth and meeting genetic diversity thresholds; 65 species were headed toward increasing difficulties; and four were in imminent danger. Similarly, out of 924 electronic studbooks (all taxa) submitted to ISIS, 58% of species had fewer than 50 individuals in the living captive population (CBSG, 2008).

6.6 Baby and bathwater!

A possible explanation for the state of captive breeding programmes in European and North American zoos, may also be the case in other parts of the world (see Stanley Price & Fa, 2007 for South American zoos), and has been linked to the constraints imposed by institutional needs, preferences and history. Many zoo managers believe that without the large, charismatic mega-vertebrates, visitor numbers would drop. This assumption has yet to be seriously tested, and more research in this area is needed. A study of attractiveness of large animals at London Zoo suggested that there was no discernible preference for large charismatic vertebrates by visitors (Balmford *et al.*, 1996). Equally important, regulatory constraints imposed by permitting processes and quarantine restrictions limit not only the movement of animals but also samples.

The conflict between what to exhibit in collections to ensure financial viability at the same time as contribute to conservation is still unresolved. However, the winner seems to be animals for exhibition. The question is, is this a symptom of still existing tensions between the Noah's Ark paradigm and what can be called the 'Hutchins' paradigm' which zoos have not been able to resolve? Robinson & Conway (1995) have perhaps come closest to declaring that the truth has to lie somewhere in the middle, with no need to throw the 'babies with the bathwater'. Hutchins *et al.* (1995) blamed the disjunction between planning and practice on the approaches developed by the CBSG. The CBSG planning process did, in some cases, promote captive breeding and reintroduction, but more importantly, overall promoted a process of systematic conservation planning. Hutchins *et al.*'s model suggested that through existing practices, zoos were able to support conservation breeding. However, close to 20 years later, there is little evidence that captive breeding and reintroduction of many threatened species by zoos has occurred. Moreover, Ark-related activity has declined as zoos have diversified their activities, re-directing efforts into areas such as funding *in-situ* conservation projects (Zimmerman & Wilkinson, 2007), or more education (Leader-Williams *et al.*, 2007). Arguably, the loss of the impetus around the Noah's Ark paradigm, in which world zoos embarked upon unprecedented regional and ultimately global levels of cooperation, may have resulted in zoo populations being in poorer shape and not achieving sustainability (Lees & Wilcken, 2009).

6.7 Effective captive breeding

6.7.1 Objectives and approaches

Captive breeding can serve several different objectives, whose strategies for demographic and genetic management vary substantially.

- Assure a viable *ex-situ* population for future exhibition in zoos (breeding for display).
- Provide a 'living museum' for species that have become extinct in the wild, or where the likelihood for species extinction in the wild is high.

- Provide suitable animals to support wild populations (population augmentation).
- Provide suitable animals to re-establish or to found new wild populations (reintroduction and introduction).

These separate aims for breeding animals in zoos require strategies for demographic and genetic management that vary substantially.

Assuring viable *ex-situ* populations for future use and display in zoos is an economic imperative for zoo management, irrespective of whether animals are bred for conservation. The popular literature and the propaganda of many zoos are full of references to participation in breeding programmes, implying active and direct support for conservation. However, breeding programmes **do not** support conservation *per se*. Because displayable animals constitute the economic core of zoos, breeding – and the science supporting it – is an essential economic activity. National and local governments are becoming increasingly concerned about their natural and genetic resources and legal export for captive breeding is becoming increasingly difficult. Obtaining new animals from endangered species is becoming increasingly difficult even if they are essential for founding or maintaining a viable *ex-situ* breeding programme aimed at subsequent population augmentation or reintroduction.

Breeding programmes not specifically aimed for conservation aim for easily manageable populations. As long as negative genetic effects do not become economically threatening or result in animal welfare issues, concerns about loss of genetic variability, inbreeding depression, adaptation to captive environments or domestication may be overlooked. Importantly, the generally benign captive environments mask the negative impact of inbreeding and inbreeding depression (Chapter 5). Whilst inbreeding avoidance through systematically planned and co-ordinated multi-facility or international cooperation is beneficial for longer-term viability, the extra cost and effort to maximally avoid inbreeding or genetic erosion will have not only little or no economic importance for captive breeding for display, but often comes with an economic cost. Because genetic variability depends on population size, even in well-designed programmes, minimising the loss of genetic variability in one target species is directly opposite to and competes with keeping and exhibiting more species, which is generally regarded as economically more attractive as it attracts visitors. The strategy to breed endangered species for future reintroduction at the smallest number possible is an epiphenomenon of this competition for available zoo spaces (Earnhardt *et al.*, 2009).

Providing animals for population augmentation, introductions or reintroductions directly supports conservation. The genetic objectives vary substantially, however. Population augmentation should provide only animals that are genetically similar to the target population in order to avoid outbreeding depression, the destruction of local adaptation, the change of evolutionary trajectories or the destruction of evolutionary history of wild populations. Unfortunately, the introduction of non-matched animals is all too common because of unknown origin of founders of captive programmes used for augmentation, failure to check genetic similarity using molecular methods or simply ignorance of the problem. For example, the captive Andean bear population in Venezuela was augmented from extra-range populations including a lineage from unknown geographic origin, which have irrevocably mixed with underrepresented wild-caught Venezuelan lineages (Rodríguez-Clark & Sánchez-Mercado, 2006). Exception of the aim not to introduce non-local animals is the genetic rescue of inbred and genetically depauperate populations by introducing new genetic materials such as in the case of the adder in Scandinavia (Chapter 5) or the Florida panther (Hedrick & Fredrickson, 2010). Introductions and reintroductions ought to establish populations with maximal genetic diversity, as this increases the likelihood for population establishment and survival and for future adaptability to environmental change.

Introductions and reintroductions ought to create populations with the maximum possible genetic variability, allowing the newly established populations to adapt to the local environment. Ideally, they should be based on captive breeding programmes that were founded from the same population, prior to extinction, or genetically related populations. This is especially important when the newly created populations will become connected with other populations of the species by dispersal. If, however, future connectivity is impossible, there is an important alternative approach to using descendants of local stock: mixed lineages of a diverse range of founding stock of the species, which maximises genetic diversity regardless of the geographic origin of founders. This approach is more likely to support future adaptability in the face of changing environmental conditions.

Genetic considerations of captive breeding as a living museum can slot in either as conservation breeding or display breeding. Because conservation breeding and display breeding follow different breeding strategies and fulfil divergent objectives, achieving objectives simultaneously will be unfeasible. Distinguishing between breeding as a living museum and breeding for conservation through re-establishment of self-sustaining wild populations is difficult as the boundaries are fluid. The crucial factor is the time-frame. Although the modern ark paradigm has a time-frame of 200 years or shorter in mind (Soulé et al., 1986), this time-frame might be over-optimistic (Chapter 5). Thus, what has started as breeding for conservation will likely mutate into breeding as a living history when time passes by without successful reintroduction into the wild. The ire of critique of zoo breeding has focussed on long-term or open-ended breeding programmes, which are unfeasible to maintain because of large population sizes required and the economic and logistic constraints (Snyder et al., 1996). All the known problems of captive breeding are becoming more likely the longer in captivity, and the transition from captive breeding for conservation to breeding for a living museum is gradual. Operationally, we should define captive breeding for conservation as only those programmes that can reasonably demonstrate a high likelihood for successful augmentation reintroduction or introduction in a reasonable time. All programmes that cannot do so should be regarded (and marketed) as breeding for display or as a living museum only. At the end of this chapter, we will summarise and attempt to define what 'reasonable' is.

6.7.2 Phases of captive breeding

Captive breeding typically follows distinct stages: (1) founder phase; (2) growth phase; (3) management phase; and (4) population augmentation, reintroduction or introduction

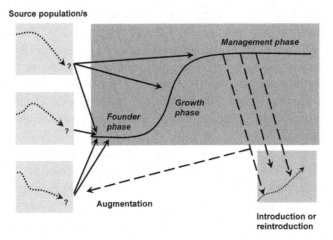

Fig. 6.6 Diagram illustrating the phases in a captive breeding programme.

of wild populations using captive stock (Fig. 6.6). These four phases only apply for 'classic' captive breeding in zoos, but not alternative approaches for conservation, in particular headstarting, in which zoos are becoming increasingly involved. Efficient captive rearing for headstarting requires the avoidance of non-heritable adaptation to captivity and supporting behavioural competence after release (Section 4.2.2) and the development and optimisation of husbandry protocols as in the founder and growth phases of 'classic' zoo breeding.

Founding phase. The founding phase sets the basis of captive breeding and the future value for conservation. Ideally, the founding population should be a fully representative sample of the wild source population. The number of founders required may be relatively small and depends on the subsequent management strategy, breeding success and aims of the programme (Chapter 5). Ten unrelated founders represent 95% of heterozygosity in an outbreeding population, but many more are required if allelic diversity is to be conserved. Soulé *et al.*'s (1986) framework of the modern ark suggest at least 20 founders as a trade-off between initial loss of heterozygosity and securing suitable founders from the wild. Whilst heterozygosity is generally assumed to be more important than allelic diversity for short-term evolutionary potential, data from wild and domestic animals increasingly stress the importance of allelic diversity for future potential for adaptive change. Adaptability is becoming crucial in the face of climate and environmental change and low allelic diversity might become an Achilles' heel in the future even if a captive or reintroduced programme seems to be initially highly successful (e.g. Tasmanian devil: Siddle *et al.*, 2007; Mauritius kestrel: Ewing *et al.*, 2008). There is also a trade-off between number of founders and the subsequently required population size to maintain heterozygosity (Chapter 5).

A very large proportion of captive populations are based on a very small number of founders, for example four Speke's gazelles, two Scandinavian wolves, six pink pigeons, two Mauritius kestrels or seven pygmy hogs. The number of founders constitutes the benchmark for the effects of subsequent captive breeding, such as retention of allelic diversity or inbreeding. Founder genome equivalents, FGEs, are defined relative to the source population. It is the expected number of unrelated, equally contributing founder genomes that would contain the same genetic diversity as in the population under study (Lacy, 1989, 1995). It is generally estimated by a simulation approach, the gene-drop analysis that is implemented in many genetic computer packages (e.g. PM2000: Pollak *et al.*, 2002) but requires known pedigrees. Not to be confused with FGE, founder equivalents, FEs, are defined relative to the founder population and are a relative measure of the variance in founder representation. It is the number of equally contributing founders that would be expected to produce the same genetic diversity as in the population under study (Lacy, 1989). If FE or FGE are lower than the actual number of founder individuals, then the data indicate that some founders reproduced disproportionately successfully and contributed more than others to the descendent population. If FGE is lower than FE, the loss of alleles due to a genetic bottleneck or random genetic drift is indicated. For example, a translocated population of New Zealand rail, the takahe, composed of 25 founders, resulted in FE = 12.5 and FGE = 6.6 (Grueber & Jamieson 2008). The Belorussian and Polish populations of European bison, founded from captive animals, contained founder equivalents of only 1.44 and 3.43 (Daleszczyk & Bunevich, 2009).

Often, it is known that founders are related, thus decreasing the effective number of founders even further (e.g. Scandinavian wolves). However, in most cases, we have little information about relatedness of founders from the wild although modern genetic techniques could solve these questions fairly easily, but this is surprisingly rarely applied (Section 6.8). Although unknown founder relationships have little impact on the effectiveness of avoiding further inbreeding during the management phase (see below), knowledge on relatedness between founders is crucial to understand how representative the sample is, the initial loss of genetic diversity and random genetic drift.

During the founder phase, there is typically a dearth of information on the natural history, husbandry, reproductive biology, disease and genetic structure of the wild and newly founded population (see Burton, 2010). The development of husbandry and research on disease and reproductive biology dominates management, producing a very large proportion of publications in journals focussing on zoo biology; often this research is being advertised as research for conservation, but breeding for display equally requires it. Lack of adequate propagation methodology introduces biases in reproductive success and selection, which reduces the effective number of founders and favours the future loss of genetic diversity and an increase of genetic problems. Variability in reproductive success reduces effective population size. This can have dramatic and long-lasting effects during the founder phase as the foundation for future genetic composition is set during this time. Equalising reproductive success among individuals is the best method to minimise genetic drift. Ideally, variation in founder's reproductive success and representation is reduced to zero, in which case effective population size might greatly exceed census size (Chapter 5).

Founding of new captive populations and augmentation or management of existing ones must consider the conservation or taxonomic unit of the source population. Except for those adapted to small geographic ranges, most species are geographically structured, often containing a complex array of populations connected with limited gene flow. Population structure is the consequence of reproductive isolation and demographic history. It may or may not represent adaptive divergence. Depending on the level of gene flow and the evolutionary past, populations within species might exhibit different levels of genetic differentiation from each other and might constitute different evolutionary trajectories or evolutionary significant units, ESUs. Populations with large genetic distances and differences in their ecological settings might be considered ESUs, or even different phylogenetic species. Demes with smaller genetic distances might be ecologically and genetically exchangeable, thus constituting a single population, but they also might represent different management units, MUs. The best defined taxonomic unit is the species, but there are two dozen different species concepts, often highly controversially discussed. At a level below species, ESU, MU or subspecies, the controversy is even higher (Crandall et al., 2000; Fraser & Bernatchez, 2001; Moritz, 1994). Hence, captive breeding must address these issues by answering the following questions.

- What is the taxonomic unit used? Which species concept is being used? How are ESUs or other units representing the different evolutionary trajectories within species defined, and how are they measured?
- What is the phylogeographic structure of the species to be brought into captivity?
- What is the purpose of the breeding programme – is it to conserve evolutionary past, local adaptation or evolutionary future?
- Which populations or ESUs should be represented in captivity – should they be maintained singly or jointly?

Additionally, the issue is also how we manage captive populations where the above questions have been ignored it has resulted in mixing different evolutionary lineages or even species. This is the case of 'cocktail' orang-utans – the mix of Bornean and Sumatran orang-utan species bred in captivity (Mallinson, 1978; Perkins, 1998).

These questions are intricately linked. Conserving each ESU will be impossible considering that zoos have not enough space and resources for all endangered species that could benefit from captive breeding. This also depends on the level of differentiation in the wild, what remains of that differentiation and what is the purpose of the captive breeding. These questions often pose conservation dilemmas, especially as the decision to maximise future adaptability by mixing lineages will irrevocably destroy existing local adaptation and evolutionary past (Funk & Fa, 2006; Young et al., 2006).

Genetic tools have a great potential to provide baseline data on the population structure of the species in question and the founder population for captive breeding. Most molecular approaches use microsatellite markers and, to a lesser extend, RFLP and AFLP markers (see textbooks such as Allendorf & Luikhardt, 2006; Frankham et al., 2010). These methods are now very powerful. For example, they enable us to infer population origin of individuals, whose origin is unknown, and population structure of the source population from animals in captivity without reliable information on origin (e.g. in confiscated

1. Aloatran Gentle Lemur

The Lac Alaotra gentle lemur, also known locally as the Bandro, is a bamboo lemur. It is endemic to the reed beds in and around Lac Alaotra, in northeast Madagascar. The Alaotran gentle lemur is the only primate specifically adapted to living in papyrus reed marshes. The classification of the Bandro is disputed, with some classifying it as a subspecies of *Hapalemur griseus*, while others see it as a separate species. (Photo by Joanna Durbin.)

2. Floreana Mockingbird

It is endemic to Floreana, one of the Galápagos Islands of Ecuador, at present only occurring on offshore islets. Its natural habitat is subtropical or tropical dry shrubland. Formerly classified as an Endangered species by the IUCN, recent research shows that its numbers are decreasing more and more rapidly, and it is on the brink of extinction. It was consequently uplisted to Critically Endangered status in 2008. (Photo by Michael Dvorak.)

3. Guenther's Gecko

This species originally occurred on Mauritius before rats and cats were introduced. Nowadays, Guenther's Gecko inhabits only Round Island, 22 km north-northeast of Mauritius. The species has been reintroduced into other islets around Mauritius. (Photo by Gregory Guida.)

4. Mangrove Finch

The Mangrove Finch is restricted to the Galápagos Islands, Ecuador. Historically, it was known from at least six mangrove patches on east Fernandina and east, south and west Isabela. Surveys on Isabela found breeding populations in only two areas, Playa Tortuga Negra and Caleta Black on the north-west coast of the island, with estimated populations of 37 and 21 pairs respectively. This species is declining due to the predation and disease due to invasive species. (Photo by Michael Dvorak.)

5. St Lucia Iguana
The Saint Lucia iguana, although considered a form of the widespread green iguana *Iguana iguana*, is scarce, with fewer than a thousand mature individuals remaining in a total area of less than 2.5 km^2. The iguana's habitat is threatened by tourism developments, sand-mining, livestock grazing and predation. (Photo by Mathew Morton.)

6. Mauritius Fody
The species is restricted to south-west Mauritius. It has suffered rapid population declines since 1975, descending from 247–260 pairs to *c.* 108–122 pairs in late 2001 owing to heavy predation by invasive mammals. Since 1993, the population has been stable. Since 2005, hand-reared chicks were released onto Ile aux Aigrettes establishing a population expected to increase further in the coming years. (Photo by Gregory Guida.)

7. St Lucia Parrot

The St. Lucia Parrot, declared the island's National Bird, was reduced to around 200 birds in the 1970s due to loss of habitat. Protected areas have been set aside and educational programmes initiated and parrot numbers currently stand at around 2000 birds. (Photo by Hester Whitehead.)

8. Flat-tailed Tortoise

The Madagascan flat-tailed tortoise or Kapidolo (ghost turtle) is currently one of the most threatened of all the world's tortoises. It is threatened with extinction through loss of its deciduous, dry forest habitat and illegal collection for the pet trade. Kapidolo is a forest floor-dwelling species found only in a small area of western Madagascar. (Photo by Quentin Bloxam.)

9. Antiguan Racer

The Antiguan Racer was re-discovered in 1995 on Great Bird Island. At the time, the species was on the brink of extinction. Today, there are more than 500 Antiguan Racers on two islands. This recovery is due to conservation efforts involving habitat restoration and translocation of animals. (Photo by Mathew Morton.)

10. Madagascar Pochard

Believed extinct until its rediscovery in 2006, the Madagascar pochard is the world's rarest duck. A flock of nine adults and four recently hatched ducklings were discovered at a lake in a remote area of northern Madagascar. A rescue plan involving the removal of a clutch of ready-to-hatch eggs from lake-side nests and incubated artificially has increased numbers to over 40 birds. (Photo by Gerardo Garcia.)

11. Giant Jumping Rat

The Madagascar Giant Jumping Rat is classified as Endangered. Through widespread loss of its dry forest habitat, the Giant Jumping Rat has declined dramatically and is now only found in a 300 km² patch of forest on the west coast of Madagascar. Currently, the main threat to this species is further loss and degradation of its habitat through logging, clearance for agriculture and subsistence use of forest products. (Photo by James Morgan.)

12. Maria Island Racer

One of the world's rarest snakes, the Maria Island or Saint Lucia Racer is only found on the 5 ha Maria Major Island, a protected area. A relatively small, non-venomous snake, this racer is distinguished by a comparatively short tail, and a stripe of dark brown that runs from the neck to the tip of the tail. Little is known of its population size. (Photo by Mathew Morton.)

13. Round Island Boa

The species is classified as Endangered. In 1996 the population was estimated to number less than 250 mature individuals. The boa is known to survive only on Round Island, but has been recorded on the islands of Gunner's Quoin, Flat Island, Ile de la Pas, and on mainland Mauritius as subfossil remains. Recent increase in numbers has been achieved by eradicating goats and rabbits from the island and restoring natural habitat which has led to an increase of the boas' natural prey. (Photo by Gregory Guida.)

14. St Lucia Whiptail

The Vulnerable St Lucia whiptail lizard, considered a single species, is the sole representative of its genus in the Caribbean region, found on Maria Major and Maria Minor islands off the coast of St Lucia. However, a recent study revealed significant morphological and phylogenetic differences between the two populations and recommended they should be managed as two separate entities. The two populations are estimated to be around 2000 and 29 individuals on Maria Major and Minor, respectively. (Photo by Mathew Morton.)

15. **Montserrat Oriole**

The Montserrat Oriole, a medium-sized black-and-yellow icterid, inhabits a small area on the island of Montserrat in the Lesser Antilles. It is threatened by habitat loss, and has been classified as Critically Endangered, with a current estimated population of between 200 and 800. Much of its habitat was destroyed by deforestation, Hurricane Hugo and the volcanic activity between 1995 and 1997. (Photo by Gregory Guida.)

16. **Blue Iguana**

The Blue Iguana is a critically endangered species of lizard of the genus *Cyclura* endemic to the island of Grand Cayman. Previously listed as a subspecies of the Cuban Iguana, it was reclassified as a separate species in 2004 because of genetic differences discovered four years earlier. Habitat destruction is the main factor threatening imminent extinction for this iguana. (Photo by Matt Goetz.)

chimpanzees: Goossens *et al.*, 2002; Western lowland gorillas: Nsubuga *et al.*, 2010). Nevertheless, there is a surprisingly large number of species in captivity where we know very little information on how "captive collections" represent population structure in the wild, which populations they descend from or whether they are admixtures of several populations. For example, whilst the population structure of captive Rodrigues fruit bat was retrospectively compared with wild populations in O'Brien *et al.*'s (2007) benchmark study (Section 6.8), we know preciously little about Livingstone's fruit bat, or most other bat species held in captivity. Moreover, where we have phylogeographic information, it typically stems from neutral genetic markers such as microsatellites. These markers represent genetic loci under no or only weak selection. However, phylogenetic structure or the identification of MUs, ESUs or other units based on neutral markers does allow little inference on the future evolutionary potential (see Section 6.8).

Growth phase. The breeding strategy during the growth phase is determined by two main aims:

- Demographic aim: grow the population as fast as possible in order to produce a large enough population to withstand environmental and demographic stochasticity.
- Genetic aim: avoid or minimise random genetic drift. This is typically achieved by equalising founder representation including an equal sex ratio, equalising family size and avoiding inbreeding.

At this stage of captive breeding, the genetic aims generally conflict with the demographic aims. Reproductive strategies and reproductive success are typically biased in wild populations, leading to an effective population size that is smaller than the census size. The mean N_e/N ratio is approximately 0.1 in free-ranging populations (Frankham, 1995). It is species- and population-specific and has a large variance but rarely exceeds 0.5. In managed populations, N_e/N ratios typically exceed those of unmanaged populations (Mace & Lande, 1991), but this requires complex breeding strategies and intensive management even under ideal husbandry conditions where genetically desirable pairings can be achieved. During the founder and growth phase, however, knowledge of reproductive biology is typically patchy and husbandry not well developed. Thus it is often difficult to establish captive conditions that foster successful reproduction let alone genetically ideal reproduction. To assure rapid increase of the population, genetic management is therefore usually de-emphasised during the growth phase as in the case of the black-footed ferret and California condor programmes. With the exception of failing reproduction of genetically important founder lineages, resulting reproductive and genetic bias can be corrected subsequently by intensive genetic management.

Management phase. The management phase is largely determined by genetic considerations. The avoidance of random genetic drift and inbreeding requires larger population sizes than the avoidance of the negative effects of demographic and environmental stochasticity especially as the latter can be more effectively controlled *ex situ* than *in situ*. Genetic management for conservation aims to maintain the genetic structure of the captive population according to the aims of the programme, ideally set during or before the founder phase (Section 6.4.2). If the aim is to maintain a safety net population, then the goal of captive management is to minimise genetic change and to minimise genetic differentiation from the founder population. If the aim is to maintain a population with the maximum genetic variability, created by more than one founder population, then the goal is to minimise loss of genetic diversity only, irrespective how differentiated the captive population is from any of the sources. For the aims and genetic goals to be realistically achievable, sound information on the founder population's provenance and relatedness is required, but in reality, there is often only little, no or even false information available (Section 6.8). Often, separate evolutionary lineages or even sister taxa were mixed. Again, modern molecular genetics are powerful tools to efficiently address these issues, but these are rarely applied.

Operationally, random genetic drift and loss of genetic variability can be achieved by four main approaches.

(1) **Maximising the N_e/N ratio**. As outlined in Chapter 5, N_e can exceed N, resulting in a N_e/N ratio of larger than one. This is most efficiently achieved by equalising family size and equalising the sex ratio of breeders.

(2) **Equalising founder representation**. Variation of reproductive success of founder individuals leads to random genetic drift. Captive breeding must account for relatedness between founder animals, which would lead to over-representation of their genetic contributions, reproductive bias introduced during the growth phase, and reproductive biology (some animals are simply 'better' breeders or genetically ideal pairings result in no offspring because of behavioural issues). Careful breeding planning is essential and can be incorporated in the approaches minimising inbreeding (see below).

(3) **Minimising the rate of random drift over time**. Demographic fluctuations increase random genetic drift. Therefore, populations are typically maintained at relatively stable population size. Target sizes are controversial and are discussed in Chapter 5. The second important aim is to maximise generation length. Delaying reproduction as long as possible would fit that aim, but it is a risky strategy as it is in practice difficult to predict the end of reproductive age. Moreover, reproduction in earlier age is beneficial for animals as parenting behaviour improves often with experience and rearing of offspring constitutes an important aspect of social behaviour in some species, especially primates (e.g. Barbary macaques). Maximising generation length can be achieved by letting animals breed from sexual maturity onwards, but euthanising previous offspring or excluding them from reproduction. However, this is ethically highly problematic and can cause serious PR issues when the visiting public becomes aware of euthanasia programmes, which are beneficial for captive breeding for conservation but rarely accepted by the general public. Cryopreservation of embryos or gametes is also highly efficient not only to maximise generation length but also to avoid the loss of genetic variability, but these reproductive technologies have been developed only for a very small number of species of conservation concern.

(4) **Minimising inbreeding**. Short-term inbreeding is often not avoidable, especially at low population sizes during the founder and growth phases. Short-term moderate inbreeding (i.e. inbreeding between distant relatives) is not of major concern as the negative effects of inbreeding vanishes after outbreeding with unrelated animals in a subsequent generation. Inbreeding is, however, a major concern when between highly related animals or when inbreeding is longer-term, because it creates random genetic drift and loss of genetic variability (Chapter 5). There are many schemes to avoid inbreeding including the MAI, MK and OCS strategies (definitions in Appendix 1). Meffert *et al.* (2005) demonstrated in an experiment on captive houseflies that the application of a MAI scheme is advantageous *versus* a scheme to select against less fit individuals disregarding relatedness. MAI resulted in significantly lower inbreeding coefficients and higher fitness. Although MAI is highly efficient, it is rarely feasible because it imposes very strict conditions on pairings. If these conditions are violated, e.g. by behavioural incompatibility within pre-determined pairs, then the positive effects of the approach collapse. In the real world of complex pedigrees, unknown ancestry, unequal founder representation, behavioural complexity and reproductive stochasticity MK, an analogue of MAI, and OCS are more efficient. They consider genome uniqueness, i.e. the identification and selection of individuals, which are carriers of rare founder alleles. Minimising mean kinship and individual's genome uniqueness are interrelated as animals with unique genomes generally have low kinship to all other individuals in a population. MK is particularly flexible and robust against departures from the ideal conditions (Fernández *et al.*, 2003) and is the most implemented breeding strategy. For example, it is the recommended approach by AZA (Cronin *et al.*, 2006). Both computer simulations and experiments with model organisms such as *Drosophila* have shown that MK retains genetic diversity better than MAI and random selection of parents (Montgomery *et al.*, 1997). In addition, it is the most effective method for maintaining allelic frequencies in realistic situations (Saura *et al.*, 2008). MK selects individuals with the lowest pairwise kinship in the population for pairings whereby kinship is computed from pedigree information. Mean kinship is each animal's kinship with the entire current population; MK is widely used in captive breeding, e.g. the black-footed ferret (Wisely *et al.*, 2008). However, MK does not account for how animals are related to the population. A medium kinship to the whole population or a very high kinship to one part and a very low kinship to the other part of a population would give the same mean kinship values. Thus, MK does not specify to which degree selected animals should contribute to the next generation, i.e. how many offspring they should produce. Several solutions for this problem have been suggested, of which OCS seems the most powerful (Oliehoek, 2009; Pong-Wong & Woolliams, 2007). OCS is increasingly being applied in domestic animal breeding and should be considered for captive breeding (Colleau & Tribout, 2008; Oliehoek, 2009). OCS selects parents together with their optimal number of progeny such that average mean kinship among selected parents is minimised. Target population sizes typically exceed the capacity of individual zoos, requiring cooperative management

across institutions whereby the individuals of each species in all institutions constitute a single population. Cooperative management is planned and implemented by member institutions on a regional basis such as the AZA and EAZA (see above). Specialist software is available to identify pairings and to plan breeding programmes (e.g. SPARKS: Scobie, 1997; PM2000: Pollak *et al.*, 2002*)*.

In populations with only partially known pedigrees, mean kinship can be estimated less precisely, resulting in suboptimal management of genetic diversity (see Oliehoek, 2009, for overview). This widespread shortcoming can be solved using molecular genetics to estimate relatedness between potential mates and to clarify kinship in pedigrees (Ivy *et al.*, 2009). Although knowing the relatedness between founders is important for equalising founder contributions and avoiding genetic drift, unknown founder relationships have little impact on the effectiveness of MK. MK strategies produce near optimal results when standard founder assumptions are made (Ivy *et al.*, 2009; Rudnick & Lacy, 2008). Pedigree information is also unavailable in species with complex mating strategies, especially in multi-male multi-female breeding groups. For these scenarios, approaches exist to minimise group inbreeding (Wang, 2004; but note a major implementation gap: see above).

Whilst the science on genetic and demographic management is now advanced, and sophisticated methods including complex computer programs have been developed to plan breeding programmes, the effective management of captive populations may be compromised by the practical limitations of the implementation of these programmes. Cronin *et al.* (2006) compared breeding and transfer recommendations with actual implementations. SSPs agree to implement recommendations whereas PMPs only agree to consider them (see above). As expected, SSPs implemented more recommendations for specific breeding and animal transfers, but both programmes fell dramatically short of recommendations. Breeding success for both programmes was less than 20% and transfer success less than 50%. These sub-optimal performances render future demographic and genetic projections for captive populations problematic and potentially endanger the breeding aims.

Most implemented captive breeding programmes for conservation have focussed on minimising loss of genetic variability and inbreeding depression, but the problems of **adaptation** for subsequent reintroduction (Chapter 4) have received less attention and management than deserved, because it can lead to severely reduced population viability (Frankham, 2008; Woodworth *et al.*, 2002). Five management options exist to minimise adaptation.

(1) **Minimising numbers of generations in captivity**. Genetic adaptation depends on reproductive output over time (Frankham, 2008). Thus, captive breeding for reintroduction ought to minimise the numbers of generations in captivity. In other words, growth and management phases should be planned to be as short as possible. Three studies empirically examined the effect of reducing generation number in captivity and demonstrated greater changes the larger the number of generations in captivity. In oldfield mice behavioural traits were affected, in Mallorcan midwife toad morphological traits and in the large white butterfly reproductive output

(see Williams & Hoffman, 2009). Maximising generation length by selecting only animals that were born to their parents late in life will minimise the numbers of generations in captivity, but may be unpractical or controversial because of ethical considerations (see above). Similarly, delayed reproduction by separating sexes or by contraception can result in behavioural abnormalities. Contraception can be a useful approach but the utility is highly species-dependent (Asa & Porton, 2005). However, physiological abnormalities can develop and the treatment may not always be reversible. Therefore delayed reproduction is currently rarely being used (Williams & Hoffman, 2009). Cryopreservation can be efficiently applied, but this technology has not been developed or has not been optimised for most endangered species (see Section 5.9). Future research on delayed reproduction, especially using reversible contraceptive and cryopreservation are urgently needed as reducing the number of generations in captivity is the most efficient method available (because of the exponential relationship with adaptation; Frankham, 2008) and the most feasible of the available methods tackling adaptation.

(2) **Creating captive conditions as close to the wild as possible**. This approach changes natural selection least. Minimising the difference between captive and wild conditions also reduces the heritability of fitness in captivity, which in turn contributes to minimise adaptation. However, creating near wild conditions is in reality impractical as it involves complex habitats including animal guilds and disease. Therefore, captivity must seek realistic trade-offs, especially as the additional monetary expense might be better invested for *in-situ* conservation. Reducing adaptation is more efficiently achieved by other means listed here. However, creating more natural captive conditions has not only major advantages for animal welfare or is essential for the success of reintroductions (e.g. anti-predator behaviour) but will provide the add-on effect of reducing adaptation.

(3) **Equalising founder representation**. Managing that founder alleles continue to be represented equally over generations ensures that no lineages are favoured against or in favour. Similarly, managing populations under the mean kinship, MK, approach and equalising family sizes can significantly reduce adaptation (Frankham *et al.*, 2000). However, despite the reduction of adaptation, which comes as a 'by-product' of avoiding inbreeding (see above), this management approach is not sufficient to minimise adaptation. Woodworth *et al.* (2002) managed their experimental *Drosophila* populations accordingly, and yet they observed large fitness reduction due to adaptation.

(4) **Maximising the proportion of immigrants**. For most endangered species, this is not feasible because there are no wild populations which could sustainably provide new founders, or extraction of founders and subsequent transfer to zoos, often abroad, faces massive socio-political and legal hurdles.

(5) **Minimising population size**. The requirements for minimising inbreeding depression and random genetic drift versus avoiding genetic adaptation are diametrically opposite as the first needs to avoid small populations and the latter larger populations (Section 4.2.2). Theoretical considerations predict that there is a medium population

size, which leads to the least loss of fitness once a wild population is being restored from captivity (Fig. 4.1). Reducing population size by fragmenting populations combines both approaches and is now being advocated to reduce genetic adaptation (see Frankham, 2008, for overview). Population fragmentation in captivity has several practical add-on effects such as reducing the risk of disease propagation and catastrophic population extinction, and keeping cost low. It supports the maintenance of genetic diversity as fragmented populations retain more genetic diversity as a whole albeit each small fragmented population loses genetic diversity more rapidly than larger populations (Margan *et al.*, 1998). However, serious data gaps exist before this approach can be utilised.

6.8 Filling the gaps

Management decisions are severely hampered by lack of suitable data (Frankham, 2008; Fraser, 2008). Priorities for applied research are: (1) monitoring and documenting effects of captivity; (2) hypothesis testing and the use of well-designed experiments; and (3) optimising procedures through simulations and laboratory experiments and subsequent testing and refinement in practical management. For example, the advantages of population fragmentation outlined above compared to the management of effectively one large population, achieved by frequent transfer of individuals, are compelling on theoretical grounds and based on the small number of experiments (Woodworth *et al.*, 2002). However, planning the fragmented metapopulation approach is not straightforward (Lehmann & Perrin, 2006). Lacking experimental data and expertise on this method from actual management, key parameters such as the optimal fragment size and migration rates remain unknown for most, if not all, captive endangered populations (Williams & Hoffman, 2009). Optimisation of protocols and use of practical case studies to further develop this approach are urgently required to tackle the serious problem of genetic adaptation to captivity.

Although research on model species such as the fruitfly give valuable insights, more empirical data are required from other species. There is a large variance in the effects of genetic adaptation and the response to captivity is not uniform and depends on the genetic background of each species (Chapter 5). Thus generalisation from one species to another, even to closely related species, can be misleading (Rego *et al.*, 2007).

Wang (2004) introduced a novel approach to manage multi-male multi-female breeding groups, which overcomes the limitations of unknown pedigrees for efficient inbreeding avoidance (Chapter 5, Section 6.7.2). Although this approach has been repeatedly recommended to improve management (e.g. in the San Marcos salamander; Lucas *et al.*, 2009), no published information is available suggesting that it is actually being applied (we searched Web of Science in September 2010 and no publication on the application of the method was found). This either indicates an implementation gap or the failure to publish actual management applications in a peer-reviewed medium, which is a re-occurring problem with many of the data collected in zoos, or which should be collected in zoos (Chapter 9).

Another major research gap in achieving competent captive breeding, especially at the founding phase, is the lack of genetic baseline data. Efficient breeding for conservation requires detailed information on the population origin of founders, relatedness, demographic history of the source population and the comparative monitoring of the genetic composition of *ex-situ* populations compared to their *in-situ* counterparts over time. Molecular genetics offers a powerful toolbox to solve many of the questions, which need urgent attention for captive breeding to support conservation optimally. Recent developments in analytical tools have become very powerful and allow, for example, the estimation of the demographic history of source populations. This allows a contextualising of the loss of heterozygosity in captivity over time, as 5% loss will constitute very different levels of loss of genetic diversity relative to the founder population: a bottlenecked source population or a source population where little loss of heterozygosity occurred before founders were extracted.

Most applied estimates of within-population diversity and between-population differentiation rely on the use of neutral or near-neutral genetic markers (see Spielman *et al.*'s, 2004, meta-analysis; Section 6.7.2). These markers do not necessarily correlate with quantitative genetic variation, i.e. the variation in gene expression, which determines future evolutionary adaptability (Reed & Frankham, 2001; Leinonen *et al.*, 2008). Whilst basing the planning of conservation units in captivity on neutral markers is already a positive quantum leap compared with the all too familiar situation where no quantitative data are available, the approach biases conservation towards maintaining demographic history of populations. The optimal conservation strategy ought to enable maximum future adaptability. Moreover, a fear of outbreeding depression has been emerging amongst some conservation managers (Section 5.5). This poses the danger not to mix populations, where past demographic processes have resulted in population differentiation but where there might be no adaptive divergence. Not mixing these lineages in captivity increases the risk of inbreeding depression, which could be avoided by mixing them. Thus, for all of these decisions to be efficient, data are urgently required on quantitative traits and their phylogeographic structure. Suitable methods have emerged and are becoming economically affordable (Tymchuk *et al.*, 2010) and we urge that these methods are utilised for applied management.

Most captive populations for conservation are now specifically founded to create safety nets readily available if wild populations decline further, or to buffer catastrophes. Yet, there is a dearth of studies which analyse how similar the genetic structures of wild and *ex-situ* populations actually are. O'Brien *et al.* (2007) compared the genetic structure of *ex-situ* and *in-situ* Rodrigues fruit bats. The study demonstrated that the *ex-situ* programme was not only highly successful in retaining genetic diversity, but also that genetic drift between *in-situ* and *ex-situ* populations was minimal. In contrast, genetic differentiation between wild and captive and differences in heterozygosity and allelic richness were high in giant pandas, suggesting that new founders need to be introduced into captivity if captive pandas are to be representative of the wild populations (Shen *et al.*, 2009). Several studies compare phenotypic and genetic characteristics of captive-bred and wild fish, especially of economically important fish such as the Atlantic salmon (Blanchet *et al.*, 2008). However, only a very small number of such studies in other species have been published. Even for high-profile species, baseline information, which could be answered by molecular tools, has not been investigated. For example, there is no genetic information available on the relatedness of the founders of the current population of captive Bali mynahs.

This dearth of information stems from several sources. Much of the work is being carried out by academic institutions, but such institutions and the founding bodies are increasingly more focussed on pure science and research papers that can be published in high-ranking academic journals. An epiphenomenon of this is the large number of peer-reviewed publications on conservation genetics, which fail to address management issues or fail to propose practical conservation solutions (Vernesi *et al.*, 2008). On the other hand, there are only a limited number of zoological gardens with capacity in genetic analysis, such as Antwerp, Henry Doorly, London, or San Diego zoos, the National Zoo in the USA or the Chengdu Giant Panda Breeding Centre. Facing the current economic crisis, molecular genetic analysis is under severe funding restrictions and often the first department to be closed (e.g. at Durrell; Cowburn, 2010). It is generally assumed that genetics is expensive especially when it involves cost-intensive development of genetic marker sets (e.g. microsatellites). There are, however, approaches such as AFLP, which can estimate relatedness relatively easily and fairly cheaply, but these approaches are rarely used. Lastly, applied zoo managers, conservation biologists and more technologically oriented biologists such as geneticists or reproductive biologists are all involved in captive breeding. All these groups are often mutually suspicious, and rarely fully understand each others' underpinning science and goals. The importance of genetics and reproductive technology is often underappreciated, which leads to the failure to capitalise on their potential benefits.

Key concepts
(1) Animals kept in zoos are bred for four main reasons, as an aid to species conservation, to sustain animal populations for exhibition (and therefore reduce the number of animals that need to be collected from the wild), for research or for education to serve as ambassadors for their wild counterparts.
(2) Effective choice of species in zoos must not just consider biological and conservation-related variables, but also economic issues. Prioritising and allocating effort, in the certain knowledge that there is insufficient capital available to save and protect all of nature's diversity, requires careful selection of species. The current strategies are fuzzy and need urgent re-evaluation, especially as powerful selection procedures have been developed.
(3) Demographic and genetic management of captive populations vary substantially whether managed for future exhibition in zoos (breeding for display), as a 'living museum' for species that have become or are likely to become extinct in the wild, as a source for population augmentation or a source for reintroduction and introduction. Assuring viable *ex-situ* populations for future use and display in zoos is an economic imperative for zoo management, but is often presented as support for conservation.

(4) Zoos need to re-think their captive breeding strategies and the targets and criteria they apply to define viable populations for conservation. Genetic changes in captive populations have potentially more severe consequences than currently assumed, especially because of genetic adaptation to captivity. Given the substantial cost of any captive breeding, the criteria to determine viable zoo populations for conservation need urgent re-evaluation, which needs to utilise the data molecular ecology, evolutionary biology and conservation economics have collected over the past decade.

7 · Returning animals to the wild

'Researchers contemplating future reintroductions [should] carefully evaluate a priori the specific goals, overall ecological purpose, and inherent technical and biological limitations of a given reintroduction . . . ' (Phillip Seddon)

7.1 Introduction

The intentional movement by humans of an animal or a population of animals from one location with free release at another to re-establish a species which has been lost, or supplement existing populations, has become an important tool in conservation biology (Fischer & Lindenmayer, 2000; Seddon *et al.*, 2007). A common goal of many animal translocations is the establishment of self-sustaining populations. Animals may be sourced from other wild populations or from captive-stock. From an ecological perspective, the implications of where the animals originate, and therefore how prepared they may be for independent life post-release, and whether release site habitats are able to support viable populations, needs assessment. Re-establishment of species in areas from which they have been extirpated has never been intended to be the only means to conserve biodiversity. But, this is a particularly useful approach that is likely to be used increasingly in the coming decades, as numbers of critically endangered species rise (Chapter 3), or as some advocate if assisted colonisation of species (also referred to as managed relocation, assisted migration, or assisted translocation) becomes a realistic intervention strategy in biodiversity management under climate change (Hoegh-Guldberg *et al.*, 2008).

Interest in mediated animal movements as a significant aid to species conservation has grown in recent years, to the extent that 'reintroduction biology' has emerged as a discipline (Seddon *et al.*, 2007). The need to understand what factors influence 'success' is crucial (Fischer & Lindenmayer, 2000). Unlike previous less quantitative analyses of what constitutes success in translocations (e.g. Beck *et al.*, 1994), Seddon *et al.* (2007) and Armstrong & Seddon (2008) highlight that there is still scope to improve reintroduction biology as a science by the greater application of the hypothetico-deductive method, where models derived from careful observation and theory are subject to testing. Additionally, rigorous experimental or adaptive management approaches can yield reliable knowledge when correctly applied.

An important role of captive populations in some conservation programmes is the supply of animals for reintroduction. Tudge (1991) strongly espouses the idea that reintroductions should be the end point of captive breeding. More explicitly, Frankham *et al.* (2010) indicate that captive breeding and reintroduction may be viewed as a process that evolves from the founding, management and maintenance of the captive population over generations, to the release of propagules and management of reintroduced populations in the wild. Reintroduction projects attempt to re-establish species within their historical ranges through the release of wild or captive-bred individuals following extirpation or extinction in the wild (IUCN, 1998). But, there is evidence that translocations using captive-bred and especially endangered animals are more risky and therefore less successful (see below) than when wild-born individuals are involved (Griffith *et al.*, 1989). The primary issue is often related to the finding of sufficiently large founder populations, and therefore the reliance of captive breeding programmes to produce a source of animals for release. Maximising genetic variation in source and new populations is crucial, as well as understanding the implications of lowered genetic variation on survival. Thus, each species (and population) differ in basic life history traits, which influence their susceptibility to extinction factors (Chapter 1), and by extension their ability to colonise new habitats (see Wolf *et al.*, 1998; Armstrong & Perrot, 2000; Bar-David *et al.*, 2005; Bretagnolle & Inchusti, 2005). Advocates of captive breeding argue that zoos are crucial in re-establishing new populations of endangered species in the wild by pointing to well-known cases such as the Arabian oryx and the California condor (but see Rahbek, 1993). The need to assess the actual and real potential of captive-born animals to return to the wild via reintroductions, and especially the importance of zoos needs testing. The question that needs answering is whether the reliance on any single strategy such as conserving depauperate wild populations actually increases the risk of extinction to an unacceptable level.

In this chapter, we first review the plethora of terms used to describe the intentional movement of animals from source to a release site, and the reasons used to justify such animal movements. We assess the literature which suggests species benefit from reintroductions, and how much zoos contribute to animal reintroductions. Finally we detail how success can be measured and predicted, and we examine the future of reintroductions including the use of assisted migrations.

7.2 Terminology

The term most often used to denote the purposeful movements of animals from one location to another has been translocation. This term has been used inconsistently resulting in considerable confusion since it has been used as both the overarching term (see Griffith *et al.*, 1989) and for a particular type of relocation, i.e. the 'capture and transfer of free-ranging animals from one part of their historic geographic range to another' (Kleiman, 1989). To avoid misunderstanding in terminology, Fischer & Lindenmayer (2000) created a neutral overarching term, relocation. However, Armstrong & Seddon (2008) propose that we return to translocation as the overarching term, being any mediated movement with free release, and then the other terms relate specifically to the motivations for different types of translocation. This is because 'translocation' is to be defined by the source of founders, in contrast to other terms such as 'reintroduction' that are defined by the primary objective. We use translocation throughout this chapter.

An early set of definitions for the different terms and sub-terms used in translocations was published by Konstant & Mittermeier (1982). In their paper, terms are defined by the source of founders but also by the intent of the animal movements, thus they suggest that translocation *sensu stricto* is the capture and transfer of feral animals from one part of their natural range to another, with minimal time spent in captivity, whilst introduction is the release of animals into a habitat in which they have never occurred naturally. Introductions can involve wild-caught individuals, but may sometimes be attempted with captive-born animals. Introductions may be intentional or inadvertent. Reintroduction is the liberation of either wild-caught or captive-born animals into an area in which they have either declined or disappeared as a result of human pressures (e.g. overhunting) or from natural causes (e.g. epidemics). A reintroduction project can require translocation of wild-caught individuals from other areas of natural habitat, it can involve release of naive, captive-born animals, or it can be attempted with equally naive, wild-caught animals captured as either infants or young juveniles and raised in captivity. In the last two cases, a reintroduction project with groups such as primates would necessarily involve rehabilitation. Rehabilitation, included in the relocation definitions by Konstant & Mittermeier (1982), is the process of training naive animals to live in their natural habitat. This is a quite restrictive definition and runs the risk of being at odds (more confusion) with the more widely applied definition of: 'the managed process whereby a displaced, sick, injured, or orphaned wild animal regains the health and skills it requires to function normally and live self-sufficiently' (IWRC, 2010). The rehabilitants may be either captive-born individuals never exposed to natural surroundings, or wild-born animals captured as infants or young juveniles and raised in captivity. In both cases, young animals have usually been deprived of important learning processes and have often become imprinted on humans as well. Rehabilitation is an important feature of reintroduction projects involving intelligent animals such as primates in which learning plays a major role in infant development; it is less significant or even unnecessary for animals in which instinctive behaviour patterns predominate (e.g. crocodilians).

Most authors now follow the original terminology outlined in the IUCN position statement on the translocation of living organisms (IUCN, 1987b) where *translocation* is defined as 'the movement of living organisms from one area with free release in another.' Three different types of translocation are defined: (1) introduction; (2) reintroduction; and (3) re-stocking (or supplementations). These definitions are clear, simple and workable, with translocation providing a useful catch-all term and the other terms being mutually exclusive of one another.

7.3 Why translocate animals?

According to Caldecott & Kavanagh (1988) conservation reasons for translocating animals may include:

- moving of a wild population threatened with local extinction away from danger,
- restocking a suitable wild range with a captive population that may be wholly or partially 'surplus',

- introducing new conspecifics to relieve a small and isolated population that may be thought to be seriously threatened by inbreeding,
- translocating part of a population where a taxon is locally or globally found in only one area to avoid having 'all eggs in one basket', or simply
- translocation may be used as an alternative to culling.

Box 7.1 · *Animal translocations in New Zealand and the kakapo*

The kakapo it is the world's only flightless parrot, the heaviest parrot, nocturnal, herbivorous, visibly sexually dimorphic in body size, has a low basal metabolic rate, no male parental care, and is the only parrot to have a polygynous lek breeding system. It is also possibly one of the world's longest-living birds. It breeds only in the infrequent years when specific trees undergo mass seeding.

Globally, the extinction of New Zealand fauna is the most recent of all the late Quaternary-period extinctions. The rich record of species in fossil deposits makes this one of the best understood extinction events. Since the arrival of humans 1000 years ago, two-thirds of New Zealand's native forest has been wiped out, converted to grasslands and urban areas. Loss of natural habitat, hunting by early settlers and the arrival of animal predators helped extinguish entire species of indigenous birds – up to one-third of land-based birds such as the moa, Haast's eagle, piopio and huia – and left other species seriously depleted.

While extinct species cannot be revived, native species in the country have long been deliberately moved around islands by humans, in most cases for conservation purposes. A review by Sherley *et al.* (2010) of animal translocations in New Zealand, other than birds, recorded a minimum of 183 animal movements before the 1960s: 2 with bats, 86 with reptiles, 10 with amphibians and 85 with invertebrates (44 molluscs, 39 insects, one centipede and one spider). However, more than 723 native bird translocations have been undertaken in New Zealand between pre-1960 and 2008. The majority of published accounts of translocations involved species that were protected by law when they were moved. In 45% of all translocations, excluding birds, the outcome was unknown or too recent to report one. Breeding was confirmed in 11% of translocations, and in 22% the animals either survived a long time or their populations expanded. Failure was recorded in 15% of cases.

Out of all the endangered New Zealand birds, the kakapo has attracted most attention because of its rarity and eccentricity. Intensive manipulation of the kakapo has had its successes. The species was once common in the three largest islands of New Zealand, but its distribution shrank following the spread of black rats and stoats introduced from Europe in the 1870s and 1880s. By the 1950s, kakapo were extinct on North Island and only 18 remained in a remote and mountainous part of South Island. The stoats are thought to have eaten not only eggs and chicks, but also incubating females, so all 18 survivors were male. The only remaining wild females were on Stewart Island (south of South Island), which stoats had not colonised, although rats and feral cats were present.

In-situ conservation of natural populations proved impracticable, and recent conservation efforts have concentrated on establishing safe populations by translocating wild-caught kakapo to offshore islands without significant predators. In 1989, a Kakapo Recovery Plan was developed and a Kakapo Recovery Group established to implement it. The first action of the plan was to relocate all the remaining kakapo to suitable islands for them to breed. None of the New Zealand islands was ideal to establish kakapo without rehabilitation by extensive revegetation and the eradication of introduced mammalian predators and competitors. Four islands were finally chosen: Maud, Hauturu/Little Barrier, Codfish and Mana. Between 1974 and 1992, 65 kakapo (43 males, 22 females) were successfully transferred onto the four islands in five translocations. Little Barrier Island was eventually viewed as unsuitable due to the rugged landscape, the thick forest and the continued presence of rats, and its birds were evacuated in 1998. Along with Mana Island, it was replaced with two new Kakapo sanctuaries, Chalky Island (Te Kakahu) and Anchor Island. The entire kakapo population of Codfish Island was temporarily relocated in 1999 to Pearl Island in Port Pegasus while rats were being eliminated from Codfish. All kakapo on Pearl and Chalky Islands were moved to Anchor Island in 2005.

To minimise transit time, radio-transmitters were attached to free-living kakapo; the radio-tagged birds were recaptured for transfer when air transport was available and they were liberated immediately upon arrival at the island (Lloyd & Powlesland, 1994). Few, if any, kakapo now remain within their former range. Regular monitoring and intensive management of the translocated populations is being undertaken. Between 63% and 85% of translocated kakapo have survived but thus far productivity has been low, only two young having survived to independence.

Individuals of a species may be removed from a community for reasons such as to relieve another rarer species from competition, to improve a population by correcting structural imbalances or weeding out unfit individuals, or to stabilise oscillations in population size that may threaten the population itself.

The deliberate movement of animals can also be motivated by educational, commercial, scientific and compassionate reasons. An example of translocation of animals for primarily educational reasons includes the establishment of free-living animal populations in new areas, such as small primates (e.g. callitrichids) in wooded areas within zoo settings (Price et al., 1989). Movements of species taken from their habitat countries far away to equivalent natural settings outside their natural range include the establishment of primate colonies to supply animals for biomedical research such as the Indian rhesus macaques introduced to Cayo Santiago Island, Puerto Rico (Rawlins & Kessler, 1986), or Morgan Island in South Carolina (Westergaard *et al.*, 1999). Reasons for moving animals for compassionate reasons (to protect the animal from pre-emptive or retaliatory attacks from humans and to protect the lives and livelihoods of the local community) are clearly exemplified by the recurring issues around the translocation of individual 'problem' carnivores. Translocation of large carnivores has been a standard management tool for decades in North America and southern Africa in response to livestock depredation and other conflict behaviours (Linnell *et al.*, 1997).

7.4 Reintroductions for conservation

Reintroduction has been seen as a valuable tool for conservation with the potential to save many species from extinction (Kleiman, 1989; MacKinnon & MacKinnon, 1991; Sarrazin & Barbault, 1996; Seal, 1991; Stuart, 1991; Tear *et al.*, 1993). There have been a number of well-publicised reintroductions, e.g. golden lion tamarin (Kleiman & Mallinson, 1998), red wolf (Oakleaf *et al.*, 2004), California condor (Snyder & Snyder, 2000), black-footed ferret (Seal *et al.*, 1989), and Arabian oryx (Stanley Price, 1989). Most of the animals used in these projects were either captive-born or brought into captivity due to their near extinct status (Chapter 4). On a much larger scale (Box 7.1), considerable success in threatened species management through reintroductions has occurred in New Zealand (Craig *et al.*, 2000; Sherley *et al.*, 2010).

Determining the potential number of species that may require recovery through re-introduction has been attempted by Stuart (1991). Using the IUCN's SSC Action Plans, primarily mammals (and especially large mammals), and thus not representative of the conservation needs of all taxonomic groups, Stuart (1991) indicated that of the 660 species listed to be under threat by the authors of the Action Plans, reintroduction was recommended for 68 (10.3%) of these, of which marsupials, crocodiles and otters (a total of 38 species) made up over half of this number. For the majority ($n = 45$) of species advocated for reintroduction, captive breeding is also recommended (Wilson & Stanley Price, 1994). Most are already being bred with varying degrees of success in zoos; only 14 are reported to have international studbooks, although others may have regional studbooks. Of the remaining 23 species for which translocation was recommended, sufficient numbers remain elsewhere in the wild (e.g. marsupials and otters). In some cases, translocation is an option where there are fears that numbers needed to establish viable zoo populations would risk remnant wild populations (e.g. Javan rhino). Assuming that there is enough habitat for the 68 species to be reintroduced, 40 of these species are native to areas outside Europe, North America, Japan and Australia. Of the remaining 28 taxa, 20 are Australian, a country where reintroductions are the subject of strict methodology and approval by state and territory governments.

Stuart (1991) also observed that the Action Plans recommended habitat protection (through protected area establishment and management) as key to species survival. This is because most threatened species have declined to low levels primarily because of destruction or alteration of their habitat. These species are usually occupying fully what

Table 7.1 *Frequency of reintroduction projects, species and individuals*

Class	Projects	Species	Individuals	Average individuals/project
Mammals	46 (32%)	39 (31%)	2317	50
Birds	65 (45%)	54 (43%)	39 054	737
Reptiles and amphibians	23 (16%)	22 (17%)	31 483	1499
Fish	9 (6%)	9 (7%)	13 201 050	3 200 263
Invertebrates	2 (1%)	2 (2%)	1391	696
Total	145	126	13 275 295	

Data from Beck *et al.* (1994).

little habitat remains, so reintroduction is unlikely to be a useful conservation tool unless large-scale ecological restoration is first carried out. It follows that for those taxa that have suffered from pressures on the species *per se*, and not at the habitat level (where substantial tracts of unoccupied suitable habitat still remain), if the original cause of decline can be removed, then reintroduction is a practical solution.

7.5 Reintroduction of captive-born animals

Beck *et al.* (1994) documented 145 known cases of reintroduction of captive-born animals (Table 7.1). These included over 13 million individuals of 126 species. Arranged by class most reintroduction projects involved mammals (32%) and birds (45%). Reptiles and amphibians made up 16% of known projects, fish (6%) and invertebrates only 1%. The average number of individual captive-born animals reintroduced by project and species shows, as expected due to their generally high fecundity and relative ease of handling and transporting eggs, fry and adults, that fish were disproportionately more available for release than other classes. Ounsted (1991) has also noted that the preponderance of bird over mammal reintroductions is due in part to the ease of manipulating and fostering eggs.

Relative to the abundance of species of each class, reintroduction of captive-born mammals and birds is used more frequently than would be predicted. Fish and especially invertebrate reintroductions (with at least 300 000 species) are less frequent. Although it is endangerment rather than abundance that should drive the frequency of use of any recovery method, the figures presented by Beck *et al.* (1994) do not distinguish between common or endangered taxa involved.

Species that have not been considered for release to the wild by using captive-bred animals in the past can become likely candidates for reintroduction in the future, if conditions for the species deteriorate. This is now the case for most of the great apes. Although much is known and has been achieved in rehabilitating Bornean and Sumatran orangutans (Russon, 2009), gorillas (Farmer & Courage, 2008) and chimpanzees (Goossens *et al.*, 2002, 2005) these species have been recently reintroduced to the wild.

Throughout their range, African great apes are threatened by deforestation, hunting for bushmeat and disease outbreaks (Barnes, 2002; Walsh *et al.*, 2003; Leroy *et al.*, 2004; Fa & Brown, 2009). Chimpanzees have a wide distribution in tropical Africa but populations are diminishing throughout the species' range. Hunting pressure results in increasing numbers of orphaned infants, and sanctuaries have been created in response to the plight of these orphan apes. There are presently 18 ape sanctuaries in Africa, housing more than 500 great apes (Farmer, 2002). However, keeping chimpanzees in captivity represents a long-term commitment (the life expectancy of chimpanzees in captivity being about 45 years), associated with a high financial burden.

Returning confiscated chimpanzees to the wild may be a possibility for some captive individuals (Tutin *et al.*, 2001). Release of wild-born chimpanzees is difficult and has led to the establishment of several semi-wild populations on islands (Tutin *et al.*, 2001). However, the natural history of chimpanzees makes their reintroduction difficult. For example, a lengthy apprenticeship with adults is needed to acquire the appropriate behaviour to survive in the wild (Custance *et al.*, 2002), and chimpanzees respond aggressively to strangers (Goodall, 1986). Although a few chimpanzee release projects have been carried out, with various degrees of success (Hladik, 1973; Brewer, 1978; Borner, 1985; Hannah & McGrew 1991; Treves & Naughton-Treves, 1997), most of these concerned chimpanzees originating from laboratories or zoos released onto forested islands, rather than into extensive forest areas. Although the wild chimpanzee population is not so low that it needs to be supplemented with captive chimpanzees, knowledge of how to release chimpanzees successfully in the future is urgently needed.

Goossens *et al.* (2005) demonstrated that after eight years of post-release monitoring of 37 wild-born, captive chimpanzees released into the Conkouati-Douli National Park, Republic of Congo, overall survival was high, with 23 (62%) individuals remaining in the release zone, and only five (14%) confirmed dead. Released females regularly interacted with wild chimpanzees. Several females appeared to have integrated into wild groups for extended periods of time, and four released females gave birth to a total of five offspring. However, encounters with wild chimpanzees were a major cause of mortality in released males, and 40%–50% of released males would have died without veterinary intervention. These results demonstrate that wild-born, captive chimpanzees can be released into the wild successfully, under certain specific conditions, with careful planning and preparation critical at all stages; a suitable release area must be identified; potential risks to existing wild populations, including the possibility of disease transmission, must be minimised; and post-release monitoring is essential.

7.6 How much are zoos involved?

The crucial issue to resolve is not whether zoos can justify their contribution to conservation through the reflected glory of iconic reintroduction projects such as the Arabian oryx, California condor or black-footed ferret. But whether zoo-originated reintroductions have actually made a significant quantitative contribution to conservation, or have the potential to do so. Stanley Price & Fa (2007) define four measures by which zoo populations might be judged for their reintroduction potential.

(1) The re-establishment of animals in the wild is usually in response either to total or local extinction; animals may also be released to reinforce small populations. Thus, reintroduction is most likely to address a situation of relative or absolute rarity. If zoos are to meet these demands for animals, they should be keeping rare species. Do they?

(2) No source population, captive or wild, should be endangered by demands for individuals for release (IUCN, 1998). Therefore, source populations for reintroduction must be self-sustaining, at least as large as the minimum size for this criterion. Are zoo populations large enough (Chapter 6)?

(3) Reintroduction projects vary greatly in the numbers of animals released and the number of releases. One attribute of successful wild-to-wild translocations is that they involve the release of many individuals and over several to many years (Griffith et al., 1989). This finding has been criticised as simplistic because projects that release a large number of animals over long periods are also those that are well resourced and have greater perceived likelihood of success.

(4) Models of swift fox releases also showed that an initial population of 100 individuals supplemented by 20 individuals per year for 10 years had the lowest probability of extinction of all models tested (Ginsberg, 1994). Thus, an adequate supply of animals must be available; are zoo populations large enough to meet such demands?

(5) Many reintroductions have now been carried out. Given the variety of situations and types of animals released, have zoos been the major provider?

Although the zoo community espouses the rationale that captive breeding should contribute to endangered species be returned back to the wild, they are still not the primary proponents, providers of release animals, funders or managers of reintroduction. State and federal wildlife agencies are involved in the great majority of reintroductions. A review of wildlife translocations in the USA carried out in one year showed that 26 out of 45 State wildlife agencies (64%) had performed animal movements (Boyer & Brown, 1988). Of these, 69% of the agencies involved projected no change in future level of translocation activity and another 20% planned an increase. Beck et al. (1994) recorded that zoo-bred animals or the captive-bred descendents of zoo animals were reintroduced in 76 (59%) out of a total of 129 reintroduction projects. On average, one in five zoos and aquaria were involved (from a total of 350 zoos and aquaria in the developed world). Zoo-bred animals were reintroduced in 37% of 76 recorded projects, birds in 41%, reptiles and amphibians in 20%, fish in 3% and invertebrates in none. Since some projects released zoo-bred and non-zoo-bred (but captive-born) animals, Beck et al. (1994) found it difficult to determine precisely how many zoo-born animals have been reintroduced but a minimum of 20 849 animals may have been involved (over half of these were reptiles and amphibians).

The argument can be made that because reintroductions are complex operations, requiring diverse skills, zoos may be providing more than just animals for release. To explore this, Stanley Price & Fa (2007) took an issue of the Reintroduction Specialist Group Newsletter (Soorae, 2003) and assessed the organisations involved in the reintroductions described and the institutional affiliations of the authors listed. Out of a total of 28 papers on reintroductions and 51 authors involved, only about 20% of authors listed a zoo affiliation, and twice as many authors came from conservation organisations, zoos were listed as involved in almost 50% projects. Where zoos were involved in a reintroduction, zoos had provided animals for release in slightly less than half of them. In just over half, the zoos had played other roles. These roles fell into three areas: (1) to provide overseas project administration services, or (2) as a provider of funds for the project, or (3) most commonly, as sources of specialised technical expertise, amongst which veterinary assistance was notable. There may be many biases in using this author information, but it does suggest that zoos are significant contributors to reintroductions, but in ways that use their particular resources and skills rather than providing animals for release.

Zoos could focus on smaller-bodied species (therefore less space-limited and even more likely to breed well in captivity, Chapter 4), which often have a large component of their behaviour non-learned and are generally expected to be easier to reintroduce. In particular, amphibians (and to lesser extent reptiles) possess a number of attributes that make them potentially good models for such programmes. In an analysis by Stanley Price & Fa (2007) of all reintroductions of amphibians and reptiles for which the RSG has been able to collect adequate data (see also Seddon et al., 2005), out of 94 species with data, more than 50% relied on wild-caught individuals that were translocated to a second in-wild destination. Where captive-bred animals were released, only 10% of cases came from zoos, and the remainder from specialised facilities of various types. More recently, Griffiths & Pavajeau (2008) reviewed the extent and effectiveness of captive breeding and reintroduction programmes for amphibians through an analysis of data from the Global Amphibian Assessment and other sources. Most captive-breeding and reintroduction programmes for amphibians have focused on threatened species from industrialised countries with relatively low amphibian diversity. Out of 110 species in such programmes, 52 were in programmes with no plans for reintroduction that had conservation research or conservation education as their main purpose. A further 39 species were in programmes that entailed captive breeding and reintroduction or combined captive breeding with translocations of wild animals. Nineteen species were in programmes with translocations of wild animals only. Eighteen out of 58 reintroduced species have subsequently bred successfully in the wild, and 13 of these species have established self-sustaining populations. As with threatened amphibians generally, amphibians in captive breeding or reintroduction programmes face multiple threats, with habitat loss being the most important. Nevertheless, only 18 out of 58 reintroduced species faced threats that are all potentially reversible. When selecting species for captive programmes, dilemmas may emerge between choosing species that have a good chance of surviving after reintroduction because their threats are reversible and those that are doomed to extinction in the wild as a result of irreversible threats. Captive breeding and reintroduction programmes for amphibians require long-term commitments to ensure success, and different management strategies may be needed for species earmarked for reintroduction and species used for conservation research and education.

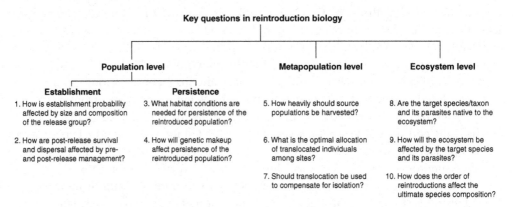

Fig. 7.1 Ten key questions for reintroduction biology, divided into questions at the population, metapopulation and ecosystem levels. Population-level questions are divided into questions about establishment and persistence of reintroduced populations. Taken from Armstrong & Sedden (2008).

7.7 Theoretical considerations of translocation success

7.7.1 Strategic approach

Translocation methodology, including results and strategy, demands rigorous analysis in order to understand its realistic value to biodiversity conservation. There is a need to know how well it works, what factors are associated with success and what strategies suggest potential success. According to May (1991), given the current state of our knowledge, any animal translocation, especially reintroductions, constitutes an experiment, so they must be deliberately planned and monitored so that we learn from them, whether they are successes or failures. A reintroduction programme should be seen as an exercise in adaptive management (Peterman *et al.*, 1978). Even so, the need for a more strategic approach where research and monitoring targets questions are identified *a priori* has been advocated by some authors, in particular Armstrong & Seddon (2008). Although translocation research will always have a strong emphasis on case studies because there is no substitute for local knowledge of species and systems, meta-analyses might have a greater role in future research. Useful meta-analyses depend on good data from individual case studies, and comparative analyses of simple statistics – such as success rates – will produce misleading or trivial results in the absence of such data.

Armstrong & Seddon (2008) envision five ways in which a more strategic approach can be developed using a framework of ten key questions (Fig. 7.1). First, the authors emphasised that at the outset, designing monitoring to address questions identified *a priori* will increase the amount of useful knowledge obtained from limited conservation funds. Second, if researchers consider the full framework of questions, the scope of translocation research will increase dramatically. Translocation research has so far focussed on only four of the ten key questions proposed (Q1–Q3, Q5), with little attention given to metapopulation and ecosystem-level questions. Third, the framework of questions can be used to improve communication between researchers and practitioners. Practitioners might be able to answer most of the questions based on prior expert knowledge and then to seek research support to address questions where the greatest uncertainty exists. Fourth, the framework of questions will encourage researchers and practitioners to think beyond their own projects. That is, monitoring programmes can be designed not just to address the key questions identified for the current reintroduction, but to address questions of interest to other projects throughout the world. Some reintroductions provide ideal model systems to address general questions and it is important to take advantage of these systems. Fifth, the framework of questions will encourage researchers and practitioners to build on the previous research. Consideration of questions to address will lead to consultation of previous research results, and those results can be taken into account when designing both management and monitoring strategies. Prior data could also be incorporated into subsequent analysis, and recent developments in Bayesian analysis provide a promising methodology for doing this. For example, population growth rates (Q3, Q4) under a particular management regime could be estimated not just from monitoring data for the current translocation, but also incorporating prior estimates, potentially improving the precision of the estimates.

From a more practical standpoint, the consideration of behavioural patterns, particularly among animals which depend on learning in an appropriate setting, is important. Social animals should be released in cohesive groups whenever possible, to minimise stress and to facilitate reproduction. There is a need to plan gradual acclimatisation of individuals to each other and to their environment. Releases of territorial animals can be more difficult, as each group may have to be released in different sites. Additionally, releases in many situations can only be effective if they do not conflict with the interests of local populations or if they have the sympathy of these. It is often too easy to lose sight of the social and political context within which programmes of reintroductions are likely to be embedded. Efforts should always be made to educate local peoples about the issues, and these should be based on surveys of the relative effectiveness of different approaches. General *a priori* considerations for any translocation require knowledge of the ecological setting and of the genetic consequences.

7.7.2 The ecological setting

Knowledge of the ecological setting into which the target species is to be released, including the causes of decline or endangerment of the original wild population, must be gathered. For example, in the case of the Hawaiian goose, knowing the causes of decline of the species would have helped in establishing a self-sustaining population from released captive-bred animals. Out of the 2150 captive-bred birds released between 1949 and 1983 there were still not enough left to maintain a wild population (Black *et al.*, 1997). Estimated annual mortality rate was up to 87%; deaths were related to year of release, age-class and method of release. Similarly, the long-term success of the black-footed ferret in North America is linked to understanding the way canine distemper interacts with wild populations of ferrets.

It is necessary to find out not only reasons for a population's decline but also details of its life-history and vital rates in natural settings. Unfortunately, there are few populations in which we have complete information of factors that regulate long-term average abundance. However, theoretical considerations based on the ecology of invading species predict that population persistence is more likely when:

- the number of founders is large;
- there is reduced environmental variation;
- the animals are herbivorous;
- there is high genetic diversity among founders.

Though often understanding is likely to be incomplete and tentative, ecological issues related to the demographic processes, but in particular density-dependent and density-independent factors affecting birth, death and movement rates will affect the establishment of new populations. Equally, the habitat needs will be determined by the animal's life-history. Thus, smaller animals with fairly precise habitat requirements or complex life-cycles are likely to be more demanding in this respect than are large generalists. Choice of appropriate release sites can become even more difficult when the species is extinct in the wild since ecological requirements must come from inferences from closely related species, research on captive animals, documented records, and observations made during pilot programmes of release.

7.7.3 Translocation genetics

Molecular tools are becoming more commonly used for the management of captive-breeding programmes, the selection of individuals for release, the identification of populations that require genetic management, the identification of captive or wild source populations and the assessment of genetic implications of deliberate or accidental translocations (Hedrick *et al.*, 1996; Frankham & Ralls, 1998; Westemeier *et al.*, 1998; Madsen *et al.*, 1999; Ralls *et al.*, 2000). However, interpretation of molecular data and devising translocation strategies are complex and case-specific, giving little scope for generalisation.

Inbreeding and outbreeding depression. Population genetic theory predicts that small populations will be affected by inbreeding and random genetic drift (Gilpin & Soulé, 1986). Nevertheless, there are populations that have lost much of their genetic diversity following severe bottlenecks without any detectable inbreeding depression (Caro & Laurenson, 1994). As a consequence, the relative importance of inbreeding depression for population persistence and for conservation in general has been challenged (Caro & Laurenson, 1994). However, the stochastic elements of random genetic drift and inbreeding mean that the survival of some inbred lineages is likely, even if inbreeding is often deleterious. Nonetheless, a large body of empirical and experimental evidence has accumulated over the past decade or so, which highlights that low genetic diversity may lead to inbreeding depression and reduced fitness (see Lacy, 1997; Saccheri *et al.*, 1998; Westemeier *et al.*, 1998; Hedrick & Kalinowski, 2000). The magnitude of inbreeding depression and the effects of purging (the removal of genetic load by selection), which may counterbalance inbreeding, are expected to vary considerably among species and among populations within the same species (Lacy & Ballou, 1998; Kalinowski et al., 2000). The effects of inbreeding depression also depend on the population's genetic composition and environmental conditions and are likely to become more severe under increasing environmental stress (Fowler & Whitlock, 1999). Therefore, the fact that some populations thrive despite low genetic diversity does not imply that there will no negative fitness consequences if environmental conditions change. These results also indicate that inbreeding in captivity in order to purge genetic load, a strategy favoured by Templeton & Read (1994), may be risky because of the environmental specificity of deleterious alleles.

In order to avoid random genetic drift and potential inbreeding depression (Chapter 5), a widely used strategy is to maximise genetic diversity within founding stocks (Lacy, 1987; Lewontin & Birch, 1996). Though this theoretically may lead to outbreeding depression by loss of local adaptation or the creation of genetic incompatibilities (see Templeton 1986), it is generally regarded as a less severe problem than inbreeding depression (Moritz, 1999) and evidence for this phenomenon on a population level is rare in captivity and in the wild (Burton et al. 1999; Marshall & Spalton, 2000). On a species level, hybridisation and genetic introgression have frequently led to population extinction, particularly in fish, and adverse effects of restocking programmes need to be addressed thoroughly (Allendorf & Leary, 1986; Keenan, 2000).

Gene flow, phylogeography and units for conservation. A general consensus is emerging that conservation management should maintain or restore evolutionary and ecological processes rather than taxonomic units or phenotypic variants (Templeton, 1986; Moritz, 1999; Crandall et al., 2000). Consequently, management by translocation should maintain or restore 'natural' levels of gene flow. However, there is considerable debate about defining 'natural' levels of gene flow and defining operational criteria for measuring population distinctiveness and setting targets for artificial gene flow (Moritz, 1999; Crandall et al., 2000).

ESUs are distinct populations meriting separate management (Ryder, 1986). Though ESUs were originally defined with an emphasis on significant adaptive variation (Ryder, 1986), the emphasis has subsequently shifted towards genetic isolation of populations (Crandall et al., 2000) because of the operational ease with which modern molecular tools allow the identification of populations between which gene flow has ceased to exist (Davis & Nixon, 1992; Moritz, 1994).

Interpreting molecular data with respect to gene flow and population isolation has proved to be not as straightforward as hoped (Barratt et al., 1999). Neutral genetic markers are by far the most common class of genetic markers used, but give little insight into the adaptive significance of observed population differentiation and the consequences of management of gene flow for evolutionary potential and population survival (Haavie et al., 2000).

Moritz (1999) advocates conserving historically isolated and independently evolving ESUs by not allowing translocations between ESUs. This approach, together with the IUCN (1998) reintroduction guidelines, which prescribe that the source population, should be genetically closely related to the original population, may enhance genetic isolation where gene flow could be more appropriate to maintain adaptive diversity. Moreover, genetic differentiation may be reinforced by random genetic drift in small, isolated populations, i.e. those that are targeted by translocations. Historical processes do not necessarily constitute adaptive significance, especially when random processes such as founder events or random lineage sorting caused phylogenetic structure. If conservation aims to preserve adaptive significance and evolutionary potential, then many ESUs that were identified by quantifying genetic isolation could and should be intermixed. No consensus over this fundamental discrepancy in the approach to conservation has yet been achieved (Moritz, 1999; Crandall *et al.*, 2000).

Genetic considerations in the post-release phase of translocations. Post-release genetic monitoring should primarily address two aspects. First, it should quantify changes in genetic composition of reintroduced or augmented populations over time. The continuous monitoring allows translocation strategies to be readjusted, if, for example, loss of genetic diversity is detected. Second, it contributes to the assessment of the success of translocations. The analysis of the success of translocations depends on knowing the fate of translocated animals and their reproductive success, the development of effective population size over time and, in case of reinforcements, the reproductive integration with the wild population. This information has traditionally not been available. Recent advances in using non-invasively collected DNA samples (Kohn *et al.*, 1999; Taberlet *et al.*, 1999) together with the development of analytical tools (e.g. detection of population bottlenecks and quantifying effective population size; Beaumont & Bruford, 1999) constitute new powerful tools for post-release monitoring. These methods not only allow assessing genetic composition after the release, but also are highly suitable additions to field-based methods for monitoring distribution and demographics.

How can genetic considerations guide translocation planning? Translocations create artificial migrants, may mix individuals from populations with differing evolutionary backgrounds and may introduce novel genes (Madsen *et al.*, 1999) into target populations. Therefore, comprehensive molecular studies should be an integral part of any translocation programme and not only part of those programmes which specifically address the re-establishment of diversity or those which were specifically designed as experiments where gene pools from different populations are mixed (Forbes & Boyd, 1997). In practice, however, the idealistic aim of integrating scientific research and practical management appears to be difficult to achieve and there remains a major dichotomy between practical management and scientific research (Breitenmoser *et al.*, 2001; Bullock & Hodder, 1997; Sarrazin & Barbault, 1996). Managers in the field tend to give genetic considerations low practical priority. Several factors contribute to this: first, translocations are rarely carried out as long-term projects, as highlighted by the general failure of long-term monitoring and reporting (Breitenmoser *et al.*, 2001). Consequently, factors affecting success in the short term, i.e. environmental and demographic variation, are of greater concern than genetic processes which will act on a longer time-scale (Caro & Laurenson, 1994). Second, translocation projects are rarely carried out in an overall framework that identifies global conservation needs and strategies. Instead aesthetic, economic or political considerations usually lead to such projects (Sarrazin & Barbault, 1996). For example, many translocations focus on 'flagship' species which are not globally endangered, whilst even baseline ecological data are missing for many endangered populations and species (Breitenmoser *et al.*, 2001). Third, genetic and evolutionary processes are complex and case-specific, which in turn requires extensive research that is normally time- and resource-intensive. However, the financial constraints of most translocation programmes lead to the neglect of many basic requirements of the IUCN Guidelines (1998) such as monitoring population demography in the post-release phase (Breitenmoser *et al.*, 2001). Expensive genetic methodology is often difficult to finance. Conservation organisations often avoid supporting molecular methodology whilst research bodies are more interested in research that is based on hypothesis testing rather than conservation management. There is an increasing tendency in molecular laboratories to utilise highly effective, but expensive screening methodology (e.g. automated sequencers), and highly specialised laboratories are often located far away from the translocation sites, usually in different countries or continents. Where possible, molecular screening should be carried out with direct involvement of the local research community and within the countries where the endangered populations exist. This can only be achieved by designing cost-efficient screening strategies, which rely only on basic equipment and methodology (such as electrophoresis with unlabelled primers and subsequent silver-staining or staining with ethidium bromide; Morgante *et al.*, 1998). A robust marker system that is powerful enough for individual genetic tagging and monitoring of the reproductive integration of released individuals into the wild population now exists to enable screening within the region without the need of expensive technology.

There remains considerable uncertainty in interpreting molecular data on population differentiation and migration rates in the context of adaptive significance and evolutionary patterns of gene flow (Haavie *et al.*, 2000). This may lead to the conclusion that molecular techniques are not adequate management tools since they rarely lead to clear-cut management strategies and often fail to predict the outcome of management interventions (Milligan *et al.*, 1994). With or without pre-release genetic screening of source and target populations for translocations (or source populations only for introductions and reintroductions), the ecological and genetic consequences are uncertain. Therefore, translocations should always be regarded as experiments and conservation management needs to monitor the outcome of translocations and to quantify the impact on population genetic structure and population viability. The recent advances in molecular methodology, in particular utilisation of non-invasively collected DNA samples, allow efficient post-release monitoring of reproductive success and spatial patterns of released individuals and their offspring (Morin *et al.*, 1994, 2001; Kohn *et al.*, 1999; Taberlet *et al.*, 1999; Vigilant *et al.*, 2001). Moreover, these methods are now a powerful alternative for estimating population size and the distribution of species where density is difficult to estimate using traditional ecological methods.

Post-release monitoring of populations is an ongoing obligation, especially in long-lived animals like chimpanzees that have a generation time of 20 years. It must be reiterated that monitoring will only contribute to the knowledge base of conservation management and science if data are published. This, however, has been largely neglected in the past (Breitenmoser *et al.*, 2001). The advance of electronic publishing now allows the effective distribution of base-line data such as individual genotypes and these should be made available electronically. Because genotyping results may systematically differ between laboratories and because genetic monitoring must be carried out over long periods of time, it is important that reference DNA samples, such as commercially available cell lines (Bradley *et al.*, 1984), are used in order to allow any monitoring and research to be directly comparable.

7.8 Empirical evaluation of animal translocation success

The question of how to define success in translocation programmes remains relatively open, although the objective is clearly long-term persistence without the need for intervention and management (Seddon, 1999). A number of comprehensive evaluations of the factors affecting success in animal translocation projects have been published (Griffith *et al.*, 1989; Stanley Price, 1991; Beck *et al.*, 1994; Beck, 1995; Wolf *et al.*, 1996; Reading & Clark, 1997; Fischer & Lindenmayer, 2000; Breitenmoser *et al.*, 2001; Seddon *et al.*, 2007). Previous reviews have highlighted several factors that appear to contribute to the success or failure of a translocation project. However, most reviews highlight biological and ecological factors contributing to project outcome, but few have examined how managers should allocate limited funds among release and monitoring activities that differ in method, cost, and probable result. Haight *et al.* (2000) used decision analysis to formulate and solve different translocation problems in which both population growth and future funding were uncertain. Performance criteria included maximising mean population size and minimising the risk of undesirable population-size outcomes. Robust optimisation provided several insights into the design of translocation strategies: (1) risk reduction is obtained at the expense of mean population size; (2) as survival of released animals becomes more important, funds should be allocated to release methods with lower risks of failure, regardless of costs; (3) the performance gain from monitoring drops as the proportion of a fixed budget required to pay for monitoring increases; and (4) as the likelihood of obtaining future funding increases, more of the existing budget should be spent on building release capacity rather than saved for future operating costs. These relationships highlight the importance of performance criteria and economic costs in determining optimal release and monitoring strategies.

A combination of the following four criteria is now generally agreed upon as indicating the success of an animal translocation:

- breeding by the first wild-born population;
- a three-year breeding population with recruitment exceeding adult death rate;
- an unsupported wild population (the number of at least 500 individuals representing a viable population has been used by some authors (e.g. Griffith *et al.*, 1989), but this is very taxon-specific and may be unachievable for many species that occur at naturally Low densities), and
- the establishment and persistence of a self-sustaining wild population.

However, there are difficulties in setting minimum success criteria (Kleiman *et al.*, 1994), as they can lead to assumptions that there is an end-point to which supplemental releases or continued monitoring of projects may no longer be required (Seddon, 1999). Therefore, the success of an animal translocation can only be examined at a specific point in time; which, in the majority of projects, is often shortly after release, hence most success criteria cannot be applied since long-term monitoring is infrequent due to time and budget constraints. Also, current analysis of success is often limited to the individual animal's adaptation to the new habitat, rather than population performance. Both elements are interlinked since the source of animals (i.e. whether they were obtained wild-caught from a sustaining wild population or from captive breeding stocks) is known to affect the outcome of a translocation. In most cases of translocating game species, the stock comes from a stable wild population. However, reintroduction and re-stocking projects are carried out because wild populations are locally extinct or declining; thus, founder stock are increasingly being sourced from captive populations (Wilson & Stanley Price, 1994). There are many risks involved when releasing captive animals; however, the main concern is that animals in captivity often show a loss of natural behaviours associated with wild fitness (Chapter 4). Deficiencies can be seen in foraging/hunting, social interactions, breeding and nesting, and locomotory skills (Rabin, 2003; Snyder *et al.*, 1996; Stoinski *et al.*, 2003; Van Heezik & Ostrowski, 2001; Vickery & Mason, 2003; Wallace, 2000). Other considerations include captive-born animals' lack of immunities to viruses/diseases prevalent in their wild counterparts (Cunningham, 1996; Woodford & Rossiter, 1994). Studies have suggested that projects using captive-born animals are less likely to be successful than projects using wild-caught animals (Mathews *et al.*, 2005). A review by Beck *et al.* (1994) estimated that only 16 out of 145 reintroduction projects using captive-born animals were successful.

Estimated average success rates range from 11% to 53% in project compilations in Beck *et al.* (1994), Fischer & Lindenmayer (2000), and Wolf *et al.* (1996), and 42% in a more detailed meta-analysis of carnivore translocations (Breitenmoser *et al.*, 2001). In particular, Griffith *et al.* (1989), Wolf *et al.* (1996, 1998) and Fischer & Lindenmayer (2000) reported significant differences between success rates of reintroduction projects and the source of animals used, and in all cases projects using captive-born animals averaged a lower success rate than those using wild-caught. Further to their 1989 paper, Griffith *et al.* (1990) statistically reported that this difference was significant; however, they did not investigate differences in survival rates between sources across species, and therefore do not account for species biases. In an examination of 49 cases of carnivore reintroductions, Jule *et al.* (2008) found evidence to support that projects using wild-caught animals are significantly more likely to succeed than projects using captive-born animals. Breitenmoser *et al.* (2001) found that projects that used animals caught in the wild, or a mixture of wild-caught and captive-bred animals, tended to be more often successful than those carried out with captive-bred animals only (Fig. 7.2). These authors also showed that with an increasing number of animals released, the chance of success increased and risk of failure declined.

Seddon *et al.* (2005) have shown that within mammals, and to some extent birds, there is a bias in reintroduction projects; two orders are particularly overrepresented in

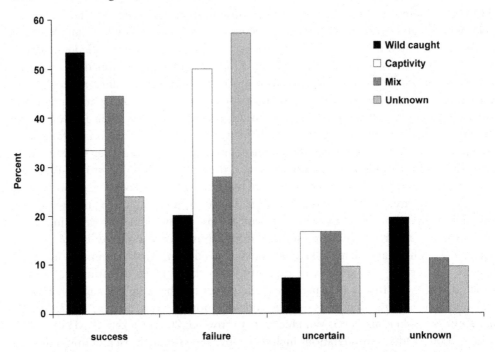

Fig. 7.2 The percentage number of carnivore reintroduction projects that were successful, failed, uncertain or unknown according to the origin of the animals released ($n = 150$). Projects using wild caught animals have a higher success ratio. This finding is however biased, as projects with smaller or more threatened species are more likely to use captive-bred stock. Data from Breitenmoser *et al.* (2001).

reintroductions, artiodactyls (e.g. ungulates) and carnivores. In a more recent systematic review, Bajomia *et al.* (2010) examined the literature on animal reintroductions in eight electronic literature databases, using seven different keyword combinations, and added the content of four bibliographies on reintroductions. They found 3826 potentially relevant publications totalling at least 29 290 pages of text. Taxonomic bias was evident; there was a marked taxonomic bias favouring vertebrates, especially birds and mammals. This may indicate that managers working with invertebrates and amphibians are less willing and/or less able to publish their results than those working with mammals and birds. The reasons for this are unclear.

Most comparative studies of translocation success (Griffith *et al.*, 1989; Wolf *et al.*, 1996, 1998) suggest that a variety of methodological, environmental, species-specific, and population-level factors are involved in the intentional release of wild-caught or captive-reared animals into new locations. Because the specific causal factors and their relative importance vary among release programmes, it can be difficult to identify general trends, but some factors are clearly of general importance. For example, methodological factors such as raise and release procedures, number and composition of animals released, and choice of source stock have been shown to influence outcomes (Beck *et al.*, 1991; Allen *et al.*, 1993; Reed *et al.*, 1993; Bright & Morris, 1994; Veltman *et al.*, 1996). Equally, environmental factors such as habitat quality and climatic conditions will affect results (Lindenmayer, 1994; Veitch, 1994) as well as the absence of predators or competitors (Crawley, 1986; Short *et al.*, 1992). Some species-specific and population characteristics considered favourable for successful invasion include high reproductive potential, an omnivorous diet, small body mass, and high genetic diversity (Crawley, 1986; O'Connor, 1986). These results are consistent with analyses of naturally invading or colonising species which show that larger founder populations are more successful, that habitat suitability is important and that increased number and size of clutches enhances successful invasion. Griffith *et al.* (1989) used multiple logistic regressions to identify seven statistically significant predictors of translocation success, although most of these variables are inter-correlated:

- taxonomic class (bird vs. mammal);
- legal status of the released species (native game vs threatened, endangered, or sensitive species);
- habitat quality of the release area (excellent, good, or fair/poor);
- location of the release area relative to the historical range of the species (core vs. periphery or outside);
- number of animals released;
- programme length (number of years over which releases occurred); and
- potential productivity of the relocated species (high vs low).

Wolf *et al.* (1996) conducted a follow-up survey, in which they up-dated the status of programmes in Griffith *et al.* (1989), increased the number of programmes available for multiple regression from 155 to 181, and tested additional variables as predictors of success. Their results, using comparative analyses, were consistent with the findings of Griffith *et al.* (1989). Wolf *et al.* (1996) produced a model which contained the first five of the variables of Griffith *et al.* (see above) plus adult diet of the species in the wild (herbivorous, omnivorous, carnivorous). A follow-up study by Wolf *et al.* (1998), using phylogenetically based multiple regression analysis on the data in Griffith *et al.* (1989) and Wolf *et al.* (1996), showed that habitat quality of the release area, range of the release site relative to the historical distribution of the relocated species, and number of individuals released, were statistically significant in explaining success of translocations.

7.9 Practical considerations in animal reintroductions

More practical issues involved in animal reintroductions involving captive-born animals have been discussed by Beck *et al.* (1994). These authors assessed projects anywhere in the world during the years 1990–1994. Their database differed in two additional ways from that of Griffith *et al.* (1989) in that it included reintroductions of the same species into distinct populations as separate projects. This database thus contained more reintroduction projects than species. Additions to the same population by successive reintroductions, even if carried out by different administrative authorities were counted as separate projects. Pre-release acclimatisation was more frequently used (76% of all projects) than pre-release training (35%). This was true for mammals, birds and reptiles and amphibians, probably reflecting the greater costs of pre-release training, and the limited evidence for its effectiveness (Kleiman *et al.*, 1986; Snyder *et al.*, 1987; but see Van Heezik & Ostrowski, 2001). Post-release training (12% of all projects) was less commonly used than pre-release training (35%), probably reflecting the logistical difficulty of training free-ranging, often widely dispersed, reintroductees.

Pre-release training was used more frequently for mammals (36% of projects) and birds (48%) than for reptiles and amphibians (7%). Likewise, acclimatisation was used more frequently for mammals (82%) and birds (83%) than for reptiles and amphibians (56%). Despite comparable levels of post-release monitoring, there was more post-release training for mammals (12%) and birds (19%) than for reptiles and amphibians (0%), and there was more post-release provisioning for mammals (69%) and birds (84%) than for reptiles and amphibians (13%). The same trends as for reptiles and amphibians are apparent in the fish and invertebrate subsamples. All these trends probably result from the conclusion that foraging, locomotor, and anti-predator behaviours, and other behaviours essential for survival, are more heavily dependent on learning and specific environmental experience in mammals and birds. Reptiles and amphibians require less pre-release preparation and post-release support. There are fewer release years for mammals (3.03 per project) than for birds (6.09) and reptiles and amphibians (7.50). To the degree that the number of release years is positively correlated with reintroduction success (Griffith *et al.*, 1989), this may retard the success of mammal reintroduction projects.

Reintroductions involve a series of procedures, each of which is complex and problematic, in terms of planning and execution. The main stages to be considered in any reintroduction programme are:

- capture,
- transport,
- captive breeding,
- training for release,
- site selection and preparation,
- transport and release,
- subsequent monitoring.

All stages are interlinked, which Stanley Price (1989) classified as biological, non-biological and an interface between the two to achieve reintroduction success (Fig. 7.3). The biological aspects (founder numbers, genetics, and ecology) refer to the intrinsic ability of the species to survive in the new environment, whereas non-biological ones are linked to institutional processes that affect the operational side of the reintroductions. The latter are by no means trivial, since in projects classified as successful (i.e. if the wild population subsequently reached 500 individuals free of provisioning or where PVAs or PHVAs predict the population to be self-sustaining), monitoring (94%), acclimatisation (76%), community education (70%) and provisioning (63%) were present (Beck *et al.*, 1994). Therefore, although problems centre on stress, disease risks, habitat suitability for

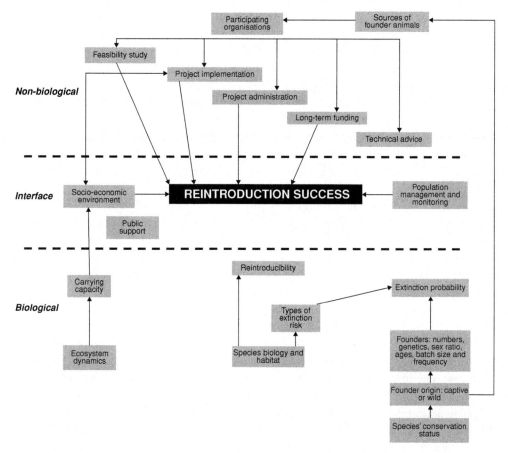

Fig. 7.3 Factors relevant to a successful reintroduction. The main concerns involved in animal reintroductions can be classified into biological, non-biological and interface between the two to achieve reintroduction success. The arrows are one way, with the exception of a dialogue between the reintroducing agency and the sources of the founder animals. Various relationships are denoted, with cause and effect prevailing on the biological side, and influence and sequence of action more evident in the non-biological and interface zones. Together they all converge on, and influence, reintroduction success. From Stanley Price (1989).

the animals to potentially survive, the following non-biological aspects of translocations can also be crucial to their success:

Local permission. The permission of the local authorities is necessary before any animals can be captured or released and in order to allow any follow-up operations. Securing this permission before any irrevocable commitment is made concerning the capture and dispensation of animals is fundamental. In particular, alternative management options for the animals concerned should not be abandoned before permission has been granted and all other obstacles have been overcome.

Capture. Capture operations may be stressful, or even fatal, to some individuals. This may require the development and/or application of new capture techniques, including the use of new drug–animal combinations. There are numerous records of animals being killed by inexperienced biologists administering wrong drug dosages or using equipment inadequately (Riney, 1982). Thus, a feasibility study by experienced professionals and with veterinary supervision is necessary. Early planning may be helped by a review of the relevant literature.

Transport. This can be as stressful as capture, being more prolonged, and veterinary supervision is essential; appropriate guidelines must be followed (see Graham-Jones, 1974; Nolan, 1975). Special care must be taken to provide adequate space, food and water, the correct temperature, adequate companionship and maternal care of infants, and protection against escape and injury. Pregnant females and infants are especially vulnerable to suffering, and delays must be minimised so that the operation is as brief as possible. Exposure to human diseases must be avoided.

Site selection. The area into which the animals are to be released requires careful investigation. The availability of food, water and sleeping sites and the presence or absence of other species (both human and non-human) have to be fully assessed. The year-round availability of food and water must be investigated, along with the reasons for the absence of that species from the area. If hunting is the reason for its absence, it must be shown that the problem can now be controlled – by effective protection of the area and/or the provision of alternative sources of meat.

Release. The immediate release of new arrivals at their destination may result in panicked, disoriented, and possibly unhealthy animals fleeing into an unfamiliar environment. This places additional stress upon the animals.

Monitoring. This is possibly the most important stage in the process. It requires several months, even years, of detailed observations to ensure that the release has been a success, where monitoring time-frames must be matched to species-specific generation times if success criteria are to be applied. Unfortunately, it has often been this stage that has been curtailed in the past because of reasons of practical and/or financial expediency. However, there is no short cut. Without detailed monitoring of the behaviour of the animals and of the productivity of their environment, the success of the venture cannot be properly ascertained, nor can important lessons be learned for the future (Kleiman *et al.*, 1986). This should involve study of all aspects of the animals' interactions with the habitat and with all other animals, including humans. Publication of the results of the monitoring is as important as the operation itself since this will allow lessons to be learnt by others making similar attempts.

7.10   Problems with animal translocations

7.10.1   Allocation of resources

Many argue that the large sums invested in translocations (particularly reintroductions of endangered species) would be better spent on the protection of habitat and existing wild populations, and halting the pet trade (e.g. MacKinnon & MacKinnon, 1991; Struhsaker

& Siex, 1998; Yaeger, 1997). Although this may be true, as argued by Lindburg (1992) the situation is complicated by the fact that the funding available for such programmes is not always available for the conservation of wild populations. In particular, arguments for zoos to divert funds spent on reintroductions to *in-situ* conservation efforts have also been raised, but it is held that those who contribute to zoo programmes may not feel the same compassion for the inhabitants of a 'distant patch of jungle'. The two approaches are probably not in competition for the same funds. However, Lindburg (1992) denotes the reasons for the resistance to reintroduction initiatives from zoos as the following.

- Zoos may be perceived, in seeking support for their programmes, as overselling re-introductions as viable strategies. Their advocacy of this admittedly costly approach adds to the perception that zoos have abundant resources and do not always use them wisely.
- Although reintroduction efforts have a number of shared elements, they may have quite different rationales.
- All reintroductions require the existence of suitable habitat and attenuation of the prior causes of population decline. Cultural and economic factors or a willingness to commit necessary resources are often insurmountable barriers.

Whatever the circumstances in a given case, reintroductions may benefit *in-situ* efforts in significant ways as well as establishing new populations of threatened taxa. Such projects should have the built-in effect of raising awareness of the plight of the taxon in question. Less frequently realised is the potential for educating zoo benefactors to broaden their support to include protection of remaining habitat. If funds for the protection or study of wild counterparts were included as part of more comprehensive captive breeding strategies, not only would *in-situ* efforts have a greater chance of succeeding but more viable partnerships between zoos and field conservationists would likely ensue.

7.10.2   Dispersal of released animals

An important factor in the success of reintroductions is the extent to which of animals to remain where released. Homing tendency is considerable in some species (Joslin, 1977). Although homing has been studied for more than 50 years, basic questions still remain as to whether animals that return 'home' do so primarily by random movements, familiarity with large areas or some means of navigation. Answers to these questions may enable managers to understand and predict movements of reintroduced animals. Movements of translocated animals have been better studied in mammals (Rogers, 1988). In general three levels of navigation ability have been defined (Griffin, 1955).

- **Type I**: simple orientation by means of familiar landmarks (visual or otherwise).
- **Type II**: the ability to move in a particular compass direction without reference to landmarks.
- **Type III**: navigation as the ability of an animal in an unfamiliar area to orient toward home or some other goal beyond the range of sensory contact, e.g. homing pigeons, swallows and certain oceanic seabirds.

Homing has been studied primarily in small mammals (Joslin, 1977). These have been based on mark–recapture of individuals so generally there is little information on whether or not they possess true navigational ability. Maximum distances that the various species have homed vary with home range size (Bovet, 1978) and therefore with body size since these are positively correlated. It is not known if this is due to differences in familiar area or to differences in inclination to travel. Information from translocated large mammals has shown that omnivores or carnivores move greater distances after release than herbivores. Where omnivores or carnivores are translocated for reintroduction, the long distances travelled after release may result in lower densities around release areas than would be true for herbivores, which could reduce chances of mating and establishment of breeding populations. Reintroduction efforts with omnivores or carnivores may require larger numbers to compensate for their greater movement. Even among some herbivores, movements may be great enough to reduce reproductive success.

The recorded high percentage of herbivores settling near release sites may indicate poor homing ability. However, where large numbers have been translocated, a few individuals have returned home from long distances. For example, a white-tailed deer individual returned from 560 km away and a return by a deer mouse from 3.2 km has been recorded.

7.10.3 Environmental carrying capacity

It may be that an environment can no longer support a population of reintroduced animals, even if there was population there in the past. It is therefore necessary to know why the species disappeared before a reintroduction programme is initiated and to decide whether or not introduced or reintroduced animals would be likely to find adequate resources for long-term survival if introduced or reintroduced. Reintroductions might unexpectedly be affected, for example, by the change in plant species composition having eliminated essential food sources or other animals. Any plans for release of animals must take into account the availability of various resources during the worst years or seasons, rather than simple averages.

If the species to be translocated is already present in the receiving area, it must either:

- be at carrying capacity of the environment; or
- be held below that level by a high rate of mortality. Hunting and trapping are the most likely causes.

The carrying capacity of a habitat refers to the quality (food, shelter, water and space) and quantity of habitat that determine the maximum number of animals that can be supported in an area. The same area may have a different carrying capacity for different life forms, and of course may vary seasonally and even annually. Determining how many released animals a new habitat can sustain is complicated and few studies have attempted this. Assessing potential carrying capacities is easier for grazers, since biomass of these herbivores is empirically correlated with habitat primary productivity. Fa (1994) argued that in the case of the Barbary macaque, a highly folivorous primate with a large surplus captive stock in Europe (see deTurkheim & Merz, 1984), the species can be viewed as a grazer. Because of this attribute, and unlike congenerics, it is possible to estimate potential densities in extant habitats in a fashion similar to predicting stocking levels for domestic herbivores. Thus, from values of consumable primary productivity for domestic stock in Mediterranean countries and the monkey's energy requirements, attainable macaque populations in studied habitats could be much higher than actual. Though these numbers may be unreachable in nature, this study shows that present macaque populations could increase after restorative management of habitats in which re-stocking with captive-born animals may play a part. However, since only 10% of potential monkey habitat in Morocco and Algeria is occupied by the species, finding areas for releasing captive-born macaques is possible.

7.10.4 Conflicts with humans

When animals are being reintroduced to former habitat, current human activities may make them unwelcome and lead to their persecution. In some cases, captive-bred animals that have lost their fear of humans through familiarity may constitute a danger to people. In the case of larger animals such as large primates or carnivores the hazards may be more acute. Candidates for release in the wild should be carefully screened for this.

7.10.5 Ecological disruption

The reintroduction of a new species runs the risk of creating a major ecological disturbance (Rolls, 1969). This might involve out-competition and elimination of other resident forms through predation, for example of eggs and nestlings, and in the case of large folivores the widespread impact upon the vegetation. Such changes could ramify throughout the ecological community. Ricciardi & Simberloff (2009) warn that impacts of biological invasions and translocations are invasions of a sort, and can cause substantial changes to biotic communities. Biological invasions, regardless of whether they are unintentional or planned, can profoundly affect the composition, and functioning of ecosystems by altering fundamental processes and key ecological interactions. They can also spread parasites and disease. Thus, planned translocations carry risks that must be considered seriously.

7.10.6 Monitoring

In order to ensure that the release has been a success it is necessary to monitor the population for several months but preferably years. This stage is often curtailed for reasons of practical and/or financial expediency. Without detailed monitoring of the behaviour of the animals and the productivity of their environment, the success of the venture cannot be properly ascertained, nor can important lessons be learned for the future. In a review of over 100 carnivore translocations, Breitenmoser et al. (2001) found that a large proportion of programmes did not integrate long-term monitoring into project design, with project managers concluding success or otherwise only after a few years. Although more projects now have long-term monitoring, approaches vary. The commitment to long-term monitoring is affected by the organisations undertaking the translocations. For example, in North America, because most carnivore projects are government initiated, some form of monitoring is carried out, but in Asia, Europe and Africa most projects are instigated by enthusiastic persons or organisations not able to make long-term commitments (Breitenmoser et al., 2001).

7.11 Costs of translocations

Any translocation operation requires the use of resources, and in most cases large amounts of money and professional expertise. It is therefore the planner's responsibility to demonstrate that the exercise in question is the best use of these assets in pursuit of the overall goal of the operation (e.g. species conservation, public education, etc.). The HELP Congo project for example cost approximately $33 800 per chimpanzee released, or $54 400 per individual known to have survived (rough estimates based on annual budgets since the release process began in 1996) (Goossens et al., 2005). For comparison, each golden lion tamarin successfully released into the wild in Brazil cost an estimated $22 563 (Kleiman et al., 1991). Post-release monitoring can be costly and in the case of the Congo chimpanzees, continues to cost approximately $5200 per chimpanzee per year ($1300 for Congolese field assistant salaries, $1400 for telemetry equipment, and $2500 for other equipment, accommodation, medicine, fuel, and maintenance). Reducing the level of post-release monitoring would of course reduce these costs for future release programmes, but would be undersirable.

In general, translocations, especially reintroductions of endangered speciess are expensive conservation projects. This is largely because they are labour intensive and monitoring must continue over several years. Costs vary with factors such as the size of the animal involved, the size of the area they move through, the animal's habits and the frequency of sighting or detail of information required after release (Stanley Price, 1989). Few translocations have been costed precisely. From data obtained from project managers in 38 mammal translocation projects (M. Smith, personal communication) costs increase positively with body size (Fig. 7.4). On average, per individual, the cost was around $28 000, ranging from $185 in the case of a Burchell's zebra translocation in Kenya to $168 000 in a European brown bear project in Italy. These costs include staffing, transport and research. Other cost data also indicate that translocations can vary enormously in their outlays depending on the circumstances in which the animals are found. For example, the translocation of 36 muskox in Canada cost $1000 per animal (Coady & Hinman, 1984), and the movement of 131 olive baboons in Kenya only $500 per animal, including travel, veterinary and monitoring costs and staff salaries (Strum & Southwick, 1986). Figures for other taxa are less available, but costs for birds, amphibians and reptiles are likely to be lower than for mammals (Chapter 6). For the two most-cited bird examples of captive breeding and reintroduction successes, the Lord Howe wood hen in Australia and the California condor in the USA, outlay was around $240 000 for the production of 78 birds to reinforce the remnant population (Fullager, 1985; NSW National Parks and Wildlife Service, 2002) whilst the condor required more than $5 million – or roughly $13 000 per bird – in annual costs (see Kettmann, 2010).

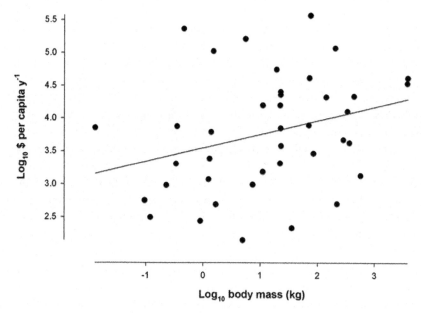

Fig. 7.4 Plot of the relationship between translocation costs (including preparatory, execution and monitoring phases) for mammals, per individual per year for animals released, and the species' adult body size ($y = 0.21x + 3.56$; $r^2 = 0.09$; $P = 0.06$). Data from M. Smith (personal communication).

7.12 Future animal translocations: assisted migrations?

Major climate events in the past are known to have caused species either to move or die out; in some cases causing mass extinctions (Erasmus *et al.*, 2002). The geographic ranges of many species would shift to higher altitudes, or towards their respective poles, in response to changes in habitats to which these species may have become adapted (modelled as the species' '*bioclimatic envelope*' denoting the relationship between climatic variables and species distributions, see Heikkinen *et al.*, 2006).

Several studies and meta-analyses have indicated that recent climatic change has already affected species' geographical distributions and the persistence of populations (Parmesan & Yohe, 2003). Animals will respond by emigration and/or changes in their numbers, both increasing and decreasing, and there will be local extinctions. Projected climate changes are likely to have an even greater impact on biota since some species are not able to disperse, or adapt quickly enough, and because land transformation, habitat destruction and landscape restructuring by humans will obstruct natural dispersal (Berry *et al.*, 2002; Hill *et al.*, 2003; Thuiller *et al.*, 2005, 2006). Additionally, loss of species is likely to result in many ecosystems ceasing to function in their current form (Hoegh-Guldberg *et al.*, 2008). Using projected species distributions under future climate scenarios for six sample regions, Thomas *et al.* (2004) predicted that 15%–37% of species would be committed to extinction under mid-range climate warming forecasts for 2050. Levinsky *et al.* (2007) assessed 120 terrestrial European mammals and predicted that up to 25% could become critically endangered within 100 years due to climate change.

It is a corollary, and yet a paradox, that climate change will result in new habitats, communities and with new distribution patterns for species. The concept of natural habitat or historical range may become so anachronistic that the release of animals into semi-wild conditions or into modified habitats may become not just acceptable but the norm, and preferable to keeping animals only in conventional zoo assurance populations. This has instigated debate amongst some scientists, resource managers and policymakers, as to whether biological units should be intentionally moved from existing areas of occupancy, to locations which they do not currently inhabit, or have not been known to occur historically, but where it is predicted the likelihood of future persistence will be improved (Richardson et al., 2009). This practice is referred to as 'assisted migration', 'assisted colonisation' or 'managed relocation', the latter term used by the Managed Relocation Working Group who are assessing its potential as a conservation strategy.

Assisted migrations are a radical solution developed in response to a pressing problem. Some believe it is a viable method for conserving species and ecosystem functions (Sax et al., 2009; Schlaepfer et al., 2009; Vitt et al., 2009) others disagree, and argue that assisted migrations could disrupt ecosystems and cause additional threats (Ricciardi & Simberloff, 2009). The idea of commencing pre-emptive action, to avoid predicted extinction risks, has been brought to the forefront by the IUCN who recently assessed species susceptibility to climate change impacts (Foden et al., 2008). The IUCN report concluded that 70%–80% of threatened birds, amphibians and corals are susceptible to climate change. These species are the least resilient to further threats, face an increased risk of extinction, and should be given high conservation priority.

Some regions may experience profound climatic shifts within the next 100 years; under these circumstances, Hoegh-Guldberg et al. (2008) argue that assisted migrations may provide the best chance of survival for some biological units. However, if assisted migration is to become a significant part of integrated conservation strategy, evaluating the benefits and dangers is essential. At present, assisted migration triggers strong, mixed feelings from conservation biologists. It builds on past efforts to save endangered species by reintroducing them to parts of their former ranges. Translocation projects have grown in number, but no organisation has yet begun an assisted migration for global warming.

The likely importance of assisted migration, relative to alternative approaches to over-coming dispersal limitation (e.g. connected reserves to facilitate species migrations or 'rewilding'), is as yet very unclear and arguments against hasty adoption of this approach have appeared (Seddon et al., 2009). An analysis of some of the costs and potential benefits of assisted migration is therefore in order, to provide timely information to assist rational conservation decision-making. Analyses are required to capture ecological risks of climate change and assisted migration at various spatial levels. Beginning the evaluation process now will allow scientists, resource managers and policymakers to develop informed decisions in the coming years, as climate change causes species extinctions to become increasingly common (Sax et al., 2009). Schlaepfer et al. (2009) and Richardson et al. (2009) recognise the need for a framework that integrates biological and socioeconomic data; however, to develop this framework, a debate on the relative (and subjective) merits of the various courses of action, based on current information, is crucial.

Managers are likely to rely on scientists to provide advice as to when assisted migration can be considered an appropriate option. Research specifically focused on assisted migration is required for scientists to answer these questions, and provide informed advice (McLachlan *et al.*, 2007).

Key concepts

(1) Species translocation can be an effective management strategy and is an important topic in conservation biology. Translocation is the movement of living organisms, by people, from one area with free release in another. An important role of captive populations can be the supply of animals for reintroduction. Interest in mediated animal movements as a significant aid to species conservation has grown in recent years. Reintroduction projects attempt to re-establish species within their historical ranges through the release of wild or captive-bred individuals.

(2) Zoos use the reflected glory of iconic reintroduction projects, such as the Arabian oryx, California condor or black-footed ferret, to argue their role in saving species. However, zoos are not the primary proponents or providers of animals for release, funders or managers of reintroductions.

(3) There is a need for a more strategic approach to animal translocations, where research and monitoring target questions are identified *a priori*. Knowledge of the ecological and genetic setting of the species to be translocated, as well as a good grasp of more practical considerations, is fundamental.

(4) Translocation success can be measured by understanding the influence of a variety of methodological, environmental, species-specific, and population-level factors. Any translocation operation requires the use of resources, and in most cases large amounts of money and professional expertise. It is therefore the planner's responsibility to demonstrate that the exercise in question is the best use of these assets in pursuit of the overall goal of the operation (e.g. species conservation, public education, etc.).

(5) Several studies and meta-analyses have indicated that recent climatic change will affected species' geographical distributions and the persistence of populations. Assisted migrations have been suggested as a radical solution in response to this pressing problem. However, the importance of assisted migration relative to alternative approaches is unclear. More research and understanding of these issues are required.

8 · Educating the public

'If we wish to save the giant pandas in the wild, what effect will it have to educate American or European children about the possible solutions to the recovery of that species?'
(Michael Hutchins)

8.1 Introduction

Educating the public is not a new role for zoos. Long established zoological institutions, such as the ZSL in London and the NYZS (now WCS) in New York, have considered public education as important since their inception in the 1800s (Sterling *et al.*, 2007). These and many other zoos have always had a profound influence on how people regard animals. Many people still receive their first exposure to live wild animals in zoos.

The behaviour of wild animals in captivity is greatly influenced by their housing (Chapter 4), and this in turn impacts the visitors' perception. The perception of an animal displayed in small, cell-like exhibits separated from the public by heavy cage bars cannot be the same as when animals are displayed in natural surroundings. Past generations of zoo visitors would have probably also been introduced to many confined creatures that nervously paced back and forth with the result that animals appeared to be distressed. The iron bars reinforced that wild animals are dangerous to people, a view that fits in very well with the general attitude that Nature was something first to be conquered, then tamed in the service of humankind.

As zoos gradually changed, and animals were moved from their cramped cages to large, open-air exhibits (and the bars replaced by chain link fences and moats) captive animals were able to behave more 'naturally' although new exhibits may not actually provide the required 'psychological space' (see Chapter 4). There is no doubt that public attitude toward wild animals in zoos began to change then, but with the advent of television, and exposure to wild animals in nature documentaries, zoo visitors expected more from zoo exhibits. Modern zoo exhibits are attempts to present wild animals to the public in naturalistic settings, both for the benefit of the animals on display as well as the zoo visitors.

Public perception of wild animals can still be shaped by zoos. The often beautifully landscaped exhibits in a modern zoo may encourage an inaccurate image of wild animals just as did the Victorian menagerie. The 'invisible barriers' between exhibit animals and public viewing areas allow zoo visitors to get 'up close and personal' with even the most exotic and potentially dangerous species. It is possible that the modern zoo exhibit may inadvertently be encouraging a perception that these now-familiar exotic animals are less dangerous to people than they actually are and could contribute to the public's desire for ever more unusual exotic pets. Some authors argue that the move from 'hard' exhibits of concrete, shotcrete and gunnite to more naturalistic 'soft' exhibit habitats took place at the same time as the emergence of environmentalism as a social movement. Subsequently, people's perception no doubt changed with the appearance of the concept of the zoo as an Ark (Chapter 3) that could prevent animal extinctions by preserving them in captivity. During the past 30 years, the public have become aware that not all environmental catastrophes are inevitable and that at least some problems caused by humans can be prevented and possibly reversed. With this increased awareness of wildlife and habitat conservation, the zoo has been perceived as a Lifeboat rather than an Ark (Campbell, 1978).

Conservation is now a significant theme in zoo education. It is commonly incorporated in programmes on vanishing species as well as other environmental issues to raise public awareness. One important means that zoo educators use in increasing public appreciation of and respect for nature is by giving zoo visitors a personal experience with living animals. Connections between people and animals in zoos commonly include adoption programmes and naming individual animals as well as keeper talks and special 'behind the scenes' visits. Developing appreciation of wild animals is an integral part of efforts by zoos to increase environmental awareness and to gain support for worldwide conservation. Close proximity to animals is often provided to the zoo visitor in animal nurseries and children's petting zoos as well as in various animal shows. In cultivating this personal appreciation for wild animals, however, it is possible that zoos may be presenting a mixed message to the public: while they may be telling the visitors that wild animals do not make good pets, in using exotic species as contact animals, zoos may inadvertently be contributing to the desire of the zoo-going public to own wild animals. This is certainly the case in many Latin American zoos (Cuarón, 2005). Honing the right message to give to the public in zoos is complicated, but essential to get right.

In this chapter, we first discuss the reasons why zoos should educate visitors and review the content and delivery of *in-situ* programmes and those supported *ex-situ*. We then review studies of visitor behaviour in the zoo and the impact of zoo education on the knowledge of, attitude towards and most importantly action for conservation.

8.2 Why should zoos educate their visitors?

Presently, zoos are bound by legislation, the goals of their umbrella associations and their own missions to educate their visitors to inspire and inform them, thereby fulfilling an essential part of their conservation function. Education is now stated as an essential purpose of zoos (Hutchins, 1996, 2003; Miller *et al.*, 2004; Sterling *et al.*, 2007; WAZA, 2005). But, if conservation education is to be effective, evidence of not only an increase in visitor knowledge, but true attitudinal and behavioural change is imperative. Such an aspiration is embodied in documents such as the WAZA's conservation strategy (2005) which states that zoos uniquely have a massive '*captive audience*' of visitors whose 'knowledge, understanding, attitude and behaviour and involvement can all be positively influenced and harnessed'.

Similarly, the education policies of zoo associations, e.g. ARAZPA now ZAA, include an aim to 'give people an understanding of their place within the natural world and the need to take individual and collective action for ecological sustainability' (ARAZPA, 2009). This statement resonates with Woollard's (2001) caution that 'knowledge, understanding and empathy don't in themselves save endangered species or the environment. Action is required'. Despite such oratory on why zoos should educate the public, going as far back as the 1800s (see above), several authors question the zoos' abilities to motivate their visitors to positive action for conservation (Mazur & Clark, 2001; Fraser & Wharton, 2007; Smith, 2009).

Some authors question whether there is a role for zoos to be conservation educators given the extensive natural history and biodiversity conservation information now available from television, the internet and other sources. Beckmann (1991) suggests that public interest in wildlife 'has been fostered by the mass media, particularly television'; with the result that zoos are educationally redundant (WSPA and Born Free Foundation, 1994; Jamieson, 1985). Broad & Smith (2004) examined the ability of visitors to recall information following a public talk on threats to wildlife as part of a guided tour at a zoo in Victoria, Australia. Of the 144 visitors questioned, 22% did not recall hearing the information. The talk could be considered effective for only the 19% of remaining visitors who were not already aware of the information in the talk. Visitors reported that television and documentaries were the major sources of their prior knowledge. However, BIAZA (2010) suggests that although television can offer valuable learning experiences, it can never have 'the same direct impact as the real, smelly, inquisitive animal, interacting with other animals and its own environment'.

The issue of whether or not zoos are providing new information to visitors is also highlighted by Smith *et al.* (2008). Their study of visitors to a bird presentation examined both the intention to and (self-reported) take up of conservation actions recommended in the talk (recycling and removing road kill to protect carrion feeders from traffic). Following the presentation, 81% of respondents recalled hearing the conservation actions during the talk and 54% stated an intention to start or increase an action. However, in thirty-eight follow-up interviews six months later, only three people had started a new action, and these actions were previously known to them. Mazur (1995) also questioned the effectiveness of zoo education programmes in Australia since it was not clear that visitors' knowledge of endangered species and habitat destruction was gained specifically through their zoo visit.

Such results have prompted some authors to suggest that zoos can have a 'reinforcing role' (Broad & Smith, 2004). They offer an alternative view that zoos can have a symbiotic relationship with wildlife documentaries; zoos are not educationally redundant simply because conservation information is available elsewhere and that education benefits would be gained from a closer linking of zoo education messages to those in the media (Broad & Smith, 2004). Perhaps zoo visits become part of a wider context of life-long learning and reinforce later experiences. Research by Falk & Dierking (2010) on the long-term impact of school field trips found that almost 100% of their sample of more than 100 adults and high-school students could recall one or more things they learnt on the trip, mostly related to the content/subject matter of the trip.

Critics argue that, by its very nature education in zoos is flawed since the subjects are out of their ecological context, may display unnatural behaviours and their captivity may emphasise negative human/animal relationships. Whitehead (1995) answers these criticisms in turn, citing that good husbandry and interpretation can overcome these potential obstacles, but that poor exhibits will present both explicit and subliminal negative messages to visitors.

8.3 Why do people visit the zoo?

For many visitors, recreation is a principal factor in the decision to visit a zoo (Rajack & Waren, 1996; Reading & Miller, 2007; Turley, 1999). However, a number of studies show that the opportunity for environmental education is also an important factor in the decision (Mazur, 1995). Visitors to the Bronx Zoo, New York rated 'good for the kids' as the primary motivation for visiting (91%), followed by 'outdoors' (89%) 'educational' (87%) and 'fun' (82%) (Gwynne, 2007).

A similar pattern was noted in the motivations of domestic visitors to Australian zoos who go for 'a family outing or to show the children the animals' (Aegis Consulting Australia & Applied Economics, 2009). However, a survey of international visitors to Australia suggested that seeing native species was the over-riding factor – 76% were interested or very interested in experiencing native wildlife and more than half preferred to visit a zoo or wildlife park rather than see the animal in the wild (Prideaux & Coghlan, 2006, as cited in Aegis Consulting Australia & Applied Economics, 2009).

Despite the efforts made by zoos to create a niche as educational, scientific and cultural centres, Turley (1999) notes that UK society is reluctant to acknowledge them as cultural or scientific establishments and as a result, they are not recipients of public money. The dichotomy between the objectives of zoos to contribute to conservation, and their lack of cultural recognition by society further exacerbates the conservation–recreation dilemma. The vast majority of zoos in the UK do not receive government funding as do museums, botanical gardens and art galleries. Without this 'cultural' status zoos are forced to operate as self-financing visitor attractions. In other parts of the world, including the USA and Germany, many zoos are publically funded and managed.

Whether publically or privately funded, attracting sufficient visitors through the gate is fundamental to the financial sustainability of zoos. Consequently there is a delicate balance between explaining the zoos' role in conservation and education and scaring away the average visitor whose fundamental aim for a day at the zoo is recreation (Turley, 1999; Tribe, 2001). An opinion poll conducted in 2004 of over 1800 British adults, and weighted to the UK population profile, asked which leisure attractions they had attended over the past year. Zoos were the seventh most visited attraction, 30% of the sample had visited a zoo in the past year (MORI, 2005).

Turley (1999) identifies an important distinction between the primary motivation of zoo visitors and their perception of the role of the zoo. Her review of several visitor studies highlighted *recreation* as a principal motivator in a zoo visit. However, her review of the public's perception of the importance of various roles of a zoo identified that *conservation* was viewed as the most important (Turley, 1999). So, although visitors believe that conservation is the primary purpose of a zoo, this is not why they choose to visit. This is surely the crux of the challenge for zoo educators, how to inform and inspire visitors who are already aware of the conservation motives of the zoo, but whose intention for the visit is recreation.

8.4   Content of zoo education programmes

It was not until 1999 that a statutory commitment, at least in Europe, was implemented to deliver conservation education through its EU Zoo Directive (European Union, 1999). A regular criticism of this Directive (Stanley Price, 2005; Eurogroup, 2006) is the lack of standards or guidance on what constitutes an adequate education programme. The Directive states simply that zoos must comply by 'promoting public education and awareness in relation to the conservation of biodiversity, particularly by providing information about the species exhibited and their natural habitats' (European Union, 1999). More recently, in the UK, the Secretary of State's Standards of Modern Zoo Practice (2004) have made some headway in formulating minimum standards, such that a zoo must have: (1) a written education strategy and an active education programme; (2) suitable facilities should be available for education purposes; and (3) accurate information about the species exhibited, as a minimum, species name (both scientific and common), its natural habitat, some of its biological characteristics and details of its conservation status.

The UK Zoos Forum (2008) suggests that the following education aims may be included in a zoo education strategy.

- To excite, enthuse and interest people in the natural world.
- To encourage public understanding of conservation issues.
- To develop public support and action to address conservation concerns.
- To provide experiences for visitors to enable them to make choices about their impact upon the environment (both positive and negative).

The SSSMZP (2004) (see also DETR, 2000) allows for education facilities to be 'commensurate to the size of the zoo'. The UK Zoos Forum (2008) has developed a set of non-mandatory benchmarks to provide guidance on the minimum provisions to be expected of zoos of different sizes (Box 8.1). The Zoos Forum clearly states that it would be expected that most zoos will exceed these requirements, which are less than ambitious in many respects. UK zoo inspectors and licensing authorities are required only to assess whether education activities taken as a whole are proportionate to the size and type of zoo. The highest recommended standards are for zoos with over 400 000 visitors annually. In the UK this equates to less than 20 establishments; around a quarter of UK zoos subject to the full inspection provisions of the legislation, and less than 10% of the total number of zoos in the UK. Only these larger establishments are required under the Zoos Forum guidance to employ a full-time member of education staff. BIAZA members as a whole employ 200 full-time and 184 part-time education staff, but in 2008 at least four collections did not employ staff specifically assigned to education (BIAZA, 2010).

Box 8.1 · *Education requirements – UK Zoos Forum*

According to the Zoos Forum (2008), the minimum requirement for education measures in zoos of *c.* 400 000+ visitors annually are as follows.

- Written education strategy outlining key target audiences and methods. Education is considered in other strategies and operations, e.g. enclosure design, species selection, etc.
- Each exhibit has identification labels – species name/range/habitat. Conservation sensitive species are highlighted. Many exhibits have additional interpretation – extra graphic panels, audio, interactives, video, etc.
- Information (e.g. signs, leaflets, guidebook, talks, demonstrations) on species, habitats and related conservation issues; conservation work undertaken by the zoo; encouraging public involvement in conservation.
- Staff can answer general questions about the animals and their care, e.g. diet, and tailor this information to different audiences (including schools/children).
- Area or room/building for public presentations and/or schools programmes. A programme of talks or lessons is available for different target groups, e.g. nursery, primary, secondary and adult groups, tailored to the curriculum.
- At least two trained members of staff for undertaking the education programme – one of these staff member's sole duty is '*education*'. Education staff are supported by other staff having education roles (e.g. keepers, presenters giving talks). If a schools programme is operated staff should be familiar with the curriculum and needs of the target age/ability groups focused upon.
- Educational resources available and designed for target groups, e.g. trails, fact sheets for families, for primary school children, etc.
- Educational elements incorporated into at least some of the zoo's conservation *in situ* projects and might be the main focus of some *in-situ* conservation work.
- Education section on the zoo's website, with additional information on some species/habitats.
- Visitors are encouraged and given ideas or opportunities to get involved/to take action that is beneficial to conservation.

Education in modern zoos must be more than showing the animal in a 'naturalistic' enclosure with accompanying signage detailing basic natural history information. Simply displaying animals to the public is not conservation education. The Zoos Forum (2008) acknowledges that education programmes have a responsibility to highlight that the captive environment is not natural and that such discussions should form part of the education programme.

In July 1994, animal welfare charities the World Society for the Protection of Animals and the Born Free Foundation issued The Zoo Inquiry (WSPA and the Born Free Foundation, 1994). This review of welfare, conservation and education in UK zoos recommended that zoo education programmes emphasise protection of ecosystems and outreach programmes that focus on field conservation and environment protection.

The Conservation Education Committee of AZA reviewed the past delivery of education in zoos and trends which are likely to shape it in the future (Ogden *et al.*, 2004). Their analysis suggested that zoos have moved on from simply teaching facts about animals to school-aged children to 'instilling caring for animals and inspiring conservation action'. The report details trends which have led to this change in education messages. These include an increase in the public's concern for animal welfare, the need for conservation organisations to demonstrate commitment to environmental policies and the public's high expectation when it comes to entertainment.

Zoos provide 'formal' education, mainly to school groups, and opportunities for 'informal' education or 'self-directed/free-choice learning' to all visitors. Formal education is characterised by the involvement of zoo staff, in the framework of a directed learning experience, usually linked to the school curriculum. Informal or self-directed education encompasses the opportunities for visitors to learn from the signage, leaflets and guidebooks, displays and informal activities such as animal shows, meet the keeper sessions and others.

8.5 What's the message?

Zoo education is not limited to species and habitat conservation or the natural history of animals in the collection, although these are important and common focuses. Education themes may encompass environmental issues such as climate change, pollution, unsustainable fishing and link these to 'green' actions such as recycling or buying sustainably harvested fish. Evolution, natural selection, population dynamics, ecosystems and anatomical adaptations are also recurring topics along with animal behaviour and conservation management techniques and can be readily aligned with school curriculums.

In addition to conservation education, zoos can also have an important role in delivering animal welfare messages, especially as they relate to the keeping of wild animals as pets and the pros and cons of this. The AZA addresses the inappropriateness of keeping wild animals as pets in its article *Why Wild Animals Don't Make Good Pets* (AZA, 2009a). In addition to risks to human health and the sustainability issues of taking animals from the wild, the article also addresses animal welfare issues such as the inability of most people to provide suitable conditions for exotic pets. The article also suggests suitable pets such as dogs and cats and recommends obtaining them from animal shelters. Similarly, the *UK Zoo Forum Handbook* (2008) recommends that animal welfare is a pertinent subject to teach zoo visitors – both through the demonstration of high standards of animal care and explicitly through advice on choosing appropriate pets.

Zoos' commitment to conservation action must also apply to their own operations, to strengthen the credibility of their conservation education messaging. As well as the more obvious actions such as moderating energy and water consumption, a zoo environmental policy should ensure building materials and products in the shop/cafe are from sustainable stocks and ethically sourced. Some zoos have designated 'green teams' to monitor the green credentials of their organisation. Several UK zoos also hold the universally recognised environmental standard 'ISO14001' award. To qualify, organisations must demonstrate an understanding of and take action on issues such as raw material consumption, energy usage, emissions and waste.

8.6 Delivering zoo education

'Interpretation' is commonly used to describe the style of delivery of both formal and informal education in zoos. Interpretation is more than simply dispensing facts and figures, it is an interactive style of delivery which aims to involve and engage the audience through active participation and the use of techniques such as storytelling, use of artefacts and demonstrations. Lewis (1980) collates the principles of learning as they relate to interpretation for park visitors (Box 8.2).

Box 8.2 · *Basic rules of interpretation*

(1) People learn better when they are actively involved.
(2) People learn better when they are using as many senses as appropriate.
(3) New learning is built on a foundation of knowledge.
(4) People prefer to learn that which is of most value to them at the present moment and knowing the usefulness of the knowledge being acquired makes learning more effective.
(5) That which people discover for themselves generates a special and vital excitement and satisfaction.
(6) Learning requires activity on the part of the learner.

In 2009, the Oregon Coast Aquarium commissioned a study to assess exhibit interpretive trends at AZA zoos and aquariums (O'Connor, 2009). Thirty education staff and consultants to zoos and aquaria were interviewed and the following is a summary of the main trends identified by participants.

- **Content** – a move from animals and habitat concepts to ecosystem conservation and the inclusion of culture and local peoples' stories. Focus on hope and success as effective approaches to changing behaviour.
- **Audiences** – exhibit interpretation based on research into how people learn. Multilingual interpretation to engage a broader audience. Targeting different levels of age and conservation literacy. Emphasis on storytelling as a technique. Interpretive panels that appeal to the emotions as much as the intellect.
- **Conservation** – providing information on the institution's involvement in local conservation and options for visitors to get involved in projects at the zoo.
- **Interaction with staff and volunteers** – live interpretation is the best way to reach guests; more staff and volunteers are now involved in exhibit interpretation.
- **Animal encounters** – enabling visitors to observe animal training and keepers interacting with animals.
- **Colour and text** – fewer, more colourful signs with shorter blocks of text and stronger content. Links may be provided to the Internet for more in-depth information.
- **Interactives** – three-dimensional objects are used throughout exhibits to engage visitors of all ages, including hands-on objects, props, and whole body experiences.

- **Technology** – technology needs to be incorporated into exhibits as this is how people are interacting with their world and accessing information. Use of mobile phone apps and text messaging is increasing. Aim to make technology family and group friendly. Using the internet and social media to stay connected with people after they leave the institution.

Box 8.3 · *An example of a comprehensive zoo education programme*

San Diego Zoo and San Diego Wild Animal Park provide comprehensive education programmes for children, students and adults, covering a wide range of subjects. School groups are catered for both within the parks and also through the outreach programme which offers assemblies in school. All programmes are aligned to California State Science Standards and pre- and post-visit materials are provided for teachers to use in the classroom.

Pre-school	'Wild Animal Moves' – uses movement-based activities, puppets and an animal presentation. Links to Art/Maths/Science/Language/Performing Arts.
Grade 8 (13 yrs)	'Flyin' To You' – focusses on the physics behind bird flight through an animal presentation, multi-media presentation and discussion session. Links to Science/Maths/Technology/Language Arts/Social Studies.
Grades 9–12 (14–17 yrs)	'Careers in Animal Science' – discusses the career opportunities available in animal sciences through an animal presentation, multi-media presentation and discussion session. Links to Science.
Field trips	School groups can stay overnight at the zoo. During 'Predator Project', children discover what it takes to be a super predator on a tour of the Wild Animal Park after hours through investigating the ecology of the lion.
Videoconferences	If a school is not able to send pupils to the zoo, videoconferences are available with San Diego Zoo educators on a variety of topics. Animal presentations by education staff include the following. Animal adaptations – how do an animal's body parts and habits help it survive in its environment? Animal classifications – what is a bird, mammal, reptile, or insect? Endangered species – what factors are threatening wild animals and plants? What can you do to help?

8.7 Types of zoo education

8.7.1 Formal education

In 2008, in the UK over one and a quarter million students went on an educational visit to a BIAZA zoo collection; of these 663 930 were taught by zoo education staff (BIAZA, 2010). Despite the aim of an all-inclusive model of education, the majority of students taught in UK zoos are still at primary level (BIAZA, 2010). This trend is reflected in zoos around the world (Mazur, 1997), although Smith & Broad (2008) note a trend towards a more inclusive approach to include the general zoo visitor.

School groups. School groups have been the traditional focus of zoo education and increasingly activities are linked to national education curriculums. One of the three aims of the UK's National Curriculum for primary children is 'to enable children to become responsible citizens who make a positive contribution to society'. Key themes within the responsible citizen aim include three which could relate directly to the education provision of zoos: 'to sustain and improve the environment, locally and globally'; 'take account of the needs of present and future generations in the choices they make'; 'can change things for the better' (National Curriculum Primary Handbook, 2010).

To illustrate the breadth of education programmes delivered by zoos, the San Diego Zoo and Zoo Safari Park (previously San Diego Wild Animal Park) education programmes are summarised in Box 8.3. The 2009 budget for education provision across these two zoos was almost $4 million (Zoological Society of San Diego, 2010). Clearly this is far from representative of the majority of zoos, but here serves as an example of the contribution zoos can make when staff and financial resources are made available.

Integrating education programmes with for example the zoo research programme can teach specific skills to students and has the added benefit of showcasing career opportunities in wildlife conservation. Barranquilla Zoo in Colombia runs an innovative programme for schoolchildren which enables them to take part in research at the zoo. '*ZooClub*' teaches children that science is one important way to conserve wildlife. In recent years, research has included creating an inventory of visiting birds at the zoo, a study of harmful garbage for the zoo environment and investigating patterns of visibility and mobility for small mammals at the zoo. The results of these studies are used as educational resources for visitors.

Outreach programmes for schools. As well as education in the zoo, almost two-thirds of BIAZA collections deliver education in local schools and other establishments (BIAZA, 2010) and this is true of many zoos around the world (e.g. San Diego Zoo, Singapore Zoo, Barranquilla Zoo). This has clear resource implications for the zoo, so many charge for this facility, but zoo education staff can potentially reach more children through assemblies, for example, than a zoo-based session. However, the very quality that makes zoos unique in their education potential – first-hand access to live animals – is essentially lost through in-school programmes. Some zoos take a selection of animals to the zoo as 'ambassadors' for the rest of the collection, but exposure to the variety of animals on site at the zoo is lost.

Overnight at the zoo. Night tours, or overnight stays at the zoo are increasingly common and are often marketed as adventures but also with an education component. 'Toad Trackers' at Houston Zoo, USA, introduces students to field research techniques and the global amphibian crisis and the importance of monitoring local amphibian populations for conservation. Students apply their newly acquired skills by actively searching for real toads on zoo grounds and weighing and measuring them under the supervision of Houston Zoo biologists.

Higher education and university students. Curriculum-tailored presentations and activities are available in many zoos on subjects such as conservation and animal husbandry but also business and tourism courses such as marketing, customer service and managing visitor attractions (e.g. Chester Zoo, UK). Some zoos partner with universities to deliver specific modules or whole courses. For example, Durrell has been running a three–four month course on Endangered Species Management, validated by the University of Kent, UK, since 1980, and is involved in the co-direction of an MSc course in Conservation Science with Imperial College, London. The latter course is run in conjunction with ZSL and Royal Kew Gardens.

Professional development and teacher training. The Wildlife Conservation Society, which runs the Bronx Zoo and others, offers both on-site and distance learning courses for teachers and educators. The six-week on-line courses include 'Environmental Education', 'Marine Biology' and 'Predators' and aim to improve participants' knowledge of zoology, ecology and conservation and engage in new science education methodologies.

Overcoming phobias. Some zoos (e.g. Bristol Zoo, UK, Taronga Zoo, Australia) run courses on overcoming phobias to arachnids and reptiles, utilising zoo animals and staff and sometimes run in conjunction with phobia experts.

Seminars for the general public. Seminars for the general public on current conservation and environmental research along with advances in biological sciences are run by many zoos in partnership with universities and research centres e.g. St Louis Zoo, USA, and ZSL, UK.

8.7.2 Informal education

Signage and interactive displays. Basic natural history facts have now given way to wider ecosystem concepts; the messages have changed from 'lions of Africa to interpreting instead how the Serengeti is endangered' (O'Connor, 2009). Graphics on signage have undoubtedly improved with the use of larger fonts, photos and attention-grabbing headlines. 'Interactive' signs and displays vary from simple 'flip book' style signs to sophisticated animations, quizzes, videos, games, websites and mobile phone audio tours. Apps for mobiles are available for some zoos; they can be used to enhance a zoo visit by allowing planning, providing maps and species information while at the zoo and details of future events after the visit. Apps and text messaging as well as social networking sites such as Facebook and Twitter provide ideal ways to engage with a younger audience and provide post-visit information and suggestions to encourage conservation action. For a comprehensive review of the evolution of signage in zoos, see Serrell (1988).

The Envirodome, an interactive visitor centre at Adelaide Zoo, opened in 2009 and offers a range of high-tech exhibits. The theme is 'We are connected to everything in our world through the air we breathe, the water we drink, the food we eat, the energy we use and the soil we live on. To keep our world healthy, all these things must work together'. Its 'Zoo to the world' exhibit is a large interactive screen which provides information on twelve endangered animal species held at the zoo and the associated conservation efforts of Zoos South Australia to protect them. The equipment can display the animal in the wild, maps of where they occur and then where the animal is located in the zoo.

'A day in the life of Jo Average' displays a series of still-frame images on tiles side by side to describe a story, which are then animated. The tiles show a range of lifestyle alternatives for the visitor to select from to create a day in the life of '*Jo Average*'. Once you've made your decision, the results of your choices play as a film while meters below the screen show the levels of environmental friendliness, general happiness and wealth that Jo Average is creating as the story proceeds.

The water sculpture interactive exhibit again encourages you to make choices over the use of resources, this time focussing on water usage. The sculpture releases water down from the ceiling through open air and into the top of the installation. The visitor activates a series of valves to control how the water is shared between the needs of the environment, domestic users, industry and agriculture.

Animal exhibits. The role of the education staff is crucial in the development of user-friendly exhibits which will deliver the intended conservation education message. High standards of animal husbandry are crucial not only to ensure good animal welfare, but also to enable appropriate education messages to be delivered to visitors.

Leaflets/guidebooks. Printed leaflets, maps and guidebooks are a common way of introducing visitors to the zoo site, providing information on some of the species and informing visitors of current field programmes. Some zoos also encourage visitors to read information on-line prior to their visit (e.g. Adelaide Zoo, Australia) in order to gain as much from the zoo visit as possible.

'Meet the animals' presentations and shows. Animal shows and presentations are a common activity in many zoos. In 2008, 48% of BIAZA collections put on animal shows for visitors, 87% gave keeper/education talks, 31% provided meet the keeper sessions, animal handling sessions, guided tours and other staff-led activities and 72% of collections used live animals in teaching (BIAZA, 2010). DEFRA (2008) provided guidance on the use of live animals in presentations or shows. The use of live animals is permitted, but the welfare of the animals, public safety and the minimum standards for education as required by all exhibits in the zoo must be ensured. Hutchins & Smith (2003) assert that 'the days of chimpanzee tea parties, elephant rides and circus-like seal or dolphin shows have passed' and of course this is thankfully true in practice in the majority of modern zoos. However, seal and dolphin displays continue to feature in many European and US zoos. Although rare, the shocking incidences of shows involving circus tricks by bears and large cats and the public feeding of live chickens to tigers by visitors in some Chinese zoos does nothing to enhance the reputation of zoos worldwide.

Keeper talks. 'Keeper talks' are now a common feature in zoos, usually run at set times during the day at different exhibits. In some zoos they are delivered by a keeper, but often by a member of the education staff. Talks usually include feeding the animals and informing the visitors of general facts about the natural history of and threats to the species and facts and stories about the particular animals in the exhibit.

'Keeper for a day' programmes. These programmes enable the public to experience the day-to-day life of a zookeeper. Participants get involved in feeding and mucking out and get a 'behind-the-scenes' tour as well as spending a day with an experienced keeper. These programmes are often several hundred pounds per person (e.g. $417 at Whipsnade Zoo, UK) so they are likely also a good money-earner for the zoo.

Observation windows. Presumably in recognition of the public's general curiosity for 'behind the scenes' experiences, some zoos have designed windows in exhibits which enable visitors to see keepers, vets and scientists at work.

Websites and on-line resources. Most zoos with an active school education programme provide pre- and post-visit on-line materials both for pupils and teachers to enhance the zoo visit and develop learning on conservation issues back at school. Some zoos provide much more than this, including detailed natural history and conservation status information for species held in the zoo. San Diego Zoo takes this further with fun science activities, several webcams and games and even recipes which include animal-related facts.

Inspiring conservation action. 'What you can do' suggestions in the zoo via talks, education materials and websites vary in the level of detail and ambition between zoos, such as the suggestions included in a number of zoo websites (Table 8.1). The common themes are energy saving (e.g. turning lights off, saving water, less car use); creating wildlife habitats at home/in the community (e.g. ponds, plant a tree); consumer awareness (e.g. don't buy tourist souvenirs made from wildlife); donating to the zoo or a conservation charity; volunteering at the zoo.

Adelaide Zoo and Monarto Zoo in South Australia are committed to working with both their shops and catering facilities to ensure they no longer use palm oil in any of their products. Their 'Go Palm Oil Free' campaign not only informs the public but highlights the zoos' own commitment to sustainability issues. Citing the current difficulty for manufacturers to source palm oil from sustainable sources, and the imminent risk of orang-utans going extinct as a result of palm oil plantations, the zoos are also encouraging visitors to 'Go Palm Oil Free' by providing free information cards advising on products containing palm oil.

Since 2000, EAZA has initiated annual campaigns to focus on specific conservation issues. Many of its members participate through designing education exhibits, promoting appropriate conservation actions and raising funds. Over three million Euros have been raised in this way and the money is used to support projects in the field. Campaigns have included European carnivores, amphibians and Madagascan biodiversity.

8.8 Education supporting *in-situ* conservation

Hutchins (2003) suggested that there is limited immediate conservation impact in educating children in developed countries about endangered species in developing countries. So perhaps zoos in developed countries should concentrate efforts in supporting conservation education programmes in developing countries. Zoos in both developed and developing countries can link their education programmes to *ex-situ* conservation programmes in the zoo and their support for field conservation. This can be through financial support, but also through utilising the skills of their education staff to work with partner

Table 8.1 *Conservation activities suggested by San Diego Zoo, London Zoo and the South East Asian Zoos Association on their website. These activities should develop awareness among visitors*

Save energy	Create and maintain wild habitats	Consumer awareness	Donate/join
Recycle	Create a wildlife refuge in your garden	Buy organic fruit and vegetables	Donate to conservation organisations
Turn off water when brushing teeth, use dishwasher on full washes	Clean up wild habitats[a]	Don't buy endangered species or products made from animal parts	Support conservation and research projects
Turn the heating down. Buy a battery charger	Don't wash soap, grease off your driveway into the gutter	Choose wood from sustainable sources	Sponsor animals or exhibits in the zoo
Turn lights off when room empty	Put food and water out for garden birds	Buy dolphin-friendly tuna	Volunteer at the zoo or your local wildlife organisation
Walk or use a bicycle, car pool	Put up bird/bat boxes up in your garden, leave an undisturbed area for frogs and hedgehogs	Eat seasonal produce	
Compost kitchen scraps and garden waste	Plant flowers to attract bees and butterflies[b]		

The suggestions in this summary require further clarification and zoos should provide more detailed information on conservation actions. For example, [a] 'clean up wild habitats' should encourage rubbish removal and wildlife sensitive management; [b] 'plant flowers...' should encourage planting of native wildflowers.

conservation organisations *in-situ* to develop locally appropriate education programmes. The following examples involve active participation by zoo staff, rather than simply providing funds:

Black Rhino Conservation Programme, Kenya. The programme is supported by Chester Zoo, UK, and focusses on the Eastern Black Rhinoceros, the subspecies of black rhino held at the zoo. In 2003, the zoo sponsored the purchase and staffing of an environmental education bus for the Laikipia Wildlife Forum, a conservation organisation in Kenya. The bus enables rural schoolchildren to visit wildlife areas and learn about environmental and conservation issues. Chester Zoo education staff helped to develop the education programme and provided training for educators. Additional support is provided for community liaison officers who work closely with Maasai communities to promote conservation awareness and sustainable development techniques (Chester Zoo, 2010).

'*Conservation Connections*', **Zimbabwe**. This three-tiered programme delivered by Werribee Open Range Zoo (Australia), engages Australian children in African conservation issues, and enables them to 'fulfil their roles as global citizens and make a tangible difference for conservation'. Students first participate in 'An African Experience' at Werribee Open Range Zoo, observing African species and through role-play explore issues such as poaching and the bushmeat crisis. The second part of the programme, the Ungana Project, tasks students to develop wildlife education resources to be utilised in conservation education in Zimbabwe. In 2007, more than 780 Australian school students participated and Werribee Open Range Zoo distributed 360 kilograms of wildlife education resources to Zimbabwe, enhancing the capacity of Kusanganisa, the *in-situ* component of the conservation education programme. Kusanganisa utilises education techniques to connect Zimbabwean schools with wildlife, promote ecological understanding and generate behaviour change for conservation (Werribee Open Range Zoo, 2010).

Threatened monkeys of the Upper Guinean forest, Ghana. West African Primate Conservation Action was founded in 2001 on the initiative of Heidelberg Zoo (Germany). The population of Roloway guenons and the white-naped mangabeys housed in the partner zoos serve as prominent 'flagship species' for the entire ecosystem of the Upper Guinean forest. WAPCA supports the work of the Ankasa Resource Reserve and Accra Zoo on the long-term protection of endangered primates *in-situ* and *ex-situ*. As part of the education programme, WAPCA organised a training course in 2004 for staff of the Accra Zoo. The education officer, curator and head of primates participated in a five week training course, sponsored by WAZA and WAPCA and supported by British zoos to improve the staff's skills within their department of the zoo. Funding was also made available for improvements at Accra Zoo upon their return (WAZA, 2010).

Conserving the maned wolf, Argentina. This project, delivered by Buenos Aires City Zoo, actively participates in the protection of this native species and of its natural habitat. The objectives of the in-zoo programme are that visitors should be able to identify this species in the zoo and list its characteristics, along with the threats to the wolf and the consequences of the species' decline. Activities include discussions, games, face painting, and videos. In addition, the *in-situ* part of the programme comprises educational campaigns in areas where the maned wolf is found. These programmes are held in rural schools which serve as a meeting place for the community and feature educational games and include teacher participation and hope to facilitate the local community to participate in conservation action (IZE, 2010).

Tackling the illegal parrot trade, Colombia. Barranquilla Zoo developed an education programme to tackle the threat of the pet trade to parrots in Colombia. The programme involved workshops in local schools using a cartoon character 'El Bola', a parrot caught in the illegal pet trade. The workshops, delivered by Barranquilla Zoo staff, focussed on the message 'Parrots do not make good pets' and highlighted the potential behavioural and physical problems associated with poor care as well as the conservation threat to the species. Over 4000 students participated and schools ran their own sessions following workshops with zoo staff (IZE, 2010).

8.9 Factors affecting visitor behaviour in the zoo

Visitor studies in zoos fall into two main categories. Firstly, those which unobtrusively observe visitors and measure the amount of time spent, e.g. reading signage, using interactive elements of the exhibit, watching the animals, communicating with others in their group. This objective approach collates empirical data which can be used to make inferences about the visitors' experience, without the problems with self-reporting inherent in other methods such as surveys and interviews (Ross & Lukas, 2005). Secondly, surveys and interviews are conducted with visitors prior to entering the zoo or a particular exhibit and on exiting. Some studies also include follow-up interviews by phone or email weeks or months later. These studies enable data to be collected on the visitor's motivation for the visit and through pre- and post-visit testing changes in knowledge, attitudes and behaviour can be quantified.

8.10 How long is long enough?

It seems reasonable to assume that a visitor who spends more time reading the signage, using interactive components of the exhibit and observing the animals has the opportunity to learn more than those who spend less time. Several studies of museum exhibits have shown a positive relationship between time spent engaged with an exhibit and the learning that takes place (Balling & Falk, 1980; Raphling & Serrell, 1993; Borun et al., 1996). Serrell (1998) comments that although time is not the most important variable, it is an important indicator of the effectiveness of an exhibit.

Many factors potentially influence the attractiveness of an exhibit, i.e. how many visitors are drawn to it, and the holding power, i.e. how long visitors stay at an exhibit. These could include personal interest in a species, visitor density at the exhibit at the time of visiting, taxonomy of the focal species of the exhibit, size and activity level of the animals, layout of the zoo, i.e. how far an exhibit is from the entrance, weather, etc. Understanding the effect of these factors on visitors can guide zoos to more active engagement with their visitors which may lead to more meaningful educational experiences.

Zoo managers make trade-offs when selecting species for the collection. Conservation status, popularity with visitors and exhibit costs (capital costs, maintenance and husbandry, e.g. food and staff resources) are three major factors. Studies of the effect of body size, length, activity level, and taxonomic group on visitor interest could usefully guide zoos in their species selection. Balmford et al.'s (1996) study at London Zoo found no evidence for visitor preference towards large-bodied animals. They concluded that since zoos can help conserve only a small proportion of threatened species, zoos could prioritise smaller-bodied species which take up less space, are often easier to breed and less costly to maintain and this would not necessarily conflict with the need for zoos to attract visitors.

Two other studies contradicted these conclusions. Bitgood et al. (1988) conducted a study of 13 zoos throughout the United States and found that increasing body size, raised activity level, presence of an infant and proximity to visitors all increased visitor viewing time. Similarly, Ward et al.'s study at Zürich Zoo (1998) found that larger animals were more popular with both adults and children and that children also showed a significant preference for larger groups of mammals. Balmford (2000b) highlights the methodological differences in data collection and analysis between the studies at London Zoo and Zürich. Following a reanalysis of the Zürich data he concludes that both studies suggest that exhibits of larger-bodied animals are less profitable in terms of popularity with visitors per unit investment. Studies at three other zoos in the UK also support this assertion. Balmford (2000b) found no relationship between body mass and visitor popularity at Whipsnade Wild Animal Park and whilst larger animals were more popular at Dudley Zoo, this did not hold when exhibit costs were controlled for. Again there was a weak positive correlation between body mass and visitor popularity observed at Chester Zoo. However, controlling for the large variation in exhibit costs showed that exhibit profitability was independent of body mass (Balmford, 2000a). Balmford (2000a) concluded that at London and Whipsnade body mass had no effect on visitor interest, and although larger animals were more popular at Zürich, Dudley and Chester, since larger exhibits were more expensive to maintain there is no increase in profitability per unit investment for larger animals.

Moss & Esson (2010) suggest the popularity of a species with visitors should be a determining factor where an education role for certain species is prescribed in a collection plan. Their study of 1863 visitors at Chester Zoo concurred with Bitgood *et al.* (1988) and Ward *et al.*'s (1998) analyses; holding time was positively correlated with increasing animal activity levels and (weakly) to body length. Their regression model comprising the independent variables of taxonomic group, animal activity level, body size (length) and whether the species was the focal one in the exhibit accounted for 63% of the total variation in holding time across 40 enclosures in the zoo. Taxonomic group was the most important predictor, alone accounting for 40% of the variation. When comparing all species, only mammals had higher than average attracting and holding power, amphibians had above average attracting power but holding time was below average. Birds and invertebrates had similarly low attracting and holding power.

Moss & Esson (2010) concluded that species should only be assigned the role of education in a zoo if they are able to attain at least a minimum level of visitor interest. This is logical since if the species does not attract and hold the visitors' attention, there will be no opportunity for learning at that exhibit. A concern in this approach is that species which are interesting to the visitor (shown by Moss & Esson (2010) to be heavily biased towards mammals) may not necessarily be those the zoo and conservation community would choose to favour in education programmes. Taken to its logical conclusion this theory could for example lead to education centred on popular animals such as meerkats (Chapter 3) which are not endangered and for which the zoo has no field programmes. Clearly this is not the intention and Moss & Esson (2010) suggest that there could be exceptions. Such as where species have a low attracting power, but unusual adaptations or an interesting conservation story and that additional interpretation or talks could be used to counter lower visitor preference for these species.

Other studies in different zoos throughout the world confirm the pattern of visitor preference for charismatic megafauna such as great apes and elephants. However, given the expectation of zoos to educate the public, viewing times even for these large mammals could be considered disappointingly low. For example, a study of the great ape exhibit at Lincoln Park Zoo (USA) tracked the behaviour of 350 visitors over a 12-month period (Ross & Lukas, 2005). The study measured time spent viewing the gorillas and chimpanzees, reading the signage and using the interactive components including a video and moulds of ape hands. Visit durations ranged from 32 s to over 41 min with a median of 7 min 23 s. There was no difference in visit duration between men and women or as a result of being accompanied by children; solitary visitors, however, spent less time than other groups. Both adults and children spent substantially more time watching the apes (average 58% of time at the exhibit) than the combined time engaged in reading signs, watching the film and handling the interpretive graphics (average 9.5%). Graphics that involved 'hands-on' interactions were used significantly more frequently than expected based on their availability.

The Trail of the Elephants at Melbourne Zoo, Australia, is a 2.5 ha immersive exhibit designed to replicate the habitat of Asian elephants. Conservation messages in the exhibit aim to convey (1) the threat of human behaviour to elephants; (2) elephants can be saved; and (3) actions visitors can take to help save the species. These messages are delivered through signs, touch screens, artefacts, static displays and presentations by keepers (Smith & Broad, 2008). The exhibit is extensive with several viewing areas, an 'Asian style' community hall, 'research station' with information on threatened Southeast Asian species and a 'make a difference' stand where visitors can sign up to receive a newsletter and donate to elephant conservation. One hundred and sixteen visitors were unobtrusively tracked throughout the exhibit at different times of day on both weekdays and weekends and both during and outside of school holidays. The average total time spent in the exhibit was 24.48 min, but only 8.48 min, i.e. 35% of the time, was spent directly engaged in either watching the animals or attending to any of the interpretive media. Of this 'active time', 5.33 min were spent viewing the elephants and other animals and of those who engaged in any of the interpretative media, the average time spent was 4.4 min with a wide range from 5 s to 25.58 min. Less than 40% of visitors in the study attended to any of the interpretation opportunities available and less than 15% interacted with the staff. Of those who passed the 'make a difference' display, around 15% made a donation. Given the extensive size of the exhibit, the array of activities available and a charismatic species as the focal animal, the active time spent in this exhibit could be seen as disappointingly short, but compares favourably with viewing times in most studies.

Given the public's general affinity with mammals over other animal groups, it is perhaps to be expected that viewing times for other groups are considerably shorter. Marcellini & Jenssen (1988) recorded viewing times of 5–6 s for lizards and 6–8 s for snakes at the Reptile House at the National Zoo, Washington. Slightly longer viewing times were recorded by Markwell & Cushing (2009) of visitors in the Lost World of Reptiles exhibit at the Australian Reptile Park, but average viewing time for the five lizard and snake exhibits in the study was less than one minute per exhibit. Pythons were the most attractive species in both studies, as measured by viewing times of almost 40 s.

8.11 Does a zoo visit affect visitors' conservation knowledge, attitude and behaviour?

In 2007, RSPCA (UK) reviewed the number and content of peer-reviewed publications evaluating education programmes in UK zoos for the period 1980–2007; only one study in a UK zoo was found. RSPCA concluded that the welfare cost to some animals in zoos means that aiming to deliver conservation education is not sufficient; zoos must demonstrate a substantial impact (RSPCA, 2007). The paucity of research on the impact of zoo education has been highlighted by others (Dierking et al., 2002; Ogden et al., 2004; Ross & Lukas, 2005; Smith, 2009; Balmford et al., 2007). However, there is some evidence to suggest that more interpretive styles of teaching, using artefacts, animal training sessions and an active presentation style is more impactful than fact-only presentations or graphics.

A study at Tierpark Goldau in Switzerland (Lindemann-Matthies & Kamer, 2005) examined the effect of using 'touch tables' overseen by zoo staff or volunteers on visitor learning. The touch table included soil stained with iron oxide and feathers to demonstrate the bearded vulture's habit of bathing in red soil, which stains its feathers; bones from prey items and vulture wing feathers. Staff/volunteers helped visitors to observe the birds and explained the material on the table. Over 600 adult visitors to the bearded vulture exhibit participated in the study. The touch table was available for only half days, enabling the study to compare visitors who saw only the standard exhibit with signage and posters with those who also used the touch table.

A questionnaire tested visitor knowledge of the vultures before and immediately after viewing the exhibit and touch table and two months later. Results revealed that visitors who interacted with the touch table were significantly more satisfied with the information available than those to whom it was not available. About 40% of visitors using the touch tables correctly answered questions regarding the vulture's diet and the reason for its red plumage compared to only 25% and 5% of those who could access only signage and posters. Two months later, 17% of participants reported seeking further information about one or more animals seen at the zoo, mostly using books; there was no difference in this between touch table users or non-users. Touch table users again scored more highly than non-users when questions on the vultures were repeated and this held when additional visits to the zoo or seeking additional information had been accounted for in the analyses.

The study did not enable the cause of these effects to be pin-pointed as many factors were involved. The authors suggest both the interactivity of the touch table and the opportunity to interact with zoo staff. The positive effect of staff interaction with visitors through keeper talks, animal shows and discussions has been noted by other authors (see Andersen, 1992, 2003; Miller et al., 2004; Ollason, 1993).

Several authors have commented on the use of animal training sessions in zoos for education purposes. Visscher et al. (2009) examined the effect of using a fact-only or interpretative style in presentations on training as an animal management technique. Three groups of children first watched a training session with a black rhinoceros. One group then received a fact-only presentation and a second group received an 'interpretive presentation'. The control group simply watched the training with no presentation. The two presentations included the same information, but the interpretative session was more active, the presenter posed and invited questions and allowed the children to handle training items such as the target pole. The results from a quiz completed immediately after the presentations showed that children watching the interpretative presentation retained more knowledge than individuals in the other two groups. Although this was a small-scale study, Visscher *et al.* suggested that the use of interpretative principles can enhance the delivery of conservation messages and that as we might intuitively expect, *how* education is delivered really is as important as the content of the messages being delivered. Anderson *et al.* (2003) similarly found that visitors to Zoo Atlanta's otter exhibit reported more positive zoo experiences, training perceptions and viewed the exhibit longer during interpretation + training sessions and training-only sessions, compared to interpretation-only or passive viewing.

Several studies indicate the difficulty in firstly encouraging visitors to read signage or use interactive displays in exhibits, the often poor uptake or retention of information when they do and the difficulty in translating any knowledge gain into conservation actions. A second study of the African ape exhibit at Lincoln Park Zoo examined visitor knowledge and conservation attitudes towards apes using a survey of 1000 visitors (Lukas & Ross, 2005). The survey revealed that visitors performed better on knowledge questions after viewing the exhibit and older and more educated visitors performed better than younger and less educated people. Visitors with higher education levels showed lower negativistic and dominionistic attitudes towards apes. Although knowledge of the apes improved following the visit, there was no change in attitudes towards apes.

Visitors to the East African Rock Kopjes exhibit at San Diego Zoo were asked a series of questions as they exited the exhibit (Derwin & Piper, 1988). Although 91% answered that they had looked at or read at least one sign, the majority were unable to correctly answer questions about the exhibit. Over half the visitors (58%) reported no change in their interest in wildlife conservation having viewed the exhibit, but 37% did.

Stoinski *et al.* (2010) investigated the effect of using explicit, disturbing or more benign photos to explain the issues of the bushmeat trade to visitors. Ninety seven per cent of visitors felt that the disturbing images were appropriate for zoo visitors except for children under the age of 12. Visitors spent significantly more time looking at the disturbing images and were significantly more likely to express being influenced by the images. However, the type of image viewed had no effect on the uptake of information about bushmeat. Stoinski *et al.* conclude that static displays of text, even if graphic images are used, may not be the most effective method for educating visitors about complex issues like bushmeat.

The 'Conservation Station' at Disney's Animal Kingdom provides an array of learning opportunities through live animal presentations, information displays, films, low and high tech interactive exhibits. Dierking *et al.* (2004) used visitors' self-reported involvement in eleven conservation activities (e.g. spend time in nature, cut down on amount of rubbish you create, help and improve habitats for wildlife, reduce car use) pre- and post-visit and 2–3 months later to examine the capacity of the Conservation Station to affect behavioural change. A significant short-term increase in the level of planned action was found immediately on exiting the Conservation Station, but follow-up interviews revealed that the intentions had not translated into concrete actions.

The largest study to date of the impact of informal education on adults in UK zoos was conducted by Balmford *et al.* (2007) with 1340 visitors across six zoos and, for comparison, one nature reserve. Pre- and post-visit questionnaires were designed to gauge the impact of a single zoo visit on visitors' conservation knowledge, concern for conservation relative to other issues and ability to propose conservation actions. Visitors were asked to allocate a hypothetical £1000 between different charitable sectors – conservation, health, domestic social concerns, international aid and animal welfare. The mean hypothetical allocation to conservation approached one-fifth of the total, i.e. as might be expected from an equal sharing between the sectors. When asked to allocate all the money to conservation, but choose between international or national, the mean spend on international conservation was less than a quarter of the total, indicating that these visitors preferred to focus on local conservation. Visitors allocated spend between habitat and species conservation very equally. Interestingly, visitors to the nature reserve scored higher on conservation knowledge, and allocated more money to conservation and to habitat protection than the zoo visitors.

Almost half of the visitors questioned could name a practical conservation action and the most common suggestion (52.8% of responses) was donating money to a conservation organisation. Other suggestions included recycling (14.4%), environmentally sensitive shopping (9.1%) and wildlife-friendly gardening (8.7%). Again visitors at the nature reserve were better able to propose conservation actions than visitors at any of the zoos.

In comparing pre- and post-visit responses, the authors detected no significant differences in departing knowledge scores, or hypothetical spend on conservation, spend on habitat or international conservation. At five of the six zoos there was also no significant difference in the visitors' ability to name conservation actions. The authors suggest that the increase in suggested actions post-visit at the remaining site may actually be due to an artefact in the data collection. There was therefore no apparent impact of a single zoo visit on the visitors' conservation knowledge, concern or ability to implement positive action for conservation. The authors suggest that expecting adults, who may also be looking after children, to absorb conservation messages through informal education during single zoo visits may be unrealistic.

8.12 Can better targeting improve the effectiveness of zoo education?

Falk (2006) proposed five categories to describe the identity-related motivations of visitors to free-choice learning institutions.

- **Explorers** are curiosity driven and seek to learn more about whatever they might encounter at the institution.

- **Facilitators** are focused primarily on enabling the experience and learning of others in their accompanying social group.
- **Professional/hobbyists** feel a close tie between the institution's content and their professional or hobbyist passions.
- **Experience seekers** primarily derive satisfaction from the fact of visiting this important site.
- **Spiritual pilgrims** are primarily seeking a contemplative and/or restorative experience.

As part of a multi-institution study conducted in collaboration with the Association of Zoos and Aquariums (US) and Monterey Bay Aquarium, these categories were used to determine the relationship between visitor motivations and changes in visitors' conservation-related cognition and affect following a zoo visit (Falk *et al.*, 2008). Interviews at two zoos and two aquariums were conducted and telephone and email interviews 7–11 months following the visit assessed any long-term impact. A single dominant identity-related motivation was identified for 55% of visitors surveyed. Explorers were common across zoos and aquariums at around 16%. Facilitators were the dominant visitor type in zoos but aquariums were more likely to attract professional/hobbyists. Experience seekers and spiritual pilgrims both comprised less than 10% each of visitors across zoos and aquariums.

The study found no overall statistically significant changes in zoo/aquarium visitors' conservation knowledge following the zoo/aquarium visit. However, analysing the total results using the identity-related categories revealed that experience seekers (around 7% of the sample) did show a significant increase in pre/post-visit knowledge. In contrast, significant overall changes in visitors' attitudes to conservation and zoos/aquariums were detected and again were correlated to identity-related visit motivation. Facilitators, professional/hobbyists and experience seekers showed large changes in their affect following the visit but explorers and spiritual pilgrims did not. Information recalled in the follow-up interviews also clustered around identity-related motivations, so interviewees described their visit in terms of, for example, the experiences of someone else in their group (facilitators).

Falk *et al.* (2008) conclude that the interpretive experiences provided for visitors in the institutions investigated were effective only for a small subset of visitors and fairly ineffective for others. There are clear lessons for practice, although we allude to shortcomings in this study in Chapter 9 (Section 9.5). Zoos must provide an array of experiences and styles of presentation to engage visitors with highly differentiated visit motivations. Since one-third of visitors interviewed had high conservation knowledge prior to the visit, perhaps zoos are underestimating the knowledge of their visitors, resulting in low post-visit knowledge gain and suggesting that the cognitive content of their programmes should be increased if new learning is to take place. Similarly, Sterling *et al.* (2007) suggest that zoos are often preaching to the converted, i.e. visitors are already conservation-minded so education messages resonate with relatively few of the real target audience, those who could make a major change in behaviour.

Smith (2009) suggests that Australian zoos are failing to identify specific behaviours to target and that this, along with a lack of staff expertise, is restricting the zoos' achievements in facilitating conservation action in visitors. A prioritisation exercise with staff and volunteers at several Australian zoos resulted in a list of potential on-site and off-site behaviours to target. The combined list for all zoos prioritised 'reduce/reuse/recycle while at the zoo; donate money or sponsor zoo animals and volunteer for zoo projects' as visitor behaviours to encourage in the zoo. The theme of recycling was again top when considering off-site behaviours, followed by 'join/support/volunteer with a conservation group and create/preserve habitats'. The exercise also revealed that learning and attitude change, rather than behaviour change was thought by participants to be the final outcome of zoo education. If the staff are unaware that behavioural change should be the ultimate goal of improved learning and attitude change, they are unlikely to be able to catalyse visitors into action for conservation.

If the ultimate aim of zoo education is the uptake of conservation actions, it is important that an explicit connection is made between the proposed conservation action and the benefit of the action to the environment. If too many cognitive steps are involved in imagining the result of their actions, or the time between the action being proposed and the visitor enacting it in their own life is too long, the connection will be lost (Smith, 2009).

Smith (2009) suggested coupling on-site behaviours with the prioritised off-site behaviours. For example, to encourage support for conservation groups, visitors could sign up at the zoo; offering free seeds, selling native plants and providing brochures on building a nest box could support the target of visitors creating wildlife habitats at home. Smith (2009) also detected a 'we do make-a-difference paradigm' operating, which is perhaps used to justify the confinement of wild animals. Such a conviction could lead to reluctance in some zoos to reorientate their programmes to target both the audiences and the behaviours that are likely to affect real benefits for conservation.

More sophisticated targeting of messages might also include tapping into the emotional responses of visitors to animals. Myers *et al.* (2004) highlight evidence from cognitive research that 'the emotional flavour of learning may determine whether a visitor wants to remember, reflect on, repeat, share or avoid what is learned'. To examine the emotional response to different animals in a zoo, Myers *et al.* (2004) asked visitors to complete questions on their feelings towards a snake, gorilla and okapi. A researcher standing close to the exhibit paged each visitor once, while they were looking directly at the animal, at which point the visitor completed the questionnaire. Seventeen emotions were measured, and wonder and respect were common responses to all three species. However, beauty, peacefulness, special privilege, caring and attraction were more common in response to the gorilla and the okapi and only the snake engendered the feelings of fear and disgust. The emotions of love, and sense of connection showed significant differences between each pair of animals; visitors were highly selective about which animals they directed these strong emotions towards.

Zoo education programmes often aim to 'inspire' and create a 'sense of wonder' and tapping into visitors' emotional response to animals may enhance the power of this

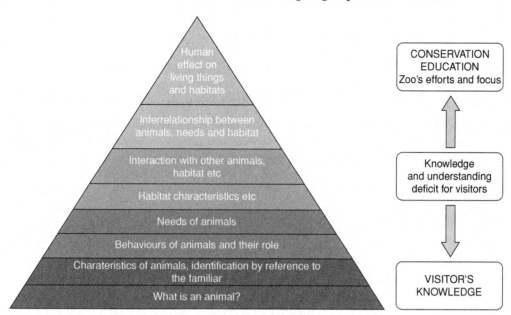

Fig. 8.1 Zoos are in a unique position to provide environmental and conservation education to large numbers of people. However, this educational task is difficult. Visitors have a limited knowledge of the complex field of conservation biology and educators need to introduce them step by step to the issues to overcome their knowledge and understanding deficit. From Tunnicliffe & Scheersoi (2009).

messaging. However, simply repeating the message and facilitating uptake of conservation actions may not be enough. Sterling *et al.* (2007) advise that long-term behavioural change is under-pinned by motivations such as commitment, altruism and intrinsic satisfaction, rather than simply reinforcement.

Since most zoos rarely undertake comprehensive studies of their visitors' prior knowledge on conservation, assessing the level to pitch conservation messages is challenging. Tunnicliffe & Scheersoi (2009) suggest a step-wise model (Fig. 8.1) for introducing the complex concepts of conservation biology, acknowledging the deficit in knowledge between many visitors and the conservation education content the zoo is trying to impart. The model begins with simple concepts such as 'what is an animal?', characteristics of animals and progresses to ecosystem-level interactions, culminating in the human effect on living things and habitats. Perhaps a further step could be 'how humans can protect biodiversity' to include the interpretation of knowledge gained in the zoo into concrete actions for conservation. Tunnicliffe & Scheersoi (2009) also emphasise the importance of situational cues, the development of an interest requires a situation-specific interaction between the person and the object (e.g. an animal or a topic). If the experience during the interaction is positive, situational interest occurs and if it endures it becomes individual interest (Tunnicliffe & Scheersoi, 2009). It is this individual interest which is the goal of all zoo educators since it is something valuable to an individual which results in their on-going investment. Educators have a valuable role to play in the development of interest since they can influence the quality of the interaction between a visitor and the object (Tunnicliffe & Scheersoi, 2009).

8.13   Are zoos expecting too much of their visitors?

If we remember that the primary intention of most zoo visitors is recreation, the seemingly poor results from published research regarding changes in knowledge, attitudes and behaviour following single zoo visits is perhaps not surprising.

If we consider formal education, although many zoos provide pre- and post-visit education materials for use in class to support school visits, the input from zoo staff and the time spent in the zoo is generally only a few hours, less than one day's school teaching. Analysis of a zoo visit, particularly for younger children, must also consider the many distractions which could interfere with effective learning such as the children being excited to be out of school, possibly nervous in a different environment, effect of weather on outdoor activities, health and safety concerns, time constraints on teachers. We are perhaps expecting too much from isolated zoo visits; studies into school-based environmental lessons can have similarly low success in changing attitude and behaviour.

Goodwin *et al.* (2010) investigated the effect of environmental lessons in school on the attitudes and behaviour of primary school children. A desirable outcome of school-based interventions is the potential for children to take the messages home to influence their families (Goodwin *et al.*, 2010). The randomised control trial of 448 primary school students and their families used questionnaires to measure the environmental attitudes and behaviours of the children before and after two types of class-based teaching. A control group answered the questionnaires but did not receive either type of lesson. Children allocated to the 'long intervention' group received two lessons of one hour each, one month apart on recycling, litter and climate change. The lessons included interactive games, a short DVD and a question-and-answer session. Each child in the long treatment group received copies of the DVD, an activity booklet to be completed at home and a series of subsequent in-class activities with accompanying lesson plans for the teacher. Children in the short treatment group received the class instruction only and the control group received only the questionnaires.

The study found no significant changes in the attitudes of children between the different lesson types, or between either lesson type or the control group; i.e. the education programme does not appear to have achieved the aim of changing the environmental attitudes of the children. Interestingly, all the experimental groups experienced an increase in pro-environmental attitudes and behaviour in the classroom survey. The authors suggest that simply being surveyed by an external research organisation was enough to raise attitudes and intended behaviours. The study suggested that longer term interventions may result in more pronounced changes, or perhaps the effect of the lessons would be demonstrated in behavioural changes beyond the time-frame of the study. The authors offer a caution to results from non-experimental studies, which may have observed positive results from education programmes but did not distinguish between the content and simply participation in the programme itself. Goodwin *et al.* (2010) suggest that 'the key drivers of attitudes remain family, peer group and media influences, rather than short interventions delivered in the classroom'.

8.14 Are zoos educating the right people?

Zoos around the world provide a variety of education opportunities for local school children and general visitors, and some provide funding and/or expertise to support education programmes in zoos abroad or as part of conservation programmes. However, even if zoo programmes are effective in changing attitudes and behaviours, the question remains whether it is actually supporting conservation either in the country the zoo is based, or abroad. Children are the decision-makers of the future, but are not able to implement the serious and imminent actions required to safeguard biodiversity.

According to a recent survey on behalf of the Convention on Biological Diversity (CBD, 2010) there is certainly work to be done to ensure the next generation of decision-makers consider the interests of the planet. The 'Airbus Bio-Index' surveyed more than 10 000 children and young people aged 5–18 from 10 countries worldwide (UK, France, Germany, Spain, USA, Japan, China, Mexico, Singapore, Australia). The results were not encouraging; 10 times more children ranked watching TV or playing computer games first compared to those who chose saving the environment (40% and 4%, respectively); 15% did not know what 'endangered species' implied. When asked which type of animal or plant they would most like to save, mammals were top with 50%, reptiles at 23%, birds at 9%. However, spending time outdoors was rated as their favourite pastime by 30% of the children, suggesting a potential for outdoor based environmental learning. The 'Wild Child Survey', carried out in 2009 and commissioned by the Zoological Society of London, interviewed 531 children in the UK about their attitudes to the natural world. The results were encouraging for zoos since 52% indicated that 'seeing animals in real life' would most inspire them to look after wildlife – more so than school lessons, television programmes or wildlife websites. The children did understand the concept of '*endangered*'; their list of top ten most endangered animals were indeed all vulnerable, endangered or critically endangered – and interestingly all non-native.

Hutchins (2003) suggests that educational efforts should focus 'where the problems are most relevant and immediate' and that efforts are often more effective when they are relevant to the audience. To highlight this he cites the example of giant pandas – if we wish to save the giant pandas in the wild, what effect will it have to educate American or European children about the possible solutions to the recovery of that species? Conway (2003) concurs and suggests that educating children and non-decision-makers is too slow and too far removed to be effective in addressing the global extinction crisis. Mazur & Clark (2001) recommend that zoos extend their influence to educating politicians, senior level bureaucrats and corporate sponsors in the habitat range of endangered species about the benefits of 'ecocentric values' (see Chapter 9).

8.15 Conservation education by non-zoo organisations

Both collection-based organisations such as museums and botanical gardens and non-collection organisations such as wildlife charities also offer education programmes for schools and general visitors on wildlife conservation, environmental issues and sustainability. The following examples highlight two collection-based organisations' commitment to life-long learning, career guidance and a facilitating role in multi-country, school-based education. These programmes expertly exploit the uniqueness of the organisations delivering them and build on the often quoted benefits children and adults derive from contact with the experts in them. Zoos are well-placed to offer similar education opportunities. One of the Eden Trust's priorities is acting as a 'convenor and agent for change' (Eden Project, 2010a), a goal the zoo world would like to emulate, but perhaps has not yet excelled in.

Eden Project, UK

The Eden Project, which is administered by the Eden Trust, is an educational charity in the UK which aims to 'promote public education and research in flora, fauna and other aspects of the natural world'. In 2008–9 it attracted 1.16 million visitors to its 'biomes' in Cornwall – impressive giant greenhouses with botanical displays, built to educate visitors on people's dependence on plants and the natural world. The Eden Trust's focus on public engagement is 'unashamedly on love and awe rather than guilt and fear', delivering positive messages for how visitors and the wider public can make a difference.

Eden's *Gardens for Life Project* has facilitated over 25 000 children in over 400 schools, in Kenya, India, the Gambia, Singapore and the USA, to develop school gardens. Eden connects schools around the world so children can share their experiences of growing food. As well as growing food, the programme helps children to explore the issues of food security, sustainable development and global citizenship. The programme is free to join and members have access to downloadable resources to support them and they share photos and experiences with Eden and each other (Eden Project, 2010b).

Natural History Museum, UK

The Natural History Museum aims to provide exciting and inspiring education opportunities to children and adults as part of life-long learning and to 'bring science to life'. The Museum also specifies its commitment to inspire children to take up scientific careers. This is facilitated through programmes such as the *Real World Science Initiative* which brings GCSE students into direct contact with scientists and it is the Museum's hope that by 2015 every secondary science student in England will be able to participate in this or a similar experience. *Student Summits*, supported by the British Council, gave hundreds of 16–18 year olds the opportunity to meet and debate issues such as climate change with scientists and decision-makers. The Museum also supports post-graduate students in taxonomy and systematics through collaborative programmes with UK universities (Natural History Museum, 2008).

8.16 Some basic principles to remember

The studies reviewed in this chapter indicate that overall, zoos are currently falling short on facilitating behavioural changes in their visitors. There are many obstacles to this worthy pursuit, but the encouraging innovations being developed in many zoos may lead to zoo education becoming a force for conservation action in the near future. Zoos must consider how to develop their role as conservation educators both in their own communities and also through supportive partnerships with zoos and conservation organisations in other countries. As Turley (1999) states, it might be argued that ultimately the survival of zoos depends on their ability to satisfy the requirements and expectations of their visitors. It is important therefore to understand visitor motivations, needs, and expectations of a zoo visit. Armed with this information, zoos will be better placed to effectively target and deliver messages to encourage visitors to make specific behavioural changes to benefit conservation.

(1) Get to know your visitors
Visitor profiles in different zoos and aquariums are not the same, it is important for each zoo to know its visitors. Design different programmes to target each group. School children, particularly in developed countries, are not in a position to conserve endangered species anytime soon – consider their education as a long-term contribution to conservation. Act in the short term to educate policy- and decision-makers and to transfer the expertise and experience of zoo educators to developing countries.

(2) Create a niche
Zoos need to be seen by their local community as a precious and useful resource. Projects to increase native species conservation in the area can help to create an association between the zoo and the local environment. Encouraging community groups to use the zoo as they perhaps would a community centre or library will attract new visitors and improve the importance of the zoo in the community. Encourage cross-organisational networking between zoo and other local conservation wildlife professionals.

(3) Target the message
Choose specific, easily comprehendible and easy to action conservation activities for visitors to participate in. Facilitate this by introducing the actions at the zoo through encouraging the use of recycling bins or providing native wild flower seeds to be planted at home.

(4) Make the most of technology and encourage long-term participation
Younger visitors will expect to be able to access additional information via the zoo website, Facebook page and increasingly zoo-specific apps for their mobiles. These are also easy ways to provide pre-visit 'orientation' to maximise the benefit and enjoyment of the zoo visit. Sign visitors up to post-visit actions and keep in touch with them to provide the necessary inspiration and encouragement for long-term participation.

(5) Use positive messaging
Positive, story-telling messages are less likely to turn visitors off who are already suffering from *'conservation fatigue'*. Include animal welfare as well as conservation messages. This will highlight good husbandry practices in the zoo, and animal welfare concepts such as animal needs are easy for children to relate to. Ensure the choice of species in the collection does not inadvertently lead to inappropriate pet purchasing such as the rise in sales of turtles and clown fish following popular films. Such species can be used to draw visitors in, but explain the species' requirements and offer alternative suggestions for more appropriate pets.

(6) Use staff as educators
Invest in staff as educators – both dedicated education staff and keepers and others who express an interest. Several studies highlight that visitors enjoy interacting with staff and learn more from keeper talks than simply reading signage. Zoos do have a unique resource, through their animal collections and also their staff from keepers to scientists to educators. Both should be used to develop a niche for zoo conservation education, both in their local community and in support of international programmes.

(7) Education is integral, not an add-on
As one of the three principal aims of the modern zoo, education must be given a stronger focus throughout all aspects of zoo planning and management. It should be at the core of exhibit planning and the visitor experience. Senior education staff should be represented on strategic committees covering these issues in the zoo. Likewise, staff and financial resources must be commensurate with the commitment and responsibility the zoo world has for delivering conservation education. Zoo educators should share experience and resources through networks such as the International Zoo Educators Association.

Key concepts
(1) Education is central to the mission of the modern zoo and the living animals can provide opportunities for unique, multi-sensorial educational experiences. However, current legislation and guidelines from zoo associations lack specific, detailed minimum standards and effective monitoring measures for education programmes.
(2) People visit the zoo primarily for recreation and as a social experience although an educational experience is also often sought. The primary visit motivation may compound the often significant knowledge gap between visitors' awareness of conservation concepts and the conservation messaging delivered by the zoo, increasing the challenge of educating visitors.
(3) Zoo education has expanded to include a wider demographic in recent years, but the majority of the recipients of formal education programmes continue to be school children. New delivery methods include a focus on interpretative techniques and deployment of high-tech, interactive exhibits.
(4) Studies have shown that visitor behaviour, as measured by holding time, is influenced by factors including taxonomy of focal animal, activity, body size and presence of

infants. There is some evidence to show that when exhibit costs are controlled for, body size of the animal does not affect visitor interest levels.

(5) To date there is insufficient evidence to support the premise that a single zoo visit has a significant effect on the knowledge, attitude or behaviour of visitors towards conservation. The strongest evidence comes from grey literature (i.e. reports by zoos), which has not been subjected to rigorous evaluation and peer-review.

9 · Turning zoos into conservation centres

'It is clear that we must mobilize our talents and arguments for conservation of biodiversity whether these are in the ethical, esthetic, social, cultural, economic, ecological, or environmental realms' (George Rabb)

9.1 Introduction

As declared by Mazur & Clark (2001), the 'zoo' is a monument to a 'long-standing tradition of people's fascination with non-human nature'. Wild animals have been maintained in captivity since early societies to satisfy human curiosity with exotica, but most western zoos today now embrace far more munificent values. There is a declared intention by zoos to help solve the problem of worldwide declines in biodiversity, and transform them from 'living natural history cabinets' to conservation centres (Rabb, 1994; WAZA, 2005).

Zoos have indeed changed significantly since their origins (Chapter 3); important and valuable shifts in zoo policy have occurred. Significantly, by participating in endangered species conservation plans and environmental education programmes, zoos support the conservation of biodiversity. But there are still discrepancies between zoos' stated conservation goals and their actual performance. There are two areas of major strain that inhibit zoos' capacity to contribute effectively to the restoration of biological diversity.

- Zoos need to resolve competing ideas, beliefs, and perceptions of how commercial and conservation aims can be made compatible.
- Zoos worldwide need to establish an operational model that allows them (jointly) to deliver clear measurable outputs and outcomes in global biodiversity conservation.

By doing so, zoos will be able to move away from more defensive oratory about their technical or logistical capabilities (Mazur & Clark, 2001) or declarations of monetary investment in conservation. Before zoos can continue to evolve to become conservation centres, more attention must be turned towards a greater understanding of what zoos can really achieve in conservation and how improvements can be made towards collective decision-making processes and organisational arrangements. Although progress will always be frustrated by some zoo professionals' understandings of and reactions to significant philosophical and practical challenges, there may be a critical mass in the zoo community to enable the realisation of adequate conservation goals.

In this chapter, we first discuss a number of conceptual posits around what zoos should understand to be their role in conservation, and how criticism of their position, whether constructive or negative, should be used to improve themselves. We attempt to understand the conflict resulting from the chimera that is being a commercial enterprise and conservation organisation at the same time. Then, we argue for zoos to delimit what they can do well. To do it better, we suggest to concentrate on species that are on the very verge of extinction. We propose a pragmatic template for zoos to deliberate and hopefully act upon.

9.2   What do zoos think they are?

What zoos purport to be has been relentlessly examined, practically throughout their entire history. The changing ecological, political and social contexts, environmental values, and economic imperatives, often against the purpose of zoos, have modified zoo policy. This has been more obvious in the case of the welfare of animals kept in captivity, possibly with relatively fast responses by zoos (Chapter 4). But, persistent criticisms of zoo practice relate mostly to the effectiveness of zoos' captive breeding and education efforts in support of biodiversity conservation. Some critics have suggested that zoos should invest less in captive breeding and release into the wild, and place greater emphasis on maintaining biodiversity through education and research programmes (Chapter 3). From the evidence presented in the previous chapters this model of indirect participation in conservation by zoos is arguably the dominant one now.

Mazur & Clark (2001) have suggested that the competing definitions of zoos' role in conserving biological diversity – direct conservation *versus* education and research – exemplify the conflicting standards that humans have about the use of environmental and natural resources (Kellert, 1996). O'Riordan (1981) distinguishes two value systems; technocentrism and ecocentrism. Technocentrism lies at one end of the spectrum. It centres on technology and its ability to affect, control and protect the environment. Technocentrics have absolute faith in technology and industry and firmly believe that humans have control over nature. Although technocentrics may accept that environmental problems exist, they do not see them as problems to be solved by a reduction in industry. Rather, environmental problems are seen as to be solved using science and technology. Ecocentrics, including deep ecologists, see themselves as being subject to nature, rather than in control of it. They promote the intrinsic value of, and our moral responsibility for, non-human nature, and endorse ecological limits to growth and low impact technologies (O'Riordan, 1981).

Zoo practices reflect elements of technocentric and ecocentric thinking. Perhaps the extreme expression of technocentrism in zoos is that around cloning and some reproductive technologies (Ballou, 1992; Pickard & Holt, 2004). Ecocentric values, on the other hand, are mostly expressed by the ideals of changing peoples' behaviour through education and inspiration (Paehlke & Torgerson, 1990; Gwynne, 2007). Mazur & Clark (2001) suggest that the presence of these two opposing sets of values within zoos demonstrates a lack of clarity about the multiple and competing values that frustrate the zoo community's conservation achievements. Zoos need to regularly and continually clarify aims, and monitor the relevance of their policies for restoring biological diversity (Mazur & Clark, 2001). There is no denying that each of these viewpoints, in addition to the more traditional environmental perspectives, has its positive points, and it is these which must be considered when searching for solutions to environmental problems. The challenge facing society is to arrive at a consensus of opinions, through global discussion about what is best not only for humans now and in the future, but also what is best for the rest of nature as well. But, with the ultimate output measure – number of species saved from extinction – zoos must reconcile differences between technocentrics and ecocentrics, and together provide much needed conservation entrepreneurship.

Evidence suggests that zoos' performance to date in terms of endangered species conservation and public education is more a function of exceptionally dedicated and motivated individual staff members, rather than a bureaucratic and corporate framework (Mazur, 1997). The zoo community can combat these problems by considering the environmental, conservation and education values best served by corporatised industry methods, and whether their organisational structures and policy development can be streamlined to provide greater support for conserving biodiversity. Frazer *et al.* (1985) propose that the basic challenge for zoos remains how to 'devise and introduce appropriate organisational changes' in line with the very rapid changes 'in the nature and size of its task, in the nature of the society it serves, and in the skills and aspirations of its staff'.

Although it may be academically attractive to identify the sways of philosophical positions that have occurred within zoos, it is the general dissatisfaction with the persistence of traditional zoo policies and practices that prevents effective communication internally, with related organisations, and the general public (Norton *et al.*, 1995; Mazur, 1997). The fact that there are still multiple and competing values among zoos has perhaps led to concerns within the conservation community about the methodological and ideological flaws of zoo-based, *ex-situ* programmes (Mazur, 1996, 1997).

Despite the zoo community's efforts to promote a conservation role and image, perceptions persist of zoos as places of entertainment rather than institutions of scholarly, scientific, or conservation pursuits (Mullan & Marvin, 1987; Bitgood, 1988; Kellert & Dunlap, 1989). If these perceptions are held by decision-makers in government wildlife agencies or non-governmental conservation organisations, they may resist zoo participation in conservation and education projects (Mazur, 1997). In counterpoint, the notion of the zoo as 'old-fashioned' has encouraged defensive policy responses from the zoo community. Thus, zoo professionals often create official position statements that may misrepresent or overstate zoos' actual contributions to conservation and education. Criticism is often answered by citing zoos' ability to deliver tangible and substantial benefits to wildlife and people (Hutchins & Wemmer, 1991; Tudge, 1991; Hutchins & Conway, 1995; Maple, 1995; Gusset & Dick, 2010). Zoo professionals also respond to fault finding by distinguishing between 'good' zoos that show concerted efforts to change and 'bad' zoos that deserve criticism and should eventually be eliminated (Bostock, 1993; Maple *et al.*, 1995). Another common response is to construe critics as 'opponents' who, because of dubious motivations or poorly constructed arguments, do not understand zoos (Seal, 1991; Allen, 1995; Hutchins *et al.*, 1996; and see Snyder *et al.*, 1996). Consequently, energy and resources are unnecessarily devoted to warding off critics and officious media through the extensive use of public relations campaigns.

The potential to learn from critics is complicated by the fact that the zoo community contains a diverse range of people with varying ideas of what constitutes appropriate conservation policies. Zoo policy is established not only by the directives of top executives, but also by the multitudes of decisions of people at all levels as they go about their daily work (Bullis & Kennedy, 1991), although not all people have equal access to formal decision-making processes. Generally, economic and market-oriented concerns held by more powerful senior managers (Smith, 1993; Beattie, 1994) tend to prevail in decision-making (Sebag-Montefiore, 1993; Hancocks, 1995; Jamieson, 1995; Mazur, 1997). Consequently, the principles and practices that constitute appropriate zoo operations may remain unclear or lack consensus. The zoo community will need to regularly clarify its aims, monitor the relevance of its policies for restoring biological diversity, and consider the full context of environmental problems it seeks to address.

9.3   Re-'thinking' zoos

9.3.1   Management structures

There is no doubt that zoos face a formidable challenge in contributing to halting biodiversity loss in the new millennium. If they are to manage wild animals in captivity for exhibit purposes, conduct inter-organisational endangered species breeding schemes and *in-situ* conservation programmes, as well as formulate and implement education and research they will require substantial resources and flexibility. These requirements become even more important as zoos attempt to regionalise their animal collection plans further and increase both their research profile and participation in endangered species recovery. Some attention has been devoted to measuring zoos' performance, fostering cultural diversity in personnel (La Rue, 1992; Chicago Zoological Society, 2010) and breaking down hierarchical divisions while adopting team-based management structures (Atkinson-Grosjean, 1992). However, Mazur (1997) argues that overall, zoos have failed to link the best of the principles contained in policy sciences with conservation practices.

Zoos' organisational structures and management are directly relevant to achieving their conservation aims. In particular, it is not unusual within the zoo world in many parts of the world to encounter bureaucratic structures, sometimes highly specialised, with a strict hierarchy of authority that maintains impersonal, rigid rule systems. These structures are effective only when their tasks and their operating environments are simple and stable, but are totally ineffective in more complicated systems (Morgan, 1986; Blau & Myer, 1987). These highly centralised systems of control and their fixed rules, roles, and regulations make them slow and ineffective in responding to changing circumstances.

The unique challenges of conserving endangered species or shaping public understanding exceed current bureaucratic capabilities (Paehlke & Torgerson, 1990). Moreover, the influence of corporate management ethos, which permeates both public and private zoos in many parts of the world, has led to expanded senior management strata, heavily represented by business expertise (Mazur & Clark, 2001). This is always accompanied by the use of corporate tools (business strategies, product formats, and performance measures) to promote a paradigm of economic rationalism. Corporate management, and the economic rationalism it embodies, has been soundly criticised since the late 1980s by Considine (1988), Painter (1988) and Sinclair (1989), and more recently by Rees (1994) and Rhodes (1996). The main criticism is that corporate management narrowly construes economic efficiency as organisational effectiveness. Corporatisation has serious ramifications for all zoo policies. For example, animals may be managed as commodities and conservation may become a public relations ploy, all justified in terms of economic efficiency. The mission of endangered species restoration and public education may easily fall prey to cost–benefit accounting (Adams, 1996). Consequently, animal welfare, wildlife conservation and public education may be overshadowed by a standard of economic efficiency common in corporate boardrooms.

Many zoos' current market-oriented approaches and corporatised organisational practices result in an emphasis on maximising and stabilising revenues (Mazur, 1997). Official pressures and budget constraints balance conservation against corporate efficiency and other demands. Hence, conservation values translate into activities 'not that the zoo must do – but that it must be able to afford to do' (Mazur & Clark, 2001). Special tensions are created when conservation programmes and animals' biological needs are balanced against zoos' financial and public relations imperatives. Since zoos consider visitors' recreational motives to be vital to their mission and survival (Chiszar et al., 1990; Bostock, 1993; Maple, 1995), it remains unclear what trade-offs are reasonable. These management structures are also promoted internally and externally, often by forceful public relations and/or mechanisms that draw on 'smoke and mirrors' to promote something that is unreal. More seriously though, the public relations game obviates measuring success and performance of zoos in more objective ways.

9.3.2 'Direct and indirect' conservation zoos – decide what you are

Zoos like many other institutions involved in conservation are influenced by non-science aspects, such as anthropomorphic (e.g. preference for protection of more 'charismatic' taxa) and anthropocentric (e.g. economic value or potential conflict with economic uses) factors that sway conservation funding decisions (Metrick & Weitzman, 1996, 1998; Restani & Marzluff, 2001, 2002). As a result, zoos focus most attention on a select number of taxa (Chapter 6) which may reflect the influence of multiple factors (e.g. societal values or even internal corporate biases). This is seen in the case of species conservation research which clearly suffers from taxonomic bias, subjectivity in the choice of research topics, and how resources are allocated (Clark & May, 2002). This is in spite of data that suggest that biodiversity conservation policies are most effective when based on current scientific knowledge and public corroboration (Babbitt, 1995; Eisner *et al.*, 1995). Taxonomic bias skews funding decisions, resulting in data collection for only a limited number of species (Male & Bean, 2005).

It is possible to argue that taxonomic bias in zoos occurs because species are often selected for exhibition (to which some conservation purpose may be attached later) based on personal interests (not just of the zoo director, but also of the institution). In some cases, species selection may or may not reflect certain actual or supposed values (Proença *et al.*, 2008). Data presented in previous chapters point to a situation similar to how conservation spending patterns and policy decisions are biased towards certain taxa (Martín-López *et al.*, 2009). Most *in-situ* conservation work on endangered species undertaken by zoos, e.g. for WAZA projects, focus on mammals, particularly on charismatic primates and carnivores, but other animal groups (e.g. amphibians and fishes) are significantly under-represented (Gusset & Dick, 2010). This is also the case for AZA and EAZA captive breeding programmes (Chapter 6), for *in-situ* projects supported by European and North American zoos (EAZA, 2010; AZA, 2010a), and also for Mexican zoos (Lascuráin *et al.*, 2009).

But there is a quandary that not only zoos are required to resolve. This is the fact that the more threatened a taxon (at least for certain vertebrate groups), the more likely funds are channelled into research and conservation of that taxon. Garnett *et al.* (2003) presented data to suggest that the direct consequence of a species reaching critically endangered or endangered status is a need for a substantial increase in the funding levels for research on that species. Spending large amounts of money on a particular priority species, however, is not the most efficient way to promote biodiversity conservation, because some of the most highly ranked species require huge conservation efforts with a small chance of success, whereas other, less threatened species might be successfully conserved for relatively little cost (Possingham *et al.*, 2002). One reason for this concentration of funds in a few threatened species is the lack of knowledge of other taxa that are less threatened but equally, or more, important from a biodiversity standpoint.

The disquiet that has arisen within and outside the zoo community through a lack of integration of zoo conservation thinking within modern environmental problem solving persists. This is evident in their inability to solve practices, such as the still prevalent preference for charismatic, exotic large-bodied fauna in zoo collections (Chapter 6). This issue is perhaps epitomised by the lack of clarity over how to adequately meet the commercial and conservation objectives of zoos. Zoos still need to re-think how much emphasis (and funds) they are willing to commit on conservation. Once they do this they can then decide whether they merely exhibit animals for education and recreation (and make money), or really get involved in direct conservation. This could mean that for those 'direct conservation' zoos, their animal collections will look different to 'indirect conservation' zoos, e.g. they would develop coherent messages exhibiting species that can change societal perceptions, and more importantly encourage adequate funding for those species needing conservation attention. But, for all zoos that want to achieve transparent and measureable conservation outcomes (ultimately meaning many more species conserved) there will be a need to work together more effectively. Mechanisms for doing this already exist (Chapter 3).

9.3.3 Applying the 'millennium ark concept' for real conservation

Zoos need to re-think their captive breeding strategies and the targets and criteria they apply to define viable populations for conservation. Since Soulé *et al.* (1986) declared their main goal of captive breeding as the 'maintenance of 90% of the genetic variation in the source (wild) population over a period of 200 years', much data have emerged highlighting the severe problems caused by genetic adaptation to captivity (Section 4.2.2), the severity and widespread occurrence of inbreeding and inbreeding depression (Chapter 5), and the limitations of effective captive breeding (Sections 6.7 and 6.8). We have learned that a very large proportion of reintroductions fail (Chapter 7), and that the most successful captive breeding programmes aimed at a time in captivity as short as possible (e.g. black-footed ferrets), albeit exceptions exist. It has emerged that the most efficient approach to limit inbreeding and genetic adaptation is to minimise the number of generations in captivity (Section 6.7). Moreover, progress in biotechnology and cryotechnology has not been as swift as Soulé *et al.* (1986) hoped (Section 5.8). However, instead of critically evaluating the implications on captive breeding or using more strict criteria, the threshold values were relaxed by applied zoo management (90% in 100 years; see Earnhardt *et al.*, 2009), mainly because of practical constraints (available 'places' for breeding) and pragmatism. Moreover, an approach has emerged which assumes that breeding for exhibition and reintroduction needs can aim at the same threshold criteria (Earnhardt *et al.*, 2009).

Genetic changes in captive populations have potentially very severe consequences, limiting their use for reintroductions. We therefore agree with Traill *et al.*'s (2010) interpretation for MVPs in wild populations, and suggest that captive populations might have a high likelihood to be managed inadvertently or implicitly for extinction. We suggest the following.

- Define clearly whether captive breeding directly and primarily aims for reintroductions, introductions or population augmentations, or whether it aims to breed for display or as a '*living museum*'.
- Critically re-evaluate and discuss criteria to determine viable populations for conservation (i.e. reintroductions) in accessible and peer-reviewed papers.
- Plan captive breeding for conservation (i.e. reintroductions) to be completed including successful reintroduction in a time-frame that is as short as possible (e.g. black-footed ferret). Captive breeding should minimise the number of generations in captivity because the number of generations is more important than number of years for captive breeding, retention of genetic diversity and adaptation to captivity. On the other hand, the total number of years is important for humans, as reflected by PVAs using normally time frames of 100 years. We suggest that the time-frame from founding captive populations to re-establishment of viable populations in the wild should aim at a time-frame as short as possible and of **40 years maximum**, whenever possible. The time-frame of 40 years maximum assures assures that there is an institutional and personal responsibility and accountability.

9.4 Advancing 'zero tolerance' conservation

Given certain conditions, many effective responses are now available for the conservation community to actively reduce biodiversity loss. However, these responses will not be sustainable or sufficient unless relevant direct and indirect drivers of change are addressed. Further progress will come through greater coherence and synergies between the *in-situ* and *ex-situ* sectors and through greater collaboration within each. Crucially though, future efforts for conservation and management of biodiversity must derive from a set of clear objectives, mechanisms for action, and commitment from all stakeholders. Apart from this, halting the process of degradation and species loss requires specialised solutions and an understanding of ecological processes. Protecting biodiversity does not merely involve setting aside portions of land as reserves. Instead, ecological processes such as predation, pollination, parasitism, seed dispersal and herbivory, involving complex interactions between several species of plants and animal, needs to be ensured in conjunction with protection of ecosystem services. This, however, is possible only if reserves are large enough to maintain such processes. There is also the need for greater involvement of human communities, and for models which decentralise management and conservation roles and responsibilities. As of now, there are still major lacunae in information resources pertaining to forests, biodiversity – whether flora and fauna, causative factors for their degradation, and major threats. The available data are alarmingly inadequate to provide a lucid picture of the current status and ongoing losses/gains. More importantly, current legislation on wild animal and habitat protection and its effective enforcement is insufficient to tackle the scale of the problem, and these insufficiencies are not being addressed with a sense of urgency.

For sure, zoos must be energetic participants in any 'surge' against biodiversity loss. They, like any other organisation involved in conservation, should aim for the most favourable cost-to-benefit ratio, i.e. 'the greatest bang for your buck'. This means that species are not seen in isolation from the ecological and human context in which they live and strategies that are practicable and more importantly that aim for cumulative or 'snowballing' effects are crucial to instigate. The term cumulative impacts has normally been used in the context of the culmination of many small-scale, independent land-use decisions or activities into a major outcome. Typically, cumulative impacts arise from uncoordinated decisions, so the outcomes are neither intended nor preferred (thus they are often negative) (Odum, 1982). Here, we offer an alternative, a mirror-image to how cumulative impacts have been described. We consider the possibility of making individual efforts in many areas to allow a massive change to occur not just within these but among them too. Over time, these individual interventions will accumulate to generate a large effect – not the 'death by a thousand cuts' or 'the tyranny of small decisions' (Kahn, 1966; Odum, 1982) but the opposite.

Presently, and not only in zoos, conservation programmes are often designed in isolation, not just from each other, but also from similar ones undertaken by others (e.g. other regions); a piecemeal approach that ignores the potential for making sure that 'snowballing' effects can be achieved. A system not dissimilar to the 'citizen science'

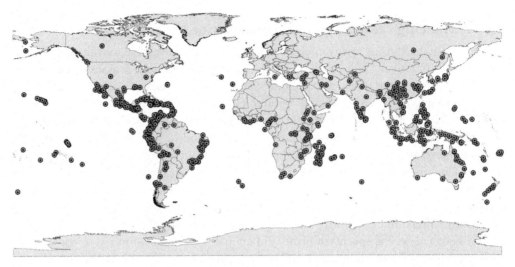

Fig. 9.1 Map of 595 sites of imminent species extinction. There are 203 fully and 87 partially contained within declared protected areas and 257 sites are completely unprotected or have unknown protection status (*n* = 48). From Ricketts *et al.* (2005).

described by Cooper *et al.* (2007) can operate over large scales by drawing on spatially dispersed participants, e.g. across multiple conservation project sites. The result is an inter-communicated system of project sites that together can achieve cumulative change for a multitude of species and landscapes. Is there already such a system in place to which the global zoo community can add and play a crucial role in saving species from extinction?

If, in a triage context, zoos are best placed at dealing with the 'worst off' species, i.e. those requiring immediate interventions (including captive breeding), then taxa that are both highly threatened and restricted to single locations should be of primary conservation interest. This approach alone is, of course, not sufficient to prevent all species extinctions, as other threatened species are not confined to single sites. However, it is a first line of defence against predictable and preventable imminent species losses, and is an urgent priority for the global conservation community. Sites containing such species, which can be managed as a discrete unit, represent the extremes of threat and irreplaceability – two widely accepted principles for prioritising conservation action (Chapter 2). With small populations, extreme vulnerability to habitat destruction, and limited conservation options, these species face imminent extinction if no appropriate conservation action is taken. Furthermore, immediate requirements for their conservation are relatively straightforward – to conserve habitat and/or augment population numbers.

Ricketts *et al.* (2005) recognised a total of 595 sites that are the last refuges for 794 of the world's most highly threatened mammals, birds, selected reptiles, amphibians and conifers (see Fig. 9.1). In a more recent iteration, 920 species have been identified from 587 'trigger' sites (Benjamin Skolnik, personal communication). Because these species are likely to become extinct unless immediate and direct action is taken, these 'trigger' species' (Chapter 2) sites require imminent protection, but almost half currently lack any legal protection and only just more than a third are fully contained within a gazetted protected area (although management effectiveness among protected areas is uneven). Average human density in these sites is 127 people km^{-2}, about three times the global mean of 45 people km^{-2} and about twice the mean recorded in adjacent areas. Similarly, mean human footprint, an aggregate index of human land use, population and infrastructure, is 25.5 units compared with a global mean of 9.9 units and a mean within ecoregions containing sites of 16.3 units. This intensity of surrounding human activity, which is nearly identical for protected and unprotected sites, suggests that the challenges facing conservation of these highly threatened species extend beyond the small tracts of land they occupy. Their protection will require a combination of site-level activities and broader-scale efforts to conserve and restore habitats, address regional threats, and maintain ecological processes.

A sobering statistic is that there are three times as many of the identified single-site species at risk of extinction as are known to have been lost in the same taxa over the last 500 years (Ricketts *et al.*, 2005). This result reinforces other estimates of accelerating extinction rates, due in part to extinctions spreading from islands containing 'ecologically naive' species toward continental terrestrial biodiversity. Broader shifts in geography are also evident. For example, 21% of extinct bird species were found in the Neotropics (the world's richest biogeographic realm); this proportion has now more than doubled to 50% of 'trigger' species. These changes do not indicate that birds, island species, or areas outside the Neotropics are now less threatened than before. Rather, they reflect the expansion of the current extinction episode beyond sensitive species and places (e.g. exploited species and island communities) as habitat destruction and other threats intensify in the planet's most biodiverse mainland regions. These regions include tropical moist forests, which contain more than one-half of all sites, emphasising their well-known importance for biodiversity.

Resulting from the identification of 'trigger' species sites, a consortium of biodiversity conservation organisations, AZE, was formed with the common aim of preventing extinctions by promoting or engaging in conservation activities in these areas. Membership includes 67 non-governmental environmental organisations (of which 11 are zoos) and is open to any institution whose primary purpose is the conservation of biological diversity. Outside the scope of the Alliance, many AZE members also work to protect highly endangered species that are more wide-ranging and require different conservation measures.

The original list of AZE sites and species in Ricketts *et al.* (2005) centred on a selected number of taxa for which data on threat status and distribution were available globally. As information for other taxonomic groups becomes available, as knowledge improves, more 'trigger' species and sites such as corals or fishes will be included in the list. To date several nations, including Brazil, Mexico and Colombia, have established national Alliances with over one hundred participating institutions in order to further refine the AZE analysis and contribute to the protection of 'trigger' sites and species. Lamentably, as human activities intensify yet more species are likely to be consigned to their last posts. Furthermore, for a number of 'trigger' species in the AZE list, so little is known about their distribution and abundance that they may be closer to extinction than currently thought. In some cases though, the species can be detected elsewhere, and this is good news. Nonetheless, the sites identified by the AZE form a critical subset of global conservation priorities, complementing other prioritisation efforts (see below) by focussing on relatively small scales and short time horizons – known places where extinctions are imminent unless immediate conservation action is taken.

The value of the AZE list of sites and species to assist global biodiversity conservation has been recognised by the CBD, with the signing of an agreement between CBD and AZE in 2010. This memorandum of cooperation allows AZE expertise to support implementation of the CBD Strategic Plan, particularly regarding the draft target of halting species extinction. AZE is able to assist the Parties to the Convention in integrating the zero-extinction target into national biodiversity strategies and action plans. AZE provides a tool for nations to comply with their obligations under the Convention, and also a cost-effective way to prioritise sites for conservation.

Alongside large-scale conservation schemes which identify broad areas of biodiversity to help protect the full range of species over the long term (Chapter 2), the AZE approach complements these efforts by focussing on a smaller spatial scale and shorter time horizon (Ricketts et al., 2005). Most large-scale prioritisation methods target endangerment more efficiently than by chance and overlap in many areas but can miss out crucial elements of global biodiversity (Brooks et al., 2006; Funk & Fa, 2010). Planning and implementing conservation strategies within broad areas must be undertaken, but this takes time, and therefore may not be rapid enough to protect individual highly threatened species. Furthermore, most AZE sites occur within the broad priority areas identified by other schemes and so can inform conservation plans and actions within them. AZE is compatible with and reinforces broader approaches.

AZE also complements existing methods to identify conservation priorities at finer scales. For example, BirdLife International's *Important Bird Areas* (Fishpool & Evans, 2001) use a series of criteria to locate sites of particular importance for bird conservation, and *Key Biodiversity Areas* (Eken et al., 2004) use a similar methodology to expand this approach to other taxa. AZE sites thus form a particularly urgent subset of *Key Biodiversity Areas* in which highly threatened species are restricted to single sites and, therefore, face imminent extinction. Some conservation organisations are already using AZE data to inform their ongoing efforts (Eken et al., 2004).

Alas, despite the expertise in small population biology, captive breeding and reintroductions that exists among zoos, active involvement with AZE sites and species is still limited. Yet, the AZE scheme is arguably exactly the sort of guidance zoos require to choose species to invest in. The AZE list could function in a way similar to the CBSG's CAMP process, i.e. allowing the prioritising of conservation activities by species. This would be compatible with the TAG system currently in place (Chapter 6), who would be able to deploy their solid experience of working at regional and global scales. The AZE system would provide clear targets for zoos, perhaps led by TAGs, to organise actions towards assisting the most endangered species and sites worldwide. Furthermore, there is no reason why AZE species cannot sit comfortably side by side within TAGs alongside taxa chosen as exhibit animals, which is largely the case now (Chapter 6).

Interventions at AZE sites by zoos would really push *ex-situ* institutions to become much more effective conservation enterprises; perhaps allowing them to take a leap, as described by Meffe (2001), from a 'science of discovery' to a 'science of engagement'. Already, zoos or *in-situ* captive breeding programmes run by zoos maintain a number of AZE 'trigger' species. Examples of these include the blue-billed curassow and the Socorro dove in the National Zoo, USA, and *Durrell's* conservation programmes involving birds and reptiles in Mauritius, the ploughshare tortoise in Madagascar, and the pygmy hog in India (Durrell, 2010). The latter two species do not appear in animal inventories such as ISIS because these taxa are not currently in international cooperative breeding programmes. This could be a reason for the low number of AZE species recorded in ISIS, but it is likely that the explanation for this is that zoos have not focussed on these species.

For this, AZE members including zoos can motivate and coordinate active species conservation actions. This conservation strategy should be flexible enough to operate at a variety of temporal and spatial scales, and with a huge potential to attack problems of continental significance. The outcome should be the exploration and improvement of the wildlife value of many landscapes, alongside building skills networks and even contribute to the capacity to face the consequences of overpopulation, disease pandemics, over-consumption of resources, and climate change. Opportunities for successful 'cumulative impacts' programmes increase especially through the use of a network of AZE conservation projects, focussing on achieving not only long-term viable populations of endangered species, but also protection of ecosystems and habitats, as well as the dependent human communities within them, thus:

- providing a high level of protection for endangered species;
- using best available science to protect the functions and values of targeted ecosystems with special consideration to conservation or protection measures necessary to preserve or enhance all species;
- furthering the goal of no net loss of ecosystem functions;
- encouraging restoration and enhancement of degraded and low quality habitats;
- complementing national and local protection measures; and
- allowing reasonable sustainable resource use by resident human communities.

That it is possible to conserve and even save from extinction many of these AZE species is exemplified by actions undertaken already by many of the Alliance partners. In the case of *Durrell*, up to 14 AZE species (two mammals, seven birds, and five reptiles) and five other single-site taxa have been aided (Table 9.1). Success has not only being achieved in actually saving species from imminent extinction (e.g. Mauritius kestrel; Jones *et al.*, 1995) and other birds on the island of Mauritius, but *Durrell's* contribution also has resulted in a number of 'cumulative impacts'. Investment in these projects has varied by site and species (in some cases more than 20 years for the Mauritius birds) and complexity of activities. But, overall, the Trust supports over 50 projects and teams in 19 countries (Durrell, 2010). Most have resulted in the creation or management support of protected areas where the species are found. Notably, the first national park in Mauritius (The Black River Gorges) was declared directly as a result of *Durrell's* involvement, and the

Table 9.1 *Examples of 'trigger' species and their cumulative impacts in projects led, or with involvement, by Durrell*

Country	'Trigger' species	Main conservation activities around the 'trigger' species	Cumulative impacts					Indicative references
			New populations established in the wild from captive stock or translocated wild animals	Human livelihoods enhanced	Protected areas declared or assisted	Ecosystem services protected	Other species protected	
AZE species								
India	Pygmy hog	Captive breeding, reintroduction	✓	✓	✓	✓	✓	Narayan et al. (2008); Funk et al. (2007)
Mauritius	Mauritius kestrel	Captive breeding, reintroduction	✓		✓		✓	Jones et al. (1995)
	Pink pigeon	Captive breeding, reintroduction	✓		✓		✓	Swinnerton et al. (2004); Bunbury et al. (2008)
	Echo parakeet	Captive breeding, reintroduction	✓		✓		✓	
	Round Island boa	Field work, captive breeding			✓		✓	Cole et al. (2009)
	Guenther's gecko	Translocations, captive breeding			✓		✓	Cole et al. (2009)
Madagascar	Giant jumping rat	Population status assessment		✓	✓	✓	✓	Young et al. (2008b)
	Madagascar pochard	Captive breeding, reintroduction	✓		✓	✓		
	Flat-tailed tortoise	Population status assessments		✓	✓	✓	✓	Young et al. (2008a)

Location	Species	Conservation action						Reference
Antigua	Ploughshare tortoise	Captive breeding, reintroduction	✓	✓	✓	✓	✓	Durrell *et al.* (1994)
	Aloatran gentle lemur	Field work, captive breeding		✓	✓	✓	✓	Lahoz-Montfort *et al.* (2010); Guillera-Arroita *et al.* (2010)
Antigua	Antiguan racer	Translocations	✓		✓			Daltry *et al.* (2001)
Montserrat	Montserrat oriole	Field work			✓		✓	Young (2008)
St. Lucia	Maria Island racer	Field work					✓	
Galapagos	Mangrove finch	Translocations	✓					Fessl *et al.* (2010)
	Floreana mockingbird	Translocations	✓					
Non-AZE single-site species								
St. Lucia	St. Lucia parrot	Field work			✓	✓	✓	Jeggo *et al.* (2000)
	St. Lucia whiptail lizard	Translocations	✓		✓		✓	Dickinson & Fa (2000); Funk & Fa (2006)
	St. Lucia iguana	Field work			✓		✓	Morton (2009)
Grand Cayman	Blue iguana	Captive breeding, reintroductions	✓		✓			Burton (2004, 2006)
Mauritius	Mauritius fody	Hand-rearing, translocations	✓		✓		✓	Cristinacce *et al.* (2008)

improvement of the management of the Menabe, Baly Bay and Lac Alaotra protected areas in Madagascar or the Manas National Park in India stem from *in-situ* commitment by the organisation (Durrell, 2010). Durrell projects have played a crucial part in the enhancement of human livelihoods in all sites in Madagascar and in India. The projects have invested in training local researchers, educators and managers and have made contributions to the dissemination of conservation science through peer-reviewed publications.

If one zoo-based organisation has been able to improve the fate of as many as 20 AZE species, this is a model that other zoos can apply to many more AZE species. This is feasible because most species in the AZE list require effective and immediate support and action using skills and knowledge zoos are well-placed to proffer. Using data from Balmford *et al.* (2003) to estimate annual costs of effective field-based conservation, Ricketts *et al.* (2005) pointed out that annual management expenditure per site in developing countries could be as low as \$470 but no more than \$3 500 000 (median \$220 000). Because a large proportion of AZE species (85%) are found in developing countries, *in-situ* conservation costs are relatively low. Even if one-time acquisition costs for unprotected sites is many times their management costs, there are possible and cost-effective opportunities through the redesignation of public lands to higher levels of protection or better enforcement of existing designations. Protection of these sites would conserve more than the individual threatened species that trigger them. A total of 103 sites contain one trigger species, but several contain five (e.g. Massif de la Hotte, Haiti, with 13). Furthermore, potential human well-being benefits of safeguarding the AZE global network of sites include: (1) climate change mitigation through avoidance of CO_2 emissions from deforestation; (2) freshwater services to downstream human populations; (3) cultural value indicated by representation of human languages; and (4) retention of option value than would other sites within the same countries or ecoregions (Larsen *et al.*, in press). Also, potential economic benefits from climate change mitigation at these sites substantially exceeded the management cost of conserving them, delivering a disproportionate value for at least one ecosystem service at 89% of AZE sites. Although many of these sites remain unprotected and all face ongoing threats, conserving them would provide substantial and cost-effective human well-being benefits.

Involvement of zoos in protection of AZE sites alongside other organisations provides the ideal opportunity for *ex-situ* conservation bodies to actively engage in direct and immediate biodiversity conservation. By patronising one or more sites, an idea not dissimilar to Tilson's (1995) *Adopt a Park*, zoos can be more effective in avoiding impending extinctions. This can be done in a number of ways, according to the zoos' internal technical abilities and financial possibilities. Donations can be used to safeguard sites through land purchase or conservation easements (i.e. the right to use the land without actually owning it). Institutions can be involved in community management, or protected area enforcement or even control of invasive species or disease. Zoos could also develop animal translocation or *ex-situ* breeding programmes where appropriate. A number of AZE species have been effectively supported through captive breeding and new wild populations established through reintroduction; e.g. the ploughshare tortoise in Madagascar (see above) or the pygmy hog in India (Box 9.1). In general though, AZE species are

Box 9.1 · *The pygmy hog – from rediscovery to recovery*

The pygmy hog is the most endangered of the world's wild suids. It was presumed to occur in early successional tall grasslands at intervals along the southern Himalayan foothills, extending from NE Uttar Pradesh and SW Nepal in the west, to NW Bengal and NW Assam in the east. However, all confirmed reports and most anecdotal accounts dating back to its description in 1847 refer only to the latter areas. The species was 'rediscovered' in 1971 after it was suspected to have become extinct. The pygmy hog is currently known to continue to exist in the Manas Tiger Reserve, though its presence has been recorded in a number of other sites. These other hog populations were confirmed or feared extinct by the early to mid 1980s (Narayan et al., 2008). However, Manas, its last refuge, is also threatened by political instability and other problems. This site has also been included on the IUCN List of Threatened Protected Areas besides being a World Heritage Site in Danger.

As a response to the precarious state of the species, the Pygmy Hog Conservation Programme (PHCP) was launched in 1995. The PHCP is a broad-based research and conservation programme that aims to protect the species and its habitat. The PHCP was formed under the aegis of a formal International Conservation Management and Research Agreement (ICMRA), signed between the Ministry of Environment and Forests (Govt of India), Forest Department (Govt of Assam), Durrell Wildlife Conservation Trust, and the IUCN/SSC Wild Pigs Specialist Group (WPSG). The agreement has been renewed twice through Memoranda of Understanding valid till 2015. The Programme is implemented in Assam by the Rare and Endangered Species Conservation Unit (RESCU) of EcoSystems-India, the local partner organisation of both Durrell and WPSG. The main aim of this collaborative programme is conservation of the pygmy hogs and other endangered species of tall grasslands of the region through field research, captive breeding and reintroductions after adequate restoration of degraded former habitats. The above Agreement stipulates that ownership of all pygmy hogs bred in captivity would lie with the Government of Assam, till perpetuity. Translocation and reintroduction of any such animal is possible only with mutual consent of the agencies involved.

The main threats to the survival of pygmy hogs are loss and degradation of habitat from expansion of human settlements, agricultural encroachment, flood control schemes and extensive and indiscriminate burning of tall grasslands. Pygmy hogs are dependent on the continuing existence of these grasslands, which are likewise crucial to the survival of a number of endangered species. However, only the pygmy hog seems inextricably linked to the continued availability of successional grasslands.

In 1996, six wild hogs (two males, four females) were caught from Manas National Park and transferred to a purpose-built research and breeding centre at Basistha, near the city of Guwahati. The three adult females, which were pregnant from wild, produced healthy litters and the captive population increased to 18. Seven more litters were born in the following year and the captive hog population almost doubled to 35 in 1997. Similar success in captive breeding in subsequent years saw the captive population at Basistha rise to 77 in 2001; a 13-fold increase in the stock in six years. This unanticipated and rapid increase in the captive population required imposition of rigorous curbs on their reproduction. A population of around 70 hogs was maintained in captivity till 2007, and since 2008, it was decided to release 10–15 hogs every year into the wild by breeding them in adequate numbers.

After extensive surveys and detailed consultations with the relevant authorities two sites were selected as being potentially suitable for reintroduction purposes, i.e. Sonai Rupai Wildlife Sanctuary and Nameri National Park. A third site, Orang National Park, was kept under observation to assess flood water levels in the rainy season, and later it was concluded that the grasslands in the northern part of the Park are suitable for releasing the hogs. These three sites fall within the species' known recent range in NW Assam, though no evidence could be found of the species' continuing occurrence in these areas, despite the presence of suitable habitats. Sonai Rupai was selected for the first releases on the basis that it contained considerably more tall grasslands than Nameri, but that this area had been generally neglected and that any such reintroduction attempt might also generate increased interest and resources to enhance future protection and management of the entire area. To these ends, the PHCP continues to work with the Sanctuary authorities and staff to improve protection and management and to control annual dry season burning of grass. Sanctuary staff was also trained in wildlife monitoring and habitat management to help in restoration of the grassland habitat and monitoring of released hogs.

Social groups of 'unrelated' (i.e. pedigree-unrelated assuming that founders are unrelated; logistics has prevented the confirmation of relatedness, so far, unfortunately) and mostly young hogs were integrated at Basistha breeding centre before being transferred to a specially constructed 'pre-release' facility in Potasali, on the outskirts of Nameri National Park, east of Sonai Rupai Wildlife Sanctuary. Every effort was made to 'pre-condition' the animals for eventual release by maintaining them in three separate social groups, in simulated natural habitats intended to encouraging natural foraging, nest-building and other behaviours; whilst also minimising human contacts to mitigate tameness and other behavioural characteristics consequent upon their captive management. After five months' tenure in the 'pre-release' enclosures at Potasali these hogs were transferred in early May to temporary 'soft-release' enclosures constructed for this purpose in a relatively secluded, but easily accessible area of natural habitat in the far interior of the Sonai Rupai Wildlife Sanctuary. These enclosures were also rigged with two lines of electric fencing and kept under

Table 9.2 *Distribution of mammal AZE trigger species according to country income (as a measure of conservation costs) and body mass (as a surrogate for captive breeding costs)*

Conservation costs	Body mass (kg)				
	0–1	2–5	6–10	10+	Total
Low income	21	1	0	1	23
Low middle income	41	3	1	2	47
Upper middle income	37	5	0	0	42
High income	17	2	1	0	20
Total	116	11	2	3	132

continual surveillance as a precaution against potential predators and to deter incursion by wild elephants. The animals were maintained for a further three days in these enclosure before being released, by the simple expedient of removing sections of fence and allowing the animals to find their own way out.

Sixteen pygmy hogs (seven males, nine females) were released in Gelgeli grasslands of Sonai Rupai in May 2008 and indirect evidence suggested that at least 10–12 of them continued to survive several months after release. Footprints of newborn hogs too were seen, indicating successful farrowing in the wild by a released female. A video camera trap was also used carefully deployed near active nests and the hogs caught on camera appeared healthy and had shiny coats, unlike the somewhat emaciated hogs captured from the wild in Manas in 1996. Some of these individuals were identified by hair-clipping marks shaved before release. That the released hogs appeared to be in good health despite harsh weather and sometimes difficult foraging conditions up to nine months after their release was most encouraging in that it not only confirmed their survival, but suggested their successful adaptation to the wild after at least one or (in most cases) two generations of captive management.

Following a similar protocol, nine hogs were released in May 2009 and ten more in May 2010, thereby releasing a total of 35 hogs in different locations of Gelgeli grasslands in Sonai Rupai. Besides numerous signs of hog activity around the release locations there were a few direct sightings of adult and even young hogs that were most certainly born in the wild.

cost-efficient for captive breeding because many are small-bodied species. All amphibians, reptiles and birds are <1 kg, and even in mammals, which have the largest spread in body mass and therefore costs (Chapter 6), half of these are less than 5 kg, with only one considerably heavier than 10 kg (the Javan rhinoceros). If we examine the matrix of body mass and conservation costs (using the country income where the species occur), half of all species are less than 5 kg and are found in low to middle income countries, cost-effective in conservation terms (Table 9.2). If species in the upper middle income countries are also included, 82% ($n = 108$) of all AZE mammals are relatively economical to conserve, in terms of both *in-situ* and *ex-situ* protection.

9.5 The future of zoo conservation biology: academic *versus* applied science

Conservation successes can often be linked to the satisfactory translation of conservation science into practice (Robinson, 2006). Nevertheless, there is evidence of disparity between the priorities of academic researchers and the needs of practitioners. This mismatch is clear in, for example, how the content of endangered species recovery plans responds to the literature (Stinchcombe *et al.*, 2002). Within zoos, research with measurable benefits for conservation is still lacking, perhaps because the assumption by zoos is that all research carried out on animals in zoo settings is useful, and instructive for the conservation of species. However, although there has indeed been a steady increase in the number of zoos undertaking research, with many carrying out conservation enquiries in the field, much published zoo research informs animal husbandry, not conservation. Analyses of the importance of zoo research abound in the literature (Finlay & Maple, 1986; Hutchins *et al.*, 1996; Stoinski *et al.*, 1998; Wharton, 2007, 2008; Anderson *et al.*, 2008). Most of these studies point to a very large proportion of published research focussing on topics unrelated to conservation. Anderson *et al.* (2008) found that almost 60% of all papers published in the journal *Zoo Biology* from 1982 to 2006 focussed on behaviour, reproduction and animal management, and only 1.8% on conservation. Often, the argument is made that information on behaviour and reproduction can also be useful in endangered species recovery. However, whether the mere accumulation of facts on animals in captivity advances species conservation is still something to be tested and probably much debated. There is no doubt that zoo biology as a discipline has grown since Heini Hediger's formulation of the term (Chapters 1 and 2). This is to be welcomed, of course, to advance knowledge of zoo animal management. But, the zoo world remains short of understanding whether key questions (and not trivial ones) are being answered in support of captive management of endangered species, much less on endangered species recovery *in-situ*.

There is a certain smugness when certain authors, e.g. Fernandez & Timberlake (2008), assume that one way of achieving better science in zoos is by engendering more collaborations between them and academia. Whilst this relationship is likely to be fruitful in some cases, the difficulty in the marriage is in the perceptions of what science is to each. Zoos can be training grounds for budding academics, in the form of university students, and publishable applied research can emanate from zoo settings. However, if research in zoos is to advance the job at hand – keeping animals in the best possible condition for exhibition, and conservation – the zoo–academic '*fusion*' may not necessarily work. This is because there are clear divides in what motivates academic research from more applied work. Much of the research carried out by academic institutions, e.g. in applied molecular genetics work for endangered species (Chapter 5), is increasingly more focussed on pure science in search of papers publishable in high-ranking academic journals. An epiphenomenon of this is that academic science which has direct management applications usually takes second place or no place at all. The most frustrating conclusion from analyses of the burgeoning high-quality, peer-reviewed publications within conservation biology, e.g. conservation genetics, is that most publications fail to address management issues or fail to propose practical conservation solutions (Vernesi et al., 2008).

Conservation academics face a dilemma. On one hand, they are expected to produce and publish peer-reviewed articles with sophisticated analyses and large sample sizes, usually requiring hypothesis testing. On the other hand, administrators and policy-makers often need research on strategies for management of small-scale problems, and require the results within short time-frames to inform imminent management decisions. Evaluating scientific quality, although a notoriously difficult problem with no standard solution, is standard practice in academia. Ideally, published scientific results should be scrutinised by true experts in the field and given scores for quality and quantity according to established rules. In practice, however, what is called peer-review is usually performed by groups of professionals with general competence rather than with the specialist's insight that is needed to assess primary research data. These individuals tend, therefore, to resort to secondary criteria like crude publication counts, journal prestige, the reputation of authors and institutions, and estimated importance and relevance of the research field, making peer-review as much of a lottery as of a rational process.

Against this background, it is hardly surprising that academics enter the 'game' of citation rates and journal impact factors, as this is the currency of their 'worth'. But, despite much criticism of the use of research assessment exercises, which primarily depend on citation data produced by the Institute for Scientific Information (ISI) in Philadelphia, academics still suffer from 'impactitis' as Van Diest et al. (2001) call it. The perception by some is not just that this growing obsession damages other crucial academic activities (see, for examples, Williams, 1998 for the medical sciences), but in the context of endangered species recovery, it may preclude good academics from publishing more applied research. Applied research journals have generally lower citation factors compared to publications in the purer sciences. Vernesi et al. (2008) suggests for conservation genetics, similar to Van Diest et al.'s (2001) argument for medicine, that publications should be judged on usefulness to conservation as well as on scientific soundness. If so, alternative methods for judging science would liberate collaboration and information exchange between practitioners and academics.

Having said this, though peer-review is not to be 'applied freely', it is a still a filter process, without which published material can be deemed invalid. A clear example of this in relation to zoos is the recent study conducted by the AZA (Falk et al., 2007) which was widely heralded as the first direct evidence that visits to zoos and aquariums produced long-term positive effects on people's attitudes toward other animals. This publication, which was not peer-reviewed, was criticised by Marino et al. (2010) for lack of method-ological soundness. The authors concluded that there were at least six major threats to methodological validity, and there remains no compelling evidence for the claim that zoos and aquariums promote attitude change, education, or interest in conservation in visitors, although further investigation of this possibility using methodologically sophis-ticated designs is warranted. Likewise, the abject failure to examine critically the 90% in 100 years assumption (Chapter 5) which is used widely, referring to managers but NEVER to scientific data is another case in point.

Another issue that bedevils progress in zoo conservation biology is that zoo managers, conservation biologists and the more technologically oriented biologists such as geneticists or reproductive biologists, all involved in captive breeding, have not addressed ways in which they can understand their respective 'sub-cultures'. It is not an exaggeration to acknowledge that these groups are often mutually suspicious, and rarely fully understand each other's underpinning science and goals. The importance of technology or sophisticated science is often underappreciated by practitioners who think it is unnecessary, while the more science-minded individuals or professions are more cautious about taking action without careful assessments. Analogous to the debate in medicine about competencies of nurse practitioners vs. doctors (see Kinnersley *et al.*, 2000), zoo conservation scientists and animal managers have compatible and complementary roles in endangered species recovery. There has to be recognition that our primary aim is to identify and deal with the factors that cause population and species declines, by using all methods and specialists at our disposal. This will also help to maintain the integrity of natural ecosystems and stem the loss of biodiversity. Only through an overall and comprehensive effort, inclusive population viability analysis as suggested by Hedrick *et al.* (1996), can extinction processes be understood and mitigated.

Above all, if zoo conservation biology is to grow, efficient deployment of appropriate specialists is fundamental alongside being able to take stock of what we do and how it is done. The replication of consensus exercises, such as those undertaken by Sutherland *et al.* (2009), where experts in the field are asked what are the crucial questions in conservation research, is definitely required to better guide developments in zoo conservation biology, and even zoo biology. Hutchins & Thompson (2008) correctly suggest that a major drawback in zoo research is that most research projects arise ad hoc from individual researchers or small consortiums, driven by a combination of staff interests and species charisma. These authors argue that prioritisation via an over-arching (they argue AZA) committee is the way forward. It is possible, however, to counter-argue (too cynically perhaps) that until we understand what the priorities and constraints are to advance species conservation, zoos are in danger of perpetuating the impression that all information gathered drives and informs.

There is no doubt that a substantial proportion of the research carried out in zoos is useful for management, but it is essential to curtail studies which advance neither animal management nor conservation. To do this, research from zoos has to be assessed in more effective ways. For example, asking zoo researchers whether science has helped accomplish outcomes or added value, as undertaken by Lawson *et al.* (2008), may not be a totally impartial way of determining the value of science to the zoo or conservation. The fear is that unless we examine the purpose and function of zoo conservation biology, we believe in the way we define it in this book, we are likely to promulgate a largely 'Baconian science'. This is the idea derived from the seventeenth century scientist, Sir Francis Bacon, that you deduce the cause of an underlying phenomenon by elimination and inductive reasoning. Essentially, a method more dependent on comparisons of accumulated facts rather than guided thought.

The legacy of Hediger's zoo biology has been a source of 'enlightenment' in the zoo world. It has generated new ways of understanding how animals can be better kept in captive situations, primarily using scientific methods. There is self-confidence in how observation and science can be used, as a result of the exponential growth in scientific knowledge around captive animals and zoos, since the 1980s. The moment may now be right to take one step further to become more effective conservation entrepreneurs and respond to the challenges facing biodiversity.

Key concepts

(1) There is no doubt that zoos have changed significantly and for the better, since their origins as menageries. Participating in endangered species conservation plans and environmental education programmes, many zoos support the conservation of bio-diversity. However, significant discrepancies between zoos' stated conservation goals and their actual performance remain, often triggered by the unresolved competition of commercial and conservation aims.

(2) Zoos are often too eager to profess the virtues of captive breeding and their contribu-tion to species conservation via this tool without much evidence for this. This is often a by-product of the current market-oriented approaches and corporatised organi-sational practices resulting in an emphasis on maximising and stabilising revenues. Animal welfare, wildlife conservation, and public education are often overshadowed by economic efficiency standards only ubiquitous in the now common corporate boardrooms.

(3) Current zoo research, as many zoo-based research projects attest, overwhelmingly addresses issues relevant for husbandry but have little relevance for *in-situ* conser-vation. Thus, many significant and urgent knowledge gaps remain unaddressed. To improve zoos' contributions to conservation, zoos need to more openly publish results and data in an accessible way, away from grey literature, to allow peer-review and scrutiny. This will allow the improvement of practices and avoid pitfalls and errors in other captive programmes.

(4) Zoos need to openly and transparently, regularly and continually clarify aims, and monitor the relevance of their policies for restoring biological diversity. Future efforts for conservation and management of biodiversity must derive from a set of clear objectives, mechanisms for action, and commitment from all stakeholders.

(5) The current main goal of captive breeding for conservation – maintenance of 90% of the genetic variation in the source (wild) population over a period of 100 years – has not incorporated the large body of genetic and demographic data we now have. Despite fulfilling this goal, many captive populations might have a high likelihood to be managed inadvertently or implicitly for extinction. Goals, management strategies and implementation need urgent re-evaluation for populations destined as sources for future re-introductions.

(6) In order to face the current biodiversity crisis and in the context of vast economic constraints, conservation programmes from zoos need to become more cost-effective

and strategic. It is imperative for conservation programmes in zoos to link seamlessly with *in-situ* efforts and together adopt rigorous prioritisation to achieve the most favourable cost-to-benefit ratio, i.e. 'the greatest bang for your buck'. This requires a re-thinking of zoos' species-centric approach to a more geographically stratified and internationally supported approach such as represented by the Alliance for Zero Extinction.

Appendix 1
Commonly used abbreviations

ACTH	Adrenocorticotropic Hormone
AFLP	Amplified Fragment Length Polymorphism
AI	Artificial Insemination
APNR	Associated Private Nature Reserves
ARAZPA	Australasian Regional Association of Zoological Parks and Aquaria
AZA	American Association of Zoos and Aquariums
AZE	Alliance for Zero Extinction
BFF	Born Free Foundation
BIAZA	British and Irish Association of Zoos and Aquariums
CAMP	Conservation Assessment and Management Plans
CARE	Committee on Animal Research and Ethics
CBD	Convention on Biological Diversity
CBSG	Conservation Breeding Specialist Group (formerly Captive Breeding Specialist Group)
CI	Conservation International
CITES	Convention on International Trade in Endangered Species of Wild Fauna and Flora
CNPPA	Commission on National Parks and Protected Areas
CR	Critically Endangered
CRSC	Census of Rare Species in Captivity
EAZA	European Association of Zoos and Aquariums
EBA	Endemic Bird Areas
EDGE	Evolutionarily Distinct and Globally Endangered
EEP	European Endangered Species Programmes
EN	Endangered
ESU	Evolutionary Significant Unit
ET	Embryo Transfer
EU	European Union
FAWAC	Farm Animal Welfare Advisory Committee
FAWC	Farm Animal Welfare Council
GCAP	Global Captive Action Plan
GNP	Gross National Product
GRB	Genome Resource Banking
IATA	International Air Transport Association

IUCN	International Union for Conservation of Nature and Natural Resources
IVF	*In-Vitro* Fertilisation
IZY	International Zoo Yearbook
LE	Lethal Equivalent
MAI	Maximum Avoidance of Inbreeding
MEA	Millennium Ecosystem Assessment
MHC	Major Histocompatibility Complex
MK	Minimizing Mean Kinship
MU	Management Unit
NYZS	New York Zoological Society
OCS	Optimal Contribution Selection
OECD	Organisation for Economic Co-operation and Development
PHVA	Population and Habitat Viability Analysis
PMP	Population Management Plans (AZA)
PPP	Purchasing Power Parity
PVA	Population Viability Analysis
RSPCA	Royal Society for the Prevention of Cruelty to Animals
SCNT	Somatic Cell Nuclear Transfer
SSC	Species Survival Commission (IUCN)
SSP	Species Survival Plan® (AZA)
TAG	Taxon Advisory Group
UFAW	Universities Federation for Animal Welfare
UNEP-WCMC	United Nations Environment Programme-Wildlife Conservation Monitoring Centre
WAPCA	West African Primate Conservation Action
WAZA	World Association of Zoos and Aquariums
WCS	Wildlife Conservation Society
WRI	World Resources Institute
WSPA	World Society for the Protection of Animals
WWF	World Wide Fund for Nature
WZACS	World Zoo and Aquarium Conservation Strategy
WZCS	World Zoo Conservation Strategy
ZAA	Zoo and Aquarium Association (previously ARAZPA)
ZAW	Zoos and Aquariums of the World
ZSL	Zoological Society of London

Appendix 2
Scientific names of species mentioned in the text

African cichlids	*Haplochromis ishmaeli, H. lividus, H. perrieri, Yssichromis sp. nov. 'argens', H. degeni*
African elephant	*Loxodonta africana*
African wild dog	*Lycaon pictus*
Alagoas curassow	*Mitu mitu*
American mink	*Mustela vison*
Andean bear	*Tremarctos ornatus*
Arabian oryx	*Oryx leucoryx*
Asian elephant	*Elephas maximus*
Atlantic salmon	*Salmo salar*
Bali mynah	*Leucopsar rothschildi*
Barbary macaque	*Macaca sylvanus*
Black–blotch pupfish	*Megupsilon aporus*
Black-footed ferret	*Mustela nigripes*
Black rat	*Rattus rattus*
Black rhinoceros	*Diceros bicornis*
Black soft-shell turtle	*Aspideretes nigricans*
Bornean orang-utan	*Pongo pygmaeus*
Brown bear	*Ursus arctos*
Brown snake	*Boiga irregularis*
Burchell's zebra	*Equus burchelli*
Butterfly splitfin	*Ameca splendens*
California condor	*Gymnogyps californianus*
Chatham Island taiko	*Pterodroma magentae*
Cheetah	*Acinonyx jubatus*
Chimpanzee	*Pan troglodytes*
Chytrid fungus	*Batrachochytrium dendrobatis*
Coho salmon	*Oncorhynchus kisutch*
Common frog	*Rana temporaria*
Common fruit fly	*Drosophila melanogaster*
Cotton-top tamarin	*Saguinus oedipus*
Deer mouse	*Peromyscus maniculatus*
Diana monkey	*Cercopithecus diana*
Dodo	*Raphus cucullatus*

Eastern wolf	*Canis lycaon* or *Canis lupus lycaon*
Echo parakeet	*Psittacula eques*
European bison	*Bison bonasus*
European rabbit	*Oryctolagus cuniculus*
Feather lice	*Degeeriella rufa*
Feathertail glider	*Acrobates pygmaeus*
Giant panda	*Ailuropoda melanoleuca*
Glanville fritillary butterfly	*Melitaea cinxia*
Golden lion tamarin	*Leontopithecus rosalia*
Golden skiffia	*Skiffia francesae*
Greater prairie chicken	*Tympanuchus cupido*
Guam rail	*Gallirallus owstoni*
Guinea pig	*Cavia aperea*
Gunther's gecko	*Phelsuma guentheri*
Haarst's eagle	*Harpagornis moorei*
Hawaiian goose	*Branta sanvichensis*
House finch	*Carpodacus mexicanus*
Housefly	*Musca domestica*
Howe Island woodhen	*Tricholimnas sylvestris*
Huia	*Heteralocha acutirostris*
Inconnu	*Stenodus leucichthys*
Japanese cedar	*Cryptomeria japonica*
Japanese primrose	*Primula sieboldii*
Javan rhinoceros	*Rhinoceros sondaicus*
Kakapo	*Strigops habroptilus*
Kemp's ridley sea turtle	*Lepidochelys kempii*
Kihansi spray toad	*Nectophrynoides asperginis*
La Palma pupfish	*Cyprinodon longidorsalis*
Lar gibbon	*Hylobates lar*
Large white butterfly	*Pieris brassicae*
Lesser bushbaby	*Galago senegalensis*
Lesser kestrel	*Falco naumanni*
Livingstone's fruit bat	*Pteropus livingstonii*
Loggerhead sea turtle	*Caretta caretta*
Lord Howe wood hen	*Gallirallus sylvestris*
Luehea	*Luehea seemannii*
Macrochelid mite	*Macrocheles subbadius*
Madagascar pochard	*Aythya innotata*
Mallorcan midwife toad	*Alytes muletensis*
Maned wolf	*Chrysocyon brachyurus*
Maria Island racer	*Liophis ornatus*
Mauritius fody	*Foudia rubra*
Mauritius kestrel	*Falco punctatus*

Meerkat	*Suricata suricata*
Moa	*Dinornis robustus/D. novaezelandiae*
Mona Island rock iguana	*Cyclura cornuta stejnegeri*
Montserrat oriole	*Icterus oberi*
Mountain gorilla	*Gorilla beringei*
Mourning dove	*Zenaida macroura*
Musk ox	*Ovibos moschatus*
Northern hairy-nosed wombat	*Lasiorhinus krefftii*
Northern white rhinoceros	*Ceratotherium cottoni*
Ochre sea star	*Pisaster ochraceous*
Okapi	*Okapia johnstoni*
Oldfield mice	*Peromyscus polionotus subgriseus*
Old World fruit bats	*Pteropus* spp.
Olive baboon	*Papio anubis*
Père David's deer	*Elaphurus davidianus*
Perrito de Potosi	*Cyprinodon alvarezi*
Pink pigeon	*Columba mayeri*
Piopio	*Turnagra capensis/T. tanagra*
Ploughshare tortoise	*Astrochelys yniphora*
Polar bear	*Ursus maritimus*
Polecat and feral ferrets	*Mustela putorius/M. p. furo*
Polynesian rat	*Rattus exulans*
Przewalski's horse	*Equus ferus Przewalskii*
Puerto Rican parrot	*Amazona vittata*
Puget blue butterfly	*Icaricia icarioides blackmorei*
Puma	*Felis concolor*
Pygmy hog	*Porcula salvania*
Red flour beetle	*Tribolium castaneum*
Red wolf	*Canis rufus* or *Canis lupus rufus*
Rhesus macaque	*Macaca mulatta*
Rock iguana	*Cyclura* spp.
Rodrigues fruit bat	*Pteropus rodricensis*
Roloway guenon	*Cercopithecus diana rollowayi*
Russian tortoise	*Testudo horsfieldii*
San Marcos salamander	*Eurycea nana*
Savannah baboon	*Papio cynocephalus*
Scandinavian adder	*Vipera berus*
Scimitar-horned oryx	*Oryx dammah*
Sea otter	*Enhydra lutris*
Siberian polecat	*Mustela sibirica*
Siberian tiger	*Panthera tigris*
Soay sheep	*Ovis aries*
Sockeye salmon	*Oncorhynchus nerka*

Socorro dove	*Zenaida graysoni*
Song sparrow	*Melospiza melodia*
Sonoran desert fruit fly	*Drosophila nigrospiracula*
Southern dunlin	*Calidris alpina schinzii*
Speke's gazelle	*Gazella spekei*
St. Lucia parrot	*Amazona versicolor*
St. Lucia whiptail lizard	*Cnemidophorus vanzoi*
Steelhead trout	*Oncorhynchus mykiss*
Stickleback	*Gasterosteus aculeatus*
Sumatran orang-utan	*Pongo abelii*
Swift fox	*Vulpes velox*
Takahe (New Zealand rail)	*Porphyrio hochstetteri*
Tasmanian devil	*Sarcophilus harrisii*
Tiro	*Skiffia francesae*
Warbiter cricket	*Decticus verrucivorus*
Western lowland gorilla	*Gorilla gorilla*
White-naped mangabey	*Cercocebus atys lunulatus*
White-tailed deer	*Odoicoileus virginianus*
Whooping crane	*Grus americana*
Wisent	*Bison bonasus*
Wyoming toad	*Bufo baxteri*
Yarkon bleak	*Acanthobrama telavivensis*

Appendix 3
Inbreeding

The coefficient of inbreeding, F, is the degree of inbreeding within individuals in a population. It is the probability that two alleles at a particular locus in an individual are identical by descent, i.e. derived from the same allele in an ancestor. The value of F ranges from 0 to 1.

Confusingly, the term '*inbreeding*' can also have other biological meanings and can be estimated by different algorithms.

- Inbreeding on a population level is estimated as a measure of genetic drift, F. It indicates the level of genetic diversity and changes thereof, but does not relate to specific individuals. The value of F is zero or larger.
- Inbreeding as a measure of the system of mating, f, estimates the deviation from random mating. The value is smaller or larger than zero or zero. Inbreeding avoidance ($f < 0$) is especially important. It describes the mating system but cannot predict population level inbreeding of individuals or the probability of individuals to exhibit inbreeding depression.
- The F-statistics is a framework describing the distribution of genetic diversity within a species by a series of inbreeding coefficients measuring the departure from Hardy–Weinberg proportions: F_{IS} estimates non-random mating within subpopulations, F_{ST} estimates the genetic divergence between subpopulations (genetic drift) and F_{IT} estimates the overall departure from Hardy–Weinberg proportions due to F_{IS} and F_{ST}.

Captive breeding programmes with small founder numbers cannot avoid inbreeding as a measure of shared ancestry (F) but can minimise the rate of increase of population main inbreeding.

Appendix 4
Population sizes – definitions and implications

Many different parameters can reduce genetic diversity in a population including: biased sex ratios, biased age structures, unequal family sizes, mating system, dispersal *versus* philopatry, and changes of population size over time. These parameters normally act together and the effects are often difficult to separate. Whether they act additively or as complex systems, they impact the effective population size (N_e) in comparison with the absolute, census, population size (N). The effective size of a population under study is the size of an ideal, randomly breeding population which has the same rate of loss of heterozygosity as that population. Skewed sex ratios and skewed fecundity can profoundly reduce N_e:

$$N_e = 4 N_m N_f / (N_m + N_f),$$

where N_m and N_f are the reproducing males and females, respectively. In this case, N_e is always smaller then or equal to N. However, this widely applied formula does not consider all the other factors impacting effective population size and can be highly misleading (Braude & Templeton, 2009). The most important factor reducing N_e is fluctuations in population size over generations (Frankham, 1995).

There are several approaches to estimate 'effective population size'. Estimations can be based on either:

- change in mean inbreeding coefficient = inbreeding effective size, N_{ei};
- degree of variation in allele frequencies = variance effective size, N_{ev}; or
- rate at which heterozygosity is lost from a population = eigenvalue effective size, $N_{e\lambda}$.

In randomly mating populations of constant population size, it is expected that $N_{ei} = N_{ev}$. In fluctuating populations, substantial discrepancies can occur. This is because the two measures are related to the population in divergent manners:

- N_{ei} relates to the number of parents = ancestors;
- N_{ev} relates to the number of progeny = descendants.

Assume the extreme case of a population with only a small number of parents. Take the following two scenarios.

- The parents have a very large number of offspring. Allele frequencies in the offspring accurately represent the allele frequencies in the parents. Thus, N_{ev} is very large. The offspring are all full-siblings. Their own offspring will be inbred and, thus, N_{ei} is very small.

- The parents have only one offspring each. Allele frequencies in the offspring do not represent the allele frequencies in the parents because of genetic drift. Thus, N_{ev} is small. The offsprings' offspring will not be inbred and, thus, N_{ei} is very large.

Appendix 5
Captive breeding and genetics – definitions

Admixture: hybridisation between genetically differentiated populations. Generally used for within-species hybridisation.

Allee effects: the effect of population density on population growth, whereby individual fitness decreases with decreasing population density from some maximum value at high density. There can be a critical threshold density above which the population grows and below which the population dynamics is unstable. Term coined after the work of W. C. Allee in the 1930s and 1940s. Allee effects are often implicitly defined by a very narrow interpretation of density-dependent effects, such as the failure of mates to find each other at low density. Here, we use the broader definition as outlined above.

Allelic diversity, A, is the average number of alleles per locus.

Effective population size: it is the size of an idealised population that would retain the same amount of genetic diversity or the same amount of inbreeding as the actual population. There are several estimators for N_e: inbreeding effective size, variance effective size and eigenvalue effective size, all with different meanings (see Appendix 4).

Founder effect: a demographic and genetic bottleneck during the founding of a new population, if the number of founders is restricted, i.e. carries less genetic variability then the parent population. Founder effects cause random genetic drift.

Gene diversity: is the expected heterozygosity, h_e.

Genetic adaptation: a change of individuals' genetic compositions from one generation to the next due to natural selection. It makes an organism better suited to its environment and leads to greater fitness. Populations with different genetic adaptations to different environments also differ in phenotypes because genetic adaptation is shaped by natural selection. Such adaptation is inherited and is an epiphenomenon of changed evolutionary trajectories. Operationally, genetic adaptation and phenotypic plasticity in different environments are difficult to distinguish (see also phenotypic plasticity).

Genetic diversity: describes the genetic variation between individuals. It can be described by several estimators, which are not equivalent to each other and which describe different aspects of diversity. Estimators include observed, h_o, and expected, h_e, heterozygosity and polymorphism at loci.

Genetic loci or, short loci: segments of DNA, which can be characterised and can be used to quantify differences within animals (each locus exist in two copies in diploid animals, which constitute the vast majority of animal species) and between individuals. Loci can encompass whole, or parts of genes, or areas of the DNA without any function. Selectively neutral loci or, short, neutral loci are those loci which are not 'tested' by selection. They encode no products, have no specific function and are the result of an evolutionary legacy.

Genotype: the genetic composition of an organism or the specific genetic composition of an organism at a set of investigated (screened) loci.

Hardy–Weinberg equilibrium, HWE: the principle that the frequency of alleles and genotypes are in equilibrium in large ideal populations. Genotype frequencies are determined by allele frequencies. The underpinning assumptions are: (1) infinite population size; (2) random mating; (3) no mutations; (4) no natural selection; (5) no immigration; and (6) non-overlapping generations.

Heterozygosity, *h*: describes the proportion of heterozygotes at all loci or at target (sampled) loci in a population, which is either observed, h_o, or expected, h_e, for an idealistic population under Hardy–Weinberg equilibrium.

Heterozygotes: are individuals that carry different alleles at a locus.

Homozygotes: are individuals that carry the same alleles at a locus.

Idealised population: it is the population on which many models in population genetics are based. The idealised population shows random mating, no selection, no overlapping generations, the same number of breeders in every generation, Poisson distribution of family sizes, and animals are hermaphrodites (individuals are both sexes). Idealised populations are well characterised, and are the foundation for a large theoretical framework in population genetics. They can be used for practical predictions of real populations, which will of course never behave as idealised populations. The genetic composition at selectively neutral loci of ideal large populations tends to conform to the predictions of the Hardy–Weinberg equilibrium.

Inbreeding depression: loss of fitness in progeny from inbreeding. Reintroductions of inbred, captive-bred animals seem to have resulted in viable wild populations without any sign of inbreeding depression. However, inbreeding does not always result in large and detectable inbreeding depression, but inbreeding depression might be small. Most fitness characters in most populations exhibit deleterious changes (Reed *et al.*, 2003). Lacy (1997) concluded that he knew of no statistical credible mammal study that did not find inbreeding depression, i.e. when it is not found it is most probable that the study has insufficient statistical power. Inbred populations that actually do not exhibit significant inbreeding depression may suffer from it in the future as for example is likely in the Mauritius kestrel (Chapter 5; Ewing *et al.*, 2008).

Inbreeding: the mating between related individuals. It increases homozygosity in the next generation. In populations, inbreeding leads to an increased proportion of homozygotes and random genetic drift.

Lethal equivalent, LE: an estimate for the cumulative effect of deleterious alleles in an individual. One LE corresponds to an allele that is lethal when homozygote.

Major histocompatibility complex, MHC: a large genomic region or gene family found in most vertebrates that plays an important role in the immune system and autoimmunity. The central function of products coded by MHC genes is in detecting pathogen antigens and triggering the acquired immune response. MHC genotypes play an important role in an individual's fitness. MHC variability in populations plays an important role in the viability of populations. MHC loci typically exhibit a very high polymorphism, which is usually being maintained by selection through pathogens and/or sexual selection.

Mutational meltdown: a feed-back loop caused by the accumulation of deleterious mutations in a small population, causing loss of fitness, causing population decline, causing further accumulation of deleterious mutations and so forth. It is a negative vortex, which eventually leads to population extinction.

Overdominance: heterozygosity is selectively advantageous over homozygosity, i.e. heterozygotes have greatest fitness. This heterozygote advantage can lead to a stable polymorphism in a population because selection favours heterozygotes. Underdominance is where heterozygosity is selectively disadvantageous over homozygosity.

Panmictic population: a randomly mating population.

Phenotype: the manifest attributes and traits of an organism. The phenotype is produced by the organism's genetic composition and the environment it grows up in and/or where it lives.

Phenotypic plasticity: an organism can activate or develop different phenotypes in response to its environment. The organism's genetic constitution allows this flexibility and this is inherited. The actual phenotypic expression is not inherited. Sometimes whole populations differ phenotypically from each other because of environmental differences. Whilst this can lead to different evolutionary trajectories, such populations are genetically exchangeable. However, it is often difficult to show whether phenotypic differences are cause by genetic differences or phenotypic plasticity. This has led (and likely still is) to the wrong designation of populations as different species.

Polymorphism: the proportion of variable loci within a sampled population as well as the presence of more than one allele at a single locus. Polymorphic loci are loci with two or more alleles. Monomorphic loci show no variation and have one single allele.

Population bottleneck: the drastic reduction of population size; genetic bottlenecks refer to population bottlenecks causing loss of genetic diversity. Typically used for transient demographic population reductions. However, the genetic effects are normally not transient except when immigration into the bottleneck occurs.

Quantitative trait loci, QTLs: genetic loci that are expressed and under selection and affecting phenotypic variation. Quantitative traits are typically determined not only by single loci, but by the complex interactions of multiple loci and environmental factors. They are identified by the association between genetic markers and:

Random genetic drift (often simply termed as 'genetic drift'): random changes in allele frequencies in populations over time due to random sampling of alleles because the offspring will represent an imperfect sample of their parent population as a consequence of stochastic, random processes. Allele frequencies can become higher or lower over time by chance. Alleles may become fixed (i.e. polymorphic loci may become monomorphic) by chance; which allele 'survives' is by chance.

Rare alleles: alleles that have a low frequency in a population. There is no general cut-off point for frequencies, but a frequency of 0.1 or less is typically regarded as rare. Rare alleles immediately impact allelic diversity, A, values, but affect heterozygosity, h, much less.

References

Aegis Consulting Australia & Applied Economics (2009). *Report on the Economic and Social Contribution of the Zoological Industry in Australia. Prepared for the Australasian Regional Association of Zoological Parks and Aquaria. 2009.* [http://www.arazpa.org.au/ArticleDocuments/12/SocioEconomic%20Contribution%20of%20Zoological%20Industry%20Report.pdf.aspx]

Adams, J. (1996). Cost-benefit analysis: the problem, not the solution. *The Ecologist*, **26**, 2–4.

Adams, W. M. (2004). *Against Extinction: The Story of Conservation.* London: Earthscan.

Agapow, P.-M., Bininda-Edmonds, O. R. P., Crandall, K. A. *et al.* (2004). The impact of species concept on biodiversity. *Quarterly Review of Biology*, **79**, 161–179.

Akçakaya, H. R. & Root, W. (2002). *RAMAS Metapop: Viability Analysis for Stage-Structured Metapopulations.* Setauket, NY: Applied Biomathematics.

Alberts, A. C. (2007). Behavioral considerations of headstarting as a conservation strategy for endangered Caribbean rock iguanas. *Applied Animal Behaviour Science*, **102**, 380–391.

Albrechtsen, L., Macdonald, D. W., Johnson, P. J., Castelo, R. & Fa, J. E. (2007). Faunal loss from bushmeat hunting: empirical evidence and policy implications in Bioko Island. *Environmental Science & Policy*, **10**, 654–667.

Allen, K. (1995). Putting the spin on animal ethics: Ethical parameters for marketing and public relations. In: *Ethics on the Ark: Zoos, Animal Welfare, and Wildlife Conservation*, eds. **B. G. Norton, M. Hutchins, E. F. Stevens & T. L. Maple.** Washington, DC: Smithsonian Institute Press, pp. 289–296.

Allen, K., Franzreb, E. & Escano, R. E. (1993). Efficacy of translocation strategies for red-cockaded wood peckers. *Wildlife Society Bulletin*, **21**, 155–159.

Allendorf, F. W. & Luikart, G. (2006). *Conservation and the Genetics of Populations.* Malden, MA, USA: Blackwell Publishing.

Allendorf, F. W. (1986). Genetic drift and the loss of alleles versus heterozygosity. *Zoo Biology*, **5**, 181–190.

Allendorf, F. W. & Leary, R. F. (1986). Heterozygosity and fitness in natural populations of animals. In: *Conservation Bidogy: The Science of Scarcity and Diversity*, ed. **M. Soulé**, Sunderland, MA, Sinauer Assoc., pp. 57–76.

ALVA (2010). *Visits Made in 2009 to Visitor Attractions in Membership with the Association of Leading Visitor Attractions.* [http://www.alva.org.uk/visitor_statistics/]

Ames, E. (2009). *Carl Hagenbeck's Empire of Entertainments.* Seattle: University of Washington Press.

Andelman, S. J. & Fagan, W. F. (2000). Umbrellas and flagships: efficient conservation surrogates, or expensive mistakes? *Proceedings of the National Academy of Sciences (USA)*, **97**, 5954–5959.

Andersen, L. L. (1992). Right enclosure design – before stories can be told. In: *Fourth International Symposium on Zoo Design and Construction*, Torquay, Devon, 14–18th May 1989, ed. **P. M. C. Stevens**, Paignton: Whitley Wildlife Conservation Trust, pp. 71–85.

Andersen, L. L. (2003). Zoo education: from formal school programmes to exhibit design and interpretation. *International Zoo Yearbook*, **38**, 75–81.

Anderson, J. R. & Chamove, A. S. (1984). Allowing captive primates to forage. In: *Standards in Laboratory Animals Management* (Part 2). Potters Bar, UK: Universities Federation for Animal Welfare.

Anderson, U. S., Kelling, A. S., Pressley-Keough, R., Bloomsmith, M. A. & Maple, T. (2003). Enhancing the zoo visitor's experience by public animal training and oral interpretation at an otter exhibit. *Environment and Behaviour*, **35**, 826–841.

Anderson, U. S., Kelling, A. S. & Maple, T. L. (2008). Twenty-five years of *Zoo Biology*: a publication analysis. *Zoo Biology*, **27**, 444–457.

Andrabi, S. M. H. & Maxwell, W. M. C. (2007). A review on reproductive biotechnologies for conservation of endangered mammalian species. *Animal Reproduction Science*, **99**, 223–243.

Araki, H., Ardren, W. R., Olsen, E., Cooper, B. & Blouin, M. S. (2007a). Reproductive success of captive-bred steelhead trout in the wild: evaluation of three hatchery programs in the Hood River. *Conservation Biology*, **21**, 181–190.

Araki, H., Cooper, B. & Blouin, M. S. (2007b) Genetic effects of captive breeding cause a rapid, cumulative fitness decline in the wild. *Science*, **318**, 100–103.

ARAZPA (2009). Australasian Association of Zoological Parks and Aquaria Education Policy 2009. [http://www.zooaquarium.org.au/Education-Policy/default.aspx Accessed 5th July 2010]

Arita, H., Robinson, J. G. & Redford, K. H. (1990). Rarity in Neotropical forest mammals and its ecological correlates. *Conservation Biology*, **4**, 181–192.

Armbruster, P. & Reed, D. H. (2005). Inbreeding depression in benign and stressful environments. *Heredity*, **95**, 235–242.

Armstrong, D. (2002). Focal and surrogate species: getting the language right. *Conservation Biology*, **16**, 285–286.

Armstrong, D. P. & Perrott, J. K. (2000). An experiment testing whether condition and survival are limited by food supply in a reintroduced Hihi population. *Conservation Biology*, **14**, 1171–1181.

Armstrong, D. P. & Seddon, P. J. (2008). Directions in reintroduction biology. *Trends in Ecology and Evolution*, **23**, 20–25.

Asa, C. S. & Porton, I. J. (eds.) (2005). *Wildlife Contraception: Issues, Methods, and Applications*. Baltimore, USA: Johns Hopkins University Press.

Asfora, P. H., Rossano, A. & Pontes, M. (2009). The small mammals of the highly impacted North-eastern Atlantic Forest of Brazil, Pernambuco Endemism Center. *Biota Neotropica*, **9**, doi: 10.1590/S1676–06032009000100004.

Asquith, P. J. (1989). Provisioning and the study of free-ranging primates: history, effects, and prospects. *Yearbook of Physical Anthropology*, **32**, 129–158.

Atkinson, I. (1989). Introduced animals and extinctions. In *Conservation for the Twenty-First Century*, eds. D. Western & M. Pearl. New York: Oxford University Press, pp. 54–75.

Atkinson-Grosjean, J. (1992). Beyond hierarchy: Team-based management at the Vancouver aquarium. In *Proceedings of the American Association of Zoological Parks and Aquariums Annual Conference*. American Association of Zoological Parks and Aquariums, Wheeling, West Virginia, pp. 151–155.

Australian Bureau of Statistics (2008). *Cultural Funding by Government*, Cat No. 4183.0.

AZA (2001). American Zoo and Aquarium Association 2001 Annual Survey New Exhibits in 2001. Wheeling, West Virginia: American Zoo and Aquarium Association. [http://www.aza.org/conservation-funding].

AZA (2009a). Why wild animals do not make good pets. [http://www.aza.org/PressRoom/detail.aspx?id=391&terms=species+survival+program].

AZA (2010a). *Association of Zoos and Aquariums. Animal Programs*. [http://www.aza.org/animal-programs/].

AZA (2010b). *Association of Zoos and Aquariums. Visitor Demographics*. [http://www.aza.org/visitor-demographics/].

AZA (2010c). *Association of Zoos and Aquariums: Conservation Funding*. [http://www.aza.org/conservation-funding].

Babbitt, B. (1995). Science opening the next chapter of conservation history. *Science*, **5206**, 1954–1955.

Bailey, N. W., Gray, B. & Zuk, M. (2010). Acoustic experience shapes alternative mating tactics and reproductive investment in male field crickets. *Current Biology*, **20**, 845–849.

Baillie, J. E. M., Hilton-Taylor, C. & Stuart, S. (2004). 2004 IUCN Red List of Threatened Species: A global species assessment. Gland, Switzerland and Cambridge, UK: IUCN.

Bajomia, B., Pullin, A. S., Stewart, G. B. & Takács-Sánta, A. (2010). Bias and dispersal in the animal reintroduction literature. *Oryx*, **44**, 358–365.

Baker, A. (2007). Animal ambassadors: an analysis of the effectiveness and conservation impact of ex-situ breeding efforts. In *Zoos in the 21st Century: Catalysts for Conservation?*, eds. **A. Zimmerman, M. Hatchwell, L. A. Dickie & C. West.** Cambridge: Cambridge University Press, pp. 139–154.

Balling, J. & Falk, J. (1980). A perspective on field trips: environmental effects on learning. *Curator*, **23**, 229–240.

Ballou, J. D. (1989). *Capacity v. 2.11*. Washington, D.C.: National Zoological Park.

Ballou, J. D. (1992). Potential contribution of cryopreserved germ plasm to the preservation of genetic diversity and conservation of endangered species in captivity. *Cryobiology*, **29**, 19–25.

Ballou, J. D. (1997). Ancestral inbreeding only minimally affects inbreeding depression in mammalian populations. *Journal of Heredity*, **88**, 169–178.

Balmford, A. (2000a). Priorities for captive breeding – which mammals should board the ark. In *Priorities for the Conservation of Mammalian Diversity: Has the Panda had its Day?* eds. **A. Entwistle & N. Dunstone.** Cambridge, UK: Cambridge University Press, pp. 291–308.

Balmford, A. (2000b). Separating fact from artefact in analysis of zoo visitor preference. *Conservation Biology*, **14**, 1193–1195.

Balmford, A., Leader-Williams, N. & Green, M. J. B. (1995). Parks or arks: where to conserve threatened mammals. *Biodiversity and Conservation*, **4**, 595–607.

Balmford, A., Mace, G. M. & Leader-Williams, N. (1996). Designing the ark: setting priorities for captive breeding. *Conservation Biology*, **10**, 719–727.

Balmford, A., Gaston, K. J., Blyth, S., James, A. & Kapos, V. (2003). Global variation in terrestrial conservation costs, conservation benefits, and unmet conservation needs. *Proceedings of the National Academy of Sciences (USA)*, **100**, 1046–1050.

Balmford, A., Leader-Williams, N., Mace, G. et al. (2007). Message received? Quantifying the impact of informal conservation education on adults visiting UK zoos. In *Zoos in the 21st Century: Catalysts for Conservation?*, eds. **A. Zimmermann, M. Hatchwell, L. Dickie & C. West**. Cambridge, UK: Cambridge University Press, pp. 120–136.

Baratay, E. & Hardouin-Fugier, E. (2004). *A History of Zoological Gardens in the West*. London: Reaktion Books.

Bar-David, S., Saltz, D., Dayan, T., Perelberg, A. & Dolev, A. (2005). Demographic models and reality in reintroductions: Persian fallow deer in Israel. *Conservation Biology*, **19**, 131–138.

Barnes, R. F. W. (2002). The bushmeat boom and bust in West and Central Africa. *Oryx*, **36**, 236–242.

Barratt, E. M., Gurnell, J., Malarky, G., Deaville, R. & Bruford, M. W. (1999). Genetic structure of fragmented populations of red squirrel (*Sciurus vulgaris*) in the UK. *Molecular Ecology*, **8**, S55–S63.

Barrowclough, G. F. & Flesness, N. R. (1996). Species, subspecies, and races: the problem of units of management in conservation. In *Wild Mammals In Captivity: Principles and Techniques*, eds. **D. G. Kleiman, M. E. Allen, K. V. Thompson, S. Lumpkin & W. Harruis.** Chicago: Chicago University Press, pp. 247–254.

Basset, L. & Buchanan-Smith, H. M. (2007). Effects of predictability on the welfare of captive animals. *Applied Animal Behaviour Science*, **102**, 223–245.

Bayne, K. (1989). Resolving issues of psychological well-being and management of laboratory non-human primates. In *Housing, Care and Psychological Wellbeing of Captive and Laboratory Primates*, ed. **E. F. Segal**. New Jersey: Noyes Publications, pp. 34–38.

Bearder, S. K. & Martin, R. D. (1980). Acacia gum and its use by bushbabies (*Galago senegalensis*). *International Journal of Primatology*, **1**, 103–128.

Beattie, T. A. (1994). Now . . . we must be more businesslike. In *Proceedings of the American Zoo and Aquarium Association Annual Conference*. Wheeling, West Virginia: American Zoo and Aquarium Association, pp. 389–391.

Beaumont, M. A. & Bruford, M. W. (1999). Microsatellites in conservation genetics. In *Microsatellites: Evolution and Applications*, eds. **D. B. Goldstein & C. Schlotterer**. Oxford: Oxford University Press, pp. 165–182.

Beck, B. (1995). Reintroduction, zoos, conservation, and animal welfare'. In *Ethics on the Ark: Animal Welfare, and Wildlife Conservation*, eds. **B. G. Norton, M. Hutchins, E. F. Stevens & T. L. Maple**. Washington and London: Smithsonian Institution Press, pp. 155–163.

Beck, B. B., Kleiman, D. G., Dietz, J. M. *et al.* (1991). Losses and reproduction in reintroduced golden lion tamarins, *Leontopithecus rosalia*. *Dodo*, **27**, 50–61.

Beck, B. B., Rapaport, L. G., Stanley Price, M. S. & Wilson, A. C. (1994). Reintroduction of captive born animals. In *Creative Conservation: Interactive Management of Wild and Captive Animals*, eds. **P. J. S. Olney, G. M. Mace & A. T. C. Feistner**. London: Chapman and Hall, pp. 256–286.

Beck, B., Walkup, K., Rodrigues, M., Unwin, S., Travis, D. & Stoinski, T. (2007). *Best Practice Guidelines for the Re-introduction of Great Apes*. Gland, Switzerland: SSC Primate Specialist Group of the World Conservation Union.

Beckmann, E. (1991). *Environmental Interpretation for Education and Management in Australia's National Parks and Other Protected Areas*. Unpublished PhD thesis, University of New England.

Beinart, W. & Coates, P. (1995). *Environment and History: The Taming of Nature in the USA and South Africa*. London: Routledge.

Beissinger, S. R. (2000). Ecological mechanisms of extinction. *Proceedings of the National Academy of Sciences of the United States of America*, **97**, 11 688–11 689.

Bélair, C., Ichikawa, K., Wong, B. Y. L. & Mulongoy, K. J. (Editors) (2010). *Sustainable Use of Biological Diversity in Socio-Ecological Production Landscapes. Background to the 'Satoyama Initiative for the Benefit of Biodiversity and Human Well-Being'*. Technical Series no. 52, Montreal: Secretariat of the Convention on Biological Diversity.

Berejikian, B. A., Tezak, E. P., Riley, S. C. & LaRae, A. L. (2001). Competitive ability and social behaviour of juvenile steelhead reared in enriched and conventional hatchery tanks and a stream environment. *Journal of Fish Biology*, **59**, 1600–1613.

Berry, P. M., Dawson, T. P., Harrison, P. A. & Pearson, R. G. (2002). Modelling potential impacts of climate change on the bioclimatic envelope of species in Britain and Ireland. *Global Ecology and Biogeography*, **11**, 453–462.

Bertram, B. (2004). Misconceptions about zoos. *Biologist*, **51**, 199–206.

Besch, E. L. & Kollias, G. V. (1994). Physical, chemical and behavioural factors in large low-density naturalistic animal facilities. In *Naturalistic Environments in Captivity for Animal Behaviour Research*, ed. **E. F. Gibbons**. Albany, NY: State University of New York Press, pp. 77–95.

Bettinger, T. & Quinn, H. (2000). Conservation funds: how do zoos and aquariums decide which project to fund? In *Proceedings of the AZA Annual Conference*, St. Louis, Missouri, pp. 88–90.

BIAZA (2010). *BIAZA Questionnaire, Summary of Results for the Year 2008*. [http://www.biaza.org.uk/resources/library/images/qreport09datafor08.pdf/]

Bibby, C. J., Crosby, M. J., Heath, M. F. *et al.* (1992). *Putting Biodiversity on the Map: Global Priorities for Conservation.* Cambridge: ICBP.

Bijlsma, R., Bundgaard, J. & Van Putten, W. F. (1999). Environmental dependence of inbreeding depression and purging in *Drosophila melanogaster. Journal of Evolutionary Biology*, **12**, 1125–1137.

Birney, B. A. (1991). *The Impact of Bird Discovery Point on Visitors' Attitudes towards Bird Conservation Issues.* Brookfield, IL: Chicago Zoological Society.

Bitgood, S. C. (1988). *Understanding the Public's Attitudes Towards and Behavior in Museums, Parks, and Zoos.* Technical Report No. 87–30. Center for Social Design, Jacksonville, Alabama.

Bitgood, S., Patterson, D., Benefield, A. & Landers, A. (1986). Understanding your visitors: Ten factors influencing their behavior. *Proceedings of the 1986 American Association of Zoological Parks and Aquariums.*

Bitgood, S., Patterson, D. & Benefield, A. (1988). Exhibit design and visitor behavior. *Environment and Behavior*, **20**(4), 474–491.

Black, J. M., Marshall, A. P., Gilburn, A. *et al.* (1997). Survival, movements, and breeding of released Hawaiian geese: An assessment of the reintroduction program. *Journal of Wildlife Management*, **61**, 1161–1173.

Blackburn, T. M. & Gaston, K. J. (1994). The distribution of body sizes of the world's bird species. *Oikos*, **70**, 127–130.

Blanchet, S., Paez, D. J., Bernatchez, L. & Dodson, J. J. (2008). An integrated comparison of captive-bred and wild Atlantic salmon (*Salmo salar*): Implications for supportive breeding programs. *Biological Conservation*, **141**, 1989–1999.

Blau, P. M. & Myer, M. W. (1987). *Bureaucracy in Modern Society*, Random House, New York: New York.

Blomqvist, D., Pauliny, A., Larsson, M. & Flodin, L. A. (2010). Trapped in the extinction vortex? Strong genetic effects in a declining vertebrate population. *BMC Evolutionary Biology*, **10**, 33.

Boakes, E. H., Wang, J. & Amos, W. (2007). An investigation of inbreeding depression and purging in captive pedigreed populations. *Heredity*, **98**, 172–182.

Bonn, A. & Gaston, K. J. (2005). Capturing biodiversity: selecting priority areas for conservation using different criteria. *Biodiversity and Conservation*, **14**, 1083–1100.

Bonn, A., Rodrigues, A. S. L. & Gaston, K. J. (2002). Threatened and endemic species: are they good indicators of patterns of biodiversity on a national scale? *Ecology Letters*, **5**, 733–741.

Borner, M. (1985). The rehabilitated chimpanzees of Rubondo Island. *Oryx*, **19**, 151–154.

Borun, M., Chambers, M. & Cleghorn, A. (1996). Families are learning in science museums. *Curator*, **39**(2), 123–138.

Bostock, S. C. (1993). *Zoos and Animal Rights: The Ethics of Keeping Animals.* New York: Routledge.

Bottrill, M. C., Joseph, L. N., Carwardine, J. *et al.* (2008). Is conservation triage just smart decision-making? *Trends in Ecology and Evolution*, **23**, 649–654.

Bovet, J. (1978). Homing in wild myomorph rodents: current problems. In *Animal Migration, Navigation and Homing*, eds. **K. Schmidt-Koenig, & K. T. Keeton,** New York: Springer-Verlag, pp. 405–412.

Bowen-Jones, E. & Entwistle, A. (2002). Identifying appropriate flagship species: the importance of culture and local contexts. *Oryx*, **36**, 189–195.

Boyer, D. A. & Brown, R. D. (1988). A survey of translocations of mammals in the United States, 1985. In *Translocation of Wild Animals*, eds. **L. Nielsen & R. D. Brown,** Milwaukee: Wisconsin Humane Society, pp. 1–11.

Boyd Group (2002). The Boyd Group Papers on the use of Non-Human Primates in Research and testing. The British Psychological Society Scientific Affairs Board Standing Advisory Committee on the Welfare of Animals in Psychology, eds. **J. A. Smith & K. M. Boyd,**

Bradley, A., Evans, M., Kaufman, M. H. & Robertson, E. (1984). Formation of germ-line chimaeras from embryo-derived teratocarcinoma cell lines. *Nature*, **309**, 255–256.

Brambell, F. W. R. (1965). Report of the Technical. Committee to inquire into the welfare of animals kept under intensive livestock husbandry systems. London: Her Majesty's Stationery Office.

Brandon, K., Redford, K. & **Sanderson, S.** (eds.) (1998). *Parks in Peril: People, Politics, and Protected Areas.* Covelo, CA, Washington, DC: Island Press.

Braude, S. & **Templeton, A. R.** (2009). Understanding the multiple meanings of 'inbreeding' and 'effective size' for genetic management of African rhinoceros populations. *African Journal of Ecology*, **47**, 546–555.

Breitenmoser, U., Breitenmoser-Wursten, C., Carbyn, L. N. & **Funk, S. M.** (2001). Assessment of carnivore reintroductions. In *Carnivore Conservation* eds. **J. L. Gittleman, S. M. Funk, D. W. Macdonald** & **R. K. Wayne.** Cambridge: Cambridge University Press, pp. 241–281.

Bretagnolle, V. & **Inchausti, P.** (2005). Modelling population reinforcement at a large spatial scale as a conservation strategy for the declining little bustard (*Tetrax tetrax*) in agricultural habitats. *Animal Conservation*, **8**, 59–68.

Brewer, S. (1978). *The Chimpanzees of Mt Assirik.* New York: Alfred A. Knopf.

Bright, P. W. & **Morris, P. A.** (1994). Animal translocation for conservation: performance of dormice in relation to release methods, origin and season. *Journal of Applied Ecology*, **31**, 699–708.

Bright, P. & **Morris, P. A.** (2000). Rare mammals, research and realpolitik. In *Priorities for the Conservation of Mammalian Diversity: Has the Panda had its Day?*, eds. **A. Entwistle** & **N. Dunstone.** Cambridge: Cambridge University Press, pp. 141–155.

Broad, S. & **Smith, L.** (2004). Who educates the public about conservation issues? Examining the role of zoos and the media. In *International Tourism and Media Conference Proceedings, 24th–26th November, 2004*, eds. **W. Frost, G. Croy** & **S. Beeton.** Melbourne: Tourism Research Unit, Monash University, pp. 15–23.

Bronikowski, J., Beck, B. & **Power, M.** (1989). Innovation, exhibition and conservation: free-ranging tamarins at the National Zoological Park. In *AAZPA Annual Conference Proceedings*, Wheeling, WV: AAZPA, pp. 540–546.

Brook, B. W., O'Grady, J. J., Chapman, A. P. *et al.* (2000). Predictive accuracy of population viability analysis in conservation biology. *Nature*, **404**, 385–387.

Brook, B. W., Tonkyn, D. W., Q'Grady, J. J. & **Frankham, R.** (2002). Contribution of inbreeding to extinction risk in threatened species. *Conservation Ecology*, **6**.

Brook, B. W., Traill, L. W. & **Bradshaw, C. J. A.** (2006). Minimum viable population size and global extinction risk are unrelated. *Ecology Letters*, **9**, 375–382.

Brooks, T. M., Mittermeier, R. A., da Fonseca, G. A. B. *et al.* (2006). Global biodiversity conservation priorities science. *Science*, **313**, 58–61.

Broom, D. M. (1983). Stereotypies as animal welfare indicators. In *Indicators Relevant to Farm Animal Welfare*, ed. **D. Smidt**, *Current Topics* in *Veterinary Medicine and Animal Science*, **23**, 81. The Hague: Martinus Nijhoff.

Broom, D. M. (1986). Indicators of poor welfare. *British Veterinary Journal*, **142**, 524–526.

Broom, D. M. (2006). Behaviour and welfare in relation to pathology. *Applied Animal Behaviour Science*, **97**, 71–83.

Bruner, A. G., Gullison, R. E., Rice, R. E. & **da Fonseca, G. A. B.** (2001). Effectiveness of parks in protecting tropical biodiversity. *Science*, **291**, 125–128.

Brussard, P. F. (1985). The current status of conservation biology. *Bulletin of the Ecological Society of America*, **66**, 9–11.

Bryant, D., Nielsen, D. & **Tangley, L.** (1997). *Last Frontier Forests.* Washngton, DC: World Resources Institute.

BTA/ETB (1997). *UK Statistics.* London: Insights.

Buchanan-Smith, H. M. (2006). Primates in laboratories: standardisation, harmonisation, variation and science. *ALTEX – Alternatives to Animal Experimentation*, **23**, 115–119.

Bullis, C. A. & Kennedy, J. J. (1991). Value conflicts and policy interpretation: Changes in the case of fisheries and wildlife managers in multiple use agencies. *Policy Studies Journal*, **19**, 542–552.

Bunbury, N., Stidworthy, M. F., Greenwood, A. G. *et al.* (2008). Causes of mortality in free-living Mauritian pink pigeons *Columba mayeri*, 2002–2006. *Endangered Species Research*, **9**, 213–220.

Burke, R. L. & Humphrey, S. R. (1987). Rarity as a criterion for endangerment in Florida's fauna. *Oryx*, **21**, 97–102.

Burton, F. J. (2004). Revision to species of *Cyclura nubila lewisi*, the Grand Cayman Blue Iguana. *Caribbean Journal of Science*, **40**, 198–203.

Burton, F. J. (2006). Blue Iguana Recovery Program. *Iguana Journal of the International Iguana Society*, **13**, 117.

Burton, F. J. (2010). *The Little Blue Book*. San Jose, CA: IRCF.

Burton, R. S., Rawson, P. D. & Edmands, S. (1999). Genetic architecture of physiological phenotypes: Empirical evidence for coadapted gene complexes. *American Zoologist*, **39**, 451–462.

Butchart, S. H. M., Stattersfield, A. J., Bennun, L. A. *et al.* (2004). Measuring global trends in the status of biodiversity: Red List indices for birds. *PLoS Biology*, **2**(12): e383.

Butchart, S. H. M., Stattersfield, A. J. & Collar, N. J. (2006). How many bird extinctions have we prevented? *Oryx*, **40**, 266–278.

Caballero, A., Rodriguez-Ramilo, S. T., Avila, V. & Fernandez, J. (2010). Management of genetic diversity of subdivided populations in conservation programmes. *Conservation Genetics*, **11**, 409–419.

Cabeza, M. & Moilanen, A. (2001). Design of reserve networks and the persistence of biodiversity. *Trends in Ecology & Evolution*, **16**, 242–247.

Caldecott, J. O. & Kavanagh, M. (1988). Strategic guidelines for nonhuman primate translocation. In *Translocations of Wild Animals*, eds. **L. Nielsen & R. D. Brown.** Madison, Wisconsin, USA: Wisconsin Humane Society, pp. 64–75.

Caldecott, J. O., Jenkins, M., Johnson, T. & Groombridge, B. (1994). *Priorities for Conserving Global Species Richness and Endemism*. Cambridge: World Conservation Press.

Campbell, S. (1978). *Lifeboats to Ararat*. New York: Times Books.

Carlstead, K., Seidensticker, J. & Baldwin, R. (1991). Environmental enrichment for zoo bears. *Zoo Biology*, **10**, 3–16.

Caro, T. M. (2003). Umbrella species: critique and lessons from East Africa. *Animal Conservation*, **6**, 171–181.

Caro, T. M. & O'Doherty, G. (1999). On the use of surrogate species in conservation biology. *Conservation Biology*, **13**, 805–814.

Caro, T. M. & Laurenson, M. K. (1994). Ecological and genetic factors in conservation: A cautionary tale. *Science*, **263**, 485–486.

Carroll, C., Noss, R. F. & Paquet, P. C. (2001). Carnivores as focal species for conservation planning in the rocky mountain region. *Ecological Applications*, **11**, 961–980.

Carter, N. (2007). *The Politics of the Environment: Ideas, Activism, Policy*, 2nd edition. Cambridge, UK: Cambridge University Press.

Case, T. J. & Bolger, D. T. (1991). The role of introduced species in shaping the distribution of island reptiles. *Evolutionary Ecology*, **5**, 272–290.

Caughley, G. (1994). Directions in conservation biology. *Journal of Animal Ecology*, **63**, 215–244.

CBSG (1992). *Ark into the 21st Century*. Apple Valley: Captive Breeding Specialist Group.

CBSG (2008). *Ex Situ Population Management Tools Working Group Report*. 2008 CBSG Annual Meeting, Adelaide, Australia. [http://www.cbsg.org/cbsg/content/files/2008_Annual_Meeting_WG_Reports/ex_situ.pdf/].

CBSG (2010). *CBSG workshop reports: Conservation Assessment and Management Plan (CAMP) reports*. [http://www.cbsg.org/cbsg/workshopreports/display.asp?catid=24].

Ceacero, F., Landete-Castillejos, T., García, A. J. *et al.* (2009). Free-choice mineral consumption in Iberian red deer (*Cervus elaphus hispanicus*) response to diet deficiencies. *Livestock Science*, **122**, 345–348.

Ceballos, G. & Ehrlich, P. R. (2009). Discoveries of new mammal species and their implications for conservation and ecosystem services. *Proceedings of the National Academy of Sciences*, **106**, 3841–3846.

Ceballos, G., Ehrlich, P. R., Soberón, J. *et al.* (2005). Global mammal conservation: what must we manage? *Science*, **309**, 603–607.

Central Zoo Authority (2010). *Central Zoo Authority*. Statutory Body under the Ministry of Environment and Forests, Government of India. [http://www.cza.nic.in/]

Chamove, A. S. & Anderson, J. R. (1989). Examining environmental enrichment. In *Ecology and Behavior of Food-Enhanced Primate Groups*, eds. **J. E. Fa** & **C. H. Southwick.** New York: Alan R. Liss Inc., pp. 231–248.

Chamove, A. S. & Rohruber, B. (1989). Moving callitrichid monkeys from cages to outside areas. *Zoo Biology*, **8**, 359–369.

Chape, S., Harrison, J., Spalding, M. & Lysenko, I. (2005). Measuring the extent and effectiveness of protected areas as an indicator for meeting global biodiversity targets. *Philosophical Transactions of the Royal Society Series B*, **360**, 443–455.

Cherfas, J. (1984). *Zoo 2000 – A Look Behind the Bars*. London: BBC.

Chester Zoo (2010). Chester Zoo Black Rhino Conservation Programme. [http://www.chesterzoo.org/~/media/Files/Conservation/Black%20Rhino.ashx]

Chicago Zoological Society (2010). Diversity Initiative [http://www.brookfieldzoo.org/czs/About-CZS/Careers/Diversity-Initiative]

Chiszar, D., Murphy, J. B. & Iliff, W. (1990). For zoos. *The Psychological Record*, **40**, 3–13.

Chittenden, C. M., Biagi, C. A., Davidsen, J. G. *et al.* (2010). Genetic versus rearing-environment effects on phenotype: hatchery and natural rearing effects on hatchery- and wild-born Coho salmon. *PLoS ONE*, **5**, e12261.

Clark, J. A. & May, R. M. (2002). Taxonomic bias in conservation research. *Science*, **5579**, 191–192.

Clubb, R. & Mason, G. (2003). Animal welfare: Captivity effects on wide-ranging carnivores. *Nature*, **425**, 473–474.

Clutton-Brock, J. (1999). *A Natural History of Domesticated Mammals*. Cambridge, UK: Cambridge University Press.

Coad, L., Burgess, N. D., Bomhard, B. & Besançon, C. (2009). *Progress towards the Convention on Biological Diversity's 2010 and 2012 Targets for Protected Area Coverage*. A technical report for the IUCN international workshop "Looking at the Future of the CBD Programme of Work on Protected Areas", Jeju Island, Republic of Korea, 14–17 September 2009. UNEP World Conservation Monitoring Centre, Cambridge. [http://www.unep-wcmc.org/protected_areas/pdf/Towardprogress].

Coady, J. W. & Hinman, R. A. (1984). Management of muskoxen in Alaska. In *Proceedings of the First International Muskox Symposium*, eds. **D. R. Klein, R. G. White** & **S. Keller,** Biological Paper of the University of Alaska Special Report, no. 4, pp. 47–51.

Cole, N., Jones, C., Buckland, S. *et al.* (2009). *The Reintroduction of Endangered Mauritian Reptiles*. Vacoas, Mauritius: The Mauritian Wildlife Foundation.

Collar, N. J. (1993–4). Red data books, action plans, and the need for site-specific synthesis. *Species*, **21/22**, 132–133.

Collar, N. J. (1996). The reasons for Red Data Books. *Oryx*, **30**,121–130.

Colleau, J. J. & Tribout, T. (2008). Optimized management of genetic variability in selected pig populations. *Journal of Animal Breeding and Genetics*, **125**, 291–300.

Collen, B., Loh, J., McRae, L. *et al.* (2009). Monitoring change in vertebrate abundance: the Living Planet Index. *Conservation Biology*, **23**, 317–327.

Coltman, D. W., Pilkington, J. G., Smith, J. A. & Pemberton, J. M. (1999). Parasite-mediated selection against inbred Soay sheep in a free-living, island population. *Evolution*, **53**, 1259–1267.

Considine, M. (1988). The corporate management framework as administrative science: a critique. *Australian Journal of Public Administration*, **47**, 4–18.

Contreras-Balderas, S. & Lozano, M. L. (1994). Water, endangered fishes and development perspectives in arid lands of Mexico. *Conservation Biology*, **8**, 379– 387.

Contreras-Balderas, S., Almada-Villela, P., Lozano-Vilano, M. L. & García-Ramírez, M. E. (2003). Freshwater fish at risk or extinct in Mexico: A checklist and review. *Reviews in Fish Biology and Fisheries*, **12**, 241–251.

Convention on Biological Diversity (CBD) (2010). COMMUNIQUÉ Alarming global survey on children's perceptions of nature. [http://www.cbd.int/doc/press/2010/pr-2010–05–18-airbus-en.pdf/]

Conway, W. G. (1986). The practical difficulties and financial implications of endangered species breeding programmes. *International Zoo Yearbook*, **24/25**, 210–219.

Conway, W. G. (1987). Species carrying capacity in the zoo alone. In *American Association of Zoological Parks and Aquariums 1987 Annual Conference Proceedings*. Wheeling, WV: AAZPA, pp. 20–32.

Conway, W. G. (1995). Wild and zoo animal interactive management and habitat conservation. *Biodiversity and Conservation*, **4**, 573–594.

Conway, W. (2003). The role of zoos in the 21st century. *International Zoo Yearbook*, **38**, 7–13.

Conway, W. G. (2007). Entering the 21st century. In *Zoos in the 21st Century: Catalysts for Conservation?*, eds. A. Zimmerman, M. Hatchwell, L. Dickie & C. West. Cambridge: Cambridge University Press, pp. 12–21.

Conway, W. G. & Hutchins, M. (2001). American Zoological Association [AZA] field conservation committee and conservation action partnerships. In *AZA Field Conservation Research Guide*, eds. W. G. Conway, M. Hutchins, M. Souza, Y. Kapetanakos & E. Paul. Wildlife Conservation Society, New York, and Zoo Atlanta, Atlanta, pp. 1–7.

Cooper, C. B., Dickinson, J., Phillips, T. & Bonney, R. (2007). Citizen Science as a tool for conservation in residential ecosystems. *Ecology and Society*, **12**(2), 11. [online] URL: http://www.ecologyandsociety.org/vol12/iss2/art11/

Courchamp, F., Clutton-Brock, T. & Grenfell, B. (1999). Inverse density dependence and the Allee effect. *Trends in Ecology and Evolution*, **14**, 405–410.

Courchamp, F., Chapuis, J.-L. & Pascal, M. (2003). Mammal invaders on islands: impact, control and control impact. *Biological Reviews*, **78**, 347–383.

Courchamp, F., Berec, L. & Gascoigne, J. (2008). *Allee Effects in Ecology and Conservation*. Oxford: Oxford University Press.

Cowburn, D. (2010). Cost cuts force out Durrell scientist. *Jersey Evening Post*. St. Helier, Jersey.

Cox, P. A., Elmqvist, T., Pierson, E. D. & Rainey, W. E. (1991). Flying foxes as strong interactors in South Pacific Island ecosystems: A conservation hypothesis. *Conservation Biology*, **5**, 448–454.

Coyne, J. A. & Orr, H. A. (2004). *Speciation*. Sunderland, MA: Sinauer Associates.

Cracraft, J. (1997). Species concepts in systematics and conservation biology – an ornithological viewpoint. In *Species the Units of Biodiversity*, eds. M. F. Claridge, H. A. Dawah, & M. R. Wilson. Systematics Association Special Volume Series 54, London: Chapman & Hall.

Cracraft, J., Feinstein, J., Vaughn, J. & Helm-Bychowski, K. (1998). Sorting our tigers (*Panthera tigris*): mitochrondial sequences, nuclear inserts, systematics, and conservation genetics. *Animal Conservation*, **1**, 139–150.

Craig, J., Anderson, S., Clout, M. *et al.* (2000). Conservation issues in New Zealand. *Annual Review of Ecology and Systematics*, **31**, 61–78.

Crandall, K. A., Bininda-Emonds, O. R. P., Mace, G. M. & Wayne, R. K. (2000). Considering evolutionary processes in conservation biology. *Trends in Ecology & Evolution*, **15**, 290–295.

Crawley, M. J. (1986). The population biology of invaders. *Philosophical Transactions of the Royal Society of London B*, **314**, 711–731.

Crissey, S. (2005). The complexity of formulating diets for zoo animals: a matrix. *International Zoo Yearbook*, **39**, 36–43.

Cristinacce, A., Ladkoo, A., Switzer, R. *et al.* (2008). Captive breeding and rearing of critically endangered Mauritius fodies *Foudia rubra* for reintroduction. *Zoo Biology*, **27**, 255–268.

Crnokrak, P. & Roff, D. A. (1999). Inbreeding depression in the wild. *Heredity*, **83**, 260–270.

Cronin, K. A., Mitchell, M. A., Lonsdorf, E. V. & Thompson, S. D. (2006). One year later: Evaluation of PMC-recommended births and transfers. *Zoo Biology*, **25**, 267–277.

Crosby, M. J. (1994). Mapping the distribution of restricted-range birds to identify global conservation priorities. In *Mapping the Diversity of Nature*, ed. **R. I. Miller.** London, UK: Chapman & Hall.

Cross, P. C. & Beissinger, S. R. (2001). Using logistic regression to analyze the sensitivity of PVA models: a comparison of methods based on African wild dog models. *Conservation Biology*, **15**, 1335–1346.

Cuarón, A. D. (2005). Further role of zoos in conservation: Monitoring wildlife use and the dilemma of receiving donated and confiscated animals. *Zoo Biology*, **24**, 115–124.

Cunningham, A. A. (1996). Disease risks of wildlife translocations. *Conservation Biology*, **10**, 349–353.

Custance, D. M., Whiten, A. & Fredman, T. (2002). Social learning and primate reintroduction. *International Journal of Primatology*, **23**, 479–499.

da Fonseca, G. A. B., Balmford, A., Bibby, C. *et al.* (2000). Following Africa's lead in setting priorities. *Nature*, **405**, 393–394.

Daleszczyk, K. & Bunevich, A. N. (2009). Population viability analysis of European bison populations in Polish and Belarusian parts of Bialowieza Forest with and without gene exchange. *Biological Conservation*, **142**, 3068–3075.

Daltry, J. C., Bloxam, Q., Cooper, G. *et al.* (2001). Five years of conserving the 'world's rarest snake', the Antiguan racer *Alsophis antiguae*. *Oryx*, **35**, 119–127.

Danzer, R. & Mormede, P. (1983). De-arousal properties of stereotyped behaviour: Evidence from pituitary-adrenal correlates in pigs. *Applied Animal Ethology*, **10**, 233–244.

Davey, G. (2007). An analysis of country, socio-economic and time factors on worldwide zoo attendance during a 40 year period. *International Zoo Yearbook*, **41**, 217–225.

Davis, J. I. (1996). Phylogenetics, molecular variation, and species concepts. *BioScience*, **46**, 502–511.

Dawkins, M. (1976). Towards an objective methods of assessing welfare in domestic fowl. *Applied Animal Ethology*, **2**, 245–254.

Dawkins, M. (1980). *The Science of Animal Welfare*. London: Chapman and Hall.

Dawkins, M. S. (2006). A user's guide to animal welfare science. *Trends in Ecology and Evolution*, **25**, 77–82.

de Queiroz, K. (1998). The general lineage concept of species, species criteria, and the process of speciation: A conceptual unification and terminological recommendations. In *Endless Forms: Species and Speciation*, eds. **D. J. Howard & S. H. Berlocher.** New York: Oxford University Press, pp. 57–75.

DEFRA (2008). *Guidance on the Requirements for Education in the Zoo Licensing Act (1981 and Amendments) with Respect to 'Animal Presentations'*. [http://archive.defra.gov.uk/wildlife-pets/zoos/documents/zoopres-edu.pdf].

Derwin, C. W. & Piper, J. B. (1988). The African Rock Kopje Exhibit. *Environment and Behaviour*, **20**, 435–451.

DETR (2000). *Secretary of State's Standards of Modern Zoo Practice*. London: Department of the Environment, Transport and the Regions.

de Turkheim, G. & Merz, E. (1984). Breeding Barbary macaques in a captive enclosure. In: *The Barbary Macaque: A Case Study in Conservation*, ed. **J. E. Fa.** New York: Plenum Press.

Diamond, J. M. (1984). 'Normal' extinction of isolated populations. In *Extinctions*, ed. **M. H. Nitecki.** Chicago: Chicago University Press, pp. 191–246.

Diamond, J. M. (1989). Overview of recent extinctions. In *Conservation for the Twenty-first Century*, eds. **D. Western** and **M. Pearl.** New York: Oxford University Press, pp. 34–37.

Dierking, L. D., Burtnyk, M. S., Büchner, K. S. & Falk, J. H. (2002). *Visitor Learning in Zoos and Aquariums: A Literature Review*, Annapolis, MD: Institute for Learning Innovation.

Dierking, L. D., Adelman, L. M., Ogden, J. et al. (2004). Using a behaviour change model to document the impact of visits to Disney's Animal Kindgom: a study investigating intended conservation action. *Curator: The Museum Journal*, **47**, 322–343.

Dickinson, H. C. & Fa, J. E. (2000). Abundance, demographics and body condition of a translocated population of St Lucia whiptail lizards (*Cnemidophorus vanzoi*). *Journal of Zoology*, **251**, 187–197.

Dixon, T. (2005). *Zoos. In Pros and Cons: A Debater's Handbook*, 18th edn, ed. **T. Sather.** London: Routledge, pp. 208–209.

Drake, A. G. & Klingenberg, C. P. (2010). Large-scale diversification of skull shape in domestic dogs: disparity and modularity. *The American Naturalist*, **175**, 289–301.

Dresser, B. L., Reece, R. W. & Maruska, E. J. (1988). *Proceedings, 5th World Conference on Breeding Endangered Species in Captivity*, October 9–12, 1988. Cincinnati, Ohio: Cincinnati Zoo and Botanical Garden.

Duncan, J. H. (2006). The changing concept of animal sentience. *Applied Animal Behaviour Science*, **100**, 11–19.

Durrell (2010). *Durrell Wildlife Conservation Trust – Saving Endangered Animals from Extinction Worldwide.* [http://www.durrell.org/In-the-field/].

Durrell, L., Rakotonindrina, R., Reid, D. & Durbin, J. (1994). The recovery of the angonoka (*Geochelone yniphora*) – an integrated approach to species conservation. In *Creative Conservation: Interactive Management of Wild and Captive Animals*, eds. **P. J. S. Olney, G. M. Mace & A. T. C. Feistner,** London: Chapman & Hall, pp. 384–393.

Earnhardt, J. M., Thompson, S. D. & Marhevsky, E. A. (2001). Interactions of target population size, population parameters, and program management of viability of captive populations. *Zoo Biology*, **20**, 169–183.

Earnhardt, J. M., Thompson, S. D. & Faust, L. J. (2009). Extinction risk assessment for the Species Survival Plan (SSP (R)) population of the Bali Mynah (*Leucopsar rothschildi*). *Zoo Biology*, **28**, 230–252.

EAZA (2010). European Association of Zoos and Aquaria. EAZA collection planning. [http://www.eaza.net/activities/cp/Pages/Collection%20Planning.aspx/].

Ebenhard, T. (1995). Conservation breeding as a tool for saving animal species from extinction. *Trends in Ecology and Evolution*, **10**, 438–443.

Eden Project (2010a). *Eden Project, Annual Review 2007/8.* [http://www.edenproject.com/annual_review_07_08.pdf]

Eden Project (2010b). *Gardens for life.* [http://www.edenproject.com/gardens-for-life]

Edmands, S. (2007). Between a rock and a hard place: evaluating the relative risks of inbreeding and outbreeding for conservation and management. *Molecular Ecology*, **16**, 463–475.

Ehrenfeld, D. (1970). *Biological Conservation.* New York: Columbia University Press.

Ehrenfeld, D. W. (1991). The management of diversity: A conservation paradox. In *Ecology, Economics, Ethics: The Broken Circle*, eds. **F. H. Borman & S. R. Kellert.** New Haven: Yale University Press, pp. 26–39.

Ehrlich, P. R. & Ehrlich, A. H. (1990). *Extinction: The Causes and Consequences of the Disappearance of Species.* New York: Random House.

Eisner, T., Lubchenco, J., Wilson, E. O., Wilcove, D. S. & Bean, M. J. (1995). Building a scientifically sound policy for protecting endangered species. *Science*, **5228**, 1231–1232.

Eken, G., Bennun, L., Brooks, T. M. *et al.* (2004). Key biodiversity areas as site conservation targets. *BioScience*, **54**, 1110–1118.

Ellis, S. (1995). Commentary on "Strategic collection planning: theory and practice". *Zoo Biology*, **14**, 49–51.

Ellis, S. & Seal, U. S. (1996). *Conservation Assessment and Management Plan (CAMP) Process Reference Manual*. Apple Valley, MN: IUCN/SSC Conservation Breeding Specialist Group.

England, P. R., Osler, G. H. R., Woodworth, L. M. *et al.* (2003). Effects of intense versus diffuse population bottlenecks on microsatellite genetic diversity and evolutionary potential. *Conservation Genetics*, **4**, 595–604.

Entwistle, A. (2000). Flagships for the future? *Oryx*, **34**, 239–240.

Erasmus, B. F. N., Van Jaarsweld, A. S. & Chown, S. L. (2002). Vulnerability of South African animal taxa to climate change. *Global Change Biology*, **8**, 679–693.

Erwin, J. & Deni, B. (1979). Reduced aggression and stereotypies in socially housed pig-tailed macaques. *Laboratory Primate Newsletter*, **28**, 3–4.

Erwin, T. L. (1982). Tropical forests: their richness in Coleoptera and other arthropod species. *Coleopterist's Bulletin*, **36**, 74–75.

Estes, J. A., Duggins, D. O. & Rathbun, G. B. (1989). The ecology of extinctions in kelp forest communities. *Conservation Biology*, **3**, 252–264.

European Union (1999). Council Directive of 29 March 1999 Relating to the Keeping of Wild Animals in Zoos. (OJL 94, 9.4.1999, p. 24) Brussels: European Union.

Eurogroup (2006). Report on the Implementation of the EU Zoo Directive. Eurogroup, Brussels. [http://www.eurogroupforanimals.org/policy/pdf/zooreportmar2006.pdf]

Evans, S. R. & Sheldon, B. C. (2008). Interspecific patterns of genetic diversity in birds: correlations with extinction risk. *Conservation Biology*, **22**, 1016–1025.

Ewbank, R. (1985). The meaning of welfare. In *The Teaching of Animal Welfare, Part I: Proceedings of a Workshop*, ed. P. M. Ray. Potter's Bar: UFAW, pp. 3–7.

Ewing, S. R., Nager, R. G., Nicoll, M. A. C. *et al.* (2008). Inbreeding and loss of genetic variation in a reintroduced population of Mauritius Kestrel. *Conservation Biology*, **22**, 395–404.

Fa, J. E. (1986). *Use of Time and Resources by Provisioned Troops of Monkeys: Social Behaviour, Time and Energy in Barbary macaques (Macaca sylvanus) at Gibraltar*. Contributions to Primatology, Vol. 23, Basel: S. Karger.

Fa, J. E. (1994). Herbivore intake/habitat productivity correlations can help ascertain re-introduction potential for the Barbary macaque. *Biodiversity and Conservation*, **3**, 309–317.

Fa, J. E. & Brown, D. (2009). Impacts of hunting on mammals in African tropical moist forests: a review and synthesis. *Mammal Review*, **34**, 231–264.

Fa, J. E. & Clark, C. C. M. (1998). Language and zoo biology training outcomes: A cautionary note. *Zoo Biology*, **18**, 71–77.

Fa, J. E. & Cavalheiro, M. L. (1998). Individual variation in food consumption and food preferences in St Lucia parrots *Amazona versicolor* at Jersey Wildlife Preservation Trust. *International Zoo Yearbook*, **36**, 199–214.

Fa, J. E. & Funk, S. M. (2007). Global endemicity centres for terrestrial vertebrates: an ecoregions approach. *Endangered Species Research*, **3**, 31–42.

Fa, J. E. & Southwick, C. H. (1988). *Ecology and Behavior of Food-enhanced Primate Groups*. New York: Alan R. Liss, Inc.

Fa, J. E., Juste, J., Perez del Val, J. & Castroviejo, J. (1995). Impact of market hunting on mammal species in Equatorial Guinea. *Conservation Biology*, **9**, 1107–1115.

Fa, J. E., Clark, C. C. & Hicks, S. (1996). Training in zoo biology at the Jersey Wildlife Preservation. Trust: A retrospective look and a glance at the future. *Dodo (Journal of the Wildlife Preservation Trusts)*, **31**, 22–32.

Fagan, W. F. & Holmes, E. E. (2006). Quantifying the extinction vortex. *Ecology Letters*, **9**, 51–60.

Falk, J. H. (2006). The impact of visit motivation on learning: using identity as a construct to understand the visitor experience. *Curator*, **49**(2), 151–166.

Falk, J. H. & Dierking, L. D. (2010). School field trips: assessing their long-term impact. *Curator: The Museum Journal*, **40**, 211–218.

Falk, J. H., Reinhard, E. M., Vernon, C. L. *et al.* (2007). *Why Zoos & Aquariums Matter: Assessing the Impact of a Visit to a Zoo or Aquarium*. Silver Spring, MD: Association of Zoos & Aquariums.

Falk, J. H., Heimlich, J. E. & Bronnenkant, K. (2008). Using identity-related visit motivations as a tool for understanding adult zoo and aquarium visitors' meaning making. *Curator: The Museum Journal*, **51**, 55–80.

Farmer, K. H. (2002). Pan-African Sanctuary Alliance: Status and range of activities for great ape conservation. *American Journal of Primatology*, **58**, 117–132.

Farmer, K. H. & Courage, A. (2008). Sanctuaries and reintroduction: a role in gorilla conservation? In *Conservation in the 21st Century: Gorillas as a Case Study*, eds. **T. S. Stoinski, H. D. Steklis & P. T. Mehlman.** Developments in Primatology: Progress and Prospects. Berlin: Springer, pp. 79–106.

Faust, L., Earnhardt, J., Schloss, C. & Bergstrom, Y. M. (2008). *ZooRisk: A Risk Assessment Tool*. Chicago, IL: Lincoln Park Zoo.

FAWC (2010). Farm Animal Welfare Council. [http://www.fawc.org.uk/]

Fernandez, E. J. & Timberlake, W. (2008). Mutual benefits of research collaborations between zoos and academic institutions. *Zoo Biology*, **27**, 470–487.

Fernández, J., Toro, M. A. & Caballero, A. (2003). Fixed contributions designs vs. minimization of global coancestry to control inbreeding in small populations. *Genetics*, **165**, 885–894.

Fessl, B., Young, G. H., Young, R. P. *et al.* (2010). How to save the rarest Darwin's finch from extinction: the mangrove finch on Isabela Island. *Philosophical Transactions of the Royal Society, B*, **365**, 1019–1030.

Finlay, T. W. & Maple, T. L. (1986). A survey of research in American zoos and aquariums. *Zoo Biology*, **5**, 261–268.

Fischer, J. & Lindenmayer, D. B. (2000). An assessment of the published results of animal translocations. *Biological Conservation*, **96**, 1–11.

Fishpool, L. D. C. & Evans, M. I. eds. (2001). *Important Bird Areas in Africa and Associated Islands: Priority Sites for Conservation*. Newbury and Cambridge, UK: Pisces Publications and BirdLife International.

Fisken, F. A., Field, D., Leus, K. *et al.* (2010). *International Zoo Yearbook 44: Bears and Canids*. London: Zoological Society of London.

Fitter, R. (1974). Most endangered mammals: An action programme. *Oryx*, **12**, 436.

Fitter, R. & Fitter, M. (eds.) (1987). *The Road to Extinction*. Gland, Switzerland: IUCN.

Fitter, R. S. R. & Scott, P. (1978). *The Penitent Butchers: The Fauna Preservation Society 1903–1978*. London: Collins.

Fjeldså, J. (2000). The relevance of systematics in choosing priority areas for global conservation. *Environmental Conservation*, **27**, 65–75.

Fleishman, E., Murphy, D. D. & Brussard, P. F. (2000). A new method for selection of umbrella species for conservation planning. *Ecological Applications*, **10**, 569–579.

Flight, P. A. (2010). Phylogenetic comparative methods strengthen evidence for reduced genetic diversity among endangered tetrapods. *Conservation Biology*, **24**, 1307–1315.

Foden, W., Mace, G., Vié, J.-C. *et al.* (2008). Species susceptibility to climate change impacts. In *The 2008 Review of The IUCN Red List of Threatened Species*, eds. **J.-C. Vié, C. Hilton-Taylor & S. N. Stuart.** Gland, Switzerland: IUCN.

Foose, T. J. (1991). Viable population strategies for reintroduction programmes. In *Beyond Captive Breeding: Reintroducing Endangered Mammals to the Wild*, ed. **J. H. W. Gipps,** Symposia, Zoological Society of London 62. Oxford: Clarendon Press, pp. 165–172.

Foose, T. J. (1991). CBSG captive action plans. *CBSG News*, **2**, 5–7.

Foose, T. J., de Boer, L., Seal, U. S. & **Lande, R.** (1995). Conservation management strategies based on viable populations. In *Population Management for Survival and Recovery*, eds. **J. D. Ballou, M. E. Gilpin,** & **T. J. Foose.** New York: Columbia University Press, pp. 273–294.

Forbes, S. & **Boyd, D.** (1997). Genetic variation of naturally colonizing wolves in the Central Rocky Mountains. *Conservation Biology*, **10**, 1082–1090.

Forthman-Quick, D. (1984). An integrative approach to environmental engineering in zoos. *Zoo Biology*, **3**, 65–77.

Foster-Turley, P. & **Markowitz, H.** (1982). A captive behavioural enrichment study with Asian small-clawed river otters (*Aonyx cinerea*). *Zoo Biology*, **1**, 19–43.

Fowler, K. & **Whitlock, M. C.** (1999). The distribution of phenotypic variance with inbreeding. *Evolution*, **53**, 1143–1156.

Fox, C. W., Scheibly, K. L. & **Reed, D. H.** (2008). Experimental evolution of the genetic load and its implications for the genetic basis of inbreeding depression. *Evolution*, **62**, 2236–2249.

Fragaszy, D. M. & **Adams-Curtis, L. E.** (1991). Generative aspects of manipulation in tufted capuchin monkey (*Cebus apella*). *Journal of Comparative Psychology*, **105**, 387–397.

Frankham, R. (1995). Effective population size/adult population size ratios in wildlife: A review. *Genetical Research*, **66**, 95–107.

Frankham, R. (2005a). Stress and adaptation in conservation genetics. *Journal of Evolutionary Biology*, **18**, 750–755.

Frankham, R. (2005b). Genetics and extinction. *Biological Conservation*, **126**, 131–140.

Frankham, R. (2008). Genetic adaptation to captivity in species conservation programs. *Molecular Ecology*, **17**, 325–333.

Frankham, R. (2010). Inbreeding in the wild really does matter. *Heredity*, **104**, 124–124.

Frankham, R. & **Loebel, D. A.** (1992). Modeling problems in conservation genetics using captive *Drosophila* populations – rapid genetic adaptation to captivity. *Zoo Biology*, **11**, 333–342.

Frankham, R. & **Ralls, K.** (1998). Conservation biology: inbreeding leads to extinction. *Nature*, **392**, 441–442.

Frankham, R., Manning, H., Margan, S. H. & **Briscoe, D. A.** (2000). Does equalization of family sizes reduce genetic adaptation to captivity? *Animal Conservation*, **3**, 357–363.

Frankham, R., Ballou, J. D. & **Briscoe, D. A.** (2002). *Introduction to Conservation Genetics*. Cambridge: Cambridge University Press.

Frankham, R., Ballou, J. D. & **Briscoe, D. A.** (2010). *Introduction to Conservation Genetics*, 2nd edition. Cambridge: Cambridge University Press.

Franklin, I. R. (1980). Evolutionary change in small populations. In *Conservation Biology: An Evolutionary-Ecological Perspective*, eds. **M. E. Soulé** & **B. A. Wilcox.** Sunderland, MA: Sinauer Associates, pp. 135–149.

Franklin, I. R. & **Frankham, R.** (1998). How large must populations be to retain evolutionary potential? *Animal Conservation*, **1**, 69–70.

Fraser, D. J. (2008). How well can captive breeding programs conserve biodiversity? A review of salmonids. *Evolutionary Applications*, **1**, 535–586.

Fraser, D. J. & **Bernatchez, L.** (2001). Adaptive evolutionary conservation: towards a unified concept for defining conservation units. *Molecular Ecology*, **10**, 2741–2752.

Fraser, J. & **Wharton, D.** (2007). The future of zoos: a new model for cultural institutions. *Curator: The Museum Journal*, **50**, 41–54.

Frazee, S. R., Cowling, R. M., Pressey, R. L., Turpie, J. K. & **Lindberg, N.** (2003). Estimating the costs of conserving a biodiversity hotspot: a case-study of the Cape Floristic Region, South Africa. *Biological Conservation*, **112**, 275–290.

Frazer, M., Dunstan, J. & **Creed, P.** (1985). *Perspectives on Organisational Change*. Sydney, Australia: Longmann-Cheshire.

Frynta, D., Lišková, S., Bültmann, S. & Burda, H. (2010). Being attractive brings advantages: the case of parrot species in captivity. *PLoS ONE*, **5**, e12568. doi:10.1371/journal.pone.0012568.

Fullager, P. J. (1985). The woodhens of Lord Howe Island. *Aviculture Magazine*, **91**, 15–30.

Funk, S. M. & Fa, J. E. (2006). Phylogeography of the endemic St. Lucia whiptail lizard *Cnemidophorus vanzoi*: conservation genetics at the species boundary. *Conservation Genetics*, **7**, 651–663.

Funk, S. M. & Fa, J. E. (2010). Ecoregion prioritization suggests an armoury not a silver bullet for conservation planning. *PLoS ONE*, **5**, e8923. doi:10.1371/journal.pone.0008923.

Funk, S. M., Verma, S. K., Larson, G. *et al.* (2007). The pygmy hog is a unique genus: 19th century taxonomists got it right first time round. *Molecular Phylogenetics and Evolution*, **45**, 427–436.

Gaines, S. D. & Lubchenco, J. (1982). A unified approach to marine plant-herbivore interactions. II Biogeography. *Annual Review of Ecology and Systematics*, **13**, 111–138.

Garnett, S., Crowley, G. & Balmford, A. (2003). The costs and effectiveness of funding the conservation of Australian threatened birds. *BioScience*, **7**, 658–665.

Gaston, K. J. (1991). The magnitude of global insect species richness. *Conservation Biology*, **5**, 283–296.

Gaston, K. J. & Blackburn, T. M. (1995). Mapping biodiversity using surrogates for species richness: macro-scales and New World birds. *Proceedings of the Royal Society, Biological Sciences*, **262**, 335–341.

Gaston, K. J. & May, R. M. (1992). Taxonomy of taxonomists. *Nature*, **356**, 281–282.

Gaston, K. J., Pressey, R. L. & Margules, C. R. (2002). Persistence and vulnerability: retaining biodiversity in the landscape and in protected areas. *Journal of Biosciences (Suppl. 2)*, **27**, 361–384.

Geiser, F. & Ferguson, C. (2001). Intraspecific differences in behaviour and physiology: effects of captive breeding on patterns of torpor in feathertail gliders. *Journal of Comparative Physiology B*, **171**, 569–576.

Giangrande, A. (2003). Biodiversity, conservation, and the taxonomic impediment. *Aquatic Conservation: Marine and Freshwater Ecosystems*, **13**, 451–459.

Gibbons, P., Zammit, C., Youngentob, K. *et al.* (2008). Some practical suggestions for improving engagement between researchers and policy-makers in natural resource management. *Ecological Management & Restoration*, **9**, 182–186.

Gilligan, D. M., Woodworth, L. M., Montgomery, M. E., Briscoe, D. A. & Frankham, R. (1997). Is mutation accumulation a threat to the survival of endangered populations? *Conservation Biology*, **11**, 1235–1241.

Gilpin, M. E. & Soulé, M. E. (1986). Minimum viable populations: processes of extinction. In *Conservation Biology: The Science of Scarcity and Diversity*, ed. **M. E. Soulé**, Sunderland, Massachusetts: Sinauer Associates, pp. 19–34.

Ginsberg, J. R. (1994). Captive breeding, reintroduction and the conservation of canids. In *Creative Conservation: Interactive Management of Wild and Captive Animals*, eds. **P. J. S. Olney, G. M. Mace & A. T. C. Feistner.** London, UK: Chapman and Hall, pp. 365–383.

Goodall, J. (1986). *The Chimpanzees of Gombe: Patterns of Behaviour.* Harvard University Press, Cambridge.

Goodwin, M., Greasley, S., John, P. & Richardson, L. (2010). Can we make environmental citizens? A randomised control trial of the effects of a school-based intervention on the attitudes and knowledge of young people. *Environmental Politics*, **19**, 392–412.

Goossens, B., Funk, S. M., Vidal, C. *et al.* (2002). Measuring genetic diversity in translocation programmes: principles and application to a chimpanzee release project. *Animal Conservation*, **5**, 225–236.

Goossens, B., Setchell, J. M., Tchidongo, E. *et al.* (2005). Survival, interactions with conspecifics and reproduction in 37 chimpanzees released into the wild. *Biological Conservation*, **123**, 461–475.

Graham-Jones, O. (1974). Some aspects of air transport in animals. *International Zoo Yearbook*, **14**, 34–37.

Grassle, J. F. (1989). Species diversity in deep-sea communities. *Trends in Ecology and Evolution*, **4**, 12–15.

Gray, T. I. (1994). The cultural diversity performance paradign: Building high performance zoos and aquariums. In *Proceedings of the American Zoo and Aquarium Association Annual Conference*. Wheeling, VA: American Zoo and Aquarium Association. pp. 398–403.

Gregory, R. D., Willis, S. G., Jiguet, F. *et al.* (2009). An indicator of the impact of climatic change on European bird populations. *PLoS ONE*, **4**, e4678. doi:10.1371/journal.pone.0004678.

Grenyer, R., Orme, C. D. L., Jackson, S. F. *et al.* (2006). Global distribution and conservation of rare and threatened vertebrates. *Nature*, **444**, 93–96.

Griffin, D. R. (1955). Bird navigation. In *Recent Studies in Avian Biology*, ed. **A. Wolfson.** Urbana: University of Illinois Press, pp. 154–197.

Griffith, B., Scott, J. M., Carpenter, J. W. & Reed, C. (1989). Translocation as a species conservation tool: status and strategy. *Science*, **245**, 477–480.

Griffith, B., Scott, J. M., Carpenter, J. & Reed, C. (1990). Translocations of captive-reared terrestrial vertebrates. *Endangered Species UPDATE*, **8**, 10–14.

Griffiths, R. A. & Pavajeau, L. (2008). Captive breeding, reintroduction, and the conservation of amphibians. *Conservation Biology*, **22**, 852–861.

Groves, C. R. (2003). *Drafting a Conservation Blueprint: A Practitioner's Guide to Planning for Biodiversity.* Washington, DC: Island Press.

Groves, C. P., Fernando, P. & Robovsky, J. (2010). The sixth rhino: a taxonomic reassessment of the critically endangered northern white rhinoceros. *PLoS ONE*, **5**, e9703. doi:10.1371/journal.pone.0009703.

Grueber, C. E. & Jamieson, I. G. (2008). Quantifying and managing the loss of genetic variation in a free-ranging population of takahe through the use of pedigrees. *Conservation Genetics*, **9**, 645–651.

Guillera-Arroita, G., Lahoz-Monfort, J. J., Milner-Gulland, E. J., Young, R. P. & Nicholson, E. (2010). Using occupancy as a state variable for monitoring the Critically Endangered Alaotran gentle lemur *Hapalemur alaotrensis*. *Endangered Species Research*, **11**, 157–166.

Gunnthorsdottir, A. (2001). Physical attractiveness of an animal species as a decision factor for its preservation. *Anthrozoos*, **14**, 204–215.

Gusset, M. & Dick, G. (2010). 'Building a Future for Wildlife'? Evaluating the contribution of the world zoo and aquarium community to in situ conservation. *International Zoo Yearbook*, **44**, 183–191.

Gwynne, J. A. (2007). Inspiration for conservation: moving audiences to care. In *Zoos in the 21st Century: Catalysts for Conservation?*, eds. **A. Zimmerman, M. Hatchwell, L. Dickie** and **C. West.** Cambridge: Cambridge University Press, pp. 51–63.

Haavie, J., Saetre, G. P. & Moum, T. (2000). Discrepancies in population differentiation at microsatellites, mitochondrial DNA and plumage colour in the pied flycatcher–inferring evolutionary processes. *Molecular Ecology*, **9**, 1137–1148.

Haight, R. G., Ralls, K. & Starfield, A. M. (2000). Designing species translocation strategies when populaton growth and future funding are uncertain. *Conservation Biology*, **14**, 1298–1307.

Hancocks, D. (1980). Bringing nature into the zoo: inexpensive solutions for zoo environments. *International Journal of Studies of Animal Problems*, **1**, 170–177.

Hancocks, D. (1995). Lions and tigers and bears, oh no! In *Ethics on the Ark: Zoos, Animal Welfare, and Wildlife Conservation*, eds. **B. G. Norton, M. Hutchins, E. F. Stevens** & **T. L. Maple.** Washington, DC: Smithsonian Institution Press, pp. 31–37.

Hancocks, D. (2001). *A Different Nature: The Paradoxical World of Zoos and Their Uncertain Future.* Berkeley: University of California Press.

Hannah, A. & McGrew, W. (1991). Rehabilitation of captive chimpanzees. In *Primate Responses to Environmental Change*, ed. **H. Box.** Chapman & Hall, London, pp. 167–186.

Hanski, I. A. & Gilpin, M. E. (1991). Metapopulation dynamics: Brief history and conceptual domain. *Biological Journal of the Linnaean Society*, **42**, 3–16.

Harcourt, A. H. (1986). Gorilla conservation: Anatomy of a campaign. In *Primates: The Road to Self-Sustaining Populations*, ed. **K. Benirschke.** New York: Springer-Verlag, pp. 31–46.

Harcourt, A. H. & Stewart, K. J. (1984). Gorilla's time feeding: aspects of methodology, body size, competition and diet. *African Journal of Ecology*, **22**, 207–215.

Hard, J. J., Berejikian, B. A., Tezak, E. P., Schroder, S. L., Knudsen, C. M. & Parker, L. T. (2000). Evidence for morphometric differentiation of wild and captively reared adult coho salmon: a geometric analysis. *Environmental Biology of Fishes*, **58**, 61–73.

Harley, E. H., Baumgarten, I., Cunningham, J. & O'Ryan, C. (2005). Genetic variation and population structure in remnant populations of black rhinoceros, *Diceros bicornis*, in Africa. *Molecular Ecology*, **14**, 2981–2990.

Hawksworth, D. L. & Kalin-Arroyo, M. T. (1995). Magnitude and distribution of biodiversity. In *Global Biodiversity Assessment*, ed. **V. H. Heywood.** Cambridge: Cambridge University Press, pp. 107–191.

Hawley, D. M., Sydenstricker, K. V., Kollias, G. V. & Dhondt, A. A. (2005). Genetic diversity predicts pathogen resistance and cell-mediated immunocompetence in house finches. *Biology Letters*, **1**, 326–329.

Hediger, H. (1950). *Wild Animals in Captivity*. London: Butterworth.

Hediger, H. (1969). *Man and Animal in the Zoo: Zoo Biology*. London: Routledge and Kegan Paul.

Hedrick, P. W. (1994). Purging inbreeding depression and the probability of extinction – full-sib mating. *Heredity*, **73**, 363–372.

Hedrick, P. W. & Fredrickson, R. T. (2010). Genetic rescue guidelines with examples from Mexican wolves and Florida panthers. *Conservation Genetics*, **11**, 615–626.

Hedrick, P. W. & Kalinowski, S. T. (2000). Inbreeding depression in conservation biology. *Annual Review of Ecology and Systematics*, **31**, 139–162.

Hedrick, P. W., Lacy, R. C., Allendorf, F. W. & Soulé, M. E. (1996). Directions in conservation biology: comments on Caughley. *Conservation Biology*, **10**, 1312–1320.

Heikkinen, R. K., Luoto, M., Araújo, M. B. *et al.* (2006). Methods and uncertainties in bioclimatic envelope modelling under climate change. *Progress in Physical Geography*, **30**, 1–27.

Hendry, A. P., Vamosi, S. M., Latham, S. J., Heilbuth, J. C. & Day, T. (2000a). Questioning species realities. *Conservation Genetics*, **1**, 67–76.

Hendry, A. P., Wenburg, J. K., Bentzen, P., Volk, E. C. & Quinn, T. P. (2000b). Rapid evolution of reproductive isolation in the wild: evidence from introduced salmon. *Science*, **290**, 516–518.

Hennemann, W. W. III (1983). Relationship among body mass, metabolic rate and the intrinsic rate of natural increase in mammals. *Oecologia (Berlin)*, **56**, 104–108.

Hess, G. R., Bartel, R. A., Leidner, A. K. *et al.* (2006). Effectiveness of biodiversity indicators varies with extent, grain, and region. *Biological Conservation*, **132**, 448–457.

Hey, J. (2001). *Genes, Categories and Species*. New York, NY: Oxford University Press.

Heywood, V. H. & Stuart, S. N. (1992). Species extinctions in tropical forests. In *Tropical Deforestation and Species Extinction*, eds. **T. C. Whitmore** & **J. A. Sayer.** London: Chapman & Hall, pp. 91–117.

Heywood, V. H., Mace, G. M. & Stuart, S. N. (1994). Uncertainties in extinction rates. *Nature*, **368**, 105.

Hiddinga, B. & Leus, K. (2006). On Regional Collection Plans and population sizes. *EAZA News*, **54**, 26–28.

Hill, J., Collingham, Y. C., Thomas, C. D. *et al.* (2001). Impacts of landscape structure on butterfly range expansion. *Ecology Letters*, **4**, 313–321.

Hill, J. K., Thomas, C. D. & Huntley, B. (2003). Modelling present and potential future ranges of European butterflies using climate response surfaces. In *Butterflies: Ecology and Evolution Taking Flight*, eds. C. Boggs, W. Watt & P. Ehrlich. Chicago: Chicago University Press. pp. 149–167.

Hill, W. G. & Rabash, J. (1986). Models of long term artificial selection in finite populations. *Genetic Research*, **48**, 41–50.

Hilton-Taylor, C., Mace, G. M., Capper, D. R. *et al.* (2000). Assessment mismatches must be sorted out: they leave species at risk. *Nature*, **404**, 541.

Hilton-Taylor, C., Pollock, C. M., Chanson, J. S. *et al.* (2009). State of the world's species. In *Wildlife in a Changing World – An Analysis of the 2008 IUCN Red List of Threatened Species*, eds. J.-C. Vié, C. Hilton-Taylor & S. N. Stuart. Gland, Switzerland: IUCN, pp. 15–42.

Hladik, C. M. (1973). Alimentation et activité d'un groupe de chimpanzés réintroduits en forêt gabonaise. *La Terre et la Vie*, **27**, 343–413.

Hobbs, R. J. & Kristjanson, L. J. (2003). How do we prioritize health care for landscapes? *Ecological Management and Restoration*, **4**, S39–S45.

Hoegh-Guldberg, O., Hughes, L., McIntyre, S. *et al.* (2008). Assisted colonization and rapid climate change. *Science*, **321**, 345–346.

Hoekstra, J. M., Boucher, T. M., Ricketts, T. H. & Roberts, C. (2005). Confronting a biome crisis: global disparities of habitat loss and protection. *Ecology Letters*, **8**, 23–29.

Hoffmann, M., Brooks, T. M., da Fonseca, G. A. B. *et al.* (2008). Conservation planning and the IUCN Red List. *Endangered Species Research*, doi:10.3354/esr00087.

Holt, W. V. & Lloyd, R. E. (2009). Artificial insemination for the propagation of CANDES: the reality! *Theriogenology*, **71**, 228–235.

Hosey, G. (1997). Behavioral research in zoos: Academic perspectives. *Applied Animal Behaviour Science*, **51**, 199–207.

Hosey, G. R. (2000). Zoo animals and their human audiences: what is the visitor effect? *Animal Welfare*, **9**, 343–357.

Hosey, G. (2005). How does the environment affect the behaviour of captive primates? *Applied Animal Behaviour Science*, **90**, 107–129.

Howard, J. G., Marinari, P. E. & Wildt, D. E. (2003). Black-footed ferret: model for assisted reproductive technologies contributing to in situ conservation. In *Reproductive Science and Integrated Conservation*, eds. W. V. Holt, A. R. Pickard, J. C. Rodger & D. E. Wildt. Cambridge: Cambridge University Press, pp. 249–266.

Howe, H. F. (1984). Implications of seed dispersal by animals for tropical reserve management. *Biological Conservation*, **30**, 261–281.

Humphries, C. J., Williams, P. H. & Vane-Wright, R. I. (1995). Measuring biodiversity value for conservation. *Annual Reviews of Ecology and Systematics*, **26**, 93–111.

Huntingford, F. A. (2004). Implications of domestication and rearing conditions for the behaviour of cultivated fishes. *Journal of Fish Biology*, **65**, Suppl. A, 122–142.

Hurlbert, A. H. & Jetz, W. (2007). Species richness, hotspots, and the scale dependence of range maps in ecology and conservation. *Proceedings of the National Academy of Sciences*, **104**, 13 384–13 389.

Hutchins, M. (1996). Education in conservation. *Communiqué*, March 26–27.

Hutchins, M. (2003). Zoo and aquarium animal management and conservation: current trends and future challenges. *International Zoo Yearbook*, **38**, 14–28.

Hutchins, M. & Conway, W. G. (1995). Beyond Noah's Ark: The evolving role of modern zoos and aquariums in field conservation. *International Zoo Yearbook*, **34**, 117–130.

Hutchins, M. & Smith, B. (2003). Characteristics of a world-class zoo or aquarium in the 21st century. *International Zoo Yearbook*, **38**, 130–141.

Hutchins, M. & Thompson, S. D. (2008). Zoo and aquarium research: priority setting for the coming decades. *Zoo Biology*, **27**, 488–497.

Hutchins, M. & Wemmer, C. (1991). In defense of captive breeding. *Endangered Species Update*, **8**, 5–6.

Hutchins, M., Hancocks, D. & Calip, T. (1978/1979). Behavioural engineering in the zoo: A critique. Parts 1, 2 and 3 *International Zoo News*, **25**, 18–23; 18, 5–18.

Hutchins, M., Hancocks, D. & Crockett, C. (1984). Naturalistic solutions to the behavior problems of captive animals. *Zoological Garten*, **54**, 28–42.

Hutchins, M., Willis, K. & Weise, R. J. (1995). Strategic collection planning: theory and practice. *Zoo Biology*, **14**, 5–25.

Hutchins, M., Paul, E. & Bowdoin, J. (1996). Contributions of zoo and aquarium research to wildlife conservation and science. In *Well-Being of Animals in Zoo and Aquarium Research*, eds. J. Bielitzki, J. Boyce, G. Burghardt & D. Schaeffer. Greenbelt, MD: Scientist's Center for Animal Welfare and Zoo Atlanta, pp. 23–39.

Hutchins, M., Wiese, R. J. & Willis, K. (1997). Captive breeding and conservation. *Conservation Biology*, **11**, 3.

ICBP (1992). *Putting Biodiversity on the Map*. Cambridge, UK: International Council for Bird Protection.

Isaac, N. J. B., Mallet, J. & Mace, G. M. (2004). Taxonomic inflation: its influence on macroecology and conservation. *Trends in Ecology and Evolution*, **19**, 464–469.

Isaac, N. J. B., Turvey, S. T., Collen, B., Waterman, C. & Baillie, J. E. M. (2007). Mammals on the EDGE: conservation priorities based on threat and phylogeny. *PLoS ONE* **2**(3), e296.

ISIS (2010). *International Species Inventory System. Find Animals*. [http://www.isis.org/Pages/findanimals.aspx]

IUCN (1987a). *Captive Breeding Policy. IUCN Policy Document*. Gland, Switzerland: IUCN.

IUCN (1987b). *IUCN Position Statement on the Translocation of Living Organisms: Introductions, Re-introductions, and Re-stocking*. Prepared by the Species Survival Commission in collaboration with the Commission on Ecology and the Commission on Environmental Policy, Law and Administration. IUCN [http://www.iucnsscrsg.org/]

IUCN (1992). *Global Biodiversity Strategy: Guidelines for Action to Save, Study and Use Earth's Biotic Wealth Sustainably and Equitably*. Gland, Switzerland: IUCN.

IUCN (1994). *IUCN Red List Categories*. Gland, Switzerland: IUCN Species Survival Commission.

IUCN (1998). *IUCN Guidelines for Re-introductions*. IUCN/SSC Reintroduction Specialist Group. Gland, Switzerland: IUCN.

IUCN (2001). *IUCN Red List Categories and Criteria: version 3.1*. Gland and Cambridge: IUCN.

IUCN (2002). *IUCN Technical Guidelines on the Management of Ex Situ Populations for Conservation*. [http://cmsdata.iucn.org/downloads/2002_dec_guidelines_management_of_ex_situ_populations_for_conservation.pdf].

IUCN (2010). *The IUCN Red List of Threatened Species*. Version 2010.1. [http://www.iucnredlist.org].

IUDZG/CBSG (IUCN/SSC) (1993). *The World Zoo Conservation Strategy: the Roles of Zoos and Aquaria of the World in Global Conservation*. Brookfield, Illinois: Chicago Zoological Society.

IUDZG/CBSG (IUCN/SSC) (2005). *The World Zoo Conservation Strategy: the Role of the Zoos and Aquaria of the World in Global Conservation*. Chicago, IL: Chicago Zoological Society.

Ivy, J. A., Miller, A., Lacy, R. C. & DeWoody, J. A. (2009). Methods and prospects for using molecular data in captive breeding programs: an empirical example using Parma Wallabies (*Macropus parma*). *Journal of Heredity*, **100**, 441–454.

IWRC (2010). *International Wildlife Rehabiliation Council*. [http://theiwrc.org/]

IZE (2010). *Programs in action – summary of education projects from selected zoos*. [http://www.izea.net/education/programs.htm]

Jablonski, D. (1991). Extinctions: a paleontological perspective. *Science*, **253**, 754–757.

Jachowski, D. & Kesler, D. (2009). Allowing extinction: are we ready to let species go? *Trends in Ecology and Evolution*, **24**, 180.

James, J. W. (1970). The founder effect and response to artificial selection. *Genetical Research*, **16**, 241–250.

Jamieson, D. (1985). *Against Zoos. In Defence of Animals*, ed. **P. Singer.** Oxford: Basil Blackwell, pp. 108–117.

Jamieson, D. (1995). Zoos revisited. In *Ethics on the Ark: Zoos, Animal Welfare, and Wildlife Conservation*, eds. **B. G. Norton, M. Hutchins, E. F. Stevens,** and **T. L. Maple.** Washington, DC: Smithsonian Institute Press, pp. 52–66.

Jamieson, I. G. (2007). Role of genetic factors in extinction of island endemics: complementary or competing explanations? *Animal Conservation*, **10**, 151–153.

Jeggo, D. F., French, H., Bellingham, L. *et al.* (2000). Breeding programme for St. Lucia Amazon. *International Zoo Yearbook*, **37**, 214–220.

Jenkins, M. (1992). Ex situ conservation of animals. In *Global Biodiversity: Status of the Earth's Living Resources*, ed. **B. Groombridge.** London: Chapman & Hall, pp. 563–575.

Jennings, M., Faber-Langendoen, D., Peet, R. *et al.* (2004). *Description, Documentation, and Evaluation of Associations and Alliances within the U. S. National Vegetation Classification*. The Ecological Society of America, Vegetation Classification Panel, Version 4.0, March 2004.

Jenkins, C. N. & Joppa, L. (2009). Expansion of the global terrestrial protected area system. *Biological Conservation*, **142**, 2166–2174.

Jones, C. G., Heck, W., Lewis, R. E. *et al.* (1995). The restoration of the Mauritius Kestrel *Falco punctatus* population. *Ibis*, **137**, S173–S180.

Jones, K. L. & Nicolich, J. M. (2001). Artificial insemination in captive whooping cranes: results from genetic analyses. *Zoo Biology*, **20**, 331–342.

Jones, M. E., Jarman, P. J., Lees, C. M. *et al.* (2007). Conservation management of Tasmanian devils in the context of an emerging, extinction-threatening disease: Devil facial tumor disease. *Ecohealth*, **4**, 326–337.

Joslin, J. K. (1977). Rodent long distance orientation ("homing"). *Advances in Ecological Research*, **10**, 63–89.

Jule, K. R., Leaver, L. A. & Lea, S. E. G. (2008). The effects of captive experience on reintroduction survival in carnivores: a review and analysis. *Biological Conservation*, **141**, 355–363.

Kahn, A. E. (1966). The tyranny of small decisions: market failures, imperfections and the limits of economics. *Kyklos*, **19**, 23–47.

Kalinowski, S. T., Hedrick, P. W. & Miller, P. S. (2000). Inbreeding depression in the Speke's gazelle captive breeding program. *Conservation Biology*, **14**, 1375–1384.

Kareiva, P. & Marvier, M. (2003). Conserving biodiversity coldspots. *American Scientist*, **91**, 344–351.

Karr, J. R. (1982). Population variability and extinction in the avifauna of a tropical land bridge island. *Ecology*, **63**, 1975–1978.

Karr, J. R. (1991). Biological integrity: A long-neglected aspect of water resource management. *Ecological Applications*, **1**, 66–84.

Kawata, K. & Hendy, M. (1978). A perspective: Zoo going and animal popularity. *International Zoo News*, **25**, 14–15.

Keenan, C. P. (2000). Should we allow human-induced migration of the Indo-West Pacific fish, barramundi *Lates calcarifer* (Bloch) within Australia? *Aquaculture Research*, **31**, 121–131.

Kellert, S. (1979). Zoological parks in American society. In American Zoo Association Annual Meeting Proceedings, Wheelings, WV: AAZPA, pp. 82–126.

Kellert, S. (1996). *The Value of Life*. Washington DC: Island Press.

Kellert, S. R. (2002). Experiencing nature: affective, cognitive and evaluative development in children. In *Children and Nature: Psychological, Sociocultural, and Evolutionary Investigations*, eds. **P. H. Kahn &** **S. R. Kellert.** Boston: The MIT Press, pp. 117–152.

Kellert, S. R. & Dunlap, J. (1989). *Informal Learning at the Zoo: A Study of Attitude and Knowledge Impacts*. A Report to the Zoological Society of Philadelphia.

Kelley, J. L., Magurran, A. E. & Macías García, C. (2006). Captive breeding promotes aggression in an endangered Mexican fish. *Biological Conservation*, **133**, 169–177.

Kelly, J. D. (1997). Effective conservation in the twenty-first century: the need to be more than a zoo. One organization's approach. *International Zoo Yearbook*, **35**, 1–14.

Kettmann, M. (2010). The great California condor comeback: after decades of costly ups and downs, the endangered species finally is poised to succeed. *The Santa Barbara Independent*, Thursday, January 7, 2010.

Kinnersley, P., Anderson, E., Parry, K. *et al.* (2000). Randomised controlled trial of nurse practitioner versus general practitioner care for patients requesting "same day" consultations in primary care. *British Medical Journal*, **320**, 1043–1048.

Kirkden, R. D. & Pajor, E. A. (2006). Motivation for group housing in gestating sows. *Animal Welfare*, **15**, 119–130.

Kirkwood, J. K. (2003). Welfare, husbandry and veterinary care of wild animals in captivity: changes in attitudes, progress in knowledge and techniques. *International Zoo Yearbook*, **38**, 124–130.

Kitchener, A. C. (1998). The Scottish wildcat – a cat with an identity crisis? *British Wildlife*, **9**, 232–242.

Kitchener, A. C. (1999). Tiger distribution, phenotypic variation and conservation issues. In *Riding the Tiger*, eds. J. Seidensticker, S. Christie & P. Jackson, Cambridge: Cambridge University Press, pp. 19–39.

Kitchener, A. C. (2004). The problem of old bears in zoos. *International Zoo News*, **51**, 283–293.

Kleiman, D. G. (1989). Reintroduction of captive mammals for conservation. *BioScience*, **39**, 152–161.

Kleiman, D. G. (1992). Behavioral research in zoos: past, present and future. *Zoo Biology*, **11**, 301–312.

Kleiman, D. G. & Mallinson, J. J. C. (1998). Recovery and management committees for lion tamarins: Partnerships in conservation planning and implementation. *Conservation Biology*, **12**, 27–38.

Kleiman, D. G., Beck, B. B., Dietz, J. M., Ballou, J. D. & Coimbra-Filho, A. F. (1986). Conservation program for the golden lion tamarin: captive research and management, ecological studies, educational strategies and reintroduction. In *Primates: The Road to Self-Sustaining Populations*, ed. K. Benirschke. New York: Springer-Verlag, pp. 960–979.

Kleiman, D. G., Beck, B. B., Dietz, J. M. & Dietz, L. A. (1991). Costs of a re-introduction and criteria for success: accountability in the golden lion tamarin conservation program. In *Beyond Captive Breeding: Reintroducing Endangered Mammals to the Wild*, ed. J. H. W. Gipps, Symposia, Zoological Society of London 62. Oxford: Clarendon Press, pp. 125–142.

Kleiman, D. G., Stanley Price, M. R. & Beck, B. B. (1994). Criteria for reintroductions. In *Creative Conservation: Interactive Management of Wild and Captive Animals*, eds. P. J. Solney, G. M. Mace & A. F. Feistner. London: Chapman and Hall, pp. 287–303.

Kohn, M. H., York, E. C., Kamradt, D. A. *et al.* (1999). Estimating population size by genotyping faeces. *Proceedings of the Royal Society of London B, Biological Sciences*, **266**, 657–663.

Konstant, W. R. & Mittermeier, R. A. (1982). Introduction, reintroduction and translocation of Neotropical primates: past experiences and future possibilities. *International Zoo Yearbook*, **22**, 69–77.

Kruska, D. (1996). The effect of domestication on brain size and composition in the mink (*Mustela vison*). *Journal of Zoology, London*, **239**, 645–661.

Kruska, D. C. T. & Sidorovich, V. E. (2003). Comparative allometric skull morphometrics in mink (*Mustela vison* Schreber, 1777) of Canadian and Belarus origin; taxonomic status. *Mammalian Biology – Zeitschrift für Saugetierkunde*, **68**, 257–276.

Künzel, C., Kaiser, S., Meier, E. & Sachser, N. (2003). Is a wild mammal kept and reared in captivity still a wild animal? *Hormones and Behavior*, **43**, 187–196.

Lacy, R. C. (1987). Loss of genetic diversity from managed populations: Interacting effects of drift, mutation, immigration, selection, and population subdivision. *Conservation Biology*, **1**, 143–158.

Lacy, R. C. (1989). Analysis of founder representation in pedigrees: Founder equivalents and founder genome equivalents. *Zoo Biology*, **8**, 111–123.

Lacy, R. C. (1993). Vortex – a computer-simulation model for population viability analysis. *Wildlife Research*, **20**, 45–65.

Lacy, R. C. (1995). Clarification of genetic terms and their use in the management of captive populations. *Zoo Biology*, **14**, 565–577.

Lacy, R. C. (1997). Importance of genetic variation to the viability of mammalian populations. *Journal of Mammalogy*, **78**, 320–335.

Lacy, R. C. & Ballou, J. D. (1998). Effectiveness of selection in reducing the genetic load in populations of *Peromyscus polionotus* during generations of inbreeding. *Evolution*, **52**, 900–909.

Lahoz-Monfort, J. J. Guillera-Arroita, G., Milner-Gulland, E. J., Young, R. P. & Nicholson, E. (2010). Satellite imagery as a single source of predictor variables for habitat suitability modelling: how Landsat can inform the conservation of a critically endangered lemur. *Journal of Applied Ecology*, DOI: 10.1111/j.1365–2664.2010.01854.

Laikre, L. (1999). Hereditary defects and conservation genetic management of captive populations. *Zoo Biology*, **18**, 81–99.

Lambeck, R. J. (1997). Focal species: a multi-species umbrella for nature conservation. *Conservation Biology*, **11**, 849–857.

Lamoreux, J. F., Morrison, J. C., Ricketts, T. H. *et al.* (2006). Global tests of biodiversity concordance and the importance of endemism. *Nature*, **440**, 212–214.

Lande, R. (1988). Genetics and demography in biological conservation. *Science*, **241**, 1455–1460.

Lande, R. (1993). Risk of population extinction from demographic and environmental stochasticity and random catastrophes. *American Naturalist*, **142**, 911–927.

Lande, R. (1994). Risk of population extinction from fixation of new deleterious mutations. *Evolution*, **48**, 1460–1469.

Lande, R. (1995). Mutation and conservation. *Conservation Biology*, **9**, 782–791.

Landres, P. B., Verner, J. & Thomas, J. W. (1988). Ecological uses of vertebrate indicator species: a critique. *Conservation Biology*, **2**, 316–328.

Larsen, F. W., Turner, W. R. & Brooks, T. M. (2011). Conserving critical sites for biodiversity provides disproportionate human well-being benefits. (In press.)

La Rue, F. (1992). Working together to resolve the historic conflict between curators and veterinarians. In *Proceedings of the American Association of Zoological Parks and Aquariums Annual Conference*. Wheeling, West Virginia: American Association of Zoological Parks and Aquariums, pp. 162–169.

Lascuráin, M., List, R., Barraza, L. *et al.* (2009). Conservación de especies ex situ. In *Capital Natural de México*, Vol. II: *Estado de Conservación y Tendencias de Cambio*. Mexico City: CONABIO, pp. 517–544.

Laurance, W. F. (1991). Ecological correlates of extinction proneness in Australian tropical rain forest mammals. *Conservation Biology*, **5**, 79–89.

Lawson, D. P., Ogden, J. & Snyder, R. J. (2008). Maximizing the contribution of science in zoos and aquariums: organizational models and perceptions. *Zoo Biology*, **27**, 458–469.

Leader-Williams, N. (1990). Black rhinos and African elephants: lessons for conservation funding. *Oryx*, **24**, 23–29.

Leader-Williams, N. & Dublin, H. T. (2000). Charismatic megafauna as 'flagship species'. In *Priorities for the Conservation of Mammalian Diversity: Has the Panda had its Day?*, eds. A. Entwistle & N. Dunstone. Cambridge: Cambridge University Press, pp. 53–81.

Leader-Williams, N., Balmford, A., Linkie, M. *et al.* (2007). Beyond the ark: conservation biologists' views of the achievements of zoos in conservation. In *Zoos in the 21st Century: Catalysts for Conservation?*, eds. A. Zimmerman, M. Hatchwell, L. Dickie & C. West. Cambridge: Cambridge University Press, pp. 236–254.

Leberg, P. L. & Firmin, B. D. (2008). Role of inbreeding depression and purging in captive breeding and restoration programmes. *Molecular Ecology*, **17**, 334–343.

Lee, T. M. & Jetz, W. (2008). Future battlegrounds for conservation under global change. *Proceedings of the Royal Society B, Biological Sciences*, **275**, 1261–1270.

Lees, C. M. & Wilcken, J. (2009). Sustaining the ark: the challenges faced by zoos in maintaining viable populations. *International Zoo Yearbook*, **43**, 6–18.

Lehmann, L. & Perrin, N. (2006). On metapopulation resistance to drift and extinction. *Ecology*, **87**, 1844–1855.

Leinonen, T., O'Hara, R. B., Cano, J. M. & Merila, J. (2008). Comparative studies of quantitative trait and neutral marker divergence: a meta-analysis. *Journal of Evolutionary Biology*, **21**, 1–17.

Leroy, E. M., Rouquet, P., Formenty, P. *et al.* (2004). Multiple Ebola virus transmission events and rapid decline of central African wildlife. *Science*, **303**, 387–390.

Levinsky, I., Skov, F., Svenning, J. C. & Rahbek, C. (2007). Potential impacts of climate change on the distributions and diversity patterns of European mammals. *Biodiversity and Conservation*, **16**, 3803–3816.

Lewis, O. T. & Thomas, C. D. (2001). Adaptations to captivity in the butterfly *Pieris brassicae* (L.) and the implications for ex situ conservation. *Journal of Insect Conservation*, **5**, 55–63.

Lewis, W. J. (1980). *Interpreting for Park Visitors*. Philadelphia, Pennsylvania: Eastern Acorn Press.

Lewontin, R. C. & Birch, L. C. (1996). Hybridization as a source of variation for adaptation to a new environment. *Evolution*, **20**, 315–336.

Lindburg, D. G. (1992). Are wildlife reintroductions worth the cost? *Zoo Biology*, **11**, 1–2.

Lindemann-Matthies, P. & Kamer, T. (2005). The influence of an interactive educational approach on visitors' learning in a Swiss Zoo. In *Science Learning in Everday Life*, eds. **L. D. Dierking** & **J. H. Falk,** section coeditors. London: Wiley Periodicals, Inc.

Lindenmayer, D. B. (1994). Future directions for biodiversity conservation in managed forests: indicator species, impact studies and monitoring programs. *Forest Ecology and Management*, **115**, 277–287.

Lindenmayer, D. B., Manning, A. D., Smith, P. L. *et al.* (2002). The focal-species approach and landscape restoration: a critique. *Conservation Biology*, **16**, 338–345.

Linnell, J. D. C., Aanes, R., Swenson, J. E., Odden, J. & Smith, M. E. (1997). Translocation of carnivores as a method for managing problem animals: a review. *Biodiversity and Conservation*, **6**, 1245–1257.

Liukkonen-Anttila, T., Saartoala, R. & Hissa, R. (2000). Impact of hand-rearing on morphology and physiology of the capercaillie (*Tetrao urogallus*). *Comparative Biochemistry and Physiology Part A*, **125**, 211–221.

Lloyd, B. D. & Powlesland, R. G. (1994). The decline of kakapo *Strigops habroptilus* and attempts at conservation by translocation. *Biological Conservation*, **69**, 75–85.

Long, A. J., Crosby, M. J., Stattersfield, A. J. & Wege, D. C. (1996). Towards a global map of biodiversity: patterns in the distribution of restricted-range birds. *Global Ecology and Biogeography Letters*, **5**, 281–304.

Lovejoy, T. E. & Hannah, L. (2005). *Climate Change and Biodiversity*. New Haven, Conn.: Yale University Press.

Lucas, L. K., Fries, J. N., Gabor, C. R. & Nice, C. C. (2009). Genetic variation and structure in *Eurycea nana*, a federally threatened salamander endemic to the San Marcos Springs. *Journal of Herpetology*, **43**, 220–227.

Lukas, K. E. & Ross, S. R. (2005). Zoo visitor knowledge and attitudes towards gorillas and chimpanzees. *Journal of Environmental Education*, **36**, 33–48.

Luo, S.-J., Kim, J.-H., Johnson, W. E., Walt, Jvd., Martenson, J., *et al.* (2004). Phylogeography and genetic ancestry of tigers (*Panthera tigris*). *PLoS Biology* **2**(12): e442. doi:10.1371/journal.pbio.0020442.

Luong, L. T., Heath, B. D. & Polak, M. (2007). Host inbreeding increases susceptibility to ectoparasitism. *Journal of Evolutionary Biology*, **20**, 79–86.

Lynch, J. M. & Hayden, T. J. (1993). Multivariate morphometrics and the biogeography of Irish mustelids. In *Biogeography of Ireland: Past, Present* and *Future*, eds. M. J. Costello & K. S. Kelly. Dublin: Irish Biogeographical Society, pp. 25–34.

Lynch, M. & Lande, R. (1998). The critical effective size for a genetically secure population. *Animal Conservation*, **1**, 70–72.

Lynch, M., Burger, R., Butcher, D. & Gabriel, W. (1993). The mutational meltdown in asexual populations. *Journal of Heredity*, **84**, 339–344.

MacArthur, R. H. (1965). Patterns of species diversity. *Biological Reviews*, **40**, 510–533.

Mace, G. M. (1994a). An investigation into methods for categorizing the conservation status of species. In *Large Scale Ecology and Conservation Biology*, eds. P. J. Edwards, R. M. May & N. R. Webb. Oxford: Blackwell, pp. 295–314.

Mace, G. M. (1994b). Classifying threatened species: means and ends. *Philosophical Transactions of the Royal Society of London*, **344**, 91–97.

Mace, G. M. & Lande, R. (1991). Assessing extinction threats: towards a reassessment of IUCN endangered species categories. *Conservation Biology*, **5**, 148–157.

Mace, G. M., Balmford, A., Boitani, L. *et al.* (2000). It's time to work together and stop duplicating conservation efforts. *Nature*, **405**, 393.

MacKenzie, J. (1988). *The Empire of Nature: Hunting, Conservation, and British Imperialism*. Manchester, UK: Manchester University Press.

MacKinnon, K. & MacKinnon, J. (1991). Habitat protection and reintroduction programmes. In *Beyond Captive Breeding: Reintroducing Endangered Mammals to the Wild*, ed. J. H. W. Gipps, Symposia, Zoological Society of London 62. Oxford: Clarendon Press, pp. 173–196.

Madsen, T., Shine, R., Olsson, M. & Wittzell, H. (1999). Restoration of an inbred adder population. *Nature*, **402**, 34–35.

Magin, C. D., Johnson, T. H., Groombridge, B., Jenkins, M. & Smith, H. (1994). Species extinctions, endangerment and captive breeding. In *Creative Conservation: Interactive Management of Captive and Wild Animals*, eds. P. J. S. Olney, G. M. Mace & A. T. C. Feistner. London: Chapman and Hall, pp. 3–31.

Male, T. D. & Bean, M. J. (2005). Measuring progress in US endangered species conservation. *Ecology Letters*, **9**, 986–992.

Mallet, J. (1995). A species definition for the modern synthesis. *Trends in Ecology and Evolution*, **10**, 294–299.

Mallet, J. (2001). The speciation revolution (Commentary). *Journal of Evolutionary Biology*, **14**, 887–888.

Mallet, J. (2007). Species, concepts of. In *Encyclopedia of Biodiversity*, ed. S. A. Levin. Elsevier, Oxford. Online update, pp. 1–15.

Mallinson, J. J. C. (1978). Cocktail orangutans and the need to preserve pure bred stock. *Dodo, Journal of the Jersey Wildlife Preservation Trust*, **15**, 69–77.

Mallinson, J. J. C. (2003). A sustainable future for zoos and their role in wildlife conservation. *Human Dimensions of Wildlife*, **8**, 59–63.

Mann, K. H. & Breen, P. A. (1972). The relationship between lobster abundance, sea urchins, lobsters and kelp beds. *Journal of the Fisheries Research Board of Canada*, **29**, 603–609.

Maple, T. L. (1979). Great apes in captivity: the good, the bad and the ugly. In *Captivity and Behaviour*, eds. J. Erwin, T. L. Maple & G. Mitchell. New York: Van Nostrand Reinhold, pp. 239–273.

Maple, T. (1995). Towards a responsible zoo agenda. In *Ethics on the Ark: Zoos, Animal Welfare, and Wildlife Conservation*, eds. **B. G. Norton, M. Hutchins, E. F. Stevens & T. L. Maple.** Washington, DC: Smithsonian Institute Press, pp. 20–30.

Maple, T., McManamon, R. & Stevens, E. (1995). Defining the good zoo: Animal care, maintenance, and welfare. In *Ethics on the Ark: Zoos, Animal Welfare, and Wildlife Conservation*, eds. **B. G. Norton, M. Hutchins, E. F. Stevens & T. L. Maple.** Washington, DC: Smithsonian Institute Press, pp. 219–234.

Marcellini, D. L. & Jenssen, T. A. (1988). Visitor behavior in the National Zoo's reptile house. *Zoo Biology*, **7**, 329–338.

Marchetti, M. P. & Nevitt, G. A. (2003). Effects of habitat enrichment on brain structures in rainbow trout (*Oncorhynchus mykiss*). *Environmental Biology of Fishes*, **66**, 9–14.

Marcot, B. G. & Flather, C. H. (2007). Species-level strategies for conserving rare or little known species. In *Conservation of Rare or Little-Known Species*, eds. **M. G. Raphael & R. Molina.** Washington, DC: Island Press, pp. 125–164.

Marešováa, J. & Frynta, D. (2008). Noah's Ark is full of common species attractive to humans: The case of boid snakes in zoos. *Ecological Economics*, **64**, 554–558.

Margan, S. H., Nurthen, R. K., Montgomery, M. E. *et al.* (1998). Single large or several small? Population fragmentation in the captive management of endangered species. *Zoo Biology*, **17**, 467–480.

Margules, C. R. & Pressey, R. L. (2000). Systematic conservation planning. *Nature*, **405**, 243–253.

Margules, C. R. & Sarkar, S. (2007). *Systematic Conservation Planning*. Cambridge: Cambridge University Press.

Margules, C. R., Pressey, R. L. & Williams, P. H. (2002). Representing biodiversity: data and procedures for identifying priority areas for conservation. *Journal of Biosciences (suppl. 2)*, **27**, 309–326.

Marino, L., Lilienfeld, S. O., Malamud, R., Nobis, N. & Broglio, R. (2010). Do zoos and aquariums promote attitude change in visitors? A critical evaluation of the American zoo and aquarium study. *Society and Animals*, **18**, 126–138.

Markowitz, H. (1982). *Behavioural Enrichment in Zoos*. Van Nostrand Reinhold, New York.

Markwell, K. & Cushing, N. (2009). The serpent's stare meets the tourist's gaze: strategies of display at the Australian Reptile Park. *Current Issues in Tourism*, **12**, 475–488.

Marriner, L. M. & Drickamer, L. C. (1994). Factors influencing stereotyped behaviour of primates in a zoo. *Zoo Biology*, **13**, 267–275.

Marshall, T. C. & Spalton, J. A. (2000). Simultaneous inbreeding and outbreeding depression in reintroduced Arabian oryx. *Animal Conservation*, **3**, 241–248.

Martín-López, B., Montes, C., Ramírez, L. & Benayas, J. (2009). What drives policy decision-making related to species conservation? *Biological Conservation*, **142**, 1370–1380.

Mason, G. J. (1993). Forms of stereotypic behaviour. In *Stereotypic Animal Behviour: Fundamentals and Applications to Welfare*, eds. **A. B. Lawrence & J. Rushen.** Wallingford, UK: CAB International, pp. 7–40.

Mason, G. J., Cooper, J. & Clareborough, C. (2001). Frustrations of furfarmed mink. *Nature*, **410**, 35–36.

Mason, P. (2000). Zoo tourism: the need for more research. *Journal of Sustainable Tourism*, **8**, 333–339.

Mathews, F., Orros, M., McLaren, G., Gelling, M., & Foster, R. (2005). Keeping fit on the ark: assessing the suitability of captive-bred animals for release. *Biological Conservation*, **121**, 569–577.

Maunder, M. & Byers, O. (2005). The IUCN Technical Guidelines on the Management of Ex Situ Populations for Conservation: reflecting major changes in the application of ex situ conservation. *Oryx*, **39**, 95–98.

May, R. M. (1988). How many species are there on earth? *Science*, **241**, 1441–1444.

May, R. M. (1991). The role of ecological theory in planning re-introduction of endangered species. In *Beyond Captive Breeding: Re-introducing Endangered Mammals to the Wild*, ed. **J. H. W. Gipps.** London: Zoological Society of London, pp. 145–164.

May, R. M. (1992). How many species inhabit the Earth? *Scientific American*, **267**, 42–48.

Mazák, J. H. & **Groves, C. P.** (2006). A taxonomic revision of the tigers (*Panthera tigris*) of Southeast Asia. *Mammalian Biology*, **71**, 268–287.

Mazur, N. (1995). Perceptions of the role of zoos in conservation: an Australasian case study. In *Proceedings of the ARAZPA/ASZK Conference*. Perth, W.A.: ARAZPA/ASZK, pp. 102–109.

Mazur, N. (1996). Zoos, conservation groups, and government wildlife agencies: Partners, colleagues, or adversaries. In *Nature Conservation: The Role of Networks*, eds. **D. A. Saunders, J. L. Craig** & **E. M. Mattiske.** Chipping Norton NSW, Australia: Surrey Beatty and Sons, pp. 460–466.

Mazur, N. A. (1997). *Contextualising the Role of the Zoo in Conservation: An Australian Experience.* Unpublished PhD dissertation, University of Adelaide, South Australia.

Mazur, N. (2001). *After the Ark: Environmental Policy-Making and the Zoo.* Victoria, Australia: Melbourne University Press.

Mazur, N. A. & **Clark, T. W.** (2001). Zoos and Conservation: Policy Making and Organizational Challenges. In *Species and Ecosystem Conservation: An Interdisciplinary Approach*, eds. **T. W. Clark, M. J. Stevenson, K. Ziegelmayer** & **M. B. Rutherford,** Bulletin Series Yale School of Forestry & Environmental Studies, No. 105. New Haven: Yale University.

McBride, M. F., Wilson, K. A., Bode, M. & **Possingham, H. P.** (2007). Incorporating the effects of socioeconomic uncertainty into priority setting for conservation investment. *Conservation Biology*, **21**, 1463–1474.

Mc Parland, S., Kearney, F. & **Berry, D. P.** (2009). Purging of inbreeding depression within the Irish Holstein-Friesian population. *Genetics Selection Evolution*, **41**. doi:10.1186/1297–9686–41–16.

McEwan, P. (1986). *Environmental Enrichment: An Artificial Termite Mound for Orangutans.* Potters Bar, UK: UFAW.

McGrew, W. C., Brennan, J. A. & **Russell, J.** (1986). An artificial "gum-tree" for marmosets (*Callithrix j. jacchus*). *Zoo Biology*, **5**, 45–50.

McIntosh, R. P. (1967). An index of diversity and the relation of certain concepts of diversity. *Ecology*, **48**, 392–404.

McKenzie, S. M., Chamove, A. S. & **Feistner, A. T. C.** (1986). Floor coverings and handing screens alter arboreal monkey behaviour. *Zoo Biology*, **5**, 339–348.

McLachlan, J. S., Hellmann, J. J. & **Schwartz, M. W.** (2007). A framework for debate of assisted migration in an era of climate change. *Conservation Biology*, **21**, 297–302.

McNeely, J. A., Miller, K. R., Reid, W. V., Mittermeier, R. A. & **Werner, T. B.** (1990). *Conserving the World's Biological Diversity.* Gland, Switzerland and Washington DC: IUCN.

McNeely, J. A. (2002). The role of taxonomy in conserving biodiversity. *Journal for Nature Conservation*, **10**, 145–153.

McNeely, J. A. & **Miller, K. R.** (eds.) (1985). *National Parks, Conservation, and Development: the Role of Protected Areas in Sustaining Society.* Washington, DC: Smithsonian Institution Press.

Meffe, G. K. (2001). The context of conservation biology. *Conservation Biology*, **15**, 815–816.

Meffe, G. K. & **Carroll, C. R.** (1994). *Principles of Conservation Biology.* Sunderland, MA: Sinauer Associates Inc.

Meffe, G. K. & **Carroll, C. R.** (1997). *Principles of Conservation Biology.* Sunderland, MA: Sinauer Associates.

Meffert, L. M., Mukana, N., Hicks, S. K. & **Day, S. B.** (2005). Testing alternative captive breeding strategies with the subsequent release into the wild. *Zoo Biology*, **24**, 375–392.

Meir, E., Andelman, S. & **Possingham, H. P.** (2004). Does conservation planning matter in a dynamic and uncertain world? *Ecology Letters*, **7**, 615–622.

Melbourne, B. A. & **Hastings, A.** (2008). Extinction risk depends strongly on factors contributing to stochasticity. *Nature*, **454**, 100–103.

Melfi, V. A. & **Feistner, A. T. C.** (2002). A comparison of the activity budgets of wild and captive Sulawesi crested black macaques (*Macaca nigra*). *Animal Welfare*, **11**, 213–222.

Melfi, V. A. & **Hosey, G. R.** (editors). (2005). Primates in zoos. *Applied Animal Behaviour Science (Special Issue)*, **90**, 93–181.

Metrick, A. & **Weitzman, M. L.** (1996). Patterns of behavior in endangered species preservation. *Land Economics*, **72**, 1–16.

Metrick, A. & **Weitzman, M. L.** (1998). Conflicts and choices in biodiversity preservations. *Journal of Economic Perspectives*, **12**, 21–34.

Meyer-Holzapfel, M. (1968). Abnormal behaviour in zoo animals. In *Abnormal Behaviour in Animals*, ed. **M. W. Fox.** Philadelphia: W.B. Saunders Company, pp. 476–503.

Meylan, A. B. & **Ehrenfeld, D.** (2000). Conservation of marine turtles. In *Turtle Conservation*, ed. **M. W. Klemens.** Washington, DC: Smithsonian Institution Press, pp. 96–125.

Millenium Ecosystem Assessment (2005). *Ecosystems and Human Well-being: Synthesis*. Washington, DC: Island Press.

Miller, B., Biggins, D., Hanebury, L. & **Vargas, A.** (1994). Reintroduction of the black-footed ferret (*Mustela nigripes*). In *Creative Conservation: Interactive Management of Wild and Captive Animals*, eds. **P. J. S. Olney, G. M. Mace** & **A. T. C. Feistner.** London: Chapman & Hall, pp. 455–464.

Miller, B., Conway, W., Reading, R. P. *et al.* (2004). Evaluating the conservation mission of zoos, aquariums, botanical gardens and natural history museums. *Conservation Biology*, **18**, 86–93.

Miller, R. M., Rodríguez, J. P., Aniskowicz-Fowler, T. *et al.* (2006). Extinction risk and conservation priorities. *Science*, **313**, 441.

Miller, R. R. & **Fitzsimmons, J. M.** (1971). *Ameca splendens*, a new genus and species of Goodeid fish from Western Mexico, with remarks on the classification of the Goodeidae. *Copeia*, **1971**, 1–13.

Mills, M. G. L., Ellis, S., Woodruffe, R. *et al.* (1998). Population and habitat viability analysis for the African wild dog (*Lycaon pictus*) in southern Africa: final report from the workshop held 13–17 October 1997 in Pretoria, South Africa. Canid Specialist Group, IUCN Species Survival Commission Conservation Breeding Specialist Group, IUCN Species Survival Commission.

Mishler, B. D. (1999). Getting rid of species? In *Species: New Interdisciplinary Essays*, ed. **R. Wilson.** Cambridge, MA: MIT Press, pp. 307–315.

Mitchell, G. F. (1994). A perspective of zoos in a changing environment. *Australian Academy of Technological Sciences and Engineering – Focus*, **81**, 23–25.

Mitrus, S. (2005). Headstarting in European pond turtles (*Emys orbicularis*): Does it work? *Amphibia-Reptilia*, **26**, 333–341.

Mittermeier, R. A. (1988). Primate diversity and the tropical forest: case studies from Brazil and Madagascar and the importance of the megadiversity countries. In *Biodiversity*, ed. **E. O. Wilson.** Washington, DC: National Academy Press, pp. 145–154.

Mittermeier, R. A., Robles Gil, P. & **Mittermeier, C. G.** (1997). *Megadiversity*. Conservation International and Agrupación Sierra Madre, Monterrey, Mexico: CEMEX.

Mittermeier, R. A., Myers, N., Thomsen, J. B., da Fonseca, G. A. B. & **Olivieri, S.** (1998). Biodiversity hotspots and major tropical wilderness areas: approaches to setting conservation priorities. *Conservation Biology*, **12**, 516–520.

Mittermeier, R. A., Myers, N., Gil, P. R. & **Mittermeier, C. G.** (1999). *Hotspots: Earth's Biologically Richest and Most Endangered Terrestrial Ecoregions*. Conservation International and Agrupación Sierra Madre, Monterrey, Mexico: CEMEX.

Mittermeier, R. A., Mittermeier, C. G., Robles-Gil, P. R. *et al.* (2002). *Wilderness: Earth's Last Wild Places*. Conservation International and Agrupación Sierra Madre, Monterrey, Mexico: CEMEX.

Mittermeier, R. A., Mittermeier, C. G., Brooks, T. M. *et al.* (2003). Wilderness and biodiversity conservation. *Proceedings of the National Academy of Sciences (USA)*, **100**, 10 309–10 313.

Mittermeier, R. A., Robles-Gil, P., Hoffmann, M. *et al.* (2004). *Hotspots Revisited: Earth's Biologically Richest and Most Endangered Terrestrial Ecoregions.* Conservation International and Agrupacion Sierra Madre, Monterrey, Mexico: CEMEX.

Mohamed Bin Zayed Species Conservation Fund (2010). What is the Mohamed bin Zayed Species Conservation Fund? [http://www.mbzspeciesconservation.org/]

Montgomery, M. E., Ballou, J. D., Nurthen, R. K. *et al.* (1997). Minimizing kinship in captive breeding programs. *Zoo Biology*, **16**, 377–389.

Montgomery, M. E., Woodworth, L. M., England, P. R., Briscoe, D. A. & Frankham, R. (2010). Widespread selective sweeps affecting microsatellites in *Drosophila* populations adapting to captivity: implications for captive breeding programs. *Biological Conservation*, **143**, 1842–1849.

Moore, J. L., Folkmann, M., Balmford, A. *et al.* (2003). Heuristic and optimal solutions for set-covering problems in conservation biology. *Ecography*, **26**, 595–601.

Morey & Associates (2000, 2001, 2004). *Cultural Attraction Attendance Report.* New York: Morey Group, Strategic Direction for Cultural Attractions.

MORI (2005). *Science in Society.* Findings from Qualitative and Quantitative Research Conducted for the Office of Science and Technology, Department of Trade and Industry [http://www.bis.gov.uk/files/file14950.pdf]

Morgan, G. (1986). *Images of Organization.* Beverly Hills, California: Sage Publications.

Morgan, K. N. & Tromborg, C. T. (2007). Sources of stress in captivity. *Applied Animal Behaviour Science*, **102**, 262–302.

Morin, P. A., Messier, J. & Woodruff, D. S. (1994). DNA extraction, amplification, and direct sequencing from hornbill feathers. *Journal of the Scientific Society of Thailand*, **20**, 31–41.

Morin, P. A., Chambers, K. E., Boesch, C. & Vigilant, L. (2001). Quantitative PCR analysis of DNA from noninvasive samples for accurate microsatellite genotyping of wild chimparzees (*Pan troglodytes*). *Molecular Ecology*, **10**, 1835–1844.

Moritz, C. (1994). Defining 'evolutionary significant units' for conservation. *Trends in Ecology & Evolution*, **9**, 373–375.

Moritz, C. (1999). Conservation units and translocations: strategies for conserving evolutionary processes. *Hereditas*, **130**, 217–228.

Morris, D. (1964). The response of animals to a restrained environment. *Symposium of the Zoological Society of London*, **13**, 99–118.

Morris, D. J. (1960). An analysis of animal popularity. *International Zoo Yearbook*, **2**, 60–61.

Morton, D. B. & Griffiths, P. H. M. (1985). Guidelines on the recognition of pain, distress and discomfort in experimental animals and an hypothesis for assessment. *Veterinary Record*, **116**, 431–436.

Morton, M. N. (2009). *Management of Critical Species on Saint Lucia: Species Profiles and Management Recommendations.* Technical Report No. 13 to the National Forest Demarcation and Bio-Physical Resource Inventory Project, FCG International Ltd, Helsinki, Finland.

Moss, A. & Esson, M. (2010). Visitor interest in zoo animals and the implications for collection planning and zoo education programmes. *Zoo Biology*, **28**, 1–17.

Mrosovsky, N. (1997). IUCN's credibility critically endangered. *Nature*, **389**, 436.

Mullan, B. & Marvin, G. (1987). *Zoo Culture*, London: Weidenfeld and Nicholson.

Munton, P. (1987). Concepts of threat to the survival of species used in Red Data books and similar compilations. In *The Road to Extinction*, eds. R. Fitter & M. Fitter. Gland, Switzerland: IUCN, pp. 72–95.

Myers Jr., O. E., Saunders, C. D. & Birjulin, A. A. (2004). Emotional dimensions of watching zoo animals: an experience sampling study building on insights from psychology. *Curator*, **47**, 299–321.

Myers, N. (1979). *The Sinking Ark: A New Look at the Problem of Disappearing Species.* Oxford: Pergamon Press.

Myers, N. (1988). Threatened biotas: 'hot spots' in tropical forests. *The Environmentalist*, **8**, 187–208.

Myers, N. (1990). The biodiversity challenge: expanded hot-spots analysis. *The Environmentalist*, **10**, 243–256.

Myers, N. (1991). Extinction "Hot Spots". *Science*, **254**, 919.

Myers, N., Mittermeier, R. A., Mittermeier, C. G., da Fonseca, G. A. B. & Kent, J. (2000). Biodiversity hotspots for conservation priorities. *Nature*, **403**, 853–858.

Nagelkerken, I., Pors, L. & Hoetjes, P. (2003). Swimming behaviour and dispersal patterns of headstarted loggerhead turtles *Caretta caretta*. *Aquatic Ecology*, **37**, 183–190.

Nagy, K. A., Girard, I. A. & Brown, T. K. (1999). Energetics of free-ranging mammals, reptiles, and birds. *Annual Review of Nutrition*, **19**, 247–277.

Narayan, G., Oliver, W., Fa, J. E. & Funk, S. M. (2008). Das Zwergwildsch-ein. In *Wilde Schweine und Flusspferde*, eds. **A. Macdonald & U. Ganslosser.** Fürth, Germany: Filander Verlag.

National Curriculum Primary Handbook (2010). *The National Curriculum Handbook for Primary Teachers in England.* London: Qualifications and Curriculum Authority.

NIH (National Institutes of Health) (1991). *Nonhuman Primate Management Plan.* Bethesda: Office of Animal Care and Use.

Natural History Museum (2008). Sharing our work 06/08. A voice of authority on the natural world. Annual Review. [http://www.nhm.ac.uk/resources-rx/files/annual-review-06-08-20962.pdf]

Naughton-Treves, L., Buck Holland, M. & Brandon, K. (2005). The role of protected areas in conserving biodiversity and sustaining local livelihoods. *Annual Review of Environment and Resources*, **30**, 219–252.

Naujokaitis-Lewis, I. R., Curtis, J. M. R., Arcese, P. & Rosenfeld, J. (2009). Sensitivity analyses of spatial population viability analysis models for species at risk and habitat conservation planning. *Conservation Biology*, **23**, 225–229.

Newmark, W. D. (1991). Tropical forest fragmentation and the local extinction of understorey birds in the eastern Usumbara Mountains, Tanzania. *Conservation Biology*, **5**, 67–78.

Nolan, M. A. (1975). Importing primates for research. In *Primate Utilization and Conservation*, eds. **G. Bermant & D. G. Lindburg.** New York: Wiley and Sons, pp. 15–19.

Norton, B. G., Hutchins, M., Stevens, E. F. & Maple, T. L. (eds.) (1995). *Ethics on the Ark: Zoos, Animal Welfare.* Washington DC: Smithsonian Institute Press.

Nsubuga, A. M., Holzman, J., Chemnick, L. G. & Ryder, O. A. (2010). The cryptic genetic structure of the North American captive gorilla population. *Conservation Genetics*, **11**, 161–172.

NSW National Parks and Wildlife Service (2002). *Approved Recovery Plan for the Lord Howe Woodhen.* Hurtsville, NSW: NSW National Parks and Wildlife Service.

Nunney, L. & Campbell, K. A. (1993). Assessing minimum viable population size: demography meets population genetics. *Trends in Ecology and Evolution*, **8**, 234–239.

Oakleaf, J. K., Stark, D., Overy, P. & Smith, N. (2004). *Mexican Wolf Recovery: Technical Component of the Five-year Program Review and Assessment.* US Fish and Wildlife Service.

O'Brien, S. J. & Evermann, J. F. (1988). Interactive influence of infectious disease and genetic diversity in natural populations. *Trends in Ecology and Evolution*, **3**, 254–259.

O'Brien, J., McCracken, G. F., Say, L. & Hayden, T. J. (2007). Rodrigues fruit bats (*Pteropus rodricensis*, Megachiroptera: Pteropodidae) retain genetic diversity despite population declines and founder events. *Conservation Genetics*, **8**, 1073–1082.

O'Connor, R. J. (1986). Biological characteristics of invaders among bird species in Britain. *Philosophical Transactions of the Royal Society of London B*, **314**, 583–598.

O'Connor, T. (2009). *Trends in Zoo and Aquarium Exhibit Interpretation. Report for the Oregon Coast Aquarium.* [http://www.izea.net/education/Trends%20in%20Zoo%20and%20Aquarium%20Exhibit%20Interpretation.pdf]

Odum, W. E. (1982). Environmental degradation and the tyranny of small decisions. *BioScience*, **32**, 728–729.

Office of National Statistics (2003). Membership of selected environmental organisations, 1971–2002: Social Trends, 33.

Office for National Statistics (2009). [http://www.statistics.gov.uk/cci/nugget.asp?id=6]

Ogden, J., Gentile, C. & Revard, B. (2004). Trends in conservation education. A primer. *AZA Communiqué*, August 2004, pp. 18–20.

Ogden, J., Routman, E., Vernon, C. *et al.* (2004). Inspiring understanding, caring and conservation action: do we or don't we? *AZA Communiqué, December* 2004, pp. 10–13.

O'Grady, J. J., Brook, B. W., Reed, D. H. *et al.* (2006). Realistic levels of inbreeding depression strongly affect extinction risk in wild populations. *Biological Conservation*, **133**, 42–51.

O'Grady, J. J., Reed, D. H., Brook, B. W. & Frankham, R. (2008). Extinction risk scales better to generations than years. *Animal Conservation*, **11**, 442–451.

Oldfield, M. L. (1984). *The Value of Conserving Genetic Resources*. US Department of Interior, Washington, D.C.: National Park Service.

Oldfield, M. L. & Alcorn, J. B. (1987). Conservation of traditional agroecosystems. *BioScience*, **37**, 199–208.

Oliehoek, P. A. (2009). *Genetic Conservation of Endangered Animal Populations*. Unpublished PhD thesis, Wageningen: Wageningen Universiteit.

Ollason, R. J. (1993). Getting the message across. *Journal of the International Association of Zoo Educators*, **29**, 186–190.

Olson, D. M. & Dinerstein, E. (1998). The Global 200: A representation approach to conserving the Earth's most biologically valuable ecoregions. *Conservation Biology*, **12**, 502–515.

Olson, D. M. & Dinerstein, E. (2002). The Global 200: priority ecoregions for global conservation. *Annals of the Missouri Botanical Gardens*, **89**, 199–224.

Olson, D. M., Dinerstein, E., Wikramanayake, E. D., *et al.* (2001). Terrestrial ecoregions of the world: a new map of life on earth. *BioScience*, **51**, 933–938.

O'Regan, H. J. & Kitchener, A. C. (2005). The effects of captivity on the morphology of captive, domesticated and feral mammals. *Mammal Review*, **35**, 215–230.

O'Riordan, T. (1981). *Environmentalism*. London: Pion.

Ortego, J., Aparicio, J. M., Calabuig, G. & Cordero, P. J. (2007). Risk of ectoparasitism and kestrel population genetic diversity in a wild lesser kestrel population. *Molecular Ecology*, **16**, 3712–3720.

Ounsted, M. L. (1991). Re-introducing birds: lessons to be learned for mammals. In *Beyond Captive Breeding: Reintroducing Endangered Mammals to the Wild*, ed. **J. H. W. Gipps,** Symposia, Zoological Society of London 62. Oxford: Clarendon Press, pp.

Paehlke, R. & Torgerson, D. (eds.) (1990). *Managing Leviathan: Environmental Politics and the Administrative State*. Peterborough, Ontario, Canada: Broadview Press.

Pagel, M., May, R. M. & Collie, A. (1991). Ecological aspects of the geographic distribution and diversity of mammal species. *American Naturalist*, **137**, 791–815.

Paine, R. T. (1966). Food web complexity and species diversity. *American Naturalist*, **100**, 65–75.

Paine, R. T. (1974). Intertidal community structure: experimental studies on the relationship between a dominant competitor and its principal predator. *Oecologia (Berlin)*, **15**, 93–120.

Painter, M. (1988). Public management: fad or fallacy. *Australian Journal of Public Administration*, **47**, 1–3.

Parmesan, C. & Yohe, G. (2003). A globally coherent fingerprint of climate change impacts across natural systems. *Nature*, **421**, 37–42.

Parrish, J. D., Braun, D. P. & Unnasch, R. S. (2003). Are we conserving what we say we are? Measuring ecological integrity within protected areas. *BioScience*, **53**, 851–860.

Paterson, S., Wilson, K. & Pemberton, J. M. (1998). Major histocompatibility complex variation associated with juvenile survival and parasite resistance in a large unmanaged ungulate population (*Ovis aries* L.). *Proceedings of the National Academy of Sciences of the United States of America*, **95**, 3714–3719.

Patrick, P. G., Mathews, C. E., Ayers, D. F. & Tunnicliffe, S. D. (2007). Conservation and education: prominent themes in zoo mission statements. *Journal of Environmental Education*, **38**, 53–59.

Patterson, B. R. & Murray, D. L. (2008). Flawed population viability analysis can result in misleading population assessment: A case study for wolves in Algonquin Park, Canada. *Biological Conservation*, **141**, 669–680.

Pedrono, M. & Smith, L. L. (2003). Testudinae, land tortoises. In *The Natural History of Madagascar*, eds. S. M. Goodman & J. P. Benstead. Chicago: The University of Chicago Press.

Pedrono, M., Smith, L. L., Clobert, J., Massot, M. & Sarrazin, F. (2004). Wild-captive metapopulation viability analysis. *Biological Conservation*, **119**, 463–473.

Pérez-Buitrago, N., García, M. A., Sabat, A. *et al.* (2008). Do headstart programs work? Survival and body condition in headstarted Mona Island iguanas *Cyclura cornuta stejnegeri*. *Endangered Species Research*, **6**, 55–65.

Perkins, L. (1998). Conservation and management of orang-utans *Pongo pygmaeus* ssp. *International Zoo Yearbook*, **36**, 109–112.

Perrow, M. R. & Davy, A. J. (2002). *Handbook of Ecological Restoration: Volume 1 Principles of Restoration*. Cambridge: Cambridge University Press.

Peterman, R. M., Walters, C. J. & Hillborn, R. (1978). Systems analysis of Pacific salmon management problems. In *Adaptive Environmental Assessment and Management*, ed. C. S. Holling. London: Wiley, pp. 158–188.

Peters, R. H. (1983). *The Ecological Implications of Body Size*. Cambridge Studies in Ecology. Cambridge: Cambridge University Press.

Pickard, A. R. & Holt, W. V. (2004). Cryopreservation as a supporting measure in species conservation; "not the frozen zoo!". In *Life in the Frozen State*, eds. B. J. Fuller, N. Lane & E. E. Benson, pp. 393–414.

Pimm, S. L. (1987). The snake that ate Guam. *Trends in Ecology and Evolution*, **2**, 293–295.

Pimm, S. (2000). Against triage, the California condor – A saga of natural history and conservation. *Science*, **289**, 2289.

Pimm, S. L., Jones, H. L. & Diamond, J. (1988). On the risk of extinction. *American Naturalist*, **132**, 757–785.

Pimm, S. L., Russell, G. J., Gittleman, J. L. & Brooks, T. M. (1995). The future of biodiversity. *Science*, **269**, 347–350.

Pollak, J. P., Lacy, R. C. & Ballou, J. D. (2002). *PM2000 (PopulationManagement 2000)*. Brookfield: Chicago Zoological Society.

Pong-Wong, R. & Woolliams, J. A. (2007). Optimisation of contribution of candidate parents to maximise genetic gain and restricting inbreeding using semidefinite programming. *Genetics Selection Evolution*, **39**, 3–25.

Poole, T. B. (1987). Environmental enrichment for captive vertebrates. In *Topics in Wild Animal Husbandry*, ed. R. Colley. Proceedings of Symposium 12 of the Association of British Wild Animal Keepers. London: ABWAK, pp. 23–30.

Poole, T. B. (1995). Behavioural problems in captivity in general and their management. In *Proceedings of the 2nd International Conference on Environmental Enrichment, Copenhagen 21–25 August 1995*, pp. 118–130.

Poole, T. B. (1998). Meeting a mammal's psychological needs. In *Second Nature: Environmental Enrichment for Captive Animals*, eds. D. J. Shepherdson, J. D. Mellen & M. Hutchins. Washington: Smithsonian Institution, pp. 83–96.

Possingham, H. P. & Davies, I. (1995). Alex – a model for the viability analysis of spatially structured populations. *Biological Conservation*, **73**, 143–150.

Possingham, H. P., Andelman, S. J., Burgman, M. A., Medellín, R. A., Master, L. L. & Keith, D. A. (2002). Limits to the use of threatened species lists. *Trends in Ecology & Evolution*, **11**, 503–507.

Poulsen, E. (1994). Think like a bird: A practical guide to enrichment. *The Shape of Enrichment*, **3**, 3–5.

Poulton, E. B. (1904). What is a species? (Presidential address to the Entomological Society of London, Jan. 1904). *Proceedings of the Entomological Society London* 1903.

Prendergast, J., Quinn, R. M., Lawton, J. H., Eversham, B. C. & Gibbons, D. W. (1993). Rare species, the coincidence of diversity hotspots and conservation strategies. Nature, **365**, 335–337.

Pressey, R. L. & Nicholls, A. O. (1989). Efficiency in conservation evaluation: Scoring versus iterative approaches. *Biological Conservation*, **50**, 199–218.

Price, E. C., Feistner, A. T. C., Carroll, J. B. & Young, J. A. (1989). Establishment of a free-ranging group of cotton-top tamarins *Saguinus oedipus* at the Jersey Wildlife Preservation Trust. *Dodo, Journal of the Jersey Wildlife Preservation Trust*, **26**, 60–69.

Price, E. O. (1988). Behavior genetics and the process of animal domestication. In *Genetics and the Behavior of Domestic Animals*, ed. T. Grandin. New York: Academic Press, pp. 31–65.

Price, E. O. (1999). Behavioral development in animals undergoing domestication. *Applied Animal Behaviour Science*, **65**, 245–271.

Prideaux, B. & Coghlan, A. (2006). *Wildlife Tourism in TNQ: an Overview of Visitor Preferences for Wildlife Experiences*. Cairns: James Cook University, Tourism Research Report 3.

Proença, V. M., Pereira, H. M. & Vicente, L. (2008). Organismal complexity is an indicator of species existence value. *Frontiers in Ecology and Environment*, **6**, 298–299.

Purvis, A. & Hector, A. (2000). Getting the measure of biodiversity. *Nature*, **405**, 212–219.

Qian, H. & Ricklefs, R. E. (2008). Global concordance in diversity patterns of vascular plants and terrestrial vertebrates. *Ecology Letters*, **11**, 547–553.

Quantum Verzeichnis (2009). Schüling, 2009, 456 Seiten, mit CD-ROM, 15 × 21 cm, Ppb., ISBN 978-3-86523-129-1.

Rabb, G. B. (1994). The changing roles of zoological parks in conserving biological diversity. *American Zoologist*, **34**, 159–164.

Rabin, L. A. (2003). Maintaining behavioural diversity in captivity for conservation: natural behaviour management. *Animal Welfare*, **12**, 85–94.

Rabinowitz, D. (1981). Seven forms of rarity. In *The Biological Aspects of Rare Plant Conservation*, ed. H. Synge. Chichester: John Wiley & Sons, pp. 205–217.

Rabinowitz, D., Cairns, S. & Dillon, T. (1986). Seven forms of rarity and their frequency in the flora of the British Isles. In *Conservation Biology: The Science of Scarcity and Diversity*, ed. M. Soulé. Chichester: Wiley, pp. 182–204.

Radwan, J., Biedrzycka, A. & Babik, W. (2010). Does reduced MHC diversity decrease viability of vertebrate populations? *Biological Conservation*, **143**, 537–544.

Rahbek, C. (1993). Captive breeding – a useful tool in the preservation of biodiversity? *Biodiversity and Conservation*, **2**, 426–437.

Rajack, L. & Waren, N. (1996). The modern zoo: how do people perceive animals? *Applied Animal Behaviour Science*, **47**, 109–118.

Ralls, K. & Ballou, J. (1983). Extinction: lessons from zoos. In *Genetics and Conservation: a Reference for Managing Wild Animal and Plant Populations*, eds. C. M. Schonewald-Cox, S. M. Chambers, B. MacBryde & W. L. Thomas. Menlo Park, CA: Benjamin/Cummings, pp. 164–184.

Ralls, K. & Ballou, J. D. (2004). Genetic status and management of California Condors. *Condor*, **106**, 215–228.

Ralls, K., Ballou, J. D. & Templeton, A. R. (1988). Estimates of lethal equivalents and the cost of inbreeding in mammals. *Conservation Biology*, **2**, 185–193.

Ralls, K., Ballou, J. D., Rideout, B. A. & Frankham, R. (2000). Genetic management of chondrodystrophy in California condors. *Animal Conservation*, **3**, 145–153.

Raloff, J. (1989). Endangered species need more help. *Science News*, **135**, 79.

Ranta, P., Blom, T., Niemela, J., Joensuu, E. & Siitonen, M. (1998). The fragmented Atlantic rain forest of Brazil: size, shape and distribution of forest fragments. *Biodiversity and Conservation*, **7**, 385–403.

Raphling, B. & Serrell, B. (1993). Capturing affective learning. *Current Trends in Audience Research and Evaluation*, **7**, 57–62.

Raudsepp-Hearne, C., Peterson, G. D. & Bennett, E. M. (2010). Ecosystem service bundles for analyzing tradeoffs in diverse landscapes. *Proceedings of the National Academy of Sciences*, **107**, 5242–5247.

Raup, D. M. (1986). Biological extinctions in earth history. *Nature*, **317**, 384–385.

Raup, D. M. (1992). Large-body impact and extinction in the Phanerozoic: an interpretation. *Paleobiology*, **18**, 80–88.

Raven, P. H. (1976). Ethics and attitudes. In *Conservation of Threatened Plants*, ed. J. B. Simmons. New York: Plenum Press, pp. 155–179.

Rawlins, R. G. & Kessler, M. J. (1986). *The Cayo Santiago Macaques*. New York: SUNY Press.

Reade, L. S. & Waran, N. K. (1996). The modern zoo: How do people perceive zoo animals? *Applied Animal Behavior Science*, **47**, 109–118.

Reading, R. P. & Clark, T. W. (1997). Carnivore reintroductions: an interdisciplinary examination. In *Carnivore Behavior, Ecology, and Evolution*, vol. 2. Ithaca, NY, Cornell University Press, pp. 296–335.

Reading, R. P. & Miller, B. J. (2007). Attitudes and attitude change among zoo visitors. In *Zoos in the 21st Century. Catalysts for Conservation?*, eds. A. Zimmerman, M. Hatchwell, L. Dickie & C. West. Cambridge: Cambridge University Press, pp. 63–91.

Reagan, T. (1995). Are zoos morally defensible? In *Ethics on the Ark: Zoos, Animal Welfare and Wildlife Conservation*, eds. B. G. Norton, M. Hutchins, E. F. Stevens & T. L. Maple. Washington and London: Smithsonian Institution Press, pp. 38–51.

RENCTAS (Rede Nacional de Combate ao Tráfico de Animais Silvestres) (2001). *1st National Report on Wild Fauna Traffic*. Brasília, Brazil: RENCTAS.

Redford, K. H., Coppolillo, P., Sanderson, E. W. et al. (2003). Mapping the conservation landscape. *Conservation Biology*, **17**, 116–131.

Redshaw, M. & Mallinson, J. J. C. (1991). Stimulation of natural patterns of behaviour: Studies of golden lion tamarins and gorillas. In *Primate Responses to Environmental Change*, ed. H. O. Box, London: Chapman and Hall, pp. 217–238.

Reed, D. H. & Frankham, R. (2001). How closely correlated are molecular and quantitative measures of genetic variation? A meta-analysis. *Evolution*, **55**, 1095–1103.

Reed, D. H., Lowe, E. H., Briscoe, D. A. & Frankham, R. (2003a). Fitness and adaptation in a novel environment: Effect of inbreeding, prior environment, and lineage. *Evolution*, **57**, 1822–1828.

Reed, D. H., Lowe, E., Briscoe, D. A. & Frankham, R. (2003b). Inbreeding and extinction: Effects of rate of inbreeding. *Conservation Genetics*, **4**, 405–410.

Reed, D. H., O'Grady, J. J., Brook, B. W., Ballou, J. D. & Frankham, R. (2003c). Estimates of minimum viable population sizes for vertebrates and factors influencing those estimates. *Biological Conservation*, **113**, 23–34.

Reed, J. M., Walters, J. R., Emigh, T. E. & Seaman, D. E. (1993). Effective population size in Red-cockaded woodpeckers. *Conservation Biology*, **6**, 283–292.

Rees, S. (1994). Economic rationalism: an ideology of exclusion. *Australian Journal of Social Issues*, **29**, 171–185.

Rees, P. A. (2005). Will the EC Zoos Directive increase the conservation value of zoo research? *Oryx*, **39**, 128–131.

Rego, C., Rose, M. R. & Matos, M. (2007). Do species converge during adaptation? A case study in *Drosophila*. *Physiological and Biochemical Zoology*, **80**, 347–357.

Reid, W. V. & Miller, K. R. (1989). *Keeping Options Alive: The Scientific Basis for Conservation Biodiversity*. Washington DC: World Resources Institute.

Reid, J. M., Arcese, P. & Keller, L. F. (2003). Inbreeding depresses immune response in song sparrows (*Melospiza melodia*): direct and inter-generational effects. *Proceedings of the Royal Society, Series B*. 2003; **270**, 2151–2157.

Restani, M. & Marzluff, J. M. (2001). Avian conservation under the Endangered Species Act: expenditures versus recovery priorities, *Conservation Biology*, **5**, 1292–1299.

Restani, M. & Marzluff, J. M. (2002). Funding extinction? Biological needs and political realities in the allocation of resources to endangered species recovery. *BioScience*, **2**, 169–177.

Rhodes, R. (1996). Looking beyond managerialism. *Australian Journal of Public Administration*, **55**, 106–109.

Ricciardi, A. & Simberloff, D. (2009). Assisted colonization is not a viable conservation strategy. *Trends in Ecology and Evolution*, **24**, 248–253.

Richardson, D. M., Hellmann, J. J., Mclachlan, J. S. *et al.* (2009). Multidimensional evaluation of managed relocation. *Proceedings of the National Academy of Sciences of the United States of America*, **106**, 9721–9724.

Ricketts, T. H., Dinerstein, E., Boucher, T. *et al.* (2005). Pinpointing and preventing imminent extinctions. *Proceedings of the National Academy of Sciences (USA)*, **102**, 18497–18501.

Richter, C. P. (1943). Total self-regulatory functions in animals and human beings. *Harvey Lectures*, **38**, 63–103.

Riney, T. (1982). *Study and Management of Large Mammals*. Chichester: Wiley and Sons.

Ritchie, M. G., Hamill, R. M., Graves, J. A. *et al.* (2007). Sex and differentiation: population genetic divergence and sexual dimorphism in Mexican goodeid fish. *Journal of Evolutionary Biology*, **20**, 2048–2055.

Roberge, J.-M. & Angelstam, P. (2004). Usefulness of the umbrella species concept as a conservation tool. *Conservation Biology*, **18**, 76–85.

Robinson, J. G. (2006). Conservation biology and real-world conservation. *Conservation Biology*, **20**, 658–669.

Robinson, J. G. & Conway, W. G. (1995). Babies and bathwater. *Zoo Biology*, **14**, 29–31.

Robinson, J. G. & Redford, K. H. (1986). Intrinsic rate of natural increase in Neotropical forest mammals: relationship to phylogeny and diet. *Oecologia (Berlin)*, **68**, 516–520.

Robinson, M. H. (1988). Education through Bioparks. *BioScience*, **38**, 630–634.

Rodrigues, A. S. L., Andelman, S. J., Bakarr, M. I. *et al.* (2004a). Effectiveness of the global protected-area network in representing species diversity. *Nature*, **428**, 640–643.

Rodrigues, A. S. L., Akçakaya, H. R., Andelman, S. J. *et al.* (2004b). Global gap analysis: priority regions for expanding the global protected-area network. *BioScience*, **54**, 1092–1100.

Rodríguez-Clark, K. M. & Sánchez-Mercado, A. (2006). Population management of threatened taxa in captivity within their natural ranges: lessons from Andean bears (*Tremarctos ornatus*) in Venezuela. *Biological Conservation*, **129**, 134–148.

Rogers, L. (1988). Homing tendencies in large mammals – A review. In *Translocation of Wild Animals*, eds. **L. Nielsen & R. D. Brown**. Milwaukee, WI, & Kingsville, TX: The Wisconsin Humane Society, Inc. and the Caesar Kleberg Wildlife Research Institute, pp. 76–92.

Rolls, E. (1969). *They All Ran Wild*. London: Angus and Robertson.

Romer, A. S. (1949). Time series and trends in animal evolution. In *Genetics, Paleontology and Evolution*, eds. **G. L. Jepson, E. Mayr** & **G. G. Simpson.** Princeton: Princeton University Press. pp. 103–121.

Rosenweig, M. L. (1997). *Species Diversity in Space and Time*. Cambridge: Cambridge University Press.

Ross, S. R. & **Lukas, K. E.** (2005). Zoo visitor behaviour at an African ape exhibit. *Visitor Studies Today*, **8**, 4–12.

Rothfels, N. (2002). *Savages and Beasts: The Birth of the Modern Zoo*. Baltimore, Maryland: The Johns Hopkins University Press.

RSPCA (2007). Evaluation of the effectiveness of zoos in meeting conservation and education objectives. In *The Welfare State: Measuring animal welfare in the UK in 2006*, ed. RSPCA, Horsham, West Sussex, UK: Royal Society for the Prevention of Cruelty to Animals, pp. 95–98.

Rudnick, J. A. & **Lacy, R. C.** (2008). The impact of assumptions about founder relationships on the effectiveness of captive breeding strategies. *Conservation Genetics*, **9**, 1439–1450.

Russon, A. E. (2009). Orangutan rehabilitation and reintroduction. In *Orangutans: Geographic Variation in Behavioral Ecology and Conservation*, eds. **S. A. Wich, S. S. Utami, T. Mitra Setia** & **C. P. van Schaik.** Oxford: Oxford University Press, pp. 327–350.

Ruzzante, D. E. (1994). Domestication effects on aggressive and schooling behavior in fish. *Aquaculture*, **120**, 1–24.

Ryder, O. A. (1986). Species conservation and systematics: the dilemma of subspecies. *Trends in Ecology and Evolution*, **1**, 1–9.

Saccheri, I., Kuussaari, M., Kankare, M. *et al.* (1998). Inbreeding and extinction in a butterfly metapopulation. *Nature*, **392**, 491–494.

Sagvik, J., Uller, T. & **Olsson, M.** (2005). Outbreeding depression in the common frog, *Rana temporaria*. *Conservation Genetics*, **6**, 205–211.

Salafsky, N. & **Margoluis, R.** (2003). What conservation can learn from other fields about monitoring and evaluation. *BioScience*, **53**, 120–121.

Samples, K. C., Dixon, J. A. & **Gowen, M. M.** (1986). Information disclosure and endangered species valuation. *Land Economics*, **62**, 306–312.

Sánchez-Azofeifa, G. A., Quesada-Mateo, C., Gonzalez-Quesada, P., Dayanandan, S. & **Bawa, K. S.** (1999). Protected areas and conservation of biodiversity in the tropics. *Conservation Biology*, **13**, 407–411.

Sanderson, E. W., Jaiteh, M., Levy, M. A. *et al.* (2002). The human footprint and the last of the wild. *BioScience*, **52**, 891–904.

Sarrazin, F. & **Barbault, R.** (1996). Reintroduction: challenges and lessons for basic ecology. *Trends in Ecology and Evolution*, **11**, 474–478.

Saunders, D. A., Hobbs, R. J. & **Margules, C. R.** (1991). Biological consequences of ecosystem fragmentation: A review. *Conservation Biology*, **5**, 18–32.

Saura, M., Perez-Figueroa, A., Fernandez, J., Toro, M. A. & **Caballero, A.** (2008). Preserving population allele frequencies in ex situ conservation programs. *Conservation Biology*, **22**, 1277–1287.

Sax, D. F. & **Gaines, S. D.** (2008). Species invasions and extinction: The future of native biodiversity on islands. *Proceedings of the National Academy of Sciences*, **105** (Supplement 1), 11 490–11 497.

Sax, D. F., Smith, K. F. & **Thompson, A. R.** (2009). Managed relocation: a nuanced evaluation is needed. *Trends in Ecology & Evolution*, **24**, 472–473.

Schauenberg, P. (1977). Longueur de l'intestin du chat forestier *Felis silvestris* Schreber. *Mammalia*, **41**, 357–360.

Schlaepfer, M. A., Helenbrook, W. D., Searing, K. B. & **Shoemaker, K. T.** (2009). Assisted colonization: evaluating contrasting management actions (and values) in the face of uncertainty. *Trends in Ecology & Evolution*, **24**, 471–472.

Schultz, C. B., Dzurisin, J. D. & **Russell, C.** (2009). Captive rearing of Puget blue butterflies (*Icaricia icarioides blackmorei*) and implications for conservation. *Journal of Insect Conservation*, **13**, 309–315.

Scobie, P. N. (1997). *Single Population Analysis and Records Keeping System [SPARKS]. Software Manual.* Apple Valley, MN: International Species Information System (ISIS).

Scott, P., Burton, J. A. & Fitter, R. (1987). Red Data Books: the historical background. In *The Road to Extinction*, eds. **R. Fitter & M. Fitter.** Gland, Switzerland: IUCN, pp. 1–5.

Scottish Agricultural College (2010). *Ostrich farming.* http://www.sac.ac.uk/consulting/services/fh/farmdiversification/database/novellivestock/ostrichfarming

Seal, U. S. (1988). Intensive technology in the care of ex-situ populations of vanishing species. In *Biodiversity*, ed. **E. O. Wilson.** Washington, DC: National Academy Press, pp. 269–295.

Seal, U. S. (1991). Life after extinction. In *Beyond Captive Breeding: Reintroducing Endangered Mammals to the Wild*, ed. **J. H. W. Gipps.** Symposia, Zoological Society of London 62. Oxford: Clarendon Press, pp. 39–56.

Seal, U. S., Foose, T. J. & Ellis, S. (1994). Conservation assessment and management plans (CAMPs) and global captive action plans (GCAPs). In *Creative Conservation: Interactive Management of Wild and Captive Animals*, eds. **P. J. S. Olney, G. M. Mace, & A. T. C. Feistner.** London: Chapman and Hall, pp. 312–325.

Seal, U. S., Thorne, E. T., Bogan, M. A. & Anderson, S. H. (1989). *Conservation Biology and The Black-Footed Ferret.* Yale University Press.

Sebag-Montefiore, H. (1993). Who's who at the zoo? *Management Today*, July, pp. 48–51.

Secretary of State's Standards of Modern Zoo Practice (2004).

Seddon, P. J., Soorae, P. S. & Launay, F. (2005). Taxonomic bias in reintroduction projects. *Animal Conservation*, **8**, 51–58.

Seddon, P. J., Armstrong, D. P. & Maloney, R. F. (2007). Developing the science of reintroduction biology. *Conservation Biology*, **21**, 303–312.

Seddon, P. J., Armstrong, D. P., Soorae, P. *et al.* (2009). The risks of assisted colonization. *Conservation Biology*, **23**, 788–789.

Seigel, R. A. & Dodd, K. C. (2000). Manipulation of turtle populations for conservation: halfway technologies or viable options? In *Turtle Conservation*, ed. **M. W. Klemens.** Washington, DC: Smithsonian Institution Press, pp. 218–238.

Selye, H. (1974). *Stress without Distress.* Philadelphia: J.B. Lippincott.

Sepkoski, J. J. Jr. (1989). Periodicity in extinction and the problem of catastrophism in the history of life. *Journal of Geological Society of London*, **146**, 7–19.

Serrell, B. (1988). The evolution of educational graphics in zoos. *Environment and Behavior*, **20**, 396–415.

Serrell, B. (1998). *Paying Attention: Visitors and Museum Exhibitions*, Washington, DC: American Association of Museums.

Seth, P. K. & Seth, S. (1986). Ecology and behaviour of Rhesus monkeys in India. In *Primate Ecology and Conservation*, eds. **J. G. Else & P. C. Lee**, pp. 89–104.

Shaffer, M. L. (1981). Minimum population sizes for species conservation. *Bioscience*, **31**, 131–134.

Shaffer, M. L. (1987). Minimum viable populations: Coping with uncertainty. In *Viable Populations for Conservation*, ed. **M. E. Soulé.** Cambridge: Cambridge University Press, pp. 69–86.

Shen, F. J., Zhang, Z. H., He, W. *et al.* (2009). Microsatellite variability reveals the necessity for genetic input from wild giant pandas (*Ailuropoda melanoleuca*) into the captive population. *Molecular Ecology*, **18**, 1061–1070.

Shepherdson, D. (1988). Environmental enrichment in the zoo. In *Why Zoos?* UFAW Courier, **24**, 45–53.

Shepherdson, D. (1989). Stereotypic behavior. What is it and how can it be eliminated or prevented? *Ratel*, **16**, 100–105.

Shepherdson, D. (1994). The role of environmental enrichment in the captive breeding and reintroduction of endangered species. In *Creative Conservation: Interactive Management of Wild and Captive*

Animals, eds. **P. J. S. Olney, G. M. Mace & A. T. C. Feistner.** London: Chapman & Hall, pp. 167–177.

Shepherdson, D., Brownback, T. & Tinkler, D. (1990). Putting the wild back into zoos: enriching the zoo environment. *Applied Animal Behaviour Science*, **28**, 300.

Sherley, G. H., Stringer, I. A. N. & Parrish, G. R. (2010). *Summary of Native Bat, Reptile, Amphibian and Terrestrial Invertebrate Translocations in New Zealand.* Science for Conservation 303. Wellington: Department of Conservation.

Short, J., Bradshaw, S. D., Giles, J., Prince, R. I. T., Wilson, G. R. (1992). Reintroduction of macropods (Marsupialia: Macropodoidea) in Australia – a review. *Biological Conservation*, **62**, 189–204.

Shropshire, T. (2000). Panda power lures thousands to Zoo Atlanta. *The Atlanta Business Chronicle. May 12, 2000.* [http://atlanta.bizjournals.com/atlanta/stories/2000/05/15/focus12.html]

Sibly, R. M., Monk, K. A., Johnson, I. K. & Trout, R. C. (1990). Seasonal variation in gut morphology in wild rabbits (*Oryctolagus cuniculus*) *Journal of Zoology*, **221**, 605–619.

Siddle, H. V., Kreiss, A., Eldridge, M. D. B. *et al.* (2007). Transmission of a fatal clonal tumor by biting occurs due to depleted MHC diversity in a threatened carnivorous marsupial. *Proceedings of the National Academy of Sciences of the United States of America*, **104**, 16 221–16 226.

Simberloff, D. (1986). Are we on the verge of a mass extinction in tropical rain forests? In *Dynamics of Extinction*, ed. **D. K. Elliott.** New York, NY: Wiley, pp. 165–180.

Simberloff, D. (1992). Do species-area curves predict extinction in fragmented forest? In *Tropical Deforestation and Species Extinction*, eds. **T. C. Whitmore & J. A. Sayer.** London: Chapman & Hall, pp. 75–89.

Simberloff, D. (1998). Flagships, umbrellas, and keystones: is single-species management passé in the landscape era? *Biological Conservation*, **83**, 247–257.

Simianer, H. (2005). Using expected allele number as objective function to design between and within breed conservation of farm animal biodiversity. *Journal of Animal Breeding and Genetics*, **122**, 177–187.

Simpson, G. G. (1951). The species concept. *Evolution*, **5**, 285–298.

Sinclair, A. (1989). Public sector culture: managerialism or multiculturalism. *Australian Journal of Public Administration*, **48**, 382–397.

Singer, P. (1995). *Animal Liberation.* London: Pimlico.

Sites, J. W. Jr. & Crandall, K. A. (1997). Testing species boundaries in biodiversity studies. *Conservation Biology*, **11**, 1289–1297.

Smith, F. A., Lyons, S. K., Ernest, S. K. M. *et al.* (2003). Body mass of late Quaternary mammals. *Ecology*, **84**, 3403–3403. Doi: 10.1890/02–9003.

Smith, G. (1993). Towards international best practice in the zoo industry. In *Proceedings of the International Union of Directors of Zoological Gardens 48th Annual Conference*, Antwerp: International Union of Directors of Zoological Gardens, pp. 15–22.

Smith, F. D. M., May, R. M., Pellew, R. *et al.* (1993). Estimating extinction rates. *Nature*, **364**, 494–496.

Smith, L. (2009). Identifying behaviours to target during zoo visits. *Curator*, **52**, 101–115.

Smith, L. & Broad, S. (2008). Do zoo visitors attend to conservation messages? A case study of an elephant exhibit. *Tourism Review International*, **11**, 225–235.

Smith, L., Broad, S. & Weiler, B. (2008). A closer examination of the impact of zoo visits on visitor behaviour. *Journal of Sustainable Tourism*, **16**, 544–562.

Smith, L. L., Reid, D., Robert, B., Joby, M. & Clément, S. (1999). Status and distribution of the angonoka tortoise (*Geochelone yniphora*) of western Madagascar. *Biological Conservation*, **91**, 23–33.

Smith, R. J. & Walpole, M. J. (2005). Should conservationists pay more attention to corruption? *Oryx*, **39**, 251–256.

Smith, R. J., Muir, R. D. J., Walpole, M. J., Balmford, A. & **Leader-Williams, N.** (2003). Governance and the loss of biodiversity. *Nature*, **426**, 67–70.

Snyder, N. F. R. & **Snyder, H.** (2000). *The California Condor: A Saga of Natural History and Conservation*. Princeton: Princeton University Press.

Snyder, N. F. R., Wiley, J. W. & **Kepler, C. B.** (1987). *The Parrots of Luquillo: Natural History and Conservation of the Puerto Rican Parrot*. Los Angeles: The Western Foundation of Vertebrate Zoology.

Snyder, N. F. R., Derrickson, S. R., Beissinger, S. R. *et al.* (1996). Limitations of captive breeding in endangered species recovery. *Conservation Biology*, **10**, 338–348.

Sokal, R. R. & **Crovello, T. J.** (1970). The biological species concept: a critical evaluation. *American Naturalist*, **104**, 127–153.

Soorae, P. (2003). *The IUCN/SSC Re-Introduction Specialist Group. Literature Database*. Abu Dhabi, UAE: IUCN/SSC Re-introduction Specialist Group.

Soulé, M. E. (1980). Thresholds for survival: Maintaining fitness and evolutionary potential. In *Conservation Biology: An Evolutionary-Ecological Perspective*, eds. **M. E. Soulé** & **B. A. Wilcox.** Sunderland, MA: Sinauer Associates, pp. 151–169.

Soulé, M. E. (1985). What is conservation biology? *BioScience*, **35**, 727–734.

Soulé, M. E. & **Wilcox, B. A.** (eds.) (1980). *Conservation Biology: An Evolutionary-Ecological Perspective*. Sunderland, MA: Sinauer Associates.

Soulé, M. E., Gilpin, M., Conway, W. & **Foose, T.** (1986). The millenium ark: how long a voyage, how many staterooms, how many passengers? *Zoo Biology*, **5**, 101–114.

Spielman, D., Brook, B. W. & **Frankham, R.** (2004). Most species are not driven to extinction before genetic factors impact them. *Proceedings of the National Academy of Sciences of the United States of America*, **101**, 15 261–15 264.

SSSMZP (2004). *Secretary of State's Standards of Modern Zoo Practice*. [http://www.defra.gov.uk/wildlife-pets/zoos/standards.htm]

Stacey, P. B. & **Taper, M.** (1992). Environmental variation and the persistence of small populations. *Ecological Applications*, **2**, 18–29.

Stanley Price, M. R. (1989). *Animal Re-introductions: The Arabian Oryx in Oman*. Cambridge: Cambridge University Press.

Stanley Price, M. R. (1991). A review of mammal re-introductions, and the role of the Re-introduction Specialist Group of IUCN/SSC. In *Beyond Captive Breeding: Re-introducing Endangered Mammals to the Wild*, ed. **J. H. W. Gipps.** Symposia, Zoological Society of London 62. Oxford: Clarendon Press, pp. 9–25.

Stanley Price, M. R. (2005). Zoos as a force for conservation: a simple ambition – but how? *Oryx*, **39**, 109–110.

Stanley Price, M. R. & **Fa, J. E.** (2007). Reintroduction from zoos: guiding light or shooting star? In *Zoos in the 21st Century: Catalysts for Conservation?*, eds. **A. Zimmerman, M. Hatchwell, L. Dickie** & **C. West.** Cambridge: Cambridge University Press, pp. 155–177.

Stanley Price, M. R., Maunder, M. & **Soorae, P. S.** (2004). Ex situ support to the conservation of wild populations and habitats: lessons from zoos and opportunities for botanic gardens. In *Ex Situ Plant Conservation Supporting Species Survival in the Wild*, eds. **E. O. Guerrant, K. Havens** & **M. Maunder.** Washington, DC: Island Press.

Stattersfield, A. J., Crosby, M. J., Long, A. J. & **Wege, D. C.** (1998). *Endemic Bird Areas of the World*. Cambridge, UK: BirdLife International.

Sterling, E. J., Lee, J. & **Wood, T.** (2007). Conservation education in zoos: an emphasis on behavioural change. In: *Zoos in the 21st Century. Catalysts for Conservation?*, eds. **A. Zimmerman, M. Hatchwell, L. Dickie** & **C. West.** Cambridge: Cambridge University Press, pp. 37–50.

Stevens, G. C. (1989). The latitudinal gradient in geographical range: how so many species coexist in the tropics. *American Naturalist*, **133**, 947–949.

Stevens, P. M. C. & McAlister, E. (2003). Ethics in zoos. *International Zoo Yearbook*, **38**, 94–101.

Stinchcombe, J. R., Moyle, L. C., Hudgens, B. R. *et al.* (2002). The influence of the academic conservation literature on endangered species recovery planning. *Conservation Ecology*, **6**, 15 [http://www.consecd.org/vol6/iss2/art15].

Stoinski, T., Lukas, K. & Maple, T. (1998). A survey of research in North American zoos and aquariums. *Zoo Biology*, **17**, 167–180.

Stoinski, T. S., Beck, B. B., Bloomsmith, M. A. & Maple, T. L. (2003). A behavioral comparison of captive-born reintroduced golden lion tamarins and their wild-born offspring. *Behaviour*, **140**, 137–260.

Stoinski, T. S., Allen, M. T., Bloomsmith, M. A., Forthman, D. L. & Maple, T. L. (2010). Educating zoo visitors about complex environmental issues: should we do it and how? *Curator: The Museum Journal*, **45**, 129–143.

Stork, N. E. (1988). Insect diversity: facts, fiction and speculation. *Biological Journal of the Linnean Society*, **35**, 321–337.

Storz, J. F., Beaumont, M. A. & Alberts, S. C. (2002). Genetic evidence for long-term population decline in a savannah-dwelling primate: Inferences from a hierarchical Bayesian model. *Molecular Biology and Evolution*, **19**, 1981–1990.

Struhsaker, T. T. & Siex, K. S. (1998). Translocation and introduction of the Zanzibar red colobus monkey: success and failure with an endangered island endemic. *Oryx*, **32**, 277–284.

Strum, S. C. & Southwick, C. H. (1986). Translocation of primates. In *Primates, the Road to Self-Sustaining Populations*, ed. **K. Bernischke.** New York: Springer-Verlag, pp. 949–958.

Stuart, S. N. (1991). Re-introductions: to what extent are they needed? In *Beyond Captive Breeding: Reintroducing Endangered Mammals to the Wild*, ed. **J. H. W. Gipps,** Symposia, Zoological Society of London 62. Oxford: Clarendon Press, pp. 27–37.

Surinova, M. (1971). An analysis of the popularity of animals. *International Zoo Yearbook*, **11**, 165–167.

Sutherland, W. J. (2002). Conservation biology: science, sex and the kakapo. *Nature*, **419**, 265–266.

Sutherland, W. J., Adams, W. M., Aronson, R. B. *et al.* (2009). One hundred questions of importance to the conservation of global biological diversity. *Conservation Biology*, **23**, 557–567.

Swarbrooke, J. (2001). *Development and Management of Visitor Attractions*. Oxford: Butterworth-Heinemann.

Swinnerton, K. J., Groombridge, J. J., Jones, C. G., Burn, R. W., Mungroo, Y. (2004). Inbreeding depression and founder diversity among captive and free-living populations of the endangered pink pigeon *Columba mayeri*. *Animal Conservation*, **7**, 353–364.

Taberlet, P., Waits, L. P. & Luikart, G. (1999). Noninvasive genetic sampling: look before you leap. *Trends in Ecology and Evolution*, **14**, 321–325.

Taubes, G. (1992). A dubious battle to save the Kemps Ridley sea turtle. *Science*, **256**, 614–616.

Taylor, A. C., Sherwin, W. B. & Wayne, R. K. (1994). Genetic-variation of microsatellite loci in a bottlenecked species – the northern hairy-nosed wombat *Lasiorhinus krefftii*. *Molecular Ecology*, **3**, 277–290.

Tear, T. H., Scott, J. M., Hayward, P. H. & Griffith, B. (1993). Status and prospects for success of the endangered species act: a look at recovery plans. *Science*, **262**, 976–977.

Templeton, A. R. (1986). Coadaptation and outbreeding depression. In *Conservation Biology: the Science of Scarcity and Diversity*, ed. **M. E. Soulé.** Sunderland, MA: Sinnauer, pp. 105–116.

Templeton, A. R. (1989). The meaning of species and speciation: a genetic perspective. In *Speciation and its Consequences*, eds. **D. Otte & J. A. Endler.** Sunderland, MA: Sinauer Associates, pp. 3–27.

Templeton, A. R. (2002). The Speke's gazelle breeding program as an illustration of the importance of multilocus genetic diversity in conservation biology: Response to Kalinowski *et al. Conservation Biology*, **16**, 1151–1155.

Templeton, A. R. & Read, B. (1984). Factors eliminating inbreeding depression in a captive herd of Speke's gazelle (*Gazella Spekei*). *Zoo Biology*, **3**, 177–199.

Templeton, A. R. & Read, B. (1994). Inbreeding: one word, several meanings, much confusion. In *Conservation Genetics*, eds. **V. Loeschcke, J. Tomiuk & S. K. Jain**. Basel: Birkhaduser Verlag, pp. 91–106.

Terborgh, J. (1974). Preservation of natural diversity: the problem of extinction prone species. *Bioscience*, **24**, 715–722.

Terborgh, J. (1986). Keystone plant species in the tropical forest. In *Conservation Biology: The Science of Scarcity and Diversity*, ed. **M. Soulé**. Sunderland, MA: Sinauer Associates, pp. 330–344.

Terborgh, J. & Winter, B. (1980). Some causes of extinction. In *Conservation Biology, an Evolutionary-Ecological Perspective*. Sunderland, MA: Sinauer Associates, pp. 119–133.

Terborgh, J., Robinson, S. K., Parker, III, T. A., Munn, C. A. & Pierpont, N. (1990). Structure and organization of an Amazonian forest bird community. *Ecological Monographs*, **60**, 213–238.

Theberge, J. B., Theberge, M. T., Vucetich, J. A. & Paquet, P. C. (2006). Pitfalls of applying adaptive management to a wolf population in Algonquin Provincial Park, Ontario. *Environmental Management*, **37**, 451–460.

Thibault, J.-C., Martin, J.-L., Penloup, A. & Meyer, J.-Y. (2002). Understanding the decline and extinction of monarchs (Aves) in Polynesian Islands. *Biological Conservation*, **108**, 161–174.

Thomas, R. K. & Lorden, R. B. (1989). What is psychological well-being? Can we know if primates have it? In *Housing, Care and Psychological Wellbeing of Captive and Laboratory Primates*, ed. **E. F. Segal**. New Jersey: Noyes Publications, pp. 12–26.

Thomas, W. W. & de Carvalho, A. M. (1993). Estudio fitossociologico de Serra Grande, Uruçuca, Bahia, Brasil. *XLIV Congresso Nacional de Botânica, São Luis, 24–30 de Janeiro de 1993, Resumos*, **1**: 224. Sociedade Botânica do Brasil, Universidade Federal de Maranhão.

Thomas, C. D., Cameron, A., Green, R. E. *et al.* (2004). Extinction risk from climate change. *Nature*, **427**, 146–148.

Thuiller, W., Araújo, M. B., Pearson, R. G., Whittaker, R. J., Brotons, L. & Lavorel, S. (2004). Uncertainty in predictions of extinction risk. *Nature*, **430**, 34.

Thuiller, W., Lavorel, S., Araújo, M. B., Sykes, M. T. & Prentice, I. C. (2005). Climate change threats to plant diversity in Europe. *Proceedings of the National Academy of Sciences, USA.* **102**, 8245–8250.

Thuiller, W., Broennimann, O., Hughes, G. O., Alkemade, J. R. M., Midgley, G. F. & Corsi, F. (2006). Vulnerability of African mammals to anthropogenic climate change under conservative land transformation assumptions. *Global Change Biology*, **12**, 424–440.

Tilson, R. (1995). In support of nature, the Minnesota Zoo's 'Adopt-a-park' program. In *The Ark Evolving: Zoos and Aquariums in Transition*, ed. **C. Wemmer**. Washington, DC: Smithsonian Institution, pp. 190–195.

Townsend Peterson, A. & Watson, D. M. (1998). Problems with areal definitions of endemism: the effects of spatial scaling. *Diversity and Distributions*, **4**, 189–194.

Traill, L. W., Bradshaw, C. J. A. & Brook, B. W. (2007). Minimum viable population size: a meta-analysis of 30 years of published estimates. *Biological Conservation*, **139**, 159–166.

Traill, L. W., Brook, B. W., Frankham, R. R. & Bradshaw, C. J. A. (2010). Pragmatic population viability targets in a rapidly changing world. *Biological Conservation*, **143**, 28–34.

Traylor-Holzer, K. & Fritz, P. (1985). Utilization of space by adult and juvenile groups of captive chimpanzees (*Pan troglodytes*). *Zoo Biology*, **4**, 115–127.

Traylor-Holzer, K., Ballou, J. D., Zhong, X. & Zhihe, Z. (2008). Development of a self-sustaining, viable captive population of giant pandas. Paper presented at the annual meeting of the International Congress for Conservation Biology, Convention Center, Chattanooga, TN. [http://www.allacademic.com/meta/p243840_index.html]

Treves, A. & **Naughton-Treves, L.** (1997). Case study of a chimpanzee recovered from poachers and temporarily released with wild conspecifics. *Primates*, **38**, 315–324.

Tribe, A. (2001). *Captive Wildlife Tourism in Australia*. Wildlife Tourism Research Report Series: No. 14. Status Assessment of Wildlife Tourism in Australia Series. Cooperative Research Centre for Sustainable Tourism.

Tribe, A. & **Booth, R.** (2003). Assessing the role of zoos in wildlife conservation. *Human Dimensions of Wildlife*, **8**, 65–74.

Tudge, C. (1991). *Last Animals at the Zoo: How Mass Extinction can be Stopped*. Oxford: Oxford University Press.

Tudge, C. (1995). Captive audiences for future conservation. *New Scientist*, **145**, 51–52.

Tunnicliffe, S. D. & **Scheersoi, A.** (2009). Engaging the interest of zoo visitors as a key to biological education. *IZE Journal*, **45**, 18–20.

Turley, S. K. (2001). Children and the demand for recreational experiences: the case of zoos. *Leisure Studies*, **20**, 1–18.

Turner, I. M. (1996). Species loss in fragments of tropical rain forest: a review of the evidence. *Journal of Applied Ecology*, **33**, 200–209.

Tutin, C. E. G., Ancrenaz, M., Paredes, J., Vacher-Vallas, M., Vidal, C., Goossens, B., Bruford, M. W. & **Jamart, A.** (2001). The conservation biology framework of the release of wild-born orphaned chimpanzees into the Conkouati Reserve, Congo. *Conservation Biology*, **15**, 1247–1257.

Tymchuk, W. V., O'Reilly, P., Bittman, J., MacDonald, D. & **Schulte, P.** (2010). Conservation genomics of Atlantic salmon: variation in gene expression between and within regions of the Bay of Fundy. *Molecular Ecology*, **19**, 1842–1859.

UFAW (1992). *Guidelines for the Reintroduction of Captive Bred Mammals to the Wild*. International Academy of Welfare Sciences. Universities Federation for Animal Welfare, 8 Hamilton Close, South Mimms, Potters Bar, Herts, EN6 3QD, UK.

UNEP WCMC (2011). A-Z Areas of Biodiversity Importance [http://www.biodiversitya-z.org]

US Census Bureau (2010). *U.S. & World Population Clocks*. [http://www.census.gov/main/www/popclock.html]

Van Dierendonck, M. & **Wallis de Vries, M. F.** (1996). Ungulate reintroductions: experiences with takhi or Przewalski horse (*Equus ferus przewalskii*) in Mongolia. *Conservation Biology*, **10**, 728–740.

Van Diest, P. J., Holzel, H., Burnett, D. & **Crocker, J.** (2001). Impactitis: new cures for an old disease. *Journal of Clinical Pathology*, **54**, 817–819.

Van Heezik, Y. & **Ostrowski, S.** (2001). Conservation breeding for reintroductions: assessing survival in a captive flock of houbara bustards. *Animal Conservation*, **4**, 195–201.

Van Valen, L. (1973). A new evolutionary law. *Evolutionary Theory*, **1**, 1–33.

Vane-Wright, R. I., Humphries, C. J. & **Williams, P. H.** (1991). What to protect? – Systematics and the agony of choice. *Biological Conservation*, **55**, 235–254.

Veasey, J. S., Waran, N. K. & **Young, R. J.** (1996). On comparing the behaviour of zoo housed animals with wild conspecifics as a welfare indicator. *Animal Welfare*, **5**, 13–24.

Veitch, C. R. (1994). Habitat repair: a necessary prerequisite to translocation of threatened birds. In *Reintroduction Biology of Australian and New Zealand Fauna*. Chipping Norton, Oxfordshire: Beatty & Sons, pp. 97–104.

Veltman, C. J., Nee, S. & **Crawley, M. J.** (1996). Correlates of introduction sucess in exotic New Zealand birds. *American Naturalist*, **147**, 542–557.

Verner Bradford, P. & **Blume, H.** (1992). *Ota Benga: The Pygmy in the Zoo*. New York: St. Martin's Press.

Vernesi, C., Bruford, M. W., Bertorelle, G. *et al.* (2008). Where's the conservation in conservation genetics? *Conservation Biology*, **22**, 802–804.

Vickery, S. & **Mason, G.** (2003). Behavioral persistence in captive bears: implications for reintroduction. *Ursus*, **14**, 35–43.

Vié, J.-C., Hilton-Taylor, C. & **Stuart, S. N.** (2009). *Wildlife in a Changing World – An Analysis of the 2008 IUCN Red List of Threatened Species.* Gland, Switzerland.

Vigilant, L., Hofreiter, M., Siedel, H. & **Boesch, C.** (2001). Paternity and relatedness in wild chimpanzee communities. *Proceedings of the National Academy of Sciences, USA*, **98**, 12 890– 12 895

Visscher, N. C., Snider, R. & **Vander Stoep, G.** (2009). Comparative analysis of knowledge gain between interpretive and fact-only presentations at an animal training session: an exploratory study. *Zoo Biology*, **28**, 488–495.

Visser, M. E. (2008). Keeping up with a warming world; assessing the rate of adaptation to climate change. *Proceedings of the Royal Society B: Biological Sciences*, **275**, 649–659.

Vitt, P., Havens, K. & **Hoegh-Guldberg, O.** (2009). Assisted migration: part of an integrated conservation strategy. *Trends in Ecology & Evolution*, **24**, 473–474.

Wagner, K., Chessler, M., York, P. & **Raynor, J.** (2009). Development and implementation of an evaluation strategy for measuring conservation outcomes. *Zoo Biology*, **28**, 473–487.

Walker, S. (1992). Biodiversity and ecological redundancy. *Conservation Biology*, **6**, 18–23.

Walker, S. (1995). Perspective on strategic planning, cooperation, and CBSG from a voluntary organization in India. *Zoo Biology*, **14**, 55–60.

Wallace, M. P. (2000). Retaining natural behaviour in captivity for re-introduction programmes. In *Behaviour and Conservation*, eds. **L. M. Gosling** & **W. J. Sutherland.** Cambridge: Cambridge University Press, pp. 300–313.

Walpole, M. J., Morgan-Davies, M., Milledge, S., Bett, P. & **Leader-Williams, N.** (2001). Population dynamics and future conservation of a free-ranging black rhinoceros (*Diceros bicornis*) population in Kenya. *Biological Conservation*, **99**, 237–243.

Walsh, P. A., Abernethy, K. A., Bermejo, M. *et al.* (2003). Catastrophic ape decline in western equatorial Africa. *Nature*, **422**, 611–614.

Wang, J. L. (2004). Monitoring and managing genetic variation in group breeding populations without individual pedigrees. *Conservation Genetics*, **5**, 813–825.

Waples, R. (2002). Definition and estimation of effective population size in the conservation of endangered species. In *Population Viability Analysis*, eds. **S. R. Beissinger** & **D. R. McCullough.** Chicago: University of Chicago Press, pp. 147–168.

Ward, A. J. W., Thomas, P., Hart, P. J. B. & **Krause, J.** (2004). Correlates of boldness in three-spined sticklebacks (*Gasterosteus aculeatus*). *Behavioural Ecology and Sociobiology*, **55**, 561–568.

Ward, P. I., Mosberger, N., Kistler, C. & **Fischer, O.** (1998). The relationship between popularity and body size. *Conservation Biology*, **12**, 1408–1411.

Washitani, I. (1996). Predicted genetic consequences of strong fertility selection due to pollinator loss in an isolated population of *Primula sieboldii*. *Conservation Biology*, **10**, 59–64.

Waugh, D. R. & **Wemmer, C.** (1994). Training in zoo biology: two approaches to enhance the conservation role of zoos in the tropics. In *Creative Conservation: Interactive Management of Wild and Captive Animals*, eds. **P. J. S. Olney, G. M. Mace** & **A. T. C. Feistner.** London: Chapman & Hall.

WAZA (2005). *Building a Future for Wildlife – The World Zoo and Aquarium Conservation Strategy.* Bern, Switzerland: WAZA Executive Office.

WAZA (2010). *Overview of WAZA Conservation Projects.* [http://www.waza.org/en/site/conservation/waza-conservation-projects/overview]

WDPA (2010). *World Database on Protected Areas.* [http://www.wdpa.org/]

Webster, J. (1994). *Animal Welfare: A Cool Eye towards Eden.* Oxford: Blackwell Publications.

Wehnelt, S. & **Wilkinson, R.** (2005). Research, conservation and zoos: the EC Zoos Directive – a response to Rees. *Oryx*, **39**, 132–133.

Wiese, R. J. (2000). Asian elephants are not self-sustaining in North America. *Zoo Biology*, **19**, 299–309.

Wemmer, C. & Derrickson, S. (1995). Collection planning and the modern zoo. *Zoo Biology*, **14**, 38–41.

Werribee Open Range Zoo (2010). *Werribee Open Range Zoo: Conservation Connections.* [http://www.zoo.org.au/Learning/Programs/Showcase/Conservation_Connections]

West, C. & Dickie, L. A. (2007). Is there a conservation role for zoos in a natural world under fire? In *Zoos in the 21st Century: Catalysts for Conservation?*, eds. **A. Zimmerman, M. Hatchwell, L. Dickie & C. West.** Cambridge: Cambridge University Press, pp. 3–11.

Westemeier, R. L., Brawn, J. D., Simpson, S. A. *et al.* (1998). Tracking the long-term decline and recovery of an isolated population. *Science*, **282**, 1695–1698.

Westergaard, G. C., Izard, M. K., Drake, J. H., Suomi, S. J. & Higley, J. D. (1999). Rhesus macaque (*Macaca mulatta*) group formation and housing: Wounding and reproduction in a specific pathogen free (SPF) colony. *American Journal of Primatology*, **49**, 339–347.

Wharton, D. (2006). Miracle under fire. In *State of the Wild*, ed. **S. Guynup.** Washington, DC: Island Press, pp. 256–264.

Wharton, D. (2007). Research by zoos. In *Zoos in the 21st Century: Catalysts for Conservation?*, eds. **A. Zimmerman, M. Hatchwell, L. Dickie & C. West.** Cambridge: Cambridge University Press, pp. 178–191.

Wharton, D. (2008). The future of zoo biology. *Zoo Biology*, **27**, 498–504.

White, J. (1993). The zoo lives: Dr Jo Gipps at London Zoo has a good story to tell, of profit and success. And he has a plan. *The Independent*, Friday 19 November, 1993. [http://www.independent.co.uk/life-style/the-zoo-lives-dr-jo-gipps-at-london-zoo-has-a-good-story-to-tell-of-profit-and-success-and-he-has-a-plan-jim-white-reports-1505285.html]

Whitehead, M. (1995). Saying it with genes, species and habitats: biodiversity education and the role of zoos. *Biodiversity and Conservation*, **4**, 664–670.

Wilcox, B. A. (1984). In situ conservation of genetic resources: determinants of minimum area requirements. In *National Parks, Conservation and Development*, eds. **A. McNeeley & K. R. Miller.** Washington, DC: Smithsonian Institute Press, pp. 639–647.

Wildt, D. E., Rall, W. F., Crister, J. K., Monfort, S. L. & Seal, U. S. (1997). Genome resource banks: 'living collections' for biodiversity conservation. *Bioscience*, **47**, 689–698.

Wildt, D. E., Ellis, S., Janssen, D. & Buff, J. (2003). Toward more effective science for conservation. In *Reproductive Science and Integrated Conservation*, eds. **W. V. Holt, A. R. Pickard, J. C. Rodger & D. E. Wildt.** Cambridge: Cambridge University Press, pp. 2–20.

Williams, G. (1998). Misleading, unscientific, and unjust: the United Kingdom's research assessment exercise. *British Medical Journal*, **316**, 1079–1082.

Williams, P., Gibbons, D., Margules, C. *et al.* (1996). A comparison of richness hotspots, rarity hotspots, and complementary areas for conserving diversity of British birds. *Conservation Biology*, **10**, 155–174.

Williams, S. E. & Hoffman, E. A. (2009). Minimizing genetic adaptation in captive breeding programs: a review. *Biological Conservation*, **142**, 2388–2400.

Willis, K. & Wiese, R. J. (1997). Elimination of inbreeding depression from captive populations: Speke's gazelle revisited. *Zoo Biology*, **16**, 9–16.

Wilson, A. C. & Stanley Price, M. R. (1994). Reintroduction as a reason for captive breeding. In *Creative Conservation: Interactive Management of Wild and Captive Animals*, eds. **P. J. S. Olney, G. M. Mace & A. T. C. Feistner.** London: Chapman and Hall, pp. 243–264.

Wilson, E. O. (1988). *Biodiversity.* Washington, DC: National Academy Press.

Wilson, E. O. (1989). Conservation: The next hundred years. In *Conservation for the Twenty-First Century*, eds. **D. Western, & M. Pearl.** Oxford: Oxford University Press, pp. 1–10.

Wilson, E. O. (1992). *The Diversity of Life.* Cambridge, MA: Belknap Press of Harvard University Press.

Wilson, M. H., Kepler, C. B., Snyder, N. F. R. *et al.* (1994). Puerto Rican parrots and potential limitations of the metapopulation approach to species conservation. *Conservation Biology*, **8**, 114–123.

Wisely, S. M., Ososky, J. J. & Buskirk, S. W. (2002). Morphological changes to black-footed ferrets (*Mustela nigripes*) resulting from captivity. *Canadian Journal of Zoology-Revue Canadienne de Zoologie*, **80**, 1562–1568.

Wisely, S. M., Santymire, R. M., Livieri, T. M. *et al.* (2005). Environment influences morphology and development for in situ and ex situ populations of the black-footed ferret (*Mustela nigripes*). *Animal Conservation*, **8**, 321–328.

Wisely, S. M., Santymire, R. M., Livieri, T. M., Mueting, S. A. & Howard, J. (2008). Genotypic and phenotypic consequences of reintroduction history in the black-footed ferret (*Mustela nigripes*). *Conservation Genetics*, **9**, 389–399.

Wolf, C. M., Griffith, B., Reed, C. & Temple, S. A. (1996). Avian and mammalian translocations: update and reanalysis of 1987 survey data. *Conservation Biology*, **10**, 1142–1154.

Wolf, C. M., Garland, T. & Griffith, B. (1998). Predictors of avian and mammalian translocation success: reanalysis with phylogenetically independent contrasts. *Biological Conservation*, **86**, 243–255.

Wolf, K. N., Wildt, D. E., Vargas, A., Marinari, P. E., Ottinger, M. A. & Howard, J. G. (2000). Reproductive inefficiency in male blackfooted ferrets (*Mustela nigripes*). *Zoo Biology*, **19**, 517–528.

Woodford, M. H. & Rossiter, P. B. (1994). Disease risks associated wildlife translocation projects. In *Creative Conservation: Interactive Management of Wild and Captive Anamils*, eds. P. J. S. Olney, G. M. Mace & A. T. C. Feistner. London: Chapmen and Hall, pp. 243–264.

Woodworth, L. M., Montgomery, M. E., Briscoe, D. A. & Frankham, F. R. (2002). Rapid genetic deterioration in captive populations: causes and conservation implications. *Conservation Genetics*, **3**, 277–288.

Woollard, S. P. (2001). Zoo education for a sustainable future. *Journal of the International Association of Zoo Educators*, **37**. [http://www.izea.net]

WSPA and the Born Free Foundation (1994). *The Zoo Inquiry*. London: WSPA and Born Free Foundation.

WWF, IUCN (1994–7). *Centres of Plant Diversity*. Gland, Switzerland: WWF and IUCN.

Yaeger, C. P. (1997). Orangutan rehabilitation in Tanjung Putting National Park, Indonesia. *Conservation Biology*, **11**, 802–805.

Yajima, M. (1991). The insect ecological land at Tama Zoo. *International Zoo Yearbook*, **30**, 7–15.

Young, R. P. (ed.) (2008). *A Biodiversity Assessment of the Centre Hills, Montserrat*. Durrell Conservation Monograph No. 1. Durrell Wildlife Conservation Trust, Jersey, Channel Islands.

Young, R. P., Fa, J. E., Ogrodowczyk, A. *et al.* (2006). The St Lucia whiptail lizard *Cnemidophorus vanzoi*: a conservation dilemma? *Oryx*, **40**, 358–361.

Young, R. P., Toto Volahy, A., Bourou, R. *et al.* (2008a). Estimating the population of the Endangered flat-tailed tortoise *Pyxis planicauda* in the deciduous, dry forest of western Madagascar: a monitoring baseline. *Oryx*, **42**, 252–258.

Young, R. P., Toto Volahy, A., Bourou, R. *et al.* (2008b). A baseline estimate of population size for monitoring the Endangered Madagascar giant jumping rat *Hypogeomys antimena*. *Oryx*, **42**, 584–591.

ZAA (2010). Zoo and Aquarium Association. Conservation overview. [http://www.zooaquarium.org.au/Conservation-Overview/default.aspx]

Zeyl, C., Mizesko, M., Arjan, J. & de Visser, G. M. (2001). Mutational meltdown in laboratory yeast populations. *Evolution*, **55**, 909–917.

Zimmerman, A. & **Wilkinson, R.** (2007). The conservation mission in the wild: zoos as conservation NGOs? In *Zoos in the 21st Century: Catalysts for Conservation?*, eds. **A. Zimmerman, M. Hatchwell, L. A. Dickie** & **C. West.** Cambridge: Cambridge University Press, pp. 303–321.

Zoos Forum (2008). *UK Zoo Forum Handbook.* [http://www.defra.gov.uk/wildlife-pets/zoos/zf-handbook.htm]

Zoological Society of San Diego (2010). *Financial Statements, Zoological Society of San Diego. Fiscal years 2009 and 2008.* [http://www.sandiegozoo.org/pressbox/annualreport/zoo_final_afs_2009.pdf]

Index

CPSIA information can be obtained at www.ICGtesting.com
Printed in the USA
LVOW02s1306011015

456515LV00008B/111/P